WORKS OF WILLIAM WINTER

POEMS—Definitive Edition
OTHER DAYS
OLD FRIENDS
LIFE AND ART OF RICHARD MANSFIELD. (2 vols.)
SHAKESPEARE'S ENGLAND. (Revised and Enlarged)
GRAY DAYS AND GOLD. (Revised and Enlarged)
OVER THE BORDER. (Scotch Companion to Above)
SHAKESPEARE ON THE STAGE. *First Series:*
    Shakespeare Spells Ruin.—King Richard III.—The Merchant of Venice.—Othello.—Hamlet.—Macbeth.—King Henry VIII
SHAKESPEARE ON THE STAGE. *Second Series:*
    Twelfth Night.—Romeo and Juliet.—As You Like It.—King Lear.—The Taming of The Shrew.—Julius Cæsar
TYRONE POWER, IN LIVES OF THE PLAYERS
THE WALLET OF TIME. (2 vols.)

THE FOLLOWING ARE IN PREPARATION

A DRAMATIC PRIMER
SHAKESPEARE ON THE STAGE. *Third Series:*
    The Tempest.—Coriolanus.—King Henry IV., 1 & 2.—The Merry Wives of Windsor.—King Henry V.—Much Ado About Nothing
SHAKESPEARE ON THE STAGE. *Fourth Series:*
    Cymbeline.—King John.—A Midsummer Night's Dream.—King Richard II.—The Two Gentlemen of Verona.—Troilus and Cressida.—Love's Labor's Lost.—Antony and Cleopatra
SHAKESPEARE ON THE STAGE. *Fifth Series:*
    Measure for Measure.—King Henry VI., 1, 2, & 3.—All's Well That Ends Well.—The Winter's Tale.—The Comedy of Errors.—Timon of Athens.—Pericles.—Titus Andronicus
SHAKESPEARE ON THE STAGE. *Supplementary*
THE SHAKESPEARE STORY AND THE BACON HUMBUG
ALMS FOR OBLIVION. (Companion to "The Wallet of Time"). (3 vols.)
HENRY IRVING AND ELLEN TERRY. (2 vols.)
LIFE AND ART OF EDWIN BOOTH. (Revised and Augmented. 2 vols.)
LIFE AND ART OF JOSEPH JEFFERSON. (Revised and Augmented. 2 vols.)
THE LIFE OF DAVID BELASCO. (2 vols.)
AMERICAN RAMBLES
IRISH RAMBLES

SHAKESPEARE ON THE STAGE
SECOND SERIES

"*The genius, and the mortal instruments.*"
JULIUS CÆSAR.

SHAKESPEARE
ON
THE STAGE

SECOND SERIES

BY

WILLIAM WINTER

"We have seen the best of our time."
—Shakespeare.

NEW YORK
MOFFAT, YARD AND COMPANY
1915

COPYRIGHT, 1915, BY
WILLIAM WINTER

All Rights Reserved

Published, March, 1915

THE QUINN & BODEN CO. PRESS
RAHWAY, N. J.

To the Memory of

HORACE HOWARD FURNESS

Whose Life Was Exemplary of Every Virtue
Whose Presence Was a Blessing to All Who Knew Him
And Whose Devotion to Shakespeare
Enriched the Scholarship of the World

I DEDICATE

These Studies of a Subject He Loved and Illumined

"In worthy hearts Sorrow hath made thy tomb."
—Sir Walter Raleigh

His gentle spirit, while on earth he dwelt,
  Spoke often to me words of love and cheer;
Perhaps he knows the gratitude I felt,
  Now, when I write his name with reverence here.

CONTENTS

CHAPTER	PAGE
Costume	332
Curiosities	337
IV. KING LEAR.—The Old Story of King Lear	342
"King Leir."—The Old Plays	343
Shakespeare's "King Lear"	345
First Performance.—Richard Burbage	350
Thomas Betterton	351
George Powell	353
Barton Booth	354
Boheme and Quin	356
David Garrick	358
Spranger Barry	360
Henry Mossop	365
Alterations of Shakespeare's "King Lear." Tate.—Colman.—Garrick.—Kemble	366
Various Performers.—British Stage	384
John Philip Kemble	388
George Frederick Cooke	391
Junius Brutus Booth and Edmund Kean	393
William Charles Macready	397
The Characters, and the Play	404
Samuel Phelps	421
Charles John Kean	425
Henry Irving	427
American Stage.—Early Representations	432
Junius Brutus Booth	435
Edwin Forrest	437
Other Players of *King Lear*	444
Edwin Booth	445
Lawrence Barrett	450
John Edward McCullough	452
Robert Bruce Mantell	462

CONTENTS

CHAPTER		PAGE
	CHARACTER AND PLAYERS OF *MERCUTIO*	194
	FEMALE PLAYERS OF *ROMEO*.—ENGLISH STAGE	198
	FEMALE PLAYERS OF *ROMEO*.—AMERICAN STAGE	201
	CHARLOTTE CUSHMAN AS *ROMEO*	205
	THE CONSUMMATE TRAGEDY OF LOVE	212
III.	AS YOU LIKE IT.—IN THE FOREST OF ARDEN	215
	TRUE SCENE OF THE ACTION	217
	SPIRIT OF THE PLAY	218
	DATE OF COMPOSITION, AND SOURCE OF THE PLOT	221
	SHAKESPEARE'S MOOD AND INSPIRATION	223
	EARLY PERFORMANCES.—SHAKESPEARE IN ECLIPSE	228
	EIGHTEENTH CENTURY PRESENTMENTS.—FROM MRS. PRITCHARD TO MRS. SIDDONS	232
	MRS. SIDDONS AND MRS. JORDAN	237
	LATER REVIVALS.—BRITISH STAGE	240
	VARIOUS PERFORMANCES OF *ROSALIND*	252
	AMERICAN STAGE.—EARLY REPRESENTATIONS	253
	LATER AMERICAN REVIVALS.—AUGUSTIN DALY'S PRODUCTIONS	259
	THE MUSIC OF "AS YOU LIKE IT"	280
	VARIOUS PRODUCTIONS AND PLAYERS.—1871 TO 1885	284
	MARY ANDERSON'S REVIVAL	293
	LATER REVIVALS.—1885 TO 1914	302
	A BAD READING	307
	HENRIETTA CROSMAN	311
	MARGARET ANGLIN'S REVIVAL	313
	JAQUES AND HIS PLAYERS	317
	TOUCHSTONE AND HIS PLAYERS	322
	ORLANDO AND HIS PLAYERS	329

CONTENTS

CHAPTER	PAGE
Miss Marlowe.—Sothern-Marlowe	89
The New Theatre Production	91
Margaret Anglin	95
II. ROMEO AND JULIET.—Date of Composition	107
Source of the Plot	110
Early Representations.—British Stage	111
David Garrick and Spranger Barry.—The Rival *Romeos*	114
Setting and Costume	118
Later Revivals.—British Stage: The Kembles and Edmund Kean	123
Various Notable *Romeos*.—From Elliston to Robinson	127
Henry Irving's Presentation	130
The Character of *Romeo*	133
Johnston Forbes-Robertson	136
The Character of *Juliet*	138
Players of *Juliet*.—British Stage	141
Helena Faucit	148
Stella Colas	150
Adelaide Neilson	151
American Stage.—Early Representations	156
Many *Romeos*.—From Snelling Powell to Edward Hugh Sothern	158
Edwin Booth's Revival	161
Various New York Productions	165
Modjeska as *Juliet*	171
Mary Anderson's Revival	172
Margaret Mather as *Juliet*	179
Various Later Productions	183
Charles Frohman's Production	187
Julia Marlowe.—Sothern-Marlowe	190

CONTENTS

CHAPTER	PAGE
I. TWELFTH NIGHT	1
DATE OF COMPOSITION	2
SOURCE OF THE PLOT	5
SPIRIT OF THE PLAY	9
EARLY REPRESENTATIONS.—BRITISH STAGE	12
THE RESTORATION REVIVALS	14
BETTERTON AND HARRIS	16
FLEETWOOD'S PRODUCTION	18
OTHER OLD REVIVALS	19
SAMUEL PHELPS	28
CHARACTER OF *MALVOLIO*	30
HENRY IRVING	32
CHARACTER OF *VIOLA*	35
ELLEN TREE	39
ADELAIDE NEILSON	41
AGUECHEEK AND *FESTE*	45
AMERICAN STAGE.—EARLY REPRESENTATIONS	47
BURTON'S PRODUCTIONS	48
SIR TOBY	52
THE ELDER WALLACK'S REVIVAL	54
LATER PLAYERS OF *MALVOLIO*	55
VARIOUS PLAYERS OF *VIOLA*.—MRS. JOHNSON TO MME. MODJESKA	57
AUGUSTIN DALY'S REVIVALS.—1869; 1893; *ET SEQ.*	62
ADA REHAN	73
VIOLA ALLEN'S PRODUCTION	76
A CURIOSITY.—"BEN" GREET'S PRODUCTION	83

CONTENTS xiii

CHAPTER	PAGE
CONTINENTAL ACTORS OF *KING LEAR*— ROSSI.—BARNAY.—SALVINI.—VON POSSART.— NOVELLI	465
V. THE TAMING OF THE SHREW.—ORIGIN, AND DATE OF COMPOSITION	481
OFFSPRING OF SHAKESPEARE'S "SHREW"	493
EARLY REPRESENTATIONS.—BRITISH STAGE.— GARRICK'S ALTERATION	496
PLAYERS OF *KATHARINE* AND *PETRUCHIO*.—BRITISH STAGE	498
SHAKESPEARE *REDIVIVUS*.—WEBSTER AND PHELPS	503
AMERICAN STAGE.—EARLY REPRESENTATIONS	506
EDWIN BOOTH AS *PETRUCHIO*	508
AUGUSTIN DALY'S REVIVAL	511
CHARACTERS OF *KATHARINE* AND *PETRUCHIO*	516
ADA REHAN'S *KATHARINE*	520
DISCURSIVE COMMENT	527
VI. JULIUS CÆSAR.—COMPOSITION, AND SOURCE OF THE PLOT	541
OLD PLAYS ABOUT JULIUS CÆSAR	545
EARLY REPRESENTATIONS.—BRITISH STAGE	549
CHARLES HART AND HIS ASSOCIATES	550
THOMAS BETTERTON	552
LATER PLAYERS OF *BRUTUS*	555
EARLY PLAYERS OF *CASSIUS*	558
WILKS.—GARRICK.—BARRY.—MOSSOP.—MILWARD	559
JOHN PHILIP KEMBLE AND CHARLES MAYNE YOUNG	563
WILLIAM CHARLES MACREADY	566
JUNIUS BRUTUS BOOTH	569

CONTENTS

CHAPTER		PAGE
	Samuel Phelps	571
	Beerbohm-Tree's Production	573
	American Stage.—Early Representations	575
	Later Players of *Brutus*, *Cassius*, and *Antony*	579
	Edwin Booth's Production	580
	Edwin Booth as *Brutus* and *Antony*	585
	Character of *Cassius*	590
	Edwin Booth as *Cassius*	592
	Lawrence Barrett as *Cassius*	593
	J. B. Booth, Jr.—Creswick.—Bangs.—Montgomery	597
	The Booth and Barrett Alliance	601
	Jarrett and Palmer's Production.—Edward Loomis Davenport	603
	John Edward McCullough	608
	At the Cincinnati Dramatic Festival	610
	The Saxe-Meiningen Production in America	612
	Various Later Productions	616
	Richard Mansfield	618
	Robert Bruce Mantell	620
	William Faversham's Production	622
VII.	INDEX	631
	Actors and Theatrical Managers	633
	Characters	647
	Titles	655
	Miscellaneous	659

ILLUSTRATIONS

Susanna Cibber, Margaret Woffington,
  Kitty Clive, Sarah Siddons,
    Dora Jordan, Ellen Tree;
      Shakespeare, *From the Chandos Portrait,*   } *Frontispiece*
Helena Faucit, Ellen Terry,
  Mary Anderson, Julia Marlowe,
    Ada Rehan, Viola Allen.

TWELFTH NIGHT.   TO FACE PAGE

  Adelaide Neilson as *Viola,* 30
    From a Photograph.

  James Lewis as *Sir Toby Belch,* 46
    From a Photograph.

  Viola Allen as *Viola,* 62
    From a Photograph.

  Edward H. Sothern as *Malvolio,* 80
    From the Oil Painting by Orlando Rouland.

  Julia Marlowe as *Viola,* 88
    From a Photograph.

  Catherine Lewis as *Maria;*
  Ferdinand Gottschalk as *Sir Andrew Aguecheek,* } . 96
    From Photographs.

ROMEO AND JULIET.

  Henry Woodward } as *Mercutio,* 114
  Charles Kemble
    From Old Prints.

xv

ILLUSTRATIONS

TO FACE PAGE

Johnston Forbes-Robertson as *Romeo*, and
Mrs. Patrick Campbell as *Juliet*, ... 136
   From a Photograph.

Adelaide Neilson as *Juliet*, ... 152
   From a Photograph.

Mary Anderson as *Juliet*, ... 174
   From a Photograph.

Edward H. Sothern as *Romeo;*
Julia Marlowe as *Juliet*, ... 190
   From Photographs.

Charlotte Cushman as *Romeo*, and
Susan Cushman as *Juliet*, ... 210
   From an Old Print.

As You Like It.

Fawcett as *Touchstone*, ... 240
   From an Old Print.

Ada Rehan as *Rosalind*, ... 266
   From a Photograph.

Lillie Langtry as *Rosalind*, ... 290
   From a Photograph.

Helena Modjeska as *Rosalind*,
Mary Anderson as *Rosalind*, ... 300
   From Photographs.

Margaret Anglin as *Rosalind*,
Fuller Mellish as *Jaques*, ... 316
   From Photographs.

King Lear.

David Garrick as *King Lear*, ... 358
   From an Old Print.

ILLUSTRATIONS xvii

TO FACE PAGE

William C. Macready as *King Lear*, and
Helena Faucit as *Cordelia*, ... 398
   From an Old Print.

Henry Irving as *King Lear*, ... 428
   From the Drawing by J. Bernard Partridge.

Edwin Forrest as *King Lear*, ... 438
   From a Steel Engraving.

Edwin Booth as *King Lear*, ... 448
   From the Painting by Jervis McEntee.

John McCullough as *King Lear*, ... 458
   From a Photograph.

Robert Mantell as *King Lear*, ... 464
   From a Photograph.

THE TAMING OF THE SHREW.

Henry Woodward as *Petruchio*, ... 496
   From an Old Print.

James E. Murdoch,
   From an Old Print.
John Drew, } as *Petruchio*. . . . 512
   From a Photograph.

Ada Rehan as *Katharine*, ... 522
   From a Photograph.

Julia Marlowe }
Elsie Leslie } as *Katharine*, ... 532
   From Photographs.

JULIUS CÆSAR.

E. L. Davenport as *Brutus*, and
William C. Macready as *Cassius*, ... 566
   From an Old Print.

ILLUSTRATIONS

TO FACE
PAGE

Edwin Booth as *Brutus*,
   After the Bust by J. C. Hartley.
Lawrence Barrett as *Cassius*,
   From a Steel Engraving. 580

Richard Mansfield as *Brutus*, ... 616
   From a Photograph.

Tyrone Power as *Brutus*,
William Faversham as *Marc Antony*, . . . 628
   From Photographs.

PREFACE

This volume continues a theatrical chronicle on which I have worked, almost incessantly, for many years, and which I hope to live long enough to finish. The labor has been hard; the product of it, I venture to believe, will prove useful. Persons who consider the Theatre to be merely a Shop and who view Theatrical Management as merely "the Show Business," cannot be, and are not, expected to feel, or pretend to feel, even the slightest interest in a work which relates to the history, and aims to illustrate the development, of the beautiful Art of Acting. Persons, on the other hand, who believe, as I do, that the Theatre exercises a vast influence on Society, and should be cherished and stimulated as a potent agent of civilization, will, I am confident, favor the pursuance of an attempt,—already approved by their cordial welcome of the First Series of these Studies, —to present, in a suitably compendious form, an authentic account of the manner in which, from the beginning, the Plays of Shakespeare have been acted. My purpose and plan are fully stated in the Preface to the first volume of my SHAKESPEARE ON THE STAGE, *but as it is designed that each volume shall be complete in itself an extract from that Preface here restates that my design is—*

"To furnish, with reference to each play that is examined, an epitome of illustrative information; to state concisely such facts of Shakespearean scholarship as are essential to spare a reader the trouble of consulting other books on the subject while reading this one; to classify and coördinate a multiplicity of widely scattered, often contradictory, opinions and records as to actors; to provide original studies, in few words, of the Shakespearean characters selected for commentary; to comprehend, define, and describe the spirit of diverse embodiments of the same parts, and in each important case to indicate the method of performance that was pursued; to note essential variations of costume, in the dressing of the same parts and plays; to record, wherever possible, such of the stage business of every influential actor named in the story of Shakespearean Acting as is most illuminative and suggestive, without lapsing into inventory and becoming wearisome; to mention the various ideals and some of the various 'readings' of many actors, particularly such as have established traditions which are still valid,—and sometimes such as have attempted mere fantastic and confusing innovations; to show changes that have been wrought, in the lapse of time, in methods of stage presentment; and, avoiding repetition wherever possible,—though at times a certain similarity is inevitable in disquistion on the same part as played by different actors,—to unite facts, theories, traditions, opinions, and conjectures into a sequent and interesting narrative."

Some dissatisfaction has been expressed by a few censors of the first volume of this work relative to my adverse views of the performances of Shakespearean parts which have been given on our Stage,—that is, on the English-speaking Stage,—by actors from Continental Europe. Those views, however, I believe to be rational and just. The genius, ability, and excellence of foreign actors, when performing in characters within their complete comprehension, have not been denied or questioned, but, on the contrary, they have been, by me, recognized and highly extolled. Great native actors arise, from time to time, in almost every civilized country. The artistic world knows and honors such names as Le Kain, Talma, Clairon, Rachel, Modena, Salvini, Ristori, Devrient, Seebach, and Bernhardt. It is when foreign actors appear, before an English-speaking audience, in translations of the plays of Shakespeare that, broadly speaking, they all fail. Those translations are, necessarily, defective. There is, in every language, especially in the poetry of it, a quality which cannot be exactly interpreted into another. France does not possess Shakespeare in French; Italy does not possess him in Italian; Germany does not possess him in German,—although the German translations of his plays are generally esteemed better than those existent in any other tongue. The ethnological distinction, furthermore, exists and operates. The best representatives of the characters in Shakespeare's plays *have been, and are, men and women of British or American origin, to whom the speaking of the English language is natural; such, for example,—to mention only a few typical names,—as Betterton, Garrick, Kemble, Kean, Cooke, Macready, Phelps, Cooper, Wallack, Forrest, Booth, Davenport, Henry Irving, Mrs. Pritchard, Mrs. Barry, Mrs. Cibber, Mrs. Siddons, Mary Duff, Charlotte Cushman, Ellen Tree, Ellen Terry, Mary Anderson, and Ada Rehan.*

Some complaint has been made that in previous chapters of this work I have considered only six of Shakespeare's Plays, whereas, to justify my title, I ought to have considered the whole thirty-seven, and also that I have not described the representations of Shakespeare which have been made in the countries of Continental Europe. Such complaint is merely captious. It was plainly stated, in the Preface to the volume containing those chapters (which I would commend to the attention of all readers of this one), that the history of the manner in which Shakespeare's Plays have been represented would be continued. Furthermore it was said, and it is true, that there is no one of those plays which, if its stage history were exhaustively written, would not require a volume of about 200,000 words, while in each of several cases three or four such volumes would be needed to contain all the materials of narrative, commentary, and stage direction that might be assembled. Such treatment of the subject is not practical. The present work is far more comprehensive than any other in the same field that has yet been attempted. Four volumes supplementary to this one will be required to complete it, and, if I live, they will be written.

There is such variety in the writings of Shakespeare that the study of them is the study of human nature and human life, in every aspect and condition, and, as every student knows, the judgment of the observer in that vast field of inquiry necessarily changes with the passage of time, as experience sheds new light upon the mind. In writing this work I have availed myself, where possible, of material contained in the large mass of commentary,—some of it published, but now long out of print, some of it privately printed, still more of it existing in my manuscript Notes and Diaries,—accumulated during my long career as a critical observer of the acted Drama; but, having perceived reason to change or modify some of my previously expressed opinions, I have in this form, which I venture to hope may prove enduring, endeavored to record only my matured, deliberate judgments regarding every subject discussed. No person, I believe, has ever entertained a more profound veneration for the genius of Shake-

speare than is cherished by me. But I have long felt that the habit of ascribing perfection to everything that Shakespeare wrote, merely because he wrote it, is one of the chief obstacles to a right understanding of his works. Much of the commentary by European Continental critics, and some of that by those of Britain and America, obscures and misrepresents those works by providing them with fictitious meanings and imputing to their author didactic purposes which it is perfectly clear that he never intended. That he was not "a moralist" it pained Dr. Johnson to discover, but the Doctor was too astute a critic to miss that fact. "He seems," says the Sage, "to write without any moral purpose," and "this fault the barbarity of his age cannot extenuate." It was not a fault, it was a merit, and therefore it needs no extenuation. Shakespeare wrote as a dramatist and poet. He saw human nature and human life as they are, and he also saw them as they might be, and what he saw he portrayed, supplementing vision with imagination, and creating a literary and dramatic fabric of inestimable value and everlasting beauty. He should, however, be venerated and extolled for his virtues, not for his faults. As an artist he was often heedless; there is not even one of his plays which, as we possess it, would not be better had it been carefully revised by him, and one object which should invariably and conscientiously be

PREFACE

sought, in the stage presentation of his plays, is the exclusion of the errors and blemishes of "the original text."

The first chapter of the first volume of this series relates to the ridiculous and pernicious parrot-cry that "Shakespeare Spells Ruin." I would here revert briefly to that subject, and would glance also at what is called "the Modern Spirit" in producing Shakespeare. In the season of 1913-'14 a production of "Much Ado About Nothing" was made in New York, with a distinguished and admired American actor as BENEDICK. *It failed, and that failure, ever since, has been glibly cited as a decisive proof that Shakespeare can no longer be profitably acted. But what are the facts? An actor of ability and experience, naturally best adapted for eccentric light comedy, domestic drama, and farce, and proficient and delightful in his proper field, has, all his life, cherished the ambition to act* BENEDICK. *For more than twenty years, however, he devotes his talents to plays which are, mostly, of an insubstantial or frivolous order; he acts one part, sometimes perhaps two, a year, and so he falls into a rut. Then, at the age of sixty, in the sophisticated city of New York, in the hot, trying month of September, with a commonplace production, an inadequate company, and an inefficient, however zealous, performer of* BEATRICE, *he emerges, for the first time, in one of the three most difficult characters in the realm of high-comedy,—and he fails. Why not? What reason was there for good judgment to expect any other result? At forty, under suitable conditions, that actor might have played* BENEDICK *for the first time, and been successful, and thus might have established himself as the chief representative of it, in his period. The venture that was made evinced nothing but worthy ambition combined with bad judgment. It wrecked itself,—and the blame for disaster is unintelligently imposed on Shakespeare!*

As to "Modern Spirit" in the acting of Shakespeare, such manifestations of it as I have seen suffice only to exhibit ignorance, incompetence, and the contemptible quest of notoriety by blatant self-advertisement. The invariable pretence of Charlatanism is Novelty, and one of the most odious humbugs of the present day is the imbecile drivel about "New Thought" and "Modern Spirit." The only novelty required for the successful acting of Shakespeare's plays is the evergreen novelty of good acting. The plays of Shakespeare require large companies and considerable scenic investiture, and, therefore, it is not, never has been, and never will be, possible to earn as much money with them as sometimes is gained by contemporaneous plays that require only small casts and small scenic sets. The public that frequents the Theatre does not care for either "old spirit" or "new spirit." It requires only the opportunity to see Shakespeare's plays intelligently represented by actors whose natural faculties fit them to act those plays, and who have been properly taught and trained for the performance of them. Thus produced, Shakespeare will never fail.

A few names of modern and of contemporary actors will be missed from my pages, thus far written, as also, perhaps, will be the tributes which are due to the labors of such old managers as Knowles, J. H. Chute, and Charles Calvert, in England, and Barry, Gilfert, and Caldwell, in America. Notable Shakespearean productions have been made, within recent years, by F. R. Benson, Arthur Bourchier, Herbert Beerbohm-Tree, Oscar Ashe, and Martin Harvey. I hope to have the opportunity of doing ample justice to the achievements of those actors. Thus far I have provided a general narrative of the stage treatment of twelve of Shakespeare's plays. The story of what has befallen the remaining twenty-five is yet to be told. The field is broad, and a complete survey of it is not instantly to be made. I venture to declare, nevertheless, that in my chapters already written no important method of producing or acting Shakespeare's plays has been left unnoticed. No account has been attempted of the methods employed by such eccentric pretenders to originality as Herr Max Rhinehart, Mr. Granville Barker, and Mr. Gordon Craig. Judgment as to their productions necessarily waits until they have been seen and studied. Their methods, —if I can trust what I have read and heard about them,—are, variously, degenerate, contemptible, and silly,—in fact, an abomination.

It is difficult, when consulting many authorities and simultaneously considering many names, dates, and miscellaneous details, to avoid making an occasional mistake. Some errors have, doubtless, crept into my work. Two or three I have perceived. In the First Volume, page 236, it is stated that "the death of Richard Burbage occurred in 1629, the fourth year of the reign of King Charles the First." The right date, of course, is 1619. The habit of reverifying every date sometimes defeats itself: it caused me, inadvertently, to be misled by the entry in "Hole's Biographical Dictionary" which (probably through a misprint) gives the date of the death of Burbage as 1629.

In my chapter on "The Merchant of Venice," when referring to Henry Irving's production, I wrote these words: "The expenditure on this revival was small,— only $6,000." The compositor generously added a cipher to those figures, which was overlooked in the reading of the proof, so that the amount became cent screen of carved oak, the gift of Queen Elizabeth, is one of the most stately old rooms that allure and impress the Shakespeare pilgrim in London. Halliwell-Phillips says, relative to that performance of "Twelfth Night": "the representation took place at the Feast of the Purification, February the 2nd, one of the two grand annual festival days of the lawyers, *on which occasion professional actors were annually engaged at the Middle Temple,* the then liberal sum of ten pounds being given to them for a single performance"; and he adds, "there is no doubt that the comedy was performed by the Lord Chamberlain's servants, and very little that Shakespeare himself was one of the actors who were engaged."

Mention is made that one of the songs in the comedy, "O mistress mine, where are you roaming?" was in print in one of the many musical works by Thomas Morley (1557-1603), a compilation entitled "The First Book of Consort Lessons, Made by Divers Authors," published in 1599; and William Chappell (1809-1888), observing this fact, infers that either "Twelfth Night" must have been written in or before 1599 "or that, in accordance with the then prevailing custom, 'O Mistress Mine' was an old song introduced into the play." The scrupulous commentator Dyce thereupon remarks that

Chappell's "latter supposition is doubtless the true one." Furness, on the contrary, contends, from internal evidence, that "'O Mistress Mine' is Shakespeare's own." In either case the inference is warranted that "Twelfth Night" was composed before 1599 or early in that year. Even Shakespeare could not have written the play over-night, and allowance of time must be made for the writing and production of it and for the obtainment of such popularity for the song "O Mistress Mine" as would have induced its insertion in Morley's book, and for the making and publishing of that work. It is unlikely, furthermore, that a play by Shakespeare,—who, in 1601, had been known as a dramatic author for, certainly, ten years, and who wrote and produced plays for subsistence, not amusement,—would have been presented for the first time in semi-privacy, and also it is unlikely that the directors would have selected an untried play for what Manningham designates their "feast." "Twelfth Night," in 1601, must have been known and popular, and the belief is rational that it was written in 1599, or even a little earlier. It is not named in the list of twelve of Shakespeare's plays given by Meres, in his "Palladis Tamia," published in 1598.

SOURCE OF THE PLOT.

It was Manningham's opinion, as stated in his "Diary," that the plot of "Twelfth Night" is "much like 'The Comedy of Errors' or 'Menechmi,' in Plautus, *but most like and neere to that in Italian called* 'Inganni,'"—"The Deceits." There is resemblance between "Twelfth Night" and two earlier Italian plays, entitled "Gl' Inganni,"—one of them by Nicolo Secchi, published in Milan, 1547; the other by Curtio Gonzaga, published in Venice, 1592,—but hardly enough resemblance to warrant assertion that it is "most like and neere to" either of them. (The fact that the poet noticed a name, Gonzago, nearly identical with that of Gonzaga appears in "Hamlet," the title of the play selected by *Hamlet* for performance before his royal uncle being "The Murder of Gonzago"; in Act III., sc. 2, the *Prince* says "Gonzago is the duke's name," and adds that the play is "extant and writ in choice Italian.") "Twelfth Night" is, however, "most like and neere to" a third Italian play, discovered by Hunter, entitled "Gl' Ingannati." The story of "Gl' Ingannati" is also told by Matthew Bandello (1480-1562), in a novel, published in 1554. Furness maintains that "Gl' Ingannati" is the source of the plot of Bandello's novel,—a work to which, as bearing on this subject, attention was first directed by Mrs. Charlotte Lennox (1720-1804). Several editions of "Gl' Ingannati" were published prior to the appearance of that novel, a composition translated from Italian into French by François de Belleforêt (1530-1583), and Edward Capell and other Shakespeare editors suggest that the dramatist derived material from Belleforêt's version of Bandello's tale. It should be considered, though, that in 1577-'78 a company of Italian actors performed in London, and also before Queen Elizabeth, at Windsor, and that "Gl' Ingannati," being a popular play, was certainly included in the repertory of that company. Shakespeare, it seems more than likely, drew material from that play, rather than from the French translation of Bandello's story.

It has been objected that Shakespeare did not know the Italian language. Dyce "suspects" that "his knowledge of Italian was small." He certainly knew "small Latin," however, and Latin is the key to Italian. But even if he was ignorant of all languages except English there is no reasonable ground for doubt that if he had wished to utilize a story extant in a foreign language he could easily have obtained at least a rough translation of it. Hack work of that kind has been utilized, in all periods of literary labor. The mention of *Twelfth Night* in the

Prologue to "Gl' Ingannati" ("the story is new, never before either seen or read, not drawn from any other source save from their industrious pates [those of the authors], just as you draw your lots on *Twelfth Night*"), taken with other considerations, warrants belief that Shakespeare was acquainted with that Italian play and that he built the serious part of the plot of his "Twelfth Night" on that basis. Furness maintains that he built it on the basis of a Latin translation of "Gl' Ingannati," entitled "Laelia," acted at Queen's College, Cambridge, in 1590 and in 1598,—a translation which that learned editor declares to be "faithful, in every main feature, to the original comedy."

Hunter's statement of the resemblance between the plots of "Gl' Ingannati" and "Twelfth Night" is instructive:

"*Fabrito* and *Lelia*, a brother and sister, are separated, at the sack of Rome, in 1527. *Lelia* is carried to Modena, where resides *Flamineo*, to whom she had formerly been attached. *Lelia* disguises herself as a boy and enters his service. *Flamineo* had forgotten *Lelia*, and was a suitor to *Isabella*, a Modenese lady. *Lelia*, in her male attire, is employed in love-embassies from *Flamineo* to *Isabella*. *Isabella* is insensible to the importunities of *Flamineo*, but conceives a violent passion for *Lelia*, mistaking her for a man. In the Third Act *Fabrito* arrives at Modena, when mistakes arise owing to the close resemblance there is between *Fabrito* and his sister in male attire. Ultimately recognitions take place: the affections of *Isabella* are easily transferred from *Lelia* to *Fabrito*, and *Flamineo* takes to his bosom the affectionate and faithful *Lelia*. . . . We have, in the Italian play, a subordinate character, named *Pasquella*, to whom *Maria* corresponds: and in the subordinate incidents we find *Fabrito* mistaken in the street for *Lelia* by the servant of *Isabella*, who takes him to her mistress' house, exactly as *Sebastian* is taken for *Viola* [*Cesario*] and led to the house of *Olivia*. . . . The name of *Fabian* given by Shakespeare to one of his characters was probably suggested to him by *Fabio*, which *Lelia*, in the Italian play, assumed in her disguise. . . ."

Shakespeare was in his prime, aged nearly thirty-five, when he wrote "Twelfth Night." His faculties were in splendid vigor, and, from whatever source he may have derived materials for the serious part of his plot,—whether from Plautus, or Secchi, or Gonzaga, or Bandello, or de Belleforêt's French translation of Bandello, or Riche's "Apolonius and Silla" (as supposed by Collier), or "Gl' Ingannati," or the Latin "faithful translation" thereof,—the borrowed persons and incidents were greatly improved by him. He invented and supplied the entire humorous portion of the comedy, including all the eccentric and comic characters. *Sir Toby Belch, Sir Andrew Aguecheek, Malvolio,* and *Feste* are his creations, while *Viola, Olivia,* and *Orsino* are persons whom his genius transfigured from ordinary shapes, common to several old romances, and made poetic. There is as much interesting human nature in "Twelfth Night" as there is in any comedy ever written, and there is, perhaps, a happier blending of humorous quaintness, airy fancy, and tender sentiment in it than there is in any other of Shakespeare's comedies.

SPIRIT OF THE PLAY.

In "Twelfth Night" the dramatic art of Shakespeare operates with an ease that is delicious. The touch is light. The mood,—now gentle, now exuberantly joyous, now pensive, now satiric, now tender,—is natural, careless, seemingly almost indifferent. You are provided with all essential knowledge of the two households of *Orsino* and *Olivia,* yet you hardly perceive how it was that you came to know them, or how it is that they are made to dwell in your mind as pictorial and typical of so much diversified character, so much human nature, and so much representative experience. The action passes frequently from one of those households to the other, but never with violence or caprice. The changes occur aptly. The persons almost imperceptibly drift into their places and into your acquaintance and favor. The variations in the style, alternating prose with verse, are made with charming flexibility and they are in perfect accordance with the variations of theme. The individuality of the speakers is consistently maintained. Incidents follow one another rapidly, yet, once surrendered to poetic glamour, they seem to be entirely natural: in Moore's happy phrase, all is "free and wandering." Though there is great moral force in the fabric, nowhere is there a trace of obtrusive didacticism. The rebuke of self-love and the warning against it are enwrapt in ridicule and sweetened with mirth. The poet's ever-present, clear-sighted sense of the incongruity of qualities in character and of circumstances in experience, the twists and turns and complexities of human life, infuse the play with a pervasive spirit of tolerant pleasantry, a kindly, careless humor, as of a genial, meditative philosopher who looks upon the great mundane spectacle as something clearly to be perceived yet never to be clearly comprehended, and always to be viewed with patience, charity, and a smiling acquiescence. From first to last it is life in little: love and loss; humor and grief; sadness and mirth; pain and pleasure; fond fidelity and capricious fancy; revel, frolic, vanity, folly, and satire; sunshine and drifting shadow, fortune all at odds, and motley the only wear:

> "A great while ago the world began,
> With hey, ho, the wind and the rain, . . .
> For the rain it raineth every day!"

The free and wandering spirit of "Twelfth Night" is manifested not only in its diversity of style but in its diversity of materials. The scene is "a city in Illyria and the sea-coast near it." The names of the characters are Italian, Spanish, and English. *Orsino* is variously called "Duke" and "Count." *Sir Toby Belch* and *Sir Andrew Aguecheek* bear English titles. *Maria* is the English stage chambermaid. *Viola* and her brother, *Sebastian,* are natives of Messaline (Mitylene), and, putatively, are Greeks, but they manifest no Grecian characteristics: in fact, they are, distinctively, as is every other character in the play, English. The *Clown, Feste,* is one of those quaint, sagacious, masquerading jesters essentially English in their humor and dear to Shakespeare's fancy, who use folly as a stalking-horse, and from behind it shoot the arrows of their wit. Love, in its tendency to create despairing melancholy, is not better portrayed in even the preliminary experience of *Romeo* with *Rosaline* than it is in the delineation of *Orsino's* passion for *Olivia.* Sorrow alternates with joy, and frolic with gravity, throughout the play, and as the funereal dirge of "Come away, Death" lapses into silence the great, strident voice of *Sir Toby Belch* brays forth, in vinous tumult, "There dwelt a man in Babylon," or the legendary catch of "Prithee, hold thy peace." Shakespeare frequently disregards those laws of form and precepts of scholarlike composition in which his philosophical and erudite contemporary Francis Bacon devoutly believed, and which his learned brother Ben Jonson scrupulously obeyed. In "Twelfth Night" he cast them to the winds. It is even more difficult to assign a place and a period for that comedy than it is to localize "As You Like It." Illyria—now Dalmatia, Croatia, and Bosnia—was a Roman province, 167 B.C. In Shakespeare's time Dalmatia was under the rule of the Venetian Republic. The custom has long prevailed of treating the play as a romantic and poetic picture of Venetian manners in the seventeenth century, but Greek dresses have sometimes been used. For the purposes of the stage there must be "local habitation"; for a reader the scene of "Twelfth Night" is the elusive and evanescent, but limitless and immortal, land of dreams.

EARLY PRESENTATIONS.—BRITISH STAGE.

It is credibly supposed, but not recorded, that "Twelfth Night" was placed on the stage for the first time in 1599 or 1600, at the Globe Theatre, Southwark, London, and acted by the Lord Chamberlain's company, of which the author was a member, but nothing is known of either the cast of the parts or the quality of the performance. Conjecture would assign *Sir Toby* to John Heminge, *Malvolio* to Joseph Taylor, and *Feste* to Robert Armin. Heminge's line of business is signified by the fact that he was the original performer of *Falstaff,* and Taylor's by the fact that he succeeded Burbage as *Hamlet,* and it is known that Armin acted some of Shakespeare's Fools or Clowns. John Shancke was one of the actors in "Twelfth Night," in Shakespeare's time, but the part he played is not named. He was dramatist as well as actor: a play by him, called "Shancke's Ordinary," was produced at the Blackfriars Theatre in 1603.

Mention of a performance of "Twelfth Night" occurs in an old manuscript preserved at the Audit Office, London, recording payment "To John Heminges, &c., upon a warrant dated April 20, 1618, for presenting two several plays before his Majesty; on Easter Monday, Twelfth Night, the play so called, and on Easter Tuesday, the Winter's Tale." In the "Diary" of Sir Henry Herbert (1595-1673), Master of the Revels, an official entry certifies that "Twelfth Night" was presented, in 1622-'23, under the title of " Malvolio." The words of this record are: "At Candlemas Malvolio was acted at Court by the King's Servants." The King was James the First. Testimony as to the currency and the popularity of

Shakespeare's plays, and, specifically, as to the favor enjoyed by "Twelfth Night," is found in the lines by Leonard Digges, prefixed to a collection of Shakespeare's poems dated 1640:

". . . . . . loe in a trice
The Cockpit, Galleries, Boxes, all are full
To hear Malvoglio, that cross garter'd Gull."

THE RESTORATION REVIVALS.

It is not till the period of the Restoration (1660) that the investigator of theatrical chronicles meets with positively designated actors in "Twelfth Night." Samuel Pepys (1632-1703) mentions the comedy several times in his "Diary," and from that valuable and interesting record we learn that it was revived by Davenant, at the Duke's Theatre (which was opened in June, 1661), in Lincoln's Inn Fields, on the following September 11, on which occasion Pepys saw the performance and made this note on it:

"Walking through Lincoln's Inn Fields observed at the Opera a new Play, 'Twelfth Night,' was acted there, and the King there: so I, against my own mind and resolution, could not forbear to go in, which did make the play seem a burthen to me; and I took no pleasure at all in it."

On January 6 (that is, on Twelfth Night), 1663, at the same theatre, he again saw the comedy, and he wrote that it was "acted well, though it be but a silly play, and not relating at all to the name or day." In 1668 he saw it for the third time, and made a note, declaring it to be "one of the weakest plays that ever I saw on the stage." Davenant's theatrical company, when he opened the Duke's Theatre, or a little later, included Thomas Betterton, —— Blagden, Henry Harris, Thomas Lovel, Matthew Medbourne, John Mosely, James Noakes, Joseph Price, —— Richards, Samuel Sandford, William Smith, Thomas Sheppy, Cave Underhill, —— Young, Mrs. Davenport, Mrs. Davies, Ann Gibbs, Mrs. Holden, Mrs. Jennings, Mrs. Long, and Mary Saunderson (afterward Mrs. Betterton). The revival of "Twelfth Night" which was effected in 1663 is particularly mentioned by Downes, in his "Roscius Anglicanus," who says that it "had mighty success by its well performance." The cast then included Betterton, as *Sir Toby Belch;* Harris, as *Sir Andrew Aguecheek;* Lovel, as *Malvolio;* Underhill, as *Feste,* and Ann Gibbs, as *Olivia.* The name of the performer of *Viola,* on that notable occasion, is not given, but it is likely that the part was played by sprightly Mrs. Davenport, young and handsome. "All the parts being justly acted,"—says the sententious old prompter, Downes,—"crown'd the play."

BETTERTON AND HARRIS.

The versatility of Betterton must have been wonderful. When we read of the gravity of his character, the sobriety of his life, the dignity of his manner, the majesty of his presence, the entrancing melody of his voice, the scope and variety of his copious, overwhelming tragic power, and the intrinsic, imperial authority and personal charm by which he could not only move an audience but inspire it with awe and hold it spellbound and almost breathless in suspense, we can readily think of him as *Hamlet* and *Brutus, Othello* and *Macbeth,* but not easily as *Sir Toby Belch:* yet we possess contemporaneous testimony that he was equally excellent in all that he did. In what manner he acted *Sir Toby* we do not know, but we know that the character, although degraded by inebriety, contains good elements,—among them courage, sagacity, humor, and formidable personality,—and we cannot doubt that Betterton, a diligent student of his author and his art, perceived, comprehended, and conveyed all that the character contains.

Harris (Pepys's "ayery man") also must have been an exceptionally versatile actor: he was the *Romeo* when Betterton played *Mercutio;* he was deemed excellent as *Cardinal Wolsey,* and yet vacuous, addle-headed *Sir Andrew* did not come amiss to him. Lovel was the "old man" of Davenant's company,—the *Polonius* when Betterton played *Hamlet,*—and, presumably, a correct actor; but particular description of his acting has not been found: he died a little before 1673. Underhill, highly praised, in particular, for his performance of the *First Grave-Digger,* in "Hamlet," seems to have been an exceptionally accomplished low comedian. "He looked," says Cibber, "as if it were not in human passions to alter a feature of him; a countenance of wood could not be more fixed than his." The essence of his presentation of *Feste* must have been waggery,—droll, but, probably, deficient of delicate suggestion. There is more than jocularity in the character of *Feste:* his temperament is agreeably whimsical, his demeanor is sprightly, and he veils, without concealing, his sapience with his caustic mirth. Underhill was also esteemed for his *Trinculo,* in "The Tempest," and his *Sir Sampson Legend,* in Congreve's "Love for Love." Ann Gibbs was one of the seven female players in Davenant's company when he opened his theatre in Lincoln's Inn Fields, but her quality as an actress is unknown.

FLEETWOOD'S PRODUCTION.

Throughout the interval, about seventy-five years, between the period of Betterton and that of Garrick, "Twelfth Night" was neglected, but on January 15, 1741, at Drury Lane, then under Charles Fleetwood's management (Garrick did not become manager of that house till 1747), it was revived, with a notably fine cast, comprising Hannah Pritchard, as *Viola;* Kitty Clive, as *Olivia;* Henry Woodward, as *Sir Andrew,* and Charles Macklin, as *Malvolio.* Mrs. Pritchard is usually brought to mind as exclusively a tragic actress, but in her youth she was a slender, elegant woman, and she was deemed incomparably good in vivacious characters. Her countenance was pleasing, her voice deliciously musical, and her deportment graceful; her eyes were brilliantly expressive, and her performances were marked by sympathetic feeling artistically controlled. Such an actress could not have been otherwise than lovely as *Viola*. Kitty Clive (Catherine Raftor) usually acted comic parts, but she was a self-assertive woman, of decided character and vigorous mind, and she would easily have made the comparatively slight part of the proud *Olivia* natural and effective. Woodward,—in private life reserved and saturnine, but a consummate artist, and, on the stage, a marvel of eccentric humor, especially able to cause laughter by means of his infectious laugh,—made what Dr. Johnson calls "natural fatuity" both ruefully actual and comically absurd. Macklin, stern in nature, aggressive in personality, and severely correct in method, was specially fitted for *Malvolio,*—possessed, as he was, of such varied talents and resources: the intense power requisite for *Shylock,* and therewithal the sturdiness and comic variety requisite for *Sir Pertinax Macsycophant.*

OTHER OLD REVIVALS.

On the London Stage, between 1746 and 1825, many important presentments of "Twelfth Night" were accomplished, and on each occasion actors of high rank participated in the performances. At Drury Lane, April 15, 1746, Macklin again being the *Steward,* the bewitching Peg Woffington acted *Viola,* for the first time, and charmed the public by her gay, sensuous assumption of the blithe and winning "boy,"—a form of artistic achievement in which she was supreme and in which her supremacy endured unchallenged till the time of Mrs. Jordan, the professional ancestor of Ada Rehan. *Feste* was played by Richard Yates, who later,—1763,—gained distinction as *Malvolio.* Participant with Yates on the latter occasion were Kitty Clive, as *Olivia;* William O'Brien, a player of rare ability, as *Sir Andrew,* and John Palmer, afterward eminent in many characters, and especially so in *Sir Toby,* as *Sebastian.* On December 10, 1771, at Drury Lane, the cast of parts in "Twelfth Night" was particularly felicitous, presenting Thomas King, as *Malvolio;* James Dodd,—so much admired and so ingeniously described and sympathetically commemorated by Charles Lamb,—as *Sir Andrew;* Mrs. Abington, as *Olivia,* in which character she sang a song, and Thomas Jefferson, great-grandfather of our Joseph Jefferson (*Rip Van Winkle*), as *Orsino.* A later *Viola* was provided by Mrs. Yates, who acted the part at Covent Garden on May 5, 1772, in association with Woodward, as *Sir Andrew;* Yates, as *Malvolio,* and Mrs. Mattocks (Isabella Hallam), as *Olivia.* On March 17, 1777, at Covent Garden, the brilliant Mrs. Spranger Barry (afterward Mrs. Crawford), who was by turns piquant and pathetic, delighted the town as *Viola,* which she then first played, the occasion being that of her benefit. John Quick was *Sir Andrew,* Mrs. Hartley *Olivia,* Mrs. Wilson *Maria,* and John Dunstall *Sir Toby.* A striking cast appears in the record, August 15, 1782, when the comedy was performed at the Haymarket, with Robert Bensley, as *Malvolio;* John Palmer, as *Sir Toby;* droll and merry John

Edwin, as *Sir Andrew;* William Parsons, as *Feste;* Mrs. Bulkley, as *Viola,* and Miss Harper, as *Olivia.* John Henderson, one of the greatest of actors (John Philip Kemble said that Henderson's performance of *Shylock* was the best piece of acting that he ever saw), played *Malvolio,* for the first time, on May 7, 1783, when "Twelfth Night" was revived at Covent Garden, for the benefit of Edwin, who played *Sir Andrew.* Mrs. Robinson was *Viola,* Mrs. Mattocks Olivia, and Tom Davies *Feste.* Henderson is known to have been an exceptionally judicious and correct speaker and to have possessed extraordinary powers of imitation: Genest says of him that "his comprehension was ample, his knowledge diversified, and his elocution accurate": his performance of the vainglorious *Steward* must have been a fine one.

Dora Jordan first acted *Viola* on November 11, 1785, at Drury Lane, and she made a brilliant hit, so that her performance became and remained a favorite and was often given. The *Malvolio* was Bensley, Dodd presented *Sir Andrew,* Palmer *Sir Toby,* and Richard Suett, the incomparable, *Feste;* Mrs. Cranch appeared as *Olivia* and John Bannister as *Sebastian.* William Dunlap, the earliest historian of the American Theatre, who saw Mrs. Jordan's performance at that time, when he was a visitor in London, records it with the remark that "Nothing could be more sweet" than her *Viola*. Mrs. Jordan, speaking to a friend (who recorded the statement) on the subject of her method in art, said that "the secret of [her] my charm, was that, 'when she had mastered the language of a part, she said to Dame Nature, my head, hands, feet, and every member of me, are at your commandment.'" Boaden, describing her appearance as *Sir Harry Wildair,* makes an observation equally applicable to her appearance as *Viola:*—"however beautiful in her figure," she "stood confessed a perfect and decided woman"; and he adds "that the mere melody of her utterance brought tears into the eyes, and that passion had never had so modest and enchanting an interpreter." Sir Joshua Reynolds, one of the most sensible and informing of observers, remarked that in "the tender and exquisite *Viola* of Shakespeare" "she combines *feeling* with sportive effect, and does as much by the music of her *melancholy* as the music of her laugh." On at least one occasion, February 10, 1790, at Drury Lane, Mrs. Jordan's brother, Bland,—who "in his figure did not tower above his disguised sister,"—by the accommodation of Kemble, acted *Sebastian* to her *Viola:* he was an indifferent actor, and the association was only notable because of the actual relationship and the personal resemblance.

Bensley's personation of *Malvolio* still lives in the

quaint, genial pages of "Elia." Bensley had been a soldier before he became an actor: he served in the British army in America, at the time of the Revolutionary War, holding the rank of lieutenant. His demeanor was stiff and formal; his gait was a "martial stalk," and he indulged a trick of glaring and of rolling his eyes. He was an actor of the artistic lineage of Quin,—the sovereign representative of the school of "dignity and declamation." His person was commanding and his mind was grave. All his peculiarities favored him as *Malvolio,* and it can well be believed that his performance of the part was perfect. He seems to have furnished a model, for some of his stage business has endured. John Bernard (1756-1828) provides, as to Bensley, the note of detraction which invariably is sounded relative to every person of distinction, in whatever period and whatever walk of life. "The system to which he belonged,"—so wrote Bernard,—"considered dignity to consist a good deal in cutting the stage at right angles, with the head up and the brows down; a coldly correct enunciation, and a full-flowing wig." James Boaden (1762-1838), the biographer of J. P. Kemble and Mrs. Jordan, said of Bensley, as *Malvolio,* that "his sliding, zigzag advance and retreat of his figure fixed the attention to his stockings and his garters"; that "his constrained smile, his hollow laugh, his lordly assumption, and his ineffable contempt of all that opposed him in the way to greatness were irresistibly diverting"; and, in another place, that "his stage-walk eternally reminded you of the 'one, two, three, hop' of the dancing master: this scientific progress of legs, in yellow stockings, most villainously cross-gartered, with a horrible laugh of ugly conceit to top the whole, rendered him Shakespeare's *Malvolio* at all points."

The most authoritative actor of *Sir Toby Belch* in the eighteenth century was John Palmer,—according to all obtainable testimony one of the best "all round" actors that ever trod the stage, while the most amusing *Sir Andrew* (if not the most correct) was the eccentric John Edwin, an actor who was spontaneously droll, yet who, according to his biographer, Pasquin, took the greatest care to be exact. John Bernard, who acted with him and knew him well, testifies that "he was always himself." Dunlap, who, if not always an accurate recorder, was a careful observer, while visiting London in 1784-'85 enjoyed the privilege of seeing, at Drury Lane, not only the vivacious Dora Jordan as *Viola* and the beautiful Elizabeth Farren as *Olivia,* but also Palmer as *Sir Toby* and Dodd as *Sir Andrew,* and to him we are indebted for an instructive glimpse of those comedians,—a sort of vignette of the after-midnight revel scene in "Twelfth Night":

"The picture presented when the two knights are discovered with their pipes and potations, as exhibited by Dodd and Palmer, is ineffaceable: The driveller, rendered more contemptible by the effect of liquor,—the actor's thin legs in scarlet stockings, his knees raised nearly to his chin by placing his feet on the front cross-pieces of the chair (the degraded drunkards being seated, with a table, tankards, pipes, and candles between them), a candle in one hand and pipe in the other, endeavoring in vain to bring the two together; while, in representing the swaggering *Sir Toby,* Palmer's gigantic limbs outstretched seemed to indicate the enjoyment of that physical superiority which Nature had given him, even while debasing it by the lowest of all vices."

Boaden remarks, of those two actors, that Palmer was "the only *Sir Toby Belch,*" and that "the smoothness, the native imbecility, of Dodd's *Sir Andrew Aguecheek* were transcendent."

On May 11, 1797, at Covent Garden, the younger Bannister, John, first acted *Malvolio,* with Suett, as *Sir Andrew,* and William Dowton, as *Feste.* Mrs. Jordan was *Viola* and Miss Mellen *Maria.* Bannister's portrayal of *Malvolio* is nowhere particularly described, but since his peculiar vein was that of *Mercutio* and *Gratiano,* and his best performance that of *Walter,* in "The Babes in the Wood," it seems reasonable to suppose that his *Malvolio* was not much more than a technically correct embodiment of eccentric character. Leigh Hunt, whose theatrical criticism is of peculiar value, highly complimented this actor, saying that he "contrived to mingle the *heart* with his broadest humor." Dowton, who first acted *Malvolio* on February 13, 1798, at Drury Lane, lives in the dramatic record as one of the best comedians of the old English Stage and as being superb in that character. It was said that "he made it his own." Dowton acted in New York in 1835 and was seen in a variety of parts, ranging from *Falstaff* to *Sir Peter Teazle,* but his *Malvolio* was not given here. A contemporary English critic, James A. Heraud, wrote of him that "unobtrusive humor was his chief characteristic," and that "because he portrayed the feelings rather than the habits of men" he was "most at home in parts which, though productive of comic effect, are yet allied to tragic emotions." Such a part, to some extent, is *Malvolio.*

Many shining names are associated with revivals of "Twelfth Night" about the beginning of the nineteenth century. On June 9, 1801, at Covent Garden, Joseph Munden was *Malvolio,* Edward Knight *Sir Andrew,* John Emery *Sir Toby,* William Blanchard *Feste,* and Mrs. D. Johnson *Viola.* Munden was an exceedingly comic actor, much given to grimace, and undoubtedly his *Malvolio* was funny, but contemporary opinion declared that the part was "not one of his best." By Lamb he was regarded as a superlative comic genius.

TWELFTH NIGHT

On January 5, 1811, at Covent Garden, John Liston acted *Malvolio,* Blanchard *Sir Andrew,* Emery *Sir Toby,* Barrymore *Orsino,* John Fawcett *Feste,* Sally Booth *Viola,* Mrs. Charles Kemble *Olivia,* and Mrs. Gibbs *Maria.* Liston, although unquestionably an excellent comedian, intrinsically and exuberantly droll, caused no memorable effect in *Malvolio;* yet so good an observer as Henry Crabb Robinson wrote (1811): "Liston's *Malvolio* was excellent. It is a character in all respects adapted to him. His inimitable gravity, till he receives the letter, and his incomparable smiles, in the Cross-gartered Scene, are the perfection of nature and art united." In a performance at Drury Lane, January 3, 1813, *Olivia* was acted by the melodious Mrs. Glover, Mrs. Davison was the *Viola,* and Miss Mellon *Maria.* William Farren (1791-1861), highly renowned for the excellence of his acting as *Sir Peter Teazle,* did not make a remarkable impression as *Malvolio,* careful and thorough artist though certainly he must have been, to have merited all the printed encomium that was lavished on his general acting. He played the part, at Covent Garden, on November 8, 1820, when "Twelfth Night" was performed as an Opera. The associate players were: Emery, as *Sir Toby;* Liston, as *Sir Andrew;* Fawcett, as *Feste;* Abbott, as *Orsino;* Maria Tree, as *Viola;* Mrs. Greene, as

Olivia, and Mrs. Gibbs, as *Maria.* Genest mentions it as "a wretched piece of business." It was acted seventeen times, and on June 3, 1825, it was revived, with a varied cast, Farren repeating his performance. The adapter of the play as an opera was Frederick Reynolds. The music was written by Bishop. Maria Tree had then been only about two years on the stage, her first notable appearance having been made in November, 1818, at Bath, when she was about sixteen years old. Mention is made of "the soft and solemn character of her singing, the simplicity which made her acting so natural, and the intelligence of one so young" (Richard Ryan). Her performance of *Viola,* admired from the first, became a favorite, and it is enthusiastically praised in various old records, but not particularly described. This actress, it is interesting to note, was the original *Clari,* in "The Maid of Milan," and therefore, probably, the first person who ever sang "Home, Sweet Home," the words of which song were written by John Howard Payne, for that opera.

SAMUEL PHELPS.

Samuel Phelps presented "Twelfth Night," at Sadler's Wells Theatre, January 26, 1848, and repeated it there, January 14, 1857,—on both occasions acting *Malvolio.* His performance was excel-

TWELFTH NIGHT

lent. To personate this part with fidelity to the dramatist's delineation, yet to avoid a painful, almost a tragic, effect in the last scenes, is difficult. Phelps studiously preserved a comedy spirit by maintaining the element of self-love to such a degree that it was an armor to him. His demeanor was not that of strutting comicality, but of arrogant grandeur. Not the least intimation was given of any tenderness of feeling toward *Olivia:* to Phelps's *Malvolio* his *Lady* was but the means of "thrusting greatness" upon him, she being happy only in loving so superlative a person. In dress and aspect he was Spanish; in demeanor, the personification of egregious self-esteem: "walled up in his own temple of flesh," said Professor Morley, "he is his own adorer." His movements were slow; his heavy lids almost closed his eyes, as though there were nothing in the external world worthy of his regard, in contrast with his perception of his own super-eminent excellence. When, at last, he perceived how notoriously he had been abused, Phelps's *Malvolio* was about to retire without condescending to speak a word to his tormentors, when *Feste's* jibe, that "the whirligig of Time brings in his revenges," "reminded him" (so wrote the same discriminative critic) "that the whirligig is still in motion," and "marching back, with as much increase of speed as is consistent with magnificence, he threatens all,—including now *Olivia* in his contempt,—'I'll be revenged on the whole pack of you!'" A discreet and informing estimate of Phelps's performance was made by Bayle Bernard, writing in 1857:

"There is a sort of frozen calm about his [Phelps's] motion as *Malvolio*, a solidified presumption, that conveys the grandest sense of his elevated consciousness. He is as little to be thawed by courtesy as he is to be shattered by collision. He sails about as a sort of iceberg, towering over spray and tumult. His *Lady* is the only sun that has power to dissolve him. There is condescension in all that he does. His vision of the future seems to suppose a crowd of listeners, whom he will oblige with the particulars. His acceptance of his *Lady's* love is quite as approving as it is grateful. He is her man, and she is wise in having him; and when, to please her, he agrees to smile, it is plain he feels he is rewarding her."

CHARACTER OF *MALVOLIO*.

King Charles the First owned a copy of the Second Folio of Shakespeare, 1632, and the fact is recorded that he drew the royal pen through the title "Twelfth Night," in that volume, and wrote the name of "Malvolio" in its stead, thereby signifying that, to his apprehension, *Olivia's Steward* was the predominant figure in the play. That book, once in the possession of George Steevens, the old Shakespeare scholar and editor (1736-1800), was bought for the private library of King George the Third,

From a Photograph by Sarony, N. Y. *Author's Collection*

ADELAIDE NEILSON AS *VIOLA*

"Cesario is your servant's name, fair princess."

Act III., Sc. 1

and when that library was given to the English nation, by his son, King George the Fourth, it was reserved, and it still remains in the archives of the English royal family. King Charles's impression of the eminence of *Malvolio* in the comedy is not wholly unwarranted, because the character is somewhat more minutely drawn than any of those which are associated with it.

Malvolio is the cause of laughter, but the observer who is not made to think and feel, as well as to laugh, by the spectacle of his infirmity, folly, and discomfiture does not fully comprehend him. The saturnine quality in his character is conspicuous and of great dramatic value. He is not to be mistaken for a mere gull. He is a person of strong individuality and austere mental constitution. He comes to grief through his colossal conceit: "His own opinion was his god," as *Queen Katharine* says of *Cardinal Wolsey;* but he is not a booby. The mirth that is derived from him is derived by devices of mischief,—as when a sportive urchin decorates a marble statue with a stovepipe hat. No plight can be more laughable than that of the pompous ass whose pomposity is made the direct means of his ridiculous disgrace. *Malvolio* falls into that plight and becomes ludicrously absurd, but his discomfiture is due to one of the chronic frailties of human nature, a frailty which, in him and by means of him, it is the purpose of the poet kindly and humorously to expose and rebuke. *Malvolio* would be a farce part, and nothing more, if he were simply a silly coxcomb, cajoled and teased by a pert chambermaid. He is intended for the image of overweening self-love, of opinionated self-esteem, of narrow-minded, strutting, consequential complacency. "Go off!" he cries; "I discard you. . . . *I am not of your element.*" The world contains many persons who have within themselves, more or less modified, the potentiality of *Malvolio's* disease. Shakespeare has covered him with confusion and laughter, making him the butt not only of the rubicund, rollicking, masterful *Sir Toby Belch,* but of trivial *Sir Andrew,* with his thimbleful of brains, and of the quaint, satiric *Feste,* and the serving-man, *Fabian,* and the shallow, prattling, skittish *Maria.* The spreading of the snare and the capture of the victim are irresistibly droll, and when all the contributary parts are well acted the resultant effect of perfect mirth is inevitable. But Shakespeare has also covered with ridicule and contempt the vicious infirmity of self-conceit.

HENRY IRVING.

The best of all the modern performances of *Malvolio,* whether in England or America, was that given

TWELFTH NIGHT

by Henry Irving,—the best for the reason that the actor completely saturated it with the inflexible egotism, innate, immovable complacence, and rigid austerity which are the dominant, pervasive attributes of the character, and also because, with that scrupulous attention to details for which his art was remarkable, he invested it with numberless characteristics of apt eccentricity of feature, manner, and costume, all expressive of the man and all coöperative to impress upon memory a definite, abiding, natural and probable image of formidable personality and substantial worth marred by unconsciously colossal conceit. He was incarnate sincerity. His make-up of the head and face,—thin, light brown hair, a scant, formal beard, a slight mustache, wasted cheeks, sallow complexion,—his tall, gaunt figure, his sober vestment, his pompous walk, his peculiar use of his staff of office,—all helped to intensify the effect of reality and to show, in strong relief, a man who truly believed himself superior to all around him. He thus set the example and provided the model which have served to inspire and guide later performers of the part.

Irving's production of "Twelfth Night" effected at the London Lyceum Theatre, July 8, 1884, was shown in New York, at the old Star Theatre, in the autumn of that year, on November 18. It did not much interest the public, either in England or

America, and Irving was critically censured for doing precisely what it is right to do,—that is, for enlisting sympathy with *Malvolio;* right, because, while the self-deluded being, because of his intrinsic, inordinate, preposterous vanity, deserves the ridicule to which he is subjected, he is, in the sequel, so cruelly ill-used as, rightly understood, to deserve compassion.

Ellen Terry, who appeared as *Viola,* did not please herself by her performance,—as she has since publicly declared in her book, "The Story of My Life,"—but she pleased many other persons. Her action was graceful and expeditious, her delivery of the text was finely intelligent, and while she did not express the gentle pathos of the part she blithely expressed its brightness. "I never liked it," she subsequently wrote, relative to the Lyceum revival of "Twelfth Night"; "I thought our production dull, lumpy, and heavy." Irving, she said, told her that he ought never to have attempted to present that play "without three great comedians." In his London production *Sir Toby* was acted by David Fisher, *Orsino* by William Terriss, *Sir Andrew* by Francis Wyatt, *Feste* by S. Calhaem, *Olivia* by Rose Leclercq, and *Sebastian* by Fred Terry. In America, Wenman acted *Sir Toby,* Norman Forbes (-Robertson) *Sir Andrew,* Samuel Johnson *Feste,* George Alexander *Orsino,* Ellen Terry *Viola,* Winifred Emery *Olivia,* and Fuller Mellish

Sebastian. During the London "run" of Irving's production Ellen Terry became seriously ill, and, on July 28, and for some time thereafter, her place, as *Viola,* was taken by her younger sister, Marion.

A remarkably fine performance of *Viola* was given, June 7, 1865, at the Olympic Theatre, London, by Kate Terry (1842-19—), and it is notable that she "doubled" the part with that of *Sebastian,* as had been done on the German stage. "Twelfth Night" was translated into German by Schlegel, and Henry Crabb Robinson, who, in 1851, at Dresden, saw a performance of Schlegel's play,—entitled "Was Ihr Wollt,"—made this record of it:

"It seemed to us admirably given. . . . A Mme. Baier Bürick played both *Viola* and *Sebastian,* and when personating the latter she gave a manliness to her voice and step which would almost have deceived us as to her identity. There was, of necessity, a change in the text at last. Another person, who managed to conceal his face, came on as *Sebastian.*"

CHARACTER OF *VIOLA.*

The prominence of *Malvolio* in the comedy does not lessen that of *Viola.* If the humor and satire eddy and crystallize around him, the loveliness, poetry, ardent, unselfish emotion, exquisite glee and radiant grace crystallize around her. *Viola* is Shakespeare's ideal of the patient idolatry and silent self-sacrifice of perfect love. In the simple, earnest words, "I'll serve this Duke," the shipwrecked, bereaved, lonely, almost destitute girl, who, cast away on a strange seacoast, must seek her fortune, practically beginning life anew, reveals more than her adventurous intention, because she also reveals the steadfast quality,—blending meek endurance with buoyant self-control,—of her strong as well as lovely character. As to the *Duke Orsino* she knows only that he is reputed noble, that he is a bachelor, and that he loves the *Lady Olivia,* who is mourning the death of her father and brother, and who will admit no one to her presence. *Viola* is not impelled by passion, or by sentiment, or by curiosity. She must find a new home, and she must obtain subsistence. Her first impulse is to serve *Olivia,* but that plan is rejected as impracticable. She will seek service in the household of the *Duke,*—for she can sing and can speak to him in many sorts of music,—and she will hide her sex, and proceed thither in disguise. A happy chance has saved her from the sea, and meanwhile the same happy chance may also have saved *Sebastian,* her brother. She will be hopeful and will go forward, and the events of her future shall be trusted to propitious time.

After her plan has succeeded and she has become a resident of *Orsino's* palace and is established, as a

Page, in the *Duke's* favor, *Viola* spreads no lure, resorts to no subterfuge. In such cases the first advance is usually made by the female. It is so made by *Rosalind,* for example,—a character commonly, and erroneously, named as the perfection of poetic spirituality and refinement,—but it is not made by *Viola.* She is a sweet, constant woman, and she is specially blessed with that cheerful courage, as to worldly fortune, for which good women are usually more remarkable than men, and she is young, handsome, attractive and, unconsciously, well qualified to prove victorious. She loves and she is simply herself and will submit, without a murmur, to any sorrow that may await her. "She never told her love." *Rosalind* is a woman. *Viola* is a poem. *Rosalind* is human. *Viola* is human, too, but also she is celestial. In her disguise, as a boy, she will follow the fortunes of her lord, and she will even plead his cause, as a lover, with the beautiful *Olivia,* who has captured his physical longing and his languishing, sentimental fancy.

A woman, under such circumstances, commonly hates her rival, with bitter resentment. *Viola* never harbors hate, never speaks one word of antagonism or malice. She does not assume that *Orsino* is her property because she happens to love him, or that he is in any way responsible for the condition of her feelings, or that *Olivia* is reprehensible because she has fascinated him. There is no selfishness in her love, because there is no selfishness in her nature. Her desire to see the face of *Olivia* is the pathetic desire to know what it is that has charmed the man whom she worships, and, through her simulated glee, when she does see it, shines the touching consciousness that the beauty of *Olivia* might well inspire a man's devotion. Nothing could be more fervent and generous than the candor and enthusiasm with which she recognizes that beauty and pleads with its possessor for compassion upon a suffering worshipper. She knows *Orsino's* sorrow by her own, and she pities him and would help him if she could. That is true love, which desires not its own happiness first, but the happiness of its object, and which feels, without conscious knowledge, that itself is the perfection of human attainment and that it may be better to lose than to win. Shakespeare has incarnated that lovely spirit in a person of equal loveliness, and has inspired it with the exuberant glee that is possible only to perfect innocence. *Viola* is as gay as she is gentle, and as guileless and simple as she is generous and sincere. The poet has emphasized his meaning, furthermore, by the expedient of contrast between the two women. *Olivia,*—self-absorbed, ostentatious in her mourning, acquisitive and voracious in her love, self-willed in her conduct, conventional in her character, physically beautiful, but spiritually insignificant, —while she is precisely the sort of woman for whom men in general go wild, serves but to throw the immeasurable superiority of *Viola* into stronger relief.

ELLEN TREE.

On the English Stage the best personation of *Viola* that was given between the time of Dora Jordan and that of Adelaide Neilson appears to have been that given by Ellen Tree,—Mrs. Charles Kean (1805-1880). Her first performance of *Viola* was given, August 31, 1836, at the Haymarket Theatre, London, Benjamin Webster being the *Malvolio;* she played the part, in a revival of the comedy effected on September 3, 1839, at the same house, the *Malvolio* being William Farren, and she was brilliantly successful in it, in still another presentment, at the Haymarket, on November 11, 1848. All contemporary critical judgment pronounced her performance beautiful. "Not a tone of voice," said "The Athenæum," "but touches the heart. *Viola* with Mrs. Kean [Ellen Tree had meantime married] puts not off the woman with her attire, but becomes yet more womanly." In 1850 she again acted *Viola,* making a profound impression of excellence, at the Princess' Theatre, London, which house Kean then opened with a splendid production of "Twelfth Night,"—the cast including Drinkwater Meadows, as *Malvolio;* Edward Philip Addison, as *Sir Toby;* Robert Keeley, as *Sir Andrew;* John Pitt Harley, as *Feste;* John Ryder, as *Antonio,* and J. F. Cathcart, as *Sebastian.* In my youth I often listened to enthusiastic praises of Ellen Tree, —whom I saw only in the latter part of her career,— by veterans who remembered her in her prime. Their admiration was boundless. An instructive estimate of her personation of *Viola* is provided by the biographer of Charles Kean, John William Cole (1859):

"Ellen Tree's *Viola* was, perhaps, the most faultless performance of the modern stage. It presented one of the sweetest creations of Shakespeare's fancy, embodied as exactly as if the accomplished representative had been foreseen by the imagination of the author. In figure, features, expression, and elegant propriety of costume; in the delicate humor of the lighter points and the exquisite pathos of the serious passages, the portrait was one in which the most exceptious caviller would have been taxed to discover a defective feature or suggest an improvement. . . . We happened to sit in the stalls of the Princess' Theatre next to an enthusiastic septuagenarian, who proved to be anything but one of Horace's types of old age, represented by the satirist as

'Difficilis, querulus, laudator temporis acti
  Se puero.'

He remembered Mrs. Jordan as *Viola* during the zenith of her reputation. . . . Mrs. Jordan, he said, was, on the whole,

TWELFTH NIGHT

inferior to Mrs. Kean. She had greater breadth, higher coloring, more exuberant spirits, and a broad-wheeled laugh, peculiar to herself, which bore down everything before it; but all this, he added, would appear coarse and vulgar to modern ideas of refinement. In personal requisites, in elegance and delicacy of manner, in the grace of sentiment and general finish, the picture was incomplete, and much less agreeable than that presented by her successor."

Ellen Tree was married to Charles Kean in 1842, and at the time of his death, January 22, 1868, she left the stage.

ADELAIDE NEILSON.

The one consummate impersonation of *Viola* made known since the golden day of Ellen Tree was that of Adelaide Neilson (1846?-1880), whose performance, given originally in England, was first presented in America, at the Fifth Avenue Theatre, New York, May 7, 1877, on which memorable occasion, and many times afterward, I saw it. The elements of soul, mind, character, temperament, and person combined in *Viola* make her the most piquant and, excepting the wonderfully feminine *Imogen,* the most subtly attractive of all Shakespeare's heroines. The atmosphere around that lovely creation is, almost exclusively, that of poetry. *Viola* is young, beautiful, gentle, spirited, arch without being coquettish, and loving without being insipid. She is not passionate. Her feeling is deep, not wild: her emotions do not distract her mind. She can be sorrowful, but not miserable. Her condition is pathetic because she has endured bereavement and because her love is involuntarily given where, seemingly, it is given in vain. The denotement of pathos in her rueful experience is the gleam of wistful sadness which now and then shows itself through the rosy flush of joy that suffuses the whole surface of her conduct. She is at heart grieved, but she suffers bravely and will keep her grief to herself. The effect of sorrow on those who see it in other persons is determined by the manner in which it is borne by the sufferer of it, and sorrow is never so affecting as when it is discerned as existent beneath a veil of gayety,—when, as Coleridge has somewhere written:

"The tear slow travelling on its way
Fills up the wrinkle of a silent laugh."

The actress seemed intended by Nature for the character, and in her embodiment of it Art perfected what Nature had ordained. Her *Viola* was incarnate April sunshine,—an embodiment of exquisitely bright and tender womanhood, dazzling yet deeply sympathetic, because, through an investiture of light and joy, there was perceptible a certain sweet melancholy, a genuine sorrow, uncomplainingly

TWELFTH NIGHT

endured. Person and temperament were completely united in that perfect achievement. The slender, lithe figure, the expressive face, so strongly indicative of sensibility and yet so radiant with mirth; the large, dark, brilliant eyes, the lovely smile, the richly modulated voice, the exuberant vitality, the unconscious grace of movement, the authority of complete self-possession, the unerring knowledge of artistic means and of the right way to use them,—all those qualifications for the part were possessed by Adelaide Neilson, and she made Shakespeare's *Viola* an actual human being, entirely beautiful and never to be forgotten.

The great representative performance given by this actress, the one that was instantly accepted and continuously admired by the multitude of play-going persons, was that of *Juliet:* the more softly feminine and winning of her impersonations were those of *Imogen* and *Viola,* and it was her inspiring excellence in those characters, more than the power of stage tradition and custom, in the time of her American career,—for her example was rapidly and largely followed,—which reanimated the vogue of "Cymbeline" and "Twelfth Night" and gave a fresh impetus to the use of the general Shakespearean repertory. Her *Viola* did not reveal her signal power, but it fully exhibited her charm. The more it was seen the lovelier it was seen to be, yet, in retrospect, the more it is considered the more difficult the task becomes of specifying the causes of the delightful effect which is produced. There is warrant in the text for spirited behavior on the part of *Viola,* and Miss Neilson's *Viola* was affluent in pretty bravado and demonstrative glee. The mock ruefulness and bubbling merriment with which she delivered the speech culminating with "*I* am the MAN!" were delicious, both as an outburst of humor and a dramatic effect. In the Challenge and Duel scenes, also, the portraiture of shrinking feminine cowardice,—commingled of amazement, consternation, fear, weakness, and dread of the disclosure of her sex,—was deliciously droll. The speech beginning "Make me a willow cabin at your gate" was spoken in a kind of ecstasy, and it flowed from her lips in perfect music. Her voice, in saying "*I* am all the daughters of my father's house," went directly to the heart, and her pause after "and all the brothers, too," with sudden, brisk transition to the business in hand ("Sir, shall I to this lady?"),—the only business of real interest to the sentimental egotist whom she loves,—were wonderfully pathetic and expressive. I remember Lamb's felicitous mention of Dora Jordan's delivery of "the disguised story of *Viola's* love for *Orsino,*"— from which it would appear that she excelled in a

similar treatment of the latter passage; but Adelaide
Neilson was not a searcher for precedents or models.
She studied her art, and she owed much to her diligence in study, but her intuitions were unerring, and
she owed much more to them. She fully comprehended *Viola,* and she merged herself in the part,
not merely imitating and assuming, but vitalizing
and interpreting both the character and the experience. The performance was a golden gem of acting,
and it has become a precious memory. Miss Neilson's
costume was Grecian in style, the prevailing colors
of it being pale blue and silver.

AGUECHEEK AND *FESTE.*

It seems a little ironical that the character of *Sir
Andrew Aguecheek,* which is both pitiable and contemptible, should have been so often cast to comedians of commanding intellect or of exuberant animal
spirits and dashing style,—Harris and Woodward, on
the early English Stage; James Dodd, John Baldwin
Buckstone, Horace Wigan (1865), and William
Blanchard, in later times, and, on the American Stage,
Charles James Mathews, Lester Wallack, George H.
Barrett, Charles M. Walcot, John Drew, and
Herbert Gresham. Buckstone acted *Sir Andrew*
in 1846, when Charlotte Cushman and her sister

Susan were performing, in London, as *Viola* and *Olivia*.

Shakespeare's Clowns or Fools,—for those terms are used by him as interchangeable,—in various ways differing one from another, are, in one way, alike,— each of them being significant of a mind that has been chastened by experience of vicissitude and trouble. The quaintest of them is *Touchstone;* the gentlest and most pitiful is the poor, faithful, wise, forlorn *Fool* who follows *Lear*. *Feste* is of the bitter-sweet species. He can be kind, he is readily jocose, but he is inclined to a cynical view of human nature, and he does not forget taunts or slights. He is shrewd, often sarcastic, and it is significant that he sings one of the saddest of the poet's songs.

This character has been personated by many talented actors, English and American. Representatives of *Feste* on the English Stage,—subsequent to Armin, Underhill, and Yates,—who have succeeded in eliciting its salient attributes of quaintness, vivacity, dry humor, and caustic sarcasm, and thus in making it effective and interesting, were William Parsons, 1782; Benjamin Webster, 1846; Alfred Wigan, 1848, and John Pitt Harley,—whose distinctive peculiarity was a delightful quaintness,—1850.

From a Photograph by Sarony, N. Y. *Author's Collection*

JAMES LEWIS AS *SIR TOBY BELCH*

"*I'll drink to her as long as there is a passage in my throat and drink in Illyria!*"

Act I., Sc. 3

TWELFTH NIGHT

AMERICAN STAGE.—EARLY REPRESENTATIONS.

In the early days of the American Stage "Twelfth Night" was seldom represented. At The Theatre in Federal Street, Boston,—opened on February 3, 1794, under the management of Charles Stuart Powell,— the comedy was acted on the following May 5, that being the first recorded performance of it in America; the cast included Snelling Powell, Miss Harrison (who later became Mrs. Powell), and Mrs. Abbott. Later, at the Chestnut Street Theatre, Philadelphia, William Warren, the Elder, acted *Sir Toby,* and William B. Wood, one of the most conscientious and correct of actors, gained particular distinction as *Malvolio.* The first production of "Twelfth Night" in New York was that effected on June 11, 1804, at the old Park Theatre. John G. Martin acted *Malvolio,* John E. Harwood *Sir Toby,* John Johnson *Sir Andrew,* Mrs. Johnson *Viola,* and Mrs. Hallam *Olivia.* Twenty years later, on August 10, 1824, the comedy was performed at the Chatham Garden Theatre,—owned and managed by Henry Barriere,— with a cast of exceptional strength, including Henry Wallack, as *Malvolio;* Thomas Kilner, as *Sir Toby;* Henry J. Finn,—excellent, versatile, and distinguished both in authorship and acting,—as *Aguecheek;* William Spiller, as *Feste;* Mrs. Henry, as

48 SHAKESPEARE ON THE STAGE

Viola; Mrs. Entwhistle, as *Olivia,* and Mrs. Durang, as *Maria.* Among those actors I remember only Henry Wallack, whom I recall as a marvel for characterization and vivacity. He was the brother of James W. Wallack, the Elder, who founded Wallack's Theatre. His impersonation of *Squire Broadlands,* in "The Country Squire,"—also sometimes billed as "The Fine Old English Gentleman,"—was a masterpiece. It is not easy to fancy him as *Malvolio,* yet he may have been excellent in that character. Other actors proficient in genial, breezy humor have proved equally capable in grim or fantastic eccentricity.

BURTON'S PRODUCTIONS.

The richly humorous comedian William Evans Burton (1804-1860) made several productions of "Twelfth Night" and, acting *Sir Toby Belch,* shone brilliantly in all of them. His first presentment of the comedy occurred at his theatre in Chambers Street, New York, on March 29, 1852. The cast included William Rufus Blake, as *Malvolio;* Lester Wallack, —then designated, in the play-bill, Mr. Lester,—as *Aguecheek;* Henry Placide, as the *Clown;* Lizzie Weston, as *Viola,* and the charming Mary Taylor, as *Maria.* The critical judgment of Burton's day declared him superlatively humorous in the bluff joviality of *Sir Toby*. I recall him as a comedian of consummate qualifications, natural and acquired, and I could not enough extol the varied excellence of his acting,—the delicious humor of it and the melting pathos. His repertory, as recorded by his judicious, sympathetic biographer, William Linn Keese, comprised one hundred and eighty-four parts: "the absolute monarch of merriment" he calls him, in *Sir Toby*. He touched, as few of the many actors within my experience have ever done, the springs of laughter and tears. Those persons who recall the exuberantly humorous, yet at times pathetic, acting of John E. Owens (1823-1886) can form an idea of Burton's dramatic genius, because Owens was of Burton's artistic kindred.

In his later presentments of "Twelfth Night,"— October 3, 1853, at his Chambers Street Theatre, and December 26, 1856, and January 17, 1858, at his New Theatre, which had been successively known as Tripler Hall, the Metropolitan, and Laura Keene's Varieties, and which he opened on September 8, 1856, —Burton's casts were varied. In 1853 the *Malvolio* was Charles Fisher, the *Aguecheek* George H. Barrett, and the *Viola* Emiline Raymond (Mrs. Marchant). In 1856 Mrs. Barrow was the *Viola,* Jane Coombs the *Olivia,* Polly Marshall the *Maria,* Mark Smith, a comedian of rare talent and great charm, the *Feste,* and Daniel E. Setchell the *Fabian.* In 1858 Charles Mathews acted *Aguecheek,* Lizzie Weston (then Mrs. A. H. Davenport) *Viola,* Amelia Parker *Olivia,* Mrs. W. H. Smith *Maria,* and Lawrence Barrett *Sebastian.* All those names, thus associated with that of Burton, speak eloquently to readers acquainted with the history of the Theatre in New York. Actors such as Placide, Blake, Lester Wallack, Charles Fisher, and Charles Mathews have been rare, in any period of stage history. Blake, who became corpulent and unwieldy as he grew old, was, in his younger days, slender and handsome, and at all times he was, in demeanor, notable for dignity and, in vocalism, for an exceptionally melodious voice and a clear, precise, crisp, incisive articulation. His superlative excellence appeared in his acting of such parts as *Mr. Hardcastle,* in "She Stoops to Conquer"; *Jesse Rural,* in "Old Heads and Young Hearts," and *Geoffrey Dale,* in "The Last Man." He was naturally dramatic, and he could be wonderfully pathetic. The record of his *Malvolio* places a strong emphasis on his maintenance of severe austerity and on the spontaneous comicality of his loftily contemptuous behavior when strutting in the garden, inflated with visions of coming greatness.

Burton's revival of "Twelfth Night" in 1852 held the stage for two weeks,—an unusual run at that

TWELFTH NIGHT

time. In the presentment made in 1853 Charles Fisher highly distinguished himself as *Malvolio.* Fisher was an actor of superior natural talent, trained faculty of impersonation, and surpassing versatility. His career on our Stage began at Burton's Chambers Street Theatre, on August 30, 1852, when he appeared as *Ferment,* in "The School of Reform," —the remarkable English comedian Lysander Thompson making, on the same occasion, his first appearance in America, as *Tyke.* Fisher could act, with equal excellence, such widely different parts as *Mercutio,* in "Romeo and Juliet," and *Mr. Peggotty,* in "David Copperfield"; *Armand Duval,* in "Camille," and *Nicholas Rue,* the miser, in "Secrets Worth Knowing"; *Vavasour,* in "Henry Dunbar," and *Beau Farintosh,* in "School"; *Theseus,* in "A Midsummer Night's Dream," and *Triplet,* in "Masks and Faces." In *Triplet* he was perfection. His performance of *Malvolio,* when at its best, exhibited a formidable personality, lofty, egotistical, austere, and dominant; the incarnation of self-importance, and only comic in being ludicrously fantastical; but, latterly, he lessened the indispensable saturnine quality of the personation, and, for the sake of the laugh, which is ever dear to the comedian, he infused into it an incongruous element of chirrupy humor.

SIR TOBY.

The best performances of *Sir Toby* that have been given on the American Stage since the time of Burton were those given by William Pleater Davidge (1814-1888), Thomas Edmund Wenman (1844-1892), James Lewis, and William F. Owen. Davidge was a student of his art and of Shakespeare, and he thought for himself, and followed precedents only when they were justified by common-sense. Sturdiness of personality and bluntness of manner were among his characteristics. His countenance and his voice were peculiarly conformable to comicality, he was naturally humorous, but beneath his humor there was deep feeling. His range of parts was wide; from *Sir Peter Teazle* to *Caliban* and from *Bishopriggs,* in "Man and Wife," to *Sir Anthony Absolute.* As *Sir Toby,* while his humor was jocund and his mirth reckless, he maintained a certain distinction of individuality, a personal importance, such as appertains to a man of mind as well as of rank: he was not merely a sottish roisterer, such as the contemporary Stage has commonly furnished as the archetype of this part. The inebriety was not overdone by him and made offensive,—as excessive inebriety necessarily is. Davidge aimed to elicit all that was laughable in the Revel Scene, and with that result was

TWELFTH NIGHT 53

content. Wenman (his family name was Newman, and he was educated and accomplished) laid emphasis on the strength of *Sir Toby's* character and gave a touch of stinging satire to his rollicking humor. This actor,—lost to the stage by untimely death,— was remarkable for scrupulous fidelity to detail, in whatever part he played, however slight it might be, and his acting invariably heightened the illusion of actuality in every scene in which he appeared. Lewis acted the part only in Daly's later revivals of "Twelfth Night" (1893-1896); his performance is considered in association with them. Owen, as *Sir Toby,* pleased by his frolicsome disposition, his amiability, sustained identification with the assumed character, and his extreme good-nature.

A deplorable perversion of "Twelfth Night," made by Charles Webb,—one of the Webb brothers, Charles and Henry, Englishmen,—for the use of the comedians William H. Crane and Stuart Robson, was produced at the Fifth Avenue Theatre, October 31, 1881, for the purpose, avowedly, of "bringing forward" *Sir Toby Belch* and *Sir Andrew Aguecheek.* The shape of the play was altered, the characters were distorted, the text mangled, new incidents and new words were inserted, and the symmetry of the work was destroyed. *Sir Toby,* for example, was made to speak of the music produced by *Sir Andrew,* "when he gets the viol-de-gambo between those spindle shanks of his." Seldom, since Tate stuck his ears through "King Lear," has any play by Shakespeare been so ruthlessly despoiled as this fine comedy was on the occasion here recalled,—and it is known that the rage for "improving" Shakespeare has impelled adapters very far. Mr. Robson, with his infantile face, bland manner, and high, thin, squeaky vocalism, gave the better performance of the two, expressing, as *Sir Andrew,* ridiculous vacuity and conceit. Mr. Crane, a comedian of fine ability in the impersonation of eccentric character, made no pretence of showing *Sir Toby* as anything but a boisterous sot.

THE ELDER WALLACK'S REVIVAL.

A notable revival of "Twelfth Night" was effected by James William Wallack, the Elder, at Wallack's Lyceum, on March 24, 1856, when *Sir Toby* was impersonated by John Brougham, *Malvolio* by John Dyott, *Aguecheek* by Charles Melton Walcot, *Orsino* by Lester Wallack,—then Mr. Lester,—and *Viola* by Mrs. Hoey. Brougham possessed the sturdiness and the rich humor requisite for *Sir Toby,* and he readily excelled in conviviality. Dyott, tall, dark, grave, sombre, was a stiff, formal, conventional actor,—well suited for such parts as *Adrastus,* in "Ion,"—and he

TWELFTH NIGHT 55

gave an effective performance of *Malvolio,* deliberate and severe. Walcot (1816-1868), who came to our Stage from London, in 1843, was prominent among the best actors of his time in whimsical, eccentric characters. He acted *Touchstone,* for example, as if he had been born to act it, and he was a model of pert conceit and abject silliness as *Aguecheek.* Lester Wallack easily made the amorous, melancholy *Orsino* pictorial and interesting. Mrs. Hoey, who was gentle and piquant as *Viola,* is remembered as one of the most elegant artistic performers who have graced our Stage. She was not persuasive in her simulation of simplicity,—which is one of *Viola's* cardinal attributes,—but in artificial comedy she excelled. She long held the position of leading lady at Wallack's Theatre and was highly respected and greatly admired.

LATER PLAYERS OF *MALVOLIO.*

Performances of *Malvolio* have been given, on the New York Stage, since the time of Blake, Fisher, and Dyott, by William Pleater Davidge, George H. Griffiths, Charles John Barton Hill, George Clarke, Edward Compton, Joseph Haworth, John Blair, Henry Jewett, Henry E. Dixey, Edward Hugh Sothern, Oswald Yorke, and Fuller Mellish.

Davidge (1814-1888), eminent among comedians

essentially Shakespearean, fully elicited the involuntary humor of the part by his portentous gravity, the solemn pomp of his walk and general demeanor, and his complete absorption in ludicrous self-conceit. This actor, a genuine humorist and a conscientious and thorough artist, came to our Stage from England in 1850, and for many years adorned it. Griffiths' performance was conventional and respectable. Barton Hill (1830-1911), an actor of large experience, who in his youth had been admired in *Maurice de Saxe, Armand Duval,* and kindred parts, and who possessed a helpfully complacent sense of personal importance, acted *Malvolio* in a dense mood of rigid gravity and fanatical self-love. Hill was associated, as the *Steward,* with Marie Wainwright, when she acted in "Twelfth Night," at the Fifth Avenue Theatre, 1890. Henry E. Dixey, who played *Malvolio,* on November 27, 1894, at Daly's Theatre, is one of many actors who have frittered away golden opportunities. He has given many good performances, but not one as good as, with serious purpose and close application to study, his signal talent would have enabled him to make it. His attempt in *Malvolio* was eminently creditable, and it procured for him a title to remembrance as an important actor. He was easily comical in showing the ridiculous proceedings of a solemn, conceited ass,—the "Fan-

TWELFTH NIGHT 57

tastical Steward," who believes the "Lady of great Beauty and Fortune" to be in love with him. His *Malvolio* ingeniously aped the gentility which he did not possess. On the occasion of his first appearance as *Malvolio* he was particularly felicitous in denoting him as, intrinsically, a type of insane egotism. His gravity was innate, not superficial. His pauses of deliberation were judicious and humorous. His use of voice,—in quality and variety of tone and inflection, —was illuminative of the character and the text. He ultimately yielded, as many other players have done, to the facile method of "horse-play," and so he converted *Malvolio* from a serious character to a buffoon. George Clarke's performance appeared to have been modelled on the later style of Fisher. The image of overweening conceit that he presented combined grimness of temperament with elaborate absurdity of fantastic behavior. Edward Compton (Mackenzie) acted *Malvolio,* in association with Adelaide Neilson, at Booth's Theatre,—that actress playing *Viola,*— April 27, 1880, and gave a competent performance.

VARIOUS PLAYERS OF *VIOLA.*—MRS. JOHNSON TO MME. MODJESKA.

On the American Stage *Viola* has been assumed by many actresses, some of them exceptionally

58 SHAKESPEARE ON THE STAGE

capable, a few highly distinguished. Mrs. Johnson (Miss Ford, 1770-1830) acted *Viola,* in the production of "Twelfth Night" which was effected at the old Park Theatre, New York, on May 30, 1804. I have not found any description of her performance. She is designated as a great beauty and an actress of signal talent, and is specially commemorated as excellent in tragedy and in ladies of distinction in high comedy. She was tall, elegant, and graceful, and, in her day, was called "the Siddons of America." Her acting was marked by refinement, deep feeling, and delicate artistic finish, but, probably, she was a woman too formidable and stately, if not majestic, to be harmonious with the gentle *Viola.*

Mrs. Shaw (Eliza Marian Trewar) was one of the loveliest women and most brilliant players of whom there is mention in the chronicles of the early American Theatre. She excelled in such comedy parts as *Beatrice* and *Rosalind,* and *Constance,* in "The Love Chase." Abundant and enthusiastic testimony to her genius and beauty was borne in contemporary records of her achievement. She came from England, appearing at the old Park Theatre, July 25, 1835, as *Mariana,* in "The Wife." In 1849 she wedded with T. S. Hamblin, of the old Bowery Theatre, where she was long a public favorite. She is mentioned as a performer of *Viola,* but her performance

TWELFTH NIGHT

is not described. It seems likely that she made no particular impression in a part to which, apparently, she could not have been well suited.

Lizzie Weston, whose appearance as *Viola* in Burton's revivals has been noted, was a daughter of A. W. Jackson (an indifferent actor, but a prosperous manager), who was known as "Black Jackson" in the time of the old Bowery Theatre and of the Winter Garden Theatre (1859-1867), of both of which houses he was, at different times, manager. She was a dazzling, vivacious brunette, handsome, clever, and unscrupulous. Her nature was not in the least sympathetic with that of *Viola,* but she was a competent actress, and her performance was piquant and pretty. Veteran votaries of the Theatre remember Lizzie Weston as having been the wife of Adolphus Hoyt Davenport ("Dolly" Davenport), who obtained a divorce from her in 1858, and, later, as the second and last wife of Charles James Mathews, the famous English light comedian.

Mrs. Barrow (Julia Bennett), a remarkably handsome woman, fair, with golden hair and gray eyes, a dashing comedian, was better suited to such parts as *Beatrice, Violante,* and *Hippolyta* than to *Viola.* She made her first appearance on the American Stage, at the old Broadway Theatre, New York, on February 24, 1851, as *Lady Teazle.* Her experience had been gained in England. Her range of character was wide, reaching from *Cicely Homespun,* in "The Heir at Law," to the *Widow Delmaine,* in "The Serious Family." The pleasing element of her performance of *Viola* was playfulness.

Fanny Davenport, while sweet in spirit and piquant in behavior as *Viola,* overweighted the part and made it mechanical and prosy. She was exceptionally handsome, possessed of abundant animal spirits, and capable of effective acting in a wide range of character,—from *Nancy,* in "Oliver Twist," to *Lady Teazle;* but she evinced little aptitude for the commingled sentiment, controlled feeling, and delicate vivacity of *Viola.* Marie Wainwright (1855-19—) has had a stage career of about thirty-seven years. She was trained in the theatrical companies of George Rignold and Lawrence Barrett, and her natural talent was developed by good instruction. She had the advantages of personal beauty and a temperament blending vivacity with sensibility. Her acting has not evinced either the capability of profound feeling or any deep sense of poetic ideals. Some of her many performances have signified artistic skill to be arch, or playful, or pensive, or demure. As *Viola* her gay behavior was pleasing; she was agreeable in her apprehension of *Olivia's* dilemma; in the Duel Scene her jaunty demeanor, hampered by

TWELFTH NIGHT

fluttering consternation, was exactly in the right vein, and happily effective. Her *Viola,* however, did not touch the heart, though it satisfied the eye and the fancy: it won the smile, but not the tear,—and *Viola* should win both.

Helena Modjeska acted *Viola* for the first time on December 9, 1881, in Washington, D. C., and her impersonation was first seen in New York on December 18, 1882, at Booth's Theatre. It blended sentiment with buoyancy. Her figure was slender; her countenance sometimes pensive, sometimes eager; her voice sympathetic; her general aspect and demeanor those of rueful perplexity. The ideal was seen to be correct, but the expression of it neither stirred the imagination nor touched the heart. Mme. Modjeska was a great actress, but for the full and fine manifestation of her art she required characters commingling much mental force with intensely passionate feeling. Her most complete performance in Shakespearean comedy was *Isabella.* The character of *Viola* did not fully arouse her spirit. Her elocution, in that as in other parts involving the use of blank verse, was artificial, by reason not so much of foreign accent as of a cadent delivery. She pleased as *Viola,*—indeed, she always pleased as a woman, for her nature was a lovely one,—but she did not enthrall. Her *Page* dress was specially rich in material and embellishment. One peculiarity of her stage business as *Viola* was that she made her first entrance in a boat (the "drifting boat" mentioned by the *Captain,* Act I., sc. 2), from which she landed on the shore of Illyria. In *Viola's* chief scene with *Orsino* she sang, to a harp accompaniment, the melancholy song, "Come Away, Death," which, by Shakespeare, is assigned to *Feste.* On the occasion of Modjeska's first presentment of "Twelfth Night" in New York *Malvolio* was acted by George H. Griffiths, *Sir Toby* by William F. Owen, *Sir Andrew* by Norman Forbes (-Robertson), *Feste* by James Cooper, *Olivia* by Maud Milton, and *Maria* by Clara Fisher.

AUGUSTIN DALY'S REVIVALS,—1869; 1893, *ET SEQ.*

The list of Shakespeare's comedies that were produced by Augustin Daly, whether when he was managing star performers or when he was managing theatres, includes "The Merry Wives of Windsor," "Much Ado About Nothing," "Twelfth Night," "Love's Labor's Lost," "A Midsummer Night's Dream," "The Merchant of Venice," "As You Like It," "The Taming of the Shrew," "The Two Gentlemen of Verona," and "The Tempest." Each of those plays received at his hands conscientious, scholar-like treatment. No one of them was forced upon public

From a Photograph by Otto Sarony Co., N. Y.   *Author's Collection*

VIOLA ALLEN AS *VIOLA*

"*I am all the daughters of my father's house,
And all the brothers, too: and yet I know not.*"

Act II., Sc. 4

attention in the tedious prolixity of an unabridged text and unadapted scenes, and no one of them was overlaid with scenic pageantry or converted into a mediæval clothes-horse. Shakespeare wrote for the mind and heart of all ages: he was not restricted by deference to contemporary fashions and the ephemeral caprices of local taste, and therefore his works did not pass away with his time. They are as real now as they were then. They can be acted in the manner of nature, which is always intelligible. The free and flexible dramatic method which prevails in the best acting of to-day, and which Daly's administrative wisdom steadily fostered, is perfectly harmonious with their spirit, and it elicits all their beauties. Ada Rehan's impersonations of *Katharine* and *Rosalind* showed women, not marionettes. Her *Rosalind* was not a theory, but a lover. The amatory creature of a poet's happy fancy became a living enchantment in her assumption of that character, and when she added *Viola* to the long chronicle of her achievements she suffused an image of romantic grace with woman-like tenderness and soft, poetic charm, and made that exquisite ideal an actual human being, of such beauty as cannot be forgotten.

Daly's first revival of "Twelfth Night" was effected at his Fifth Avenue Theatre, in West Twenty-fourth Street, New York, then newly opened, on October 4, 1869, on which occasion Mrs. Scott-Siddons appeared as *Viola,* Fanny Davenport as *Maria* (of which part she gave a sparkling performance), Davidge as *Sir Toby,* and George Clarke as *Malvolio.* Mrs. Scott-Siddons was effective in her exhibition of the mingled consternation and arch enjoyment with which, in the disguise of *Cesario, Viola* perceives the perplexity of "poor Olivia," but she was more notable as a handsome woman than as an artist. The actress was descended from the illustrious Sarah Siddons, and that renowned woman's niece, Fanny Kemble, said that "her features presented the most perfect living miniature of her great-grandmother's beauty."

Daly's second production of "Twelfth Night" was accomplished at his second Fifth Avenue Theatre, situated in West Twenty-eighth Street, on May 7, 1877. Adelaide Neilson was the *Viola,* and Charles Fisher was the *Malvolio.* Daly's best presentment of the comedy, however, was not effected till February 21, 1893, when he revived it at Daly's Theatre,—the house in which his career was fulfilled and ended. That presentment was judicious, correct, tasteful, and charming, and it satisfied every reasonable requirement. The play was compressed within four acts, comprising ten scenes. Six places were represented: A Sea-coast of Illyria; a Room in the Pal-

TWELFTH NIGHT

ace of *Orsino;* a Room in the House of *Countess Olivia;* a Street Before One of the Gates of the City; a Garden Before the House of *Countess Olivia,* and a Prison Under the House of the *Countess.* Daly has been censured, on the ground that he overlaid and disfigured his productions of Shakespeare's plays,—in particular, "Twelfth Night," —with "popular, extraneous, un-Shakespearean" musical embellishment and other fripperies. The censure is undeserved and unjust, because the accusation is groundless. Daly's production of "Twelfth Night" exhibited no "extraneous" embellishments. The comedy not only admits of musical embellishment, but imperatively requires it, and in making his final arrangement of it the judicious manager only supplied the music for which occasions are so abundantly provided. The musical numbers that were *introduced* were exactly two in number. The first was a chorus, "Come unto these yellow sands," taken from "The Tempest," which, as a prelude to the play, was sung by fishermen and peasants of Illyria, strolling by the seashore. The second was a serenade, "Who is Sylvia?" taken from "The Two Gentlemen of Verona,"—the name of "Olivia" being substituted for that of "Sylvia." The serenade was sung to Schubert's well-known music, deftly rearranged by the accomplished musician Henry Widmer (1845-1895), whose treatment of the score was sympathetic and eminently felicitous. Daly's employment of this serenade, which was introduced at the close of the Third Act, in the scene representing the *Countess Olivia's* Garden, greatly enhanced the effect of one of the most expressive and touching dramatic and poetic pictures ever shown in a theatre,—a picture (invented and executed solely by Daly) in which, amid precisely appropriate accessories, the three lovers, *Viola, Olivia,* and *Orsino,* exhibited, with a significance beyond the reach of words, the essential theme of the comedy,—love at odds and all things drifting. The earlier part of the act was played in the fading, mellow light of afternoon, which, at the end, was succeeded by the dusk of evening. *Viola,* in her disguise as "the Duke's man, Cesario," having, in the scene with *Antonio,* received the intimation that perhaps her brother, *Sebastian,* was not drowned, had spoken her joyous soliloquy upon that auspicious thought, and had sunk into a seat, in meditation. The silver moon was rising over the distant sea, and in the fancied freshness of the balmy night breeze you could almost hear the gentle lapping of the water and the murmuring ripple of the leaves. The lovelorn *Orsino* entered, with musicians, and, half concealed among the garden shrubbery, they sang beneath the windows of *Olivia's* house.

The proud beauty came forth upon the balcony, and, parting her veils, looked down, perceived *Orsino,* and was about to withdraw, when her gaze fell upon *Viola,*—the supposed man, *Cesario,* with whom she had fallen in love. Meantime *Orsino* was gazing up at *Olivia,* whom he worshipped; while *Viola,* aroused from revery by the music, was gazing on *Orsino,* whom she adored. The garden was all in moonlight; the delicious music flowed on, and over that perfect pageant of romance the curtain slowly fell.

It is not extravagant to declare that every note of music sung in Daly's production of "Twelfth Night" was required by the text or authorized by the scheme of the play. The opening chorus was appropriate and well vocalized, and, aside from its dramatic utility in attuning the mind of the auditory to a mood of sentiment and fancy, it served another good purpose, conclusively defensive of its use. The English-speaking public, in one particular, almost customarily treats the Stage and the actors with thoughtless incivility,—coming into the theatre after the curtain has been raised and making a noisy disturbance during the first moments after a performance has begun. Actors are annoyed and disconcerted by that behavior, considerate auditors are disquieted and offended, and representations on the stage are marred. Daly was not only a man of fine intellectual purpose and poetic imagination in his treatment of the Stage, but a sagacious, practical manager in his treatment of the Public; and in this employment of an opening chorus, as well as in some other adroit devices, he provided means of abating or lessening the injurious effect of heedless impropriety.

"There is not, perhaps, any play of Shakespeare's," said Dr. Johnson, in 1765, "which could be represented on the modern stage, as originally written." That statement, true then, is emphatically true now. In Daly's final revival of "Twelfth Night" the mirth of the revel scenes was, for the first time in the stage history of the play, elicited without coarseness. *Sir Toby's* carousal and *Maria's* plot were expedited with enjoyable veracity. *Malvolio's* scenes were slightly condensed. The Dungeon Scene and *Malvolio's* expostulation, toward the end of the play, were, ultimately, omitted,—an elision unquestionably open to censure. Daly told me that he made it because, after long observation, he had become convinced that the ordeal to which *Malvolio* is subjected, in his colloquy with the disguised *Feste,* is both painful and tiresome, and had perceived that his audiences were distinctly averse to it. In making a stage version of "Twelfth Night" I should not, for any reason, omit the passages specified, but Daly's

TWELFTH NIGHT 69

defence,—that he elicited the essential spirit and full dramatic effect of the comedy without them,—is an entirely respectable one.

"Twelfth Night" is a long play, and it would, in the acting, drag somewhat, unless suitably cut. In every practical version of Shakespeare made for use on the modern stage (which, in every particular, is much better equipped than was the stage of Shakespeare's time) the dialogue is, necessarily and rightly, curtailed. There are 2,684 lines in the original of "Twelfth Night," and Daly excised about 600. He also accelerated the action of the play, by several transpositions. The two songs, "Come Away, Death" and "O Mistress Mine," were transposed, and, eventually, "Come Away, Death" was omitted. About 370 lines of this comedy, besides three of the lyrics, are discarded, even from the Flower version, customarily acted at the Shakespeare Memorial Theatre, in Stratford-upon-Avon, where they insist on having as much of the divine bard as possible,— "the original text," in its pristine purity, or, as *Mrs. Battle* says, "the rigor of the game."

George Clarke acted *Malvolio* in Daly's final presentment of the comedy, and the authority of his art was explicitly manifested. James Lewis acted *Sir Toby,* giving a performance that merits particular remembrance and encomium, because of its preservation, without any sacrifice of humor, of an air of consequence befitting the social rank of the knight, and because of a tone of artistic decency governing his portrayal. It is an error of taste and judgment to make the scene of the midnight revel offensive with swinish grossness of drunken ribaldry. The spirit in which it should be played is that of jovial, vinous carousal. "It is a night of revels." Tipsy *Sir Toby* is bent on mirth; he knows *Sir Andrew* to be an ass, and he is intent on indulging himself in "a good time" and amusing himself by chaffing his gull. To impersonate a coarsened gentleman, rioting, singing, quaffing "potations pottle deep," to indicate drunkenness, yet to avoid seeming to be literally and offensively drunk—this artistic exigency requires rare discretion and skill. This discretion was deftly used by Lewis; while he was, in that scene, continuously jocular and "reeling ripe," he was never vulgar. The native humor of Lewis was dry, quizzical, and whimsically, waggishly sapient, and at times mordant with an acid sting of satirical pungency. There was nothing about him of the unctuous order, and he was not intended by nature for *Falstaff* or any of that kindred. Nevertheless, he adroitly suggested *Sir Toby's* exultant animal delight in his capability of sensual enjoyment and in his bibulous diversions. He contrived to lay strong emphasis on the mirth, and in the scene of the midnight revel he was the incarnation of tipsy jocularity, while to the mental quality of the knight, —the comic sagacity of a selfish, good-natured worldling, the inveterate purpose of predominance and profit,—he rendered ample justice. The relation of *Sir Toby* to *Sir Andrew* is kindred with that of *Falstaff* to *Justice Shallow;* in both cases the knight seeks from the gudgeon the replenishment of his purse. The preservation of that attitude by Lewis was perfect. He was correct and felicitous, also, in his amatory bearing toward *Maria,* whom the knight eventually marries. It was seen to be a pity that this *Sir Toby* should have unlaced his reputation for the name of a night-brawler, yet it was seen that, being what he had become, it was fitting he should marry the waiting-maid, frequent the buttery bar, and round out his life in sensual indulgence. As a work of art in a vein not natural to the actor that performance of *Sir Toby* may fairly be called one of the most notable of its period. The coöperation of Catherine Lewis, as *Maria,* proved of much value to the Revel Scene and to other humorous portions of the comedy, contributing abundant animal spirits, mischievous merriment, vivacious action, and a nimble, crisp method of speech,—attributes that are appropriate and delightful in characters like *Maria,*— of brittle sprightliness and roguish duplicity. Catherine Lewis (Mrs. Donald Robertson) was an actress of rare talent, and the most sparkling performer of chambermaid parts who has illumined and cheered our Stage since the merry springtime of the charming Mrs. John Wood.

The associates of Clarke, Lewis, and Miss Lewis in Daly's 1893 revival of "Twelfth Night" included Creston Clarke, as *Orsino;* Adelaide Prince, as *Olivia;* Charles Leclerq, as *Antonio,* and Herbert Gresham, as *Sir Andrew.* Creston Clarke acted *Orsino* at very short notice, taking the place of the English actor, Arthur Bourchier, who had been, for some time, a member of Daly's company, and who quarrelled with the manager and refused to appear. On January 8, 1894, Daly presented his version of "Twelfth Night" at his theatre in London, where it was abundantly successful, receiving 111 representations. The run ended May 7, 1894.

In later repetitions of Daly's presentment of the play William F. Owen (1844-1906), after the death of Lewis, acted *Sir Toby,* and Sybil Carlyle, and later the beautiful Maxine Elliott, and also Margaret St. John, acted *Olivia.* John Craig, Francis Carlyle, and, for a few nights, Frank Worthing played *Orsino,* and Dixey, during his short association with Daly's Theatre, replaced Clarke as *Malvolio:* but, from the first and until the end, the most brilliant feature of the revival was the *Viola* of Ada Rehan.

ADA REHAN.

Ada Rehan's delightful performance of *Viola* is not yet (1914) so distant that it has passed entirely from public remembrance, though possibly it is not as distinct in the general memory as her matchless *Rosalind* is, or her brilliant *Katharine*. She acted *Viola* for the first time on February 21, 1893. Long before she joined Daly's company she had played, in "Twelfth Night," with Adelaide Neilson, and had become acquainted with the method of that actress in the treatment of *Viola,* and in assuming this character she, wisely and rightly, followed, to some extent, that excellent model, which she admired and could not forget. The spirit of her personation was the same,—combining deep tenderness of feeling with glittering gayety of demeanor,—but the form of it was more massive and the execution more bold. Her *Viola* was less a dreamer and more an executant. Her repulse of *Malvolio,* at "No, good swabber, I am to hull here a little longer," struck a defiant note and exhibited an airy truculence. A little of the temperament of *Rosalind* was infused into that of *Viola.* When she said "I am all the daughters of my father's house" her manner and the despairing sadness of her tone almost revealed her sex to the *Duke,* and, as *Orsino* turned toward her with a look of mingled surprise and inquiry, she, rapidly, confusedly, and also *comically,*—added, "a-a-and all the *brothers,* too!"—thus obtaining a laugh instead of a tear. Those touches, slight but significant, indicated that the actress had formed an independent ideal of the part, and intended her personation to be in no wise deficient of the glitter of comedy. It was a performance not less brilliant than gentle. Its salient qualities were poetic condition, physical beauty, innate refinement, and ardent feeling artfully restrained. In this *Viola's* replies to *Orsino's* questions about *Cesario's* love ("of *your* complexion"; "about *your* years, my lord") there was a delicious blending of roguishness and wistfulness. While listening to the song "O Mistress Mine" (which, in Daly's stage version of the comedy, was sung, for *Orsino,* instead of "Come Away, Death"), she sat at the foot of the couch on which the lovelorn *Duke* was reclining, and at "Journeys end in lovers meeting" she slowly turned her head toward that entranced sentimentalist, and bent her gaze upon him, with an expression of fond longing, supremely indicative of perfect love. This was a beautiful use of art, but the supreme beauty of the performance was its manifestation of the magnanimity which makes the character so noble as well as so lovely—*Viola's* generous, gentle, sympathetic consideration for *Olivia,* the woman beloved by the man to whom she is herself devoted. In Ada Rehan's denotement of that feature there was a felicity all her own.

In the opening scene of Daly's version, the seacoast of Illyria, Ada Rehan's *Viola* wore a loose, flowing white robe, trimmed with golden fringe, not a well-chosen garment, because it augmented the size of a person who, though large, was one of the most beautifully formed and proportioned women ever seen on the stage. In *Viola's* first scene with *Orsino,* and until the end of the Second Act, she wore a costume of delicate purple color, silk tights and shoes. Her doublet, heavily embroidered with gold, was open at the throat, where it was edged with white. Her garb was completed by a silk sash, fringed with gold, and a small, plumed cap. In the Third and Fourth acts she wore a costume similar in detail and general design, but of a delicate light-green color, and this she augmented with a short armhole cloak, made of light brown, ribbed velvet. Her dresses all were Italian.

VIOLA ALLEN'S PRODUCTION.

Since the fine presentment of "Twelfth Night" was effected by Daly in 1893 the comedy has been acted many times and in many places in our country, but that presentment has not been equalled. On February 8, 1904, Viola Allen,—an actress of exceptional ability, noble ambition, large and varied experience, and ardent zeal in the service of her art,—produced the play in New York, at the Knickerbocker Theatre, and acted *Viola*. Among her associates in the performance were John Craig, as *Orsino;* John Blair, as *Malvolio;* Clarence Handyside, as *Sir Toby Belch;* Frank Currier, as *Sir Andrew Aguecheek;* Edwin Howard, as *Feste,* and Zeffie Tilbury, as *Maria*. The representation was, in various ways, defective, and therefore the venture did not succeed. Mr. Craig, who had, when associated with Daly's company, impersonated *Orsino* well,—suggesting the languid melancholy, fitful moodiness, and romantic grace which it requires,—made the dreaming lover ostentatious, demonstrative, and vehement, thus sacrificing the poetic charm of the character to the mistaken notion that it should be bold and aggressive. This is a common error with actors who do not know, or who forget, that artistic reserve is more winning than showy self-

TWELFTH NIGHT

assertion, and that sometimes it is more attractive to retire than to obtrude. It seemed strange that Mr. Craig should take an erroneous course in his treatment of *Orsino,* because he had given several admirable performances, and shown himself to be an actor of exceptional natural talent. The fact that, after leaving Daly's thoroughly trained dramatic company, Mr. Craig associated himself with various "stock" companies and gradually became habituated to a rough method of action and speech, might explain the difference between his later and former personation of *Orsino.*—This actor has happily prospered in his profession, and he now conducts, ably and tastefully, the Castle Square Theatre, in Boston.—Mr. Blair, as *Malvolio,* made his only approach to personification of the character when, in the scene of the midnight carousal, the indignant *Steward* interferes, and endeavors to quell the tumult of the revellers: at "My masters, are you mad? or what are you?" he was, for a moment,—in his array of dressing-gown and night-cap, with his beard and moustache crimped in long curl-papers,—a veritable ludicrous image of egregious self-importance and conceit, and therefore an appropriate, effective semblance of the *Malvolio* of the play. His general treatment of the part, however, had the effect of burlesque. His delivery was painfully artificial, monotonous, and inexpressive. Much of the text was intoned, in a thin, high, hollow voice, some of it was bleated, and some of it was sung: most of it might as well have been whistled, for all the intelligible effect it was made to cause. This actor possesses experience and zeal, and, possibly, there are parts to which he is suited, but he did not show *Malvolio* to be one of them. Mr. Handyside signified his total misunderstanding of the character of *Sir Toby,* whom he presented as merely a rank, unmitigated, offensive vulgarian, whereas the knight is, by birth, a gentleman, while his language implies education, and certainly he is a person of sagacious mind and masterful character, though coarsened and degraded by sensual self-indulgence: especially is he a humorist,—having a strain of the humor of *Falstaff*. Mr. Handyside provided all of the *Belch,* but nothing of the *Sir Toby,*—"my lady's kinsman." The spectator saw a large, somewhat corpulent man, having an expansive face, dull and heavy in expression, and pendulous cheeks. His attempt to simulate jocular inebriety, in the Revel Scene, resulted only in vulgar clowning. There is, in some aspects of intoxication, a comicality which can be made effectively humorous in acting,—as was often shown by Burton, Owens, Raymond, and Rowe, in such parts as *Mr. Toodle, Mr. Gilman,* and *Micawber,*

TWELFTH NIGHT 79

—but fine art is required in the showing of it. Mr. Handyside's *Sir Toby,* in the midnight revel, fell over everything and everybody he came near; thrust first his hands and then his feet into a bowl of drink, at which the knights were shown regaling themselves; afterward dipped liquid from it with a ladle, drank from the ladle, and finally threw the dregs into the faces of his companions. Mr. Currier,—an old and experienced actor, who should have known better than to misrepresent a perfectly obvious type of vacuity, asininity, and conceit,—made *Aguecheek* a sort of senile, pottering, toothless, scarce-audible Pantaloon, and appeared to think it funny to straddle, and try to "ride," a chair, and to put his hand into a mug and pretend that he could not withdraw it. Such antics are merely mournful. At the close of that scene the tipplers,—with merciless prolixity, —did the traditional business with the pipes and candles, and then sprawled on the floor, dead drunk, as the curtain fell. Miss Tilbury, coarse in style but vigorous in action, sufficiently expressed the spirit of merry mischief and rampant roguery which animates *Maria.* Mr. Howard, as *Feste,* disported himself sometimes like Harlequin, in the Circus Ring, and sometimes like Nadab, in the Music Hall, but never once appeared the sapient, quizzical, droll, caustic yet humorous *Clown* of Shakespeare's "Twelfth Night."

It is not strange that Viola Allen,—accomplished actress though she is, and by superiority of mind, sensibility of temperament, proficient artistic skill, and personal beauty, fitted to act *Viola,*—did not, when thus surrounded with depressing impediments, make the part as effective as certainly she is capable of making it. There was, moreover, another cause adverse to her success. Whether affected by the influence of prosy, commonplace, professional associates, or guided by deference to the deplorably prevalent proclivity to "realism" on the stage, the actress seemed determined that a play essentially fanciful and romantic should be interpreted as a portrayal of actual, every-day life, and that a heroine almost ethereal in quality should be made literal, probable, and matter-of-fact. The persons in "Twelfth Night" were to be considered such as are not only possible but usual. The incidents, some of which are forced and, indeed, in the light of cold reason, preposterous, were to be viewed and treated as entirely credible. The instantaneous marriage of *Sebastian* and *Olivia* was to be accepted as rational. The delicate, almost spiritual, yet absolutely feminine *Viola,* lovelorn for the lord whom she serves, was not only to be so perfectly disguised in male apparel as to be esteemed, by all her interlocutors, a young man; she was to appear so to her auditors.

From the Oil Painting by Orlando Rouland. Courtesy of Mr. Rouland

EDWARD H. SOTHERN AS *MALVOLIO*

"This does make some obstruction in the blood, this cross-gartering."

Act III., Sc. 4

TWELFTH NIGHT

The abnegation of sex was to be literal, as in the instances occasionally reported in contemporaneous life, wherein a woman, for a long time, passes for a man. Poetic license was to be ignored and poetry converted into prose. This could not, and can not, be done in such plays as "Twelfth Night" and "As You Like It," without incurring failure. The charm of a performance, whether of *Viola* or *Rosalind,* depends on the performer's consistent preservation and exhibition of many commingled elements of loveliness in the woman pretending to be a man. The scheme is a delightful fiction, and it cannot be successfully treated as a bald fact. Miss Allen, in trying to be seemingly a literal boy, succeeded only in depleting the essential beauty of feminine allurement, permeating her performance with a prosy instead of a poetic spirit (which, as subsequently shown in her *Imogen,* she could easily have supplied), and thus sacrificing loveliness of quality and sympathetic effect in a useless endeavor to invest an ethereal being,—the Egeria of a poet's imagination,—with the common garb of reality. It is true that women do sometimes succeed in passing themselves off as men. Not long ago a woman died, in an Old Soldiers' Home, who had successfully pretended to be a man, had participated as a soldier in the Civil War, and had for years drawn a pension as a veteran of that conflict: her secret was discovered only after her death. Miss Allen's notion about *Viola* seems to have rested on the fact that such deception is *possible*. But it is "to consider too curiously" so to consider the poetic drama. The woman of fact who succeeds in passing herself off as a man is abnormal, unfeminine, and the success of her imposition depends on her being so. Shakespeare's *Viola* is not a woman of that kind. The masquerade is an allowed premise. Something, in these cases, must be left to the imagination.—It should be mentioned that Miss Allen, in appearing in the American metropolis as *Viola,* gratified herself by the fulfilment of a life-long desire and purpose, yet at the last moment was suddenly stricken with a dangerous illness. Her appearance on the date appointed was forbidden by her physician, who warned her that she would risk her life if she ventured to act. She nevertheless insisted on acting, but after the performance she collapsed, and the next day she underwent the dreadful operation for mastoiditis. She happily recovered and, on March 14, at the Harlem Opera House, resumed her occupation, reappearing as *Viola.* She again presented "Twelfth Night," on January 11, 1905, at the Knickerbocker Theatre, with the same cast as before, except that the part of *Malvolio* was assigned to Mr. Henry

TWELFTH NIGHT

Jewett, who showed no comprehension of its complexity and importance, but seemed to have apprehended it as that of an obsequious flunky.

A CURIOSITY.—"BEN" GREET'S PRODUCTION.

On February 22, 1904, Mr. "Ben" Greet, succeeding Viola Allen at the Knickerbocker Theatre, effected a revival of "Twelfth Night," ostensibly "in the Elizabethan manner," himself appearing as *Malvolio*, and presenting Miss Edith Wynne Matthison as *Viola*. Mr. Greet's aim, as declared on this and other occasions, was "mainly an educational design," to be accomplished by pursuing "a middle way between an antiquarian revival and the modern style of presenting a maximum of stage settings with a minimum of Shakespeare." Exact and complete knowledge of the manner in which plays were presented in Shakespeare's time cannot be obtained. Something is known,—not everything. The authorities, for example, disagree as to the character and use of scenery. The Masques presented at Court appear to have been embellished with scenes that were elaborate, ingenious, and costly, and there is evidence that the stage, in Queen Elizabeth's time and that of King James the First, was, in some respects, well though not lavishly equipped. The model followed by Mr. Greet in his presentment of "Twelfth Night" was, measurably, the setting which he conjectured to have been used when the comedy was acted in the Hall of the Middle Temple, February 2, 1601, as recorded in the "Diary" of Manningham. A single scene, boxed and panelled, with a raised platform at the back, draped doorways, and a timbered and bannered ceiling, served for the whole performance. The effect, though monotonous, was not otherwise unpleasant.

The truth, as to scenic illustration, lies in a nutshell. Investiture if excessive is injurious to illusion and effect and is then objectionable, but a judicious, tasteful investiture helps to create and maintain illusion, and, in as far as it accomplishes that result, it is useful, desirable, and commendable. Color, light, picture, and ornament can be, and often are, misused, but within rational limits they are not only helpful but essential to dramatic effect. The method of the modern stage, in the setting of plays, whatever be its faults, is, in any competent instance, superior to any method that was employed in "the spacious times of great Elizabeth." Mr. Greet, however, who began management in America by introducing Miss Matthison to our Stage, October 13, 1902, in the Morality of "Everyman," has, from the first, found it advantageous to employ a quasi-antique manner of stage-setting, and his method was exemplified by his presentment of "Twelfth Night," which aroused some curiosity and attracted some favor. Rational objection to this manager's method is that it pretends to accomplish something which is not, and cannot be, fully accomplished,—and which, even if it were fully accomplished, would serve only to exemplify, which is needless and useless, the deficiencies of the early English Theatre. In Shakespeare's time, and long afterward, the female characters were assumed by males: in Mr. Greet's presentments of Shakespeare's plays they are assumed by females,—according to the proper usage of the regular stage. These presentments, furthermore, are illumined with electric lights, and the performers in them use modern wigs and likewise a style of "make-up" accordant to the theatrical customs of the present day. Mr. Greet is aware, and he has so signified in print, that the old mode of producing Shakespeare's plays "can only be *reflected* to a *limited extent*,"—in which case the reflection is, practically, barren of "educational" value. This manager's actual purpose, as distinguished from his pretended one, is commercial, and as such a purpose is honest it should not be associated with a sophistical and fatuous pretence, which smacks of humbug. To produce plays as, probably or certainly, they were produced three hundred years ago, before Science had made discoveries and Ingenuity had contrived inventions which Taste has employed to revolutionize all the old processes of industry and art, is only to do badly that which can be done well; and to do this under the pretence of serving the cause of "education" is to be disingenuous. Mr. Greet, desiring to succeed in theatrical management, in the face of great competition, presents a curiosity instead of a regular dramatic performance, and for curiosities, however tiresome, there seems to be an audience:

"New customs,
Though they be never so ridiculous,
Nay, let 'em be unmannerly, yet are followed,"

and so, too, are old ones when sprinkled over with the gilt of "novelty." Mr. Greet's policy aims to escape the large expense of manufacturing elaborate, costly costumes and heavy scenery, and of transporting them from town to town, over all the wide area of the country, and to make possible the giving of remunerative exhibitions in places otherwise generally inaccessible, and in circumstances otherwise prohibitive. That is not a discreditable policy, but it ought to be pursued without any cant about "education."

Mr. Greet has brought out several of Shakespeare's plays in what he styles the "middle way," and some of his presentments,—notably that of "Macbeth,"—because of the inadequacy of his method and the inefficiency of his actors, have been little better than desecrations. In his production of "Twelfth Night" he manifested discretion and taste and was creditably successful. The merit of the representation did not, indeed, consist in the scenical poverty which that other learned Shakespearean scholar and sapient theatrical speculator, Mr. Charles Frohman, designated its "simple grandeur,"—because there was no "grandeur" about it, simple or complex; the merit, for a wonder, consisted in the acting. Almost half of the parts were well played, with skill of impersonation, with sense, taste, and correct delivery, and, in general, the treatment of the play was wise and right. Mr. B. A. Field lacked both stature and humor for *Sir Toby,* but he knew the meaning of the character, and he made it evident. Mr. Cecil Collins lacked quaintness and drollery for *Feste,* but he showed vivacity, gave the requisite touch of malice to his mischief, and sang as the *Jester* should, in a spontaneous, simple style, and not like a modern professional concert singer. Miss Alys Rees was over-mature and was "contemporary" in method as *Olivia,* but she evinced refinement and distinction, and she spoke the text so as to impart all its meaning. John Crawley's performance of *Sir Andrew* was deficient only in emphasis. *Antonio,* acted by George Riddell, and the *Sea Captain,* by St. Clair Bayfield, stood forth in fine relief, as little parts exceedingly well played. It was a comfort to hear the words of the play correctly spoken, and to see the tipsy Revel Scene acted with natural jollity, and almost entirely without horse-play. Miss Matthison was elderly and heavy for *Viola,* and her endeavor to show the blithe, joyous aspect of the character was ineffective; but her intimation of its sadness, its submissive endurance, its sweet, gentle patience, its restrained passion, and its grace, was natural, fluent, and sympathetic, while her vocalism was delightfully melodious and expressive. Mr. Charles Rann Kennedy, as *Orsino,* was prosy and commonplace, but he read with precision, and his action was definite. Mr. Greet manifested an intelligent comprehension of the essential spirit of *Malvolio,*—that of diseased self-love,—a keen sense of character, ample discretion in leaving untouched the effects he had once produced, and remarkable technical skill in the execution of his design. A purpose was visible in his acting to elicit all possible laughter, and to that end he indulged in some extravagance,—in the carriage of the body, and in a demeanor almost clownish in the episode of the yellow stockings and cross-garters. That discrepancy of performance, however, was in-

From a Photograph by White, N. Y. *Courtesy of T. R. Smith, Esq.*

JULIA MARLOWE AS *VIOLA*

"Most excellent accomplished lady, the heavens rain odors on you!"

Act III., Sc. 1

evitable in an actor who is, intrinsically, a low comedian. Mr. Greet's obvious self-complacency, not to say assurance, and his high, thin voice suit well with *Malvolio,* and, though the lack of genuine austerity, individual weight, and almost truculent dignity made itself apparent,—those qualities being essential to justify this actor's passionate intensity at the moment of *Malvolio's* final exit,—the impersonation was highly commendable, and it is remembered as by far the best that Mr. Greet has given on our Stage.

MISS MARLOWE.—SOTHERN-MARLOWE.

Julia Marlowe first acted *Viola* in 1887,—appearing in that part at the old Star Theatre, December 14, that year, with Joseph Haworth as *Malvolio,*—and, since then, she has repeated and developed her impersonation by performances in many different places and in various associations. Her best and representative embodiment of *Viola,* rounded and polished in the light of her mature experience alike of life and art, has been given within comparatively recent years, in association with E. H. Sothern, as *Malvolio.* The production of "Twelfth Night" that those actors accomplished at the Knickerbocker Theatre, New York, on November 13, 1905, was remarkable chiefly for the excellence of their acting.

Miss Marlowe's *Viola* is remembered as the most truthful, effective, and charming realization of that romantic character which has been placed before the American audience within recent years. It is the best of all her Shakespearean personations, because true in ideal, lovely in spirit, and definite in execution. She possessed the personal beauty, the sensibility of temperament, and the melodious, sympathetic voice requisite for the part, and, in the acting of it, her art was so fine and under such admirable control that she created the illusion of truth without sacrificing the enchantment of poetry. *Viola* is a perfect ideal of beauty, and such an ideal, suitably presented on the stage, as it was by Miss Marlowe, sinks into the mind, remains in the memory, and beneficently influences the conduct of life.

Mr. Sothern's personation of *Malvolio* was admirable for a correct ideal, authority, sincerity, and smooth execution. In the Letter Scene and the Yellow Stockings Scene the humor of it and the intolerable egotism were exactly elicited. Indeed, the actor's fidelity to Shakespeare and to Nature, alike in his ideal and in his presentation of it, was almost painful; it was literally so in the Dungeon Scene, when the unhappy man is badgered by *Feste,* disguised as the curate. Sothern embodied a *Malvolio* who might well have been prized by *Olivia* at the value of the half of her dowry; who might well write the sturdy, incisive letter, in which he says, "I leave my duty a little unthought of, and speak out of my injury"; a *Malvolio* worthy to be so esteemed that *Olivia* should offer to make him "both the plaintiff and the judge" of his own "notorious wrong," and that *Orsino* should "entreat him to a peace": in a word, he presented *Malvolio* as a natural, possible person, of substantial character, however grotesquely eccentric, and this he did without sacrifice of the requisite effect of humor, satire, and mirth.

THE NEW THEATRE PRODUCTION.

The presentment of "Twelfth Night" effected at the New Theatre,—now (1914) the Century,—on January 26, 1910, was more pretentious than efficient. The scenery and costumes then shown were, indeed, handsome, and in the main appropriate, but the acting, while, as a whole, intelligent and earnest, was, except in two personations,—those of *Sir Andrew* and *Feste,*—essentially commonplace. The cast included Annie Russell, as *Viola;* Oswald Yorke, as *Malvolio;* Louis Calvert, as *Sir Toby;* Ferdinand Gottschalk, as *Sir Andrew;* Jacob Wendell, Jr., as *Feste;* Matheson Lang, as *Orsino;* Leah Bateman-Hunter, as *Olivia;* and Jessie Busley, as *Maria*. Miss

Russell, an actress of much experience,—having been on the stage since 1872, when she was only eight years old,—proved rather elderly for *Viola,* and in other particulars besides that of aspect she was seen to be deficient. The imperative requirements of the part have been sufficiently specified, and it will be enough here to say that the attributes of girlish loveliness, fervent feeling, sensibility, romantic tone, and spiritual exaltation were not visible in Miss Russell's performance. Her vocalism was weak, and she did not succeed in speaking the blank verse (few actors ever do) in such a way as to make it seem the language of nature, without sacrificing its poetic quality. Mr. Yorke clearly indicated comprehension of the character of *Malvolio,* and his acting was, technically, proficient, but the personality which he disclosed was unsubstantial and unimpressive. He is an amiable man and a competent and useful actor, not, however, possessed of distinction, weight, massive authority, or exceptional individuality, and therefore his *Malvolio,* while correct in form, was superficial and practically insignificant. In the last analysis every dramatic performance is dependent, alike for immediate effect and enduring appreciation, not merely on what the actor does or the manner in which it is done, but also on what the actor *is.* Mr. Calvert, who has shown himself able and expert in the impersonation of a

TWELFTH NIGHT 93

variety of characters, exhibited a singular lack of humor, as *Sir Toby,* and was lethargic, mechanical, and dull. Mr. Wendell (1869-1911), an actor of promise, untimely taken away, gave a fine performance of *Feste,* sympathetic with the droll, whimsical, half-cynical, half-rueful spirit of the part, and in the scene of the revel he sang the song in an easy, off-hand manner, precisely as the *Jester* ought to sing it. Miss Bateman-Hunter was pretty and pleasing as *Olivia,* and Miss Busley was rampant and noisy, without either infectious mirth or sportive mischief, as *Maria.* Mr. Lang, as *Orsino,* was intolerable,—plebeian in quality, stolid in demeanor, and metallic in vocalism: "So they sell bullocks."

A remarkably fine performance, however, was given by Ferdinand Gottschalk, as *Aguecheek,* and this, in some degree, redeemed the dulness of the general representation, giving pleasure by the excellence of its art, and providing a subject for thought. Almost for the first time, certainly for the first time in recent years, *Aguecheek* was shown as a possible human being, and not as a grotesque caricature of humanity,—such as, usually, seems to be considered a true "Shakespearean" low-comedy character. The vacuity of the conceited, silly knight was shown to be that of an actually fatuous mind, being most evident when it made him at once most entirely the victim and sport of his false friend *Sir Toby* and most complacent in his self-satisfied conviction of his own sense and superiority. That which he least understood he most approved, and his vanity, enwrapping him like a mantle, kept him warm in his own approbation. The physical peculiarities assumed by the comedian were completely and happily appropriate to the character. His face wore an expression compounded of foolishness, pertness, meanness, and arrogance. He walked with a mincing strut, wagging his head, and turning his thin, bedizened body, now to one side and now to the other, with a preening, bird-like motion, exceedingly ridiculous and admirably expressive of the inflation of conceit. His voice was thin and high; his articulation and intonation were clear and peculiarly fitted to convey the due effect of every word he spoke. The resentment of this *Aguecheek* because of *Olivia's* favor toward "the Duke's man" was shown to be sincere, angry, bitter with the gall of a vain, mean, paltry, contemptible nature, and vindictive with the malignity of a coward who believes himself secure in assailing a weaker person than himself. His terror, in the Duel Scene, was that of the veritable poltroon impelled by vanity into a situation of apparent peril, who is too frightened to perceive the fear and dismay of his antagonist, and who, while vaguely conscious of his

TWELFTH NIGHT

despicable position in the view of his companions, is frantically desirous to escape, by any expedient whatsoever, from the danger that confronts him. Mr. Gottschalk's embodiment of the "dear venom" will long be remembered. The best stage pictures in this production of "Twelfth Night" were the one showing *Olivia's* House and the one showing the rock-bound sea-coast and a dark expanse of stormy ocean, canopied by wild, lowering cloud, illumined by a single rift of angry red. The music, which is so essential in the representation of this comedy, was,—whether played or sung,—delightfully performed.

MARGARET ANGLIN.

The first of Shakespeare's plays produced by Miss Margaret Anglin,—an actress of good natural ability, much force of character, and worthy professional reputation,—was "Twelfth Night." She brought it out on October 24, 1908, at Melbourne, Australia: she first presented it in America, at San Francisco, on September 29, 1913, and on March 25, 1914, acted in it for the first time in New York, at the Hudson Theatre. Her version is in four acts, and, according to her published play-bill, in eleven scenes, representing eight different places. These places are the Sea-coast of Illyria, a Passage in the

House of *Olivia,* a Room in the House of *Orsino,* a Garden by the House of *Olivia,* Another Place on the Sea-coast of Illyria, a Room in the House of *Olivia,* a Street (near "the City"), and a Cellar (beneath the house of *Olivia*). The arrangement of the scenes as noted in the play-bill would have required the acting of the scene in which *Antonio* gives his purse to *Sebastian after* the arrest of Antonio. In the action this absurdity was avoided by an abrupt expedient: the two scenes between *Antonio* and *Sebastian* (that in which *Sebastian* takes leave of *Antonio,*—"If you will not undo what you have done," etc.,—in the original, Act II., sc. 1, and that which closes with the appointment to meet "at the Elephant," in the original, Act III., sc. 4) were cut, combined in one, and acted in a set showing a distant seashore, visible from a place overhung by trees. *Sebastian* therefore proposed to view "the reliques of this town," and *Antonio* specified the danger incurred by him in walking in "these streets," with nothing in sight to signify the proximity of either town or streets or relics.

The scenery used in this production, designed by Mr. Livingston Platt and painted by Messrs. Unitt and Wicks, was merely utilitarian. In general it was light in color, and that is an advantage in presenting a "joyous comedy," but the investiture

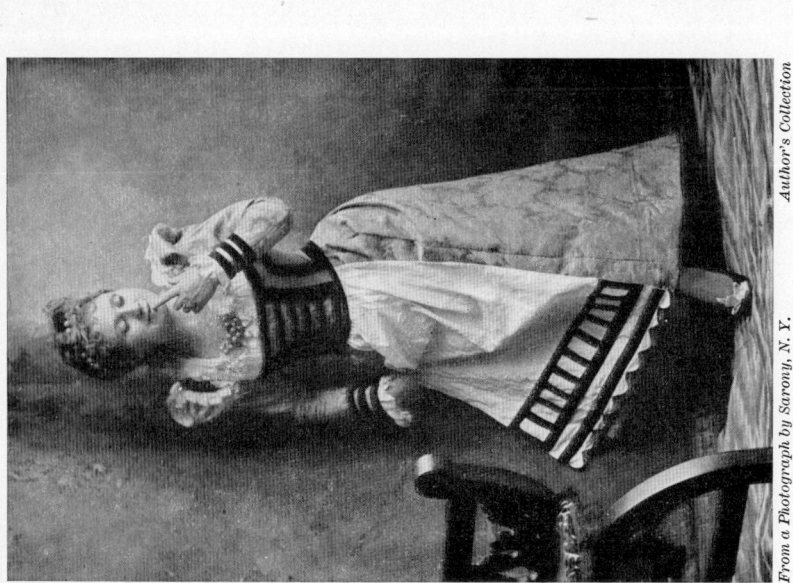

CATHERINE LEWIS AS MARIA
"Peace, you rogue, no more o' that!"
Act I, Sc. 5

FERDINAND GOTTSCHALK AS SIR ANDREW AGUECHEEK
"Good Mistress Accost, I desire better acquaintance!"
Act I, Sc. 3

was neither handsome, attractive, nor interesting, the general effect, in most of the scenes, being that of huddle and insipidity. The dressing of the play was more appropriate. The raiment worn by *Orsino,* indeed, seemed fantastic, comprising, as it did, a violet or purple cloak, richly embroidered, depending almost to the ankles, tights of the same color, and a close-fitting body garment, with a parti-colored sash, green and gold predominating. The sleeves of the coat-cloak, which were long, hanging from above the elbow, were lined with gold color, and the player's head was encircled with a turban of silk, the color of which varied from cream to gold, according as the light changed under which it was seen: this turban was thick-sewn with pearls. The effect was neither Grecian, Italian, nor Elizabethan, but Moorish. Miss Anglin's *Page* dress was Grecian in design, and of a greenish-gray color,—called, I believe, "French gray." The lighting of the stage was often insufficient; it was particularly so in the first scene, which, practically, was played in the dark, and in *Viola's* second scene with *Orsino.* In the former (which seemed intended to represent a rock-ribbed ravine, near the seashore) Miss Anglin, as *Viola,* was discovered perched upon what appeared to be the prow of a boat, but which may have been anything, for it could not be distinctly discerned.

From that queer eminence, after a portentous pause, the actress delivered the inquiry, "What country, friends, is this?" speaking in a radically artificial, affected voice. The *Sea Captain,* in order to reply, "This is Illyria, lady," entered, from the right, carrying a lighted lantern, which he raised so as to illumine *Viola's* face. The keynote of staginess was thus struck, and throughout the performance the tone of artificiality was consistently maintained.

Miss Anglin is a person of large stature, mature physique, formidable aspect, commanding demeanor, and, apparently, somewhat insusceptible temperament. Her voice is unsympathetic, and her articulation is marred by a slight impediment. She is professionally expert, evincing sense of character and the executive facility which comes of long experience. Her method is familiar and colloquial: she is not in any degree poetic. Her performance of *Viola* showed distinct purpose, conscientious study, and careful, laborious preparation. Authority, sincerity, and flexibility of action were its salient characteristics, but, not possessing the personal beauty,—girl-like, delicate, and bewitching,—which is essential to the representative of *Viola,* and having no natural proclivity to the character or affinity with it, the actress succeeded only in giving a mechanical representation, such as might have been expected from a practised performer. Her nearest approach to an indication of the spirit of the part was made in *Viola's* first colloquy with *Orsino:* at "I'll do my best," etc., she indicated the tender longing and rueful, lovely resignation of the gentle girl who must go a-wooing to another woman, for the man she loves. Her comedy tone and manner, at "I will return into the house," were effective, and she manifested the necessary blending of feminine terror and affected courage, in the mock Duel Scene, exceedingly well. Some of her stage business was singularly injudicious, and some of it was amazing in its ineptitude. In *Viola's* first scene with *Olivia,* when she asks, "The honorable lady of the house, which is she?" Miss Anglin produced a scroll, and so deported herself as to signify that *Viola* intended to read her "commission." In the text she says that the speech in praise of *Olivia's* beauty has been learned,—declaring "I took great pains *to study it,*" and she deplores not being permitted to recite the "poetical" effusion. The fact that a device in acting is new should not be a bar to its use, but the introduction of a device at once unwarranted, unnecessary, and commonplace cannot be approved as sensible. In *Viola's* second scene with *Orsino* the *Duke's* room had been closed in with curtains, his couch, on which he was reclining, shifted from its first position, and a large, gilded vessel, resembling the kind of structure often placed in gardens as a fountain, had been placed in front of him,—this receptacle being filled with roses, which *Viola,* kneeling beside it, was occupied in arranging. The object of this floricultural display became manifest as the colloquy proceeded: it was to allow the speakers to "suit the action to the word, the word to the action." When *Orsino* was declaring his views on the suitability of mating, in marriage, he hesitated on the words "For women are," and then, observing the mass of flowers before him, added, *"as roses,* whose fair flower," etc. That proceeding, obviously, was artificial to an extreme degree and in the worst taste. As I viewed it, I thought that its foolish, prosy dulness could not be exceeded; yet a moment later it was exceeded by Miss Anglin herself (who, indeed, was responsible for all the defects of stage management, as the play was "produced and staged" by her), for, when she was speaking that most exquisite speech,—that perfect strain of pure feeling which flows from the woman's heart,—"She never told her love," etc.,—she, too, hesitated, pausing on the words "but let concealment," and then, gaining inspiration from the flower-pot, indicated an opening rose and significantly added, "like a worm i' the bud." "W-i-n-d-e-r," says *Mr. Squeers* to one of his pupils, at Dotheboys Hall, "spells winder: now you go and *wash* the winder, and you'll remember how to spell it." No actress capable of such "business" as that, in the poetic drama, could reasonably be expected to act *Viola*. Illusion is difficult to create and it is easily destroyed. I remember seeing a performance of *Rosalind* by a female who remarked that "men have died—and *woems* have eaten them—but not for love."

Recourse to the sometimes dubious text of the First Folio of Shakespeare is one of the expedients of the "producer" of his plays, when straining after novelty. That expedient has been employed by Miss Anglin, in her work of arranging the Shakespearean plays which are included in her repertory, "Twelfth Night," "As You Like It," and "The Taming of the Shrew." The Folio print of "Twelfth Night" makes *Viola* address the words, "No, good swabber," to the waiting woman, *Maria:* that, probably, is an error—though the text of "Twelfth Night" is, as a rule, exceptionally correct. The words, in fitness, should be addressed to *Malvolio*. Miss Anglin follows the Folio. It would be well if some of the attention bestowed on the quest for "original readings" could be, instead, bestowed on correct use of the English language. Miss Anglin prescribed, or at least sanctioned, the pronunciation of "humble" as "ŭm'-bl," and "humor" as "hue-mor";—both vulgarisms.

Miss Anglin's associates in the representation of "Twelfth Night" were Pedro de Cordoba, as *Orsino;* Fuller Mellish, as *Malvolio;* Sidney Greenstreet, as *Sir Toby;* Wallace Widdecombe, as *Sir Andrew;* Max Montesole, as *Feste;* Miss Ruth Holt Boucicault, as *Olivia,* and Miss Lillian Thurgate, as *Maria.* The most prominent characteristic of the entire performance was the overweening, obtrusive, self-satisfaction of the performers. Mr. de Cordoba was intelligent, earnest, and mechanically efficient, as *Orsino,* but more intent on showing himself than the character. Mr. Greenstreet's proceedings as *Sir Toby* were clownish and vulgar, displaying no sense of the character, not a particle of humor, exceedingly boisterous, and physically and vocally repellent. A worse performance of the part,—more completely mistaken as to its meaning, and more grossly common,—has not been given. Mr. Widdecombe showed no distinct idea of *Sir Andrew,* seeming to suppose that the humor of that part, such as it is, consists in monotonous fussiness of movement and insistent, shrill, nasal vocalism. In Mr. Montesole's assumption of *Feste* there was abundance of caper, but no tinge of character, no humor, no sapience, no quaintness. Toward the end of the revel, as acted by this absurd trio, *Feste,* who had been asleep, on a bench, at the back of the scene, rose and walked away, yawning and emitting sepulchral groans. *Sir Andrew* and *Sir Toby,* hearing those sounds, showed signs of fear, and turned in their seats, so slowly that when they were able to look behind themselves *Feste* had disappeared. Then, as they prepared to make their exit, pursuant of *Sir Toby's* intention to "go burn some sack," *Feste,* who had returned and concealed himself behind a parapet, suddenly elevated before them a "ghost,"—a scarecrow figure made of white sheeting, on a wooden cross-frame and head-piece, on which a "face" had been painted,—such a figure as mischievous boys sometimes employ, in their silly sports at Halloween; and, seeing that apparition, Mr. Greenstreet and Mr. Widdecombe, emitting loud shrieks, fell backward on the floor and lay there, waving their legs in the air, as the curtain descended. This asinine device I first saw in the production of "Twelfth Night" at the New Theatre: in it ignorance, folly, and vulgarity were shown at their height. Miss Thurgate presented *Maria* as a violent and vehement hoyden, laborious and stridulous in her mischief, and not in the least piquant or frolicsome. The performance of *Olivia* by Miss Boucicault was discreet, sensible, and refined.

Much was expected of Mr. Mellish, as *Malvolio.* He is one of the most experienced and able actors now on our stage. He comes of a theatrical family; he was trained in one of the best of histrionic schools, having been for years a member of Henry Irving's dramatic company; he is a reverent disciple of that actor, and he is possessed of exceptional dramatic talent, which has been shown in many fine performances. Expectation as to his *Malvolio* was, in the main, disappointed. He had evidently perceived the complexity of the character and the difficulty of impersonating it in such a way as to show its inherent worth and essential gravity without obscuring the effect of humor, but his execution was artificial, his manner was extravagant, not fantastic and pompously important, and some of the expedients to which he resorted in abortive effort for comic effect were clownish. *Malvolio's* egotistical fancies impel him to supposititious eminence and the practising of behavior only when he is alone; he does not assume "greatness" until it has been "thrust upon him," until after he has read the forged letter and fallen into *Maria's* trap: up to that time, when in company, "he is sad and civil." Mr. Mellish made him, from the first, a churl to all persons except *Olivia,* while Miss Anglin, as "producer," permitted a manner toward him, on the part of his interlocutors,—especially *Maria,*—such as could not have been tolerated for even a moment toward a man of his character,

TWELFTH NIGHT

esteemed and trusted as he is by his mistress. On both sides the attitude was wrong, and possibly the actor had been enjoined to play *Malvolio* not after his own design, but after that of some one else. In the Letter Scene the boisterous, noisy conduct of the three espials,—who, whether improperly crossing from side to side of the stage, or lurking "in the box-tree" or on the parapet, deported themselves so as to be continually visible,—was destructive of all effect of any acting that might be done by *Malvolio*. It is a settled principle of dramatic art that, in scenes of individual predominance, all the performers implicated must work together to promote the essential prominence of the central figure. If ever a scene belonged entirely to one actor, it is the Letter Scene in "Twelfth Night." Criticism would be wasted on the porcine folly of such antics as were practised during Mr. Mellish's performance in that scene.

In reading the letter, at "If this fall into thy hand, revolve," Mr. Mellish paused, with an air of perplexity, looked up from the paper, then spun round on his heel, and resumed reading,—as though *Malvolio* had understood the word "revolve" as a command to rotate his body. At "put thyself into the trick of singularity," he misread the last word, stopping on the first syllable of it, saying "put thyself into the trick of sin," repeated "sin" twice, with an air of amazement, then perceived the other syllables, read the word "singularity," and proceeded with an air of pleased relief;—all this rank foolery, uncharacteristic and not in the least comic, being, presumably, indulged because of the bad example of Beerbohm-Tree, who introduced it, several years ago. Such silly stage business illustrates what is considered a "modern" and "progressive" spirit, in the treatment of Shakespeare's plays. Mr. Mellish was at his best in *Malvolio's* last two scenes, because he was convincing and touching in his denotement of the distress and indignation of the imprisoned *Steward,* and dignified and pathetic in the reproach to *Olivia,* —"Madam, you have done me wrong," etc. The business of returning, at the close, and casting his official chain at the feet of *Olivia* has been done by many players of *Malvolio,* since the time of Phelps, if not from an earlier time, but it seems incorrect. It is true that "men in rage strike wild," but *Malvolio* does not include *Olivia* in his "I'll be revenged on the whole pack of you!"—he must, of course, have perceived the truth of her denial of complicity in the plot to disgrace him.

II.

ROMEO AND JULIET.

"Oh, lovers of Verona, fair and young,
Are ye indeed return'd? What spell sublime—
What effort, like the backward glance of time,
Hath borne ye hither?—Passionate still, and hung
Round with enchantment, like the days of yore,
When joy was one large dream, and life no more."

Bryan Waller Procter.

DATE OF COMPOSITION.

UNLESS Shakespeare wrote "Titus Andronicus," which, for cogent reasons, is incredible, though possibly he touched it here and there, the first tragedy that he composed is "Romeo and Juliet," and, notwithstanding errors of taste and blemishes of style,—meaning occasional vulgarity, a florid excess of fanciful images, and the dissonant artifice of many rhymed couplets,—it is one of the most profoundly affecting, and therefore most salutary, tragedies in existence. The precise date of its composition has not been ascertained, nor has the precise date of its first representation. The weight of such testimony as diligent research has collected tends to prove that it was written, and acted, not earlier than 1591 and not later than 1595, and that, subsequently, it was by Shakespeare rewritten and much improved. It was first published in 1597, in quarto form, that publication being piratical and not bearing the author's name. It is positively known to have been acted prior to that publication, the dramatic company of which Shakespeare was a member having presented it, at the Curtain Theatre, Holywell, London, in 1596, or early in 1597. The title page of the First Quarto states that it is therein printed "as it hath been often (with great success) played publicly by the Right Honourable the Lord of Hunsdon his Servants." The title page of the Second Quarto states that the tragedy is therein printed "As it hath been sundry times publicly acted by the Lord Chamberlain his Servants." Henry, Lord Hunsdon, the Lord Chamberlain, died on July 22, 1596, and his son, George, Lord Hunsdon, was appointed Lord Chamberlain in April, 1597. The title page of the First Quarto shows that "Romeo and Juliet" had been acted, and, later, probably, published, in the interim between the death of Henry Hunsdon and the appointment of his son, George Hunsdon, as Lord Chamberlain; otherwise that title page would, more importantly, have advertised its performance (as the title page of the Second Quarto does) as having been given by the actors of "the Lord Chamberlain" (Malone).

Knight records his opinion that the statement of the title page of "Romeo and Juliet," when printed in 1597, that it had been acted by Lord Hunsdon's servants, is not evidence that the tragedy was not publicly acted long before. That statement, while not "evidence" that "Romeo and Juliet" was not acted earlier, *is* constructive *testimony* to that effect. Knight maintains that this tragedy was originally written and first produced in 1591, because of the particular emphasis that (Act I., sc. 3) is laid on the memory of the *Nurse* concerning "the great earthquake," April 5, 1580: " 'Tis since the earthquake now eleven years," "and since that time [the earthquake] it is eleven years."

"Romeo and Juliet" was a notably successful play: besides the two quartos already mentioned three others were printed; one undated, one in 1607 (Knight), and one in 1609. It is at least somewhat unlikely that a play popular enough to warrant publication of five editions within twelve years would have remained unprinted and unrecorded for six years after its first performance, an assumption which we must accept as sound if we accede to Knight's reasoning on this point. That it was successful from the first the number of editions tends to show, and it is certain that, when competently performed, it has ever since been successful. The Second Quarto, "newly corrected, augmented, and amended," appeared in 1599, and in that volume the tragedy stands as the world now possesses it. In the First Folio, 1623, the play was reprinted from the "amended" quarto.

SOURCE OF THE PLOT.

Even in his earliest writings Shakespeare exhibits intuitive knowledge of human nature, but theorists who have ascribed to him subtle, complex purposes in his "Romeo and Juliet" have forgotten, or been willing to forget, that in almost every fibre of it the play is a dramatic amplification of "The Tragical History of Romeus and Juliet" (1562), a labored poem by Arthur Brooke (died 1563). It is a marvellous amplification, indeed, ingenious, affluent, eloquent, fervent, beautiful; one which gives limbs to the story, causes it to move, and thus to become dramatic; but, all the same, it is the elaborate expansion of an earlier work by another hand. The only new ingredients of invention in the play are the delightful character of *Mercutio* (a similar name occurs in Brooke's poem) and the dramatic employment of *Paris* in the Churchyard Scene. In

ROMEO AND JULIET

development of plot and arrangement of incidents the drama follows the poem. If, accordingly, any person had a darker design than that of telling a tragical love-story in a plain, straightforward manner, it was Brooke, not Shakespeare. Brooke's poem was based on material derived from old Italian writings,—chiefly those of Matthew Bandello,—and from a play that had been produced prior to the making of his poem, and therefore prior to the composition of Shakespeare's tragedy. "It is certain," says Collier, "that there was an English play upon the story of Romeo and Juliet before the year 1562."

EARLY REPRESENTATIONS.—BRITISH STAGE.

The first representative of *Romeo* was Richard Burbage, but no description of his performance is known. The contemporary "Elegy" on his death, which came to light in 1825, implies that his acting was effective, lamenting that

> "Poor *Romeo* nevermore shall tears beget
> For *Juliet's* love and cruel *Capulet*."

The first representative of *Juliet* was a male, and it is difficult to believe that the spectacle thus presented could have created the requisite illusion.

From the time of Richard Burbage, who died in 1619, to that of Thomas Betterton (1635-1710)

"Romeo and Juliet" remained unacted; but on March 1, 1662, Sir William Davenant presented it, at the theatre in Lincoln's Inn Fields, with a fine cast, including the admired actor Henry Harris as *Romeo*, Betterton as *Mercutio*, and Mary Saunderson as *Juliet*. Harris's performance of *Romeo* is not described, but probably it was sympathetic and winning. Harris possessed the advantages of fine face and person, as is shown by authentic portraits of him, and he was a versatile and accomplished actor, as indicated by the record, sparse though it be, of his professional achievements. Miss Saunderson, who, in December, 1662, became Mrs. Betterton, and was one of the first female players to appear on the English stage, is, in the old records, highly commended as an actress, and doubtless her *Juliet* was competent. Some time after effecting this revival of Shakespeare's tragedy Davenant produced, apparently with the same cast, an adaptation of it made by James Howard, brother-in-law and close friend of the poet Dryden, the peculiarity of which was "a happy ending," the lovers being preserved alive. Howard's play was not printed, and presumably it is lost. Davenant alternated that adaptation with the unchanged original of Shakespeare, so that the performance was that of tragedy on one day and that of tragi-comedy on another.

ROMEO AND JULIET

Eighty-two years passed before the next revival of Shakespeare's "Romeo and Juliet" was accomplished. The fine dramatic genius Thomas Otway (1651-1685) had, meanwhile, incorporated much of the language of Shakespeare's tragedy into a play, comprehensive of political incidents in the life of the Roman consul Caius Marius, as related by Plutarch, which was acted at Dorset Garden in 1680, Betterton appearing as *Caius Marius* and Elizabeth Barry as *Lavinia*. The juvenile hero of that play, *Marius the Younger,* is virtually *Romeo,* while the juvenile heroine, *Lavinia,* is *Juliet*. Otway's tragedy, entitled "Caius Marius," held the stage intermittently for more than sixty years, Shakespeare's "Romeo and Juliet" remaining abeyant. It reappeared, however, September 11, 1744, at the Haymarket Theatre, "revived and altered" by Theophilus Cibber, the son of old Colley. The adapter played *Romeo,* and his daughter, Jane Cibber, played *Juliet*. The character of their performances is unknown. One of the memoirs of T. Cibber states that his person was "far from pleasing," his voice a "shrill treble," and his features "rather disgusting," in which case he could not have looked like *Romeo*. His adaptation excluded all that part of the original which relates to *Romeo's* passion for his first charmer, *Rosaline,* and all that relates to old *Capulet's* Feast, and it used the expedient, taken from Bandello's novel about those lovers, of causing *Juliet* to awaken in the tomb before the death of *Romeo*,—who, meanwhile, had swallowed poison,—so that the wretched husband and wife were permitted to have a brief farewell, this being terminated by *Romeo's* decease and *Juliet's* suicide. That expedient was afterward adopted by David Garrick, to whom the invention of it has been incorrectly attributed. Garrick wrote and inserted a prosy, spasmodic colloquy of sixty-one lines, long and short, to close the tragedy. It is to him we owe the familiar couplet:

> "Fathers have flinty hearts, no tears can melt 'em,—
> Nature pleads in vain; children must be wretched."

DAVID GARRICK AND SPRANGER BARRY.—THE RIVAL ROMEOS.

Garrick's first presentment of "Romeo and Juliet,"—not the original, which he never produced, but his alteration of it,—was made on November 29, 1748, at Drury Lane. The cast included Spranger Barry as *Romeo,* Mrs. Cibber (Susanna Maria Arne,—1714-1766,—the most pathetic and tragic actress of her day) as *Juliet,* and Henry Woodward as *Mercutio.* Garrick had attended the rehearsals precedent to that production and, according to Arthur

HENRY WOODWARD AS MERCUTIO

"Sometimes she gallops o'er a courtier's nose,
And then dreams he of smelling out a suit."

ACT I., Sc. 4

CHARLES KEMBLE

"O, then, I see Queen Mab hath been with you."

ACT I., Sc. 4

Murphy's "Life" of him (1801), "solicitous for the success of his alterations, had communicated all his ideas to the performers." Abundant success attended the revival, but dissension ensued, and Barry and Mrs. Cibber left Drury Lane and went to Covent Garden, where James Quin and Peg Woffington joined them, making John Rich's company very strong. Then arose between Garrick and Barry a determined competition for the supreme popularity. On September 28, 1750, "Romeo and Juliet" was presented by both factions. At Covent Garden the *Romeo* was Barry, the *Juliet* Mrs. Cibber, the *Mercutio* Charles Macklin: Rich introduced into his production "a grand funeral procession" (a form of embellishment to which he was specially partial), on which "he laid out almost as much as the play brought him." At Drury Lane Garrick (who labored under the serious disadvantage of having previously given Barry the benefit of his thought) acted *Romeo,* Henry Woodward *Mercutio,* and George Anne Bellamy *Juliet.* The softer, more sensuous, and more convincing *Romeo* was that of Barry; the more intense, passionate, tragical *Juliet* that of Mrs. Cibber. The better *Mercutio* was Woodward, an exceptionally brilliant player. According to contemporary records, all the performances were good, and the chief of them, excepting that of *Mer-*

cutio, by Macklin, whose forbidding aspect and manner marred the effect of his intelligent acting, were excellent. Barry surpassed in the expression of amorous rapture; Garrick and Mrs. Cibber in that of tragic passion. A contemporary female observer of the rival performances said that Garrick's animation in the Garden Scene was so eager that, had she been *Juliet,* she should have thought he was going to jump up to her, while Barry was so tender and magnetically attractive that, in the same position, she should have felt inclined to jump down to him. The anecdote has become trite in repetition, but it is too instructively significant to be omitted. Garrick's characteristic powers were exhibited in the scene in which *Romeo* is told of the sentence of "banishment," in the scene with the *Apothecary,* and in the Tomb Scene. Mrs. Bellamy, a handsome, blue-eyed young woman of the languishing, seductive, fascinating order, captivated the populace. She was not deficient of dramatic talent, but in feeling and the tragic expression of it she could not bear comparison with Mrs. Cibber. Her *Juliet* possessed the advantage of being younger and prettier than that of the better actress. Mrs. Bellamy (whose "Apology" mentions her rival as "the incomparable Cibber") declares that "the contest was long, and it was universally allowed that, except in the scenes with the

ROMEO AND JULIET

Friar, Mr. Barry excelled in *Romeo.*" Mrs. Cibber, according to Thomas Davies, who often saw her, was not symmetrical in form; but her features were regular, her eyes dark and brilliant, her manner was elegant, her voice magical, and of the tender emotions her command was supreme: "In love, grief, and tenderness she greatly excelled all competitors." Tate Wilkinson says:

"Mr. Barry was at that time in the prime of life, as to health and vigor, and Mrs. Cibber also at her best. No wonder such a pair of lovers obtained the triumph they were entitled to: indeed it was a pity they were ever separated, for no two persons were so calculated to assist each other, by voice, manner, and real feeling, as Mr. Barry and Mrs. Cibber."

One of the recorders of theatrical gossip tells a somewhat amusing story of a conversation between Macklin and Garrick, relative to this rivalry of Garrick and Barry as *Romeo.* Macklin, having declared that the town had not correctly decided which of the two actors was the better, told Garrick that he intended to settle the question in the course of a lecture which he purposed to deliver at a literary coffee-house he had opened. "Ah, my dear Mac," said Garrick, "how will you bring this about?" "I'll tell you, sir," answered Macklin; "I mean to show your different methods in the Garden Scene.

Barry comes into it, sir, as great as a lord, swaggering about his love, and talking so loud that, if we don't suppose the servants of the *Capulet* family almost dead with sleep, they must have come out and tossed the fellow in a blanket. Well, sir, after having fixed my auditors' attention to this part, then I shall ask, 'But how does Garrick act this?' Why, sir, sensible that the family are at enmity with him and his house, he comes creeping in upon his toes, whispering his love, and looking about him, *just like a thief in the night.*" The narrator adds that Garrick thanked the veteran for his good-will, but suggested that the point might better be left to the public judgment. On one night, after the defection of Barry and Mrs. Cibber from Garrick, while these competitive performances of "Romeo and Juliet" were going on, at Drury Lane and Covent Garden, when Mrs. Bellamy as Garrick's *Juliet,* in the Garden Scene, uttered the mournful interrogatory, "O Romeo, Romeo, wherefore art *thou* Romeo?" a voice of some one in the audience instructively replied, "Because *Barry* has gone to *the other house!*"

SETTING AND COSTUME.

The scenic investiture anciently provided for this tragedy was barren, and the dressing, while opulent

ROMEO AND JULIET

in some particulars, was never even approximately correct. In Shakespeare's time it was customary to dress his characters in raiment of his period, and although for more than a century afterward some of those characters were invariably dressed as they had been when first shown on the stage, the practice of arraying them in accordance with contemporary English fashions was adopted in the time of King Charles the Second,—when the theatres, which had long been closed, were again opened,—and it prevailed in the time of Queen Anne and in the later times of King George the Second and King George the Third. Burbage, as *Romeo,* looked like Queen Elizabeth's Essex or Leicester. Harris, as *Romeo,* and Betterton, as *Mercutio,* looked like the ruffled, bewigged courtiers of the Merry Monarch. Barry's costume, as *Romeo,* consisted of a square-cut coat, a figured waistcoat, knee-breeches, silk stockings, buckled shoes, a small sword, and a heavy periwig. Mrs. Cibber's *Juliet* costume was "a full white satin dress, with the then indispensable hoop." Garrick, who arrayed *Hamlet* in a court-dress of the time of King George the Second, and *Macbeth* in the scarlet, white, and gold garb of an English military officer, adhered, as *Romeo,* to his invariable custom of clothing Shakespeare's characters in English habiliments of his own time: his *Romeo* was described as presenting the appearance of "a beau in a new birthday embroidery." Woodward's costume for *Mercutio* comprised a periwig, a square-cut coat, an ample waistcoat, which depended over his thighs,—the material being velvet,—knee-breeches, silk stockings, high-heeled shoes garnished with gold buckles, a muslin scarf trimmed with lace, a sword, and a three-cornered black hat, edged with gold lace.

The players of *Juliet* in Shakespeare's time were males, but they wore such garments as were worn by the ladies of the courts of Queen Elizabeth and King James the First. The *Juliets* of the later time of Betterton and of the still later time of Garrick dressed themselves in accordance with the female fashions of their respective periods. The old actor and manager Tate Wilkinson, writing, 1790, about the dressing of stage characters forty years earlier (1750), declares that the performers, particularly at Covent Garden, "wore the old laced clothes which had done many years' service at Lincoln's Inn Fields, besides having graced the original owners" (meaning the fashionable persons who had bestowed their discarded fine apparel on the playhouse), and that "the ladies were in large hoops and the velvet petticoats, heavily embossed, [which] proved extremely inconvenient and troublesome." There was, he adds, "always a page behind, to hear the lovers' secrets and keep the train in graceful decorum": and he appends, in a facetious spirit, the remark that "if two princesses met on the stage, with the frequent stage-crossing then practised," the spectators would "behold a page dangling at the tail of each heroine." The same writer records that a large hoop was a requisite and indispensable mode of dress; that Mrs. Woffington's wardrobe had only the increase of one tragedy suit in the course of the season, in addition to the clothes allotted to her, unless she indulged herself; and that he had "seen Mrs. Woffington dressed in high taste for *Mrs. Phillis,* for then all ladies' companions or gentle-women's gentle-women actually appeared in that style of dress: even the comical Clive dressed her chambermaids, *Lappet, Lettice,* etc., in the same manner, authorized from what custom had warranted in their younger days."

Reform, whether in stage setting or in costume, proceeded slowly: gold-laced hats and brilliant scarlet waist-coats decorated with broad bands of gold lace, hoops, powdered wigs, feathers, and gaudy finery in general, whether appropriate or not, lingered till the early years of the nineteenth century. Some of the dresses of even the scholar-like Kemble were garish and incongruous. Mary Robinson, "Perdita," the lovely, hapless victim of the licentious Prince Regent, arrayed her *Juliet* in a pale pink satin frock, trimmed with white crape and spangled with silver, and a head-dress of white feathers, changing, for the last scene, to a garb which included a robe of plain white muslin, a long veil of white, transparent gauze, and a girdle of beads sustaining a gold cross. Fanny Kemble's first *Juliet* costume, 1829, was a plain white satin gown, having a low bodice, short sleeves, and a long train, and being ornamented with a belt of fine paste brilliants. Later she devised and wore what she deemed a more appropriate one.

According to Corte's "History of Verona," in which the story of "Romeo and Juliet" is related as true, the time of the catastrophe of their loves was 1303, and it is accordingly maintained by some authorities that the costumes used in presenting the play should accord with the fashions of dress prevalent in Italy about six hundred years ago; but as Italian dresses of that period present in general a somewhat cumbersome appearance, inhibitory of graceful demeanor and detrimental to romantic seeming, the use of them is destructive of pleasing effect. Historical accuracy of costume is instructive and, within reason, desirable, but the paramount object in dressing "Romeo and Juliet" should be the creation of poetic atmosphere. A young man swathed in tunics, super-tunics, and cloaks, with rows of buttons sewn up and down the front and arms of his garments, with a capuchin shaped like a pedler's bag hanging down his back, and with his head incased in fantastic gear, might, indeed, feel, and a good actor thus attired could still simulate, the passion and agony of *Romeo;* but in theatrical representation such a costume would seem grotesquely absurd, and it would distract attention from both play and acting. The right way, manifestly, is to take as a basis the ascertained fashion of the known or accepted period of any specific old play, and then, wherever essential for effect, vary the costume and accoutrement sufficiently to insure picturesque, romantic, pleasing semblance for all the characters. That is, substantially, the method which has been employed in the best modern productions of Shakespeare's plays, notably, in the case of the tragedy of "Romeo and Juliet," in the presentments made by Edwin Booth (1869), Henry Irving (1882), Mary Anderson, after she had become established (first in London, 1884, then in New York, 1885), and E. H. Sothern and Julia Marlowe (1904).

LATER REVIVALS—BRITISH STAGE: THE KEMBLES AND EDMUND KEAN.

In the long interval between the Garrick period and that of Henry Irving and Johnston Forbes-Robertson many presentations of "Romeo and Juliet" have been made on the British Stage, and in the list of distinguished performers who have assumed *Romeo,* and who, in theatrical chronicles, have been variously commended or condemned, conspicuous names are those of David Ross, 1760; William Powell, 1767; Charles Holland, 1760; John Jackson, 1762; Richard Wroughton, 1771; Henry Ward, 1776; William Brereton, 1776; John Philip Kemble, 1783; Joseph George Holman, 1784; William Barrymore (whose family name was Blewitt), 1796; Robert William Elliston, 1796; Henry Johnston, 1797; Charles Kemble, 1805; John Howard Payne, 1813; William Augustus Conway, 1813; Edmund Kean, 1815; Charles Mayne Young, 1815; William Charles Macready, 1815; Thomas Abthorpe Cooper, 1828; Charles John Kean, 1829; William Abbott, 1830; William Creswick, 1839; James Robert Anderson, 1840, Leigh Murray, 1840; William Rowles Belford, 1855; J. F. Warden, 1858; Frank Clements, 1861; Charles Warner (Lickfold), 1864; John Henry Barnes, 1871; William Terriss (Lewin), 1871; George Rignold, 1872; C. W. Gathorne, 1873; Frederick Henry Macklin, 1874; Henry B. Conway (Coulson), 1876; Johnston Forbes-Robertson, 1880, and Henry Irving, 1882.

Wroughton, who played many parts, ranging from *Jaques* to *Young Mirabel,* was "a sterling, sound,

ROMEO AND JULIET

sensible performer," and his *Romeo* was respectable. John Philip Kemble, one of the most intellectual of actors, a man of philosophic, meditative habit of mind, proved too massive for *Romeo*. "Youthful love," says his reverent, faithful biographer, James Boaden, "was never well expressed by Kemble: the thoughtful strength of his features was at variance with juvenile passion." His brother Charles, on the contrary, as *Romeo*, filled a perfect ideal of a youthful lover, precisely as, when acting *Mercutio*, he filled a perfect ideal of the gay comrade and galliard gentleman. The critical opinion of his time, indeed, without a dissenting voice, accounted him supreme in both those characters. Dr. Doran wrote, of his performance as *Mercutio*, contrasted with those of some of his predecessors in the part, that "he walked, spoke, looked, fought, and died like a gentleman," and "was as truly Shakespeare's *Mercutio* as ever Macklin was Shakespeare's *Jew*." His daughter, Fanny Kemble, testified that "he was one of the best *Romeos*, and incomparably the best *Mercutio*, that ever trod the English stage."

Edmund Kean did not like the part of *Romeo*, and his appearance in it at Drury Lane, January 2, 1815, made against his inclination, was not successful. He was indifferent and tame until he reached *Romeo's* apprehension of the *Prince's* edict, but in that scene he gave startling effect to the lines:

> "Ha, banishment! be merciful, say 'death';
> For exile hath more terror in her look,
> Much more, than death! . . .
> Hence banished is banish'd from the world,
> And world's exile is death."

In the Tomb Scene, likewise, he put forth his utmost skill in the use of pathos, and deeply moved his audience. Hazlitt, an enthusiast of Kean, greatly admired the performance, and said that the actor's utterance of the word "banished" was, in particular, of transcendent dramatic value; adding, "He treads close indeed upon the genius of the author,"—meaning Shakespeare. Kean, in fact, used Garrick's perversion of the original play. It is probable that, in the course of his performance of *Romeo,* he gave a moving presentment of Edmund Kean in a frenzy, and a signally effective portrayal of the agonies of death by poison. He could be overwhelmingly pathetic, and he could be irresistibly terrific. His aspect of brooding melancholy, when he sat silent, as the *Stranger,* caused spectators to weep, and Byron, who greatly admired him, and who was once so completely overcome that he fainted at a point in his personation of *Sir Giles Overreach,* thought that one just impression of him as an actor was indicated in four lines of "The Corsair":

"There was a laughing devil in his sneer
That raised emotions both of rage and fear;
And where his frown of hatred darkly fell
Hope, withering, fled, and Mercy sighed farewell."

VARIOUS NOTABLE *ROMEOS*—FROM ELLISTON TO ROBINSON.

Elliston, a dashing comedian, a paragon of effrontery, and, as a stage lover, coarsely animal, could not have been a good *Romeo*. Conway was an actual *Romeo:* he loved Eliza O'Neill, famous as *Juliet,* with whom he acted, and loved her in vain. His performance was much admired. Disappointment in love and the malignantly hostile criticisms of Theodore Hook drove him from the English Stage and from his native land. He came to America, and, in 1828, a confirmed victim of melancholia, he committed suicide by leaping overboard from a steamship, at the mouth of Charleston Harbor. As to Charles Kean as *Romeo,* critical praise is languid. My vivid remembrance of his personality and his acting persuades me that he was constitutionally unfit for that character. Abbott was the *Romeo* on the memorable occasion when Fanny Kemble, as *Juliet,* made her first appearance on the stage, October 10, 1829, at Covent Garden, London, saving the fortunes of that theatre, then imperilled, by 120 consecutive performances, which elicited general admiration and earned much money. Abbott's *Romeo* was a failure. Long afterward, Fanny Kemble wrote of him:

"Mr. Abbott was not a bad actor, though a perfectly uninteresting one in tragedy. His performances were always respectable, though seldom anything else. He was an old, established favorite with the public, a very amiable and worthy man, old enough to have been my father, whose performance [of *Romeo*], not certainly of the highest order, was nevertheless not below inoffensive mediocrity."

It was as *Romeo* that Macready made his first appearance on the stage, June 7, 1810, at Birmingham, and he long retained the part in his repertory. His performance was comparatively little admired except by himself. It must have been a fine study of the operation of love upon a romantic temperament in youth, because from the first and always there was discriminative mind in Macready's acting; and also it must have been powerful in the tragic portions and artistically formed and rounded. In the early part of his career that great actor had not adopted the peculiar method of elocution, marred by gasps, grunts, and long pauses, which he used in later years, but spoke naturally and freely. It is, however, difficult to believe that a man of Macready's austere visage, stalwart figure, dominant mentality, and sternly authoritative manner ever really caused the effect of being identified with *Romeo* or with any other juvenile lover. He was the original impersonator of *Alfred Evelyn,* in "Money," and in embodying the rather grim kind of lover indicated by that character he was facile and entirely successful.

Macready's *Romeo* did not entirely lack commendation. Almost all acting is praised by somebody. He played the part, December 15, 1817, at Covent Garden, with Eliza O'Neill as *Juliet,* and "The Theatrical Inquisitor" stated that the performance exhibited his superiority, in tenderness and energy, "in a gorgeous and conclusive manner": he has himself recorded that the applause was enthusiastic. When manager of Covent Garden he produced the tragedy, April 30, 1837, playing *Friar Lawrence,* and giving *Romeo* to Anderson, a handsome actor, whose performance was correct, ardent, and pleasing. Helena Faucit was the *Juliet.* In 1841 Macready made an elaborate stage version of "Romeo and Juliet," but did not produce it. The first recorded restoration, according to the text of Shakespeare, was that made by Charlotte Cushman, in 1845.

Samuel Phelps, Macready's compeer and rival, always scrupulously careful to use as much as possible of the original text of Shakespeare, rejected altogether the Cibber-Garrick hash and effected a scholar-like revival of the tragedy at Sadler's Wells

Theatre, on September 16, 1846. *Romeo* was assumed by William Creswick,—afterward well known on the New York Stage as *Wolsey, Brutus,* and *Macbeth,*—and *Juliet* by Laura Addison; while Phelps acted *Mercutio,* a part in which he exulted and excelled. On a later occasion, September 10, 1859, the play was again presented by Phelps, *Romeo* being performed by Frederick C. P. Robinson (in 1865-'66 a member of Lester Wallack's company, in New York; he died in 1912) and *Juliet* by Caroline Heath, afterward Mrs. Wilson Barrett. On November 30 Phelps's production of "Romeo and Juliet" was acted before Queen Victoria, at Windsor Castle.

HENRY IRVING'S PRESENTATION.

The most carefully made, the longest, and, I believe, the best version of "Romeo and Juliet" presented on the stage in our time is the one that was made by Henry Irving, and first produced by him at the London Lyceum Theatre (where I saw and studied the performance), on March 8, 1882. It contained twenty-two scenes, and adhered to the text of Shakespeare. Irving's most effective restoration was that of the scene in which the supposed death of *Juliet* is discovered (Act IV., sc. 5), on the morning of the day appointed for her marriage to

Paris. The stage picture was exceedingly beautiful. The gradual increase of light, the songs of newly awakened birds, the music made by serenaders, and the entrance and distraction of the *Nurse* combined to cause a thrilling effect. The part of the play which relates to *Romeo's* first love, *Rosaline,* of whom *Mercutio,* humorously commiserating his comrade's distressful condition, declares she "torments him so that he will sure run mad," has generally been excised on the stage; but it is of value as a study of the operation of love in youth and because of the light which it casts on *Romeo's* temperament and the morbid nature of his first amatory passion. By Irving that portion of the play was in part retained. The setting for the Tomb Scene surpassed in detail and in weird, sepulchral, melancholy beauty any other stage picture of the subject that ever has been devised. The Tomb was a huge, gloomy crypt occupying the whole stage, accessible from the top by an irregular flight of stone steps. The body of *Tybalt,* covered with an ample purple pall, was conspicuous, and near it, "uncover'd, on the bier," was the lovely *Juliet,* in snow-white robes of death. There *Romeo* entered, high up at the back, dragging with him the body of dead *Paris:* "I'll bury thee in a triumphant grave," etc. Irving acted *Romeo,* Ellen Terry *Juliet,* William Terriss *Mercutio,* Mrs. Stirling the *Nurse.*

Other specially notable features of the production were the scene of the *Capulets'* "solemnity" and that of the street in Mantua where the *Apothecary* dwells. "Romeo and Juliet" was one of the most profitable of all Irving's productions. It received 161 performances and during the first five mouths the gross receipts were about $170,000 and the profits, notwithstanding extraordinary expenses, $50,000. Irving, distinctively and superlatively intellectual, overweighted the part of *Romeo,* seeming, while he conveyed all its meaning, to *expound* rather than to *impersonate* it. The actor who is distinctively and superlatively intellectual must naturally find it difficult to identify himself with *Romeo,* for the reason that intellect inclines to look with either amused tolerance or scornful contempt on amatory passion; but Irving's performance was thoroughly illuminative and exceedingly interesting, and a more romantic figure than he presented could not easily be imagined. He was at his best in the killing of *Tybalt* and in the scene with the *Apothecary* Ellen Terry, though somewhat mature for *Juliet,* was incarnate beauty and feeling, one of the loveliest and most sympathetic beings ever beheld. Terriss was agreeably buoyant and merry as *Mercutio.* The *Nurse,* in the person of Mrs. Stirling, was perfection: kindly, garrulous, pettish, coarse, salacious, sordid—the veritable old, familiar servitor so deftly drawn in Shakespeare's text.

THE CHARACTER OF *ROMEO*.

Romeo is a well-born, well-bred young man, ardent in temperament, chivalrous, romantic, brave, impulsive, governed by feeling, seldom amenable to reason, and absorbed by love and the longing for love. His sensibility is excessive. He has been first attracted and then repulsed by one girl, an object of his juvenile idolatry, and in the dejection consequent on that bitter experience he has become morosely melancholy, and is oppressed by a presentiment of impending evil, "some consequence yet hanging in the stars." Shakespeare, in transfiguring the hero of Brooke's poem, made *Romeo* a tragic character, a man predestined to calamity; and in the long annals of the Stage the most affecting embodiments of the part have been presented by actors who could grasp and make actual that ideal, comprehending *Romeo* as the hapless victim of a malign, inevitable fate.

Hazlitt designated *Romeo* as "*Hamlet* in love," and that phrase has, with the "damnable iteration" peculiar to the parrot cry, often been cited as felicitously illuminative of the character. It seems true, however, only until it is examined. *Hamlet* suffers under the burden of mere living: *Romeo,* notwithstanding his sentimental indulgence in "the luxury of woe" relative to *Rosaline's* rejection of his suit, is ardently conscious of the potential happiness in life. *Hamlet* reasons, darkly, indeed, at times, but logically; *Romeo,* comparatively speaking, reasons not at all. *Hamlet's* melancholy proceeds from a profound, fixed, corrosive consciousness of the immitigable misery inherent in the mortal state of man. *Romeo's* melancholy is sentimental, and proceeds, in the first instance, from unrequited, boyish love, if that much-abused word can rightly be used to designate his regard for *Rosaline;* later it proceeds from a vague apprehension of disaster, such as is common to excessive sensibility. *Hamlet* broods on the terrible and eternal mystery of life, death, and "after death," and contemplates suicide,—thinks, but cannot act. *Romeo* is not in the least concerned about the state of Man, nor does he ever *meditate* on suicide and "the ills that flesh is heir to"; but immediately, when apprised that *Juliet* is dead, he obtains a poison, goes to the Tomb of the *Capulets,* and kills himself beside her. *Hamlet,* after seeing the corpse of his once loved *Ophelia* laid in the grave, to which she has been brought by his slaughter of her father, can moralize on life, augury, providence, and death, and within a short time engage in a fencing-bout with her brother:

Hamlet, be it remembered, is always an eminently and entirely sane person! *Romeo* is a lover, and nothing else; a young man besotted by love and the love of being in love; one to whom love is everything, and all else nothing; and his passion is of a kind usual at the period of adolescence,—romantic, ardent, and sensuous. He has no thought of denying himself, of sacrificing himself for the sake of a woman, or a parent, or anything else, and he would never inquire of his *Juliet,* as *Hamlet* does of *Ophelia,* "why wouldst thou be a breeder of sinners?" or counsel her to "get you to a nunnery." And *Romeo's* despair and hysterical behavior,—which are mindless of the assured advantages of his position,—are exactly typical of a common experience of youthful passion, and utterly at variance with an intellectual, introspective nature. Indeed, at the vital crisis of his affairs, when reason and self-possession are most required, *Romeo's* behavior, so far from being that of a thinking, reasoning person, is such as causes his friend and counsellor, *Friar Lawrence,* to exclaim:

> "Art thou a man? thy form cries out thou art:
> Thy tears are womanish; thy wild acts denote
> The unreasonable fury of a beast."

No two men could be more radically unlike in nature than are *Romeo* and *Hamlet:* the one all emotion, the other a profound, saddened intellect, trembling on the verge of madness.

JOHNSTON FORBES-ROBERTSON.

The view of *Romeo* thus indicated is the one that was taken by Johnston Forbes-Robertson, whose portrayal of that character was the most sympathetic, impressive, and winning that has been given in recent years. It was intense, fervidly emotional, profoundly sincere, subtly suffused with an elusive spiritual quality ominous of predestinate ruin, artistically finished in every detail of action, and conveyed through the medium of a clear, refined, exquisite elocution, delicious to hear. Forbes-Robertson's first presentment of *Romeo* was made in association with Helena Modjeska as *Juliet,* when that great actress began her second engagement in London, March 26, 1881, at the Court Theatre. In 1885-'86 he acted *Romeo* to the *Juliet* of Mary Anderson, in England and also in America. On September 21, 1895, making his first venture in theatrical management, he produced "Romeo and Juliet" at the Lyceum Theatre, London, acting *Romeo* to the *Juliet* of Mrs. Patrick Campbell. The impersonation of that representative lover had become to him "a property of easiness," and, as

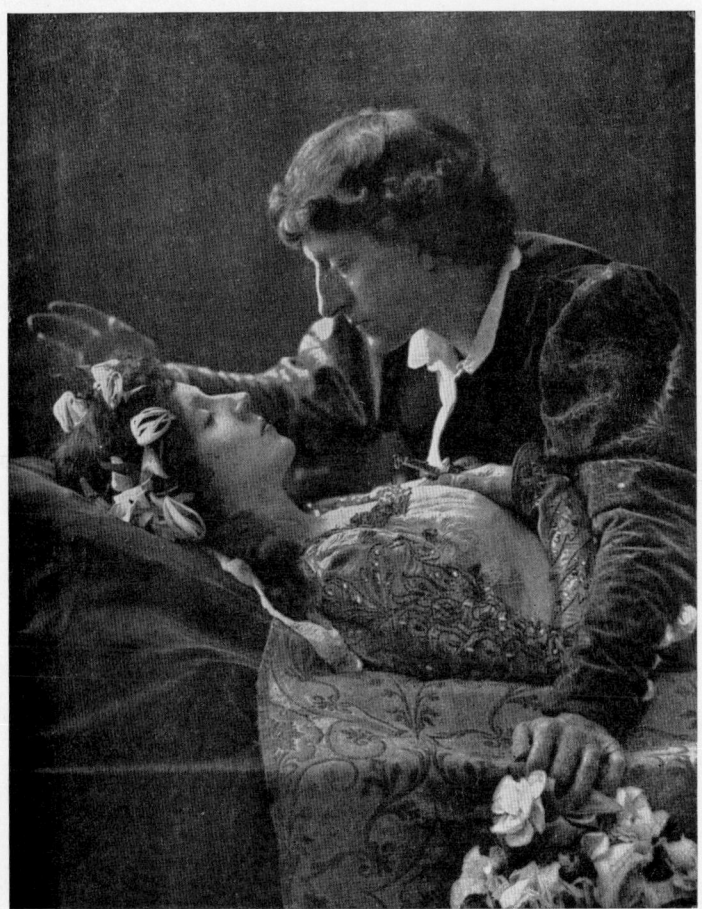

From a Photograph by W. & D. Downey, London   *Author's Collection*

JOHNSTON FORBES-ROBERTSON AS *ROMEO*
MRS. PATRICK CAMPBELL AS *JULIET*

"O my love, my wife!
Death, that hath suck'd the honey of thy breath,
Hath had no power yet upon thy beauty:
Thou art not conquer'd!"

ACT V., Sc. 3

shown in that revival, it admirably exemplified clarity of correct ideal and sustained fluency and power of artistic expression. His acting, in the frenzied killing of *Tybalt,* lacked a little of the "torrent, tempest, and whirlwind of passion"—the distinctively tragical impetuosity and fury which, at that climax, are indispensable—yet it was brilliantly effective. In the manifestation of *Romeo's* anguish and delirium when told of the edict of banishment he evinced a complete capability of portraying alternate despair and frenzy in a natural manner, and therefore without extravagance. His demeanor when *Romeo* is told of *Juliet's* death was superb in its stony calm, and pathetically expressive alike of his knowledge of affliction and his skill to reveal it. Mrs. Patrick Campbell, while her *Juliet* was obviously a sophisticated woman, was interesting and effective during the first half of her performance, evincing the appearance of sensibility, and the reality of physical charm. There was a show of something like girlish artlessness and grace in her acting throughout the Balcony Scene, and, while she could not entirely divest herself of an artificial manner, she aided in conveying the meaning of that exquisite scene and enforcing its dramatic value. In the subsequent tragic passages her acting was flaccid and ineffective. There was neither imagination, passion, nor pathos in her conduct of the Potion Scene, and her manner of effecting *Juliet's* suicide was ludicrous: she placed the handle of a dagger against the wall of the Tomb and pressed her person upon the point. That proceeding might, no doubt, effect a lethal purpose, but on the stage it seemed more singular than appropriate, and such as never could have occurred to a desperate mind. Charles F. Coghlan (1842-1899) acted *Mercutio,* in Robertson's revival, and it was a great pleasure to see that fine comedian in a character so well suited to him, and of which he was an admirable representative. His acting showed the effect of illness and physical pain, but it was suffused with *Mercutio's* buoyant, brilliant, gayly reckless spirit, and the actor indicated perfectly the maturity of *Mercutio's* experience, the inherent virtue and force of his character, and the golden glow and limpid fluency of his humor.

THE CHARACTER OF *JULIET.*

In drawing *Juliet* the dramatist placed emphasis more on feeling than on character, but the attributes of her character are discernible, and they are seen to comprise nobility, which includes chastity, integrity, and fidelity; decision, courage, fortitude, inflexibility of purpose, and the capability of passionate devotion. She is a beautiful girl, of a pure spirit, an ardent temperament, and an imaginative mind. She loves,—once and forever. Thenceforward she lives for love and only for love. She is romantic, but also she is discreet, resolute, and expeditious; she possesses the courage of her love, and, however fettered by circumstance and thrilled by fear and dread, she can bravely confront all perils and persist in her devotion, even unto death. It is true of *Juliet,* as it is of *Romeo,* that she is an idolater: one who loves madly, blindly, excessively, and therefore disastrously,—for the reason that amorous idolatry generally, if not invariably, impels its victims, even those naturally the most prudent, to utter recklessness of conduct and thus, almost necessarily, precipitates ruin.

Shakespeare has placed the age of *Juliet* at fourteen years, which is an absurdity, and one that has made much trouble for actors of the part and for commentators on the play. When the tribute of veneration has been paid to transcendent genius there is no reason why common-sense should forbear to specify and condemn obvious defects and errors. In adapting "Romeo and Juliet" to the stage I should not hesitate to change "fourteen" to "eighteen," in the passages relative to *Juliet's* age, and I should cut and change the context to harmonize with that alteration. It is a fact of wide general knowledge that, physically, the inhabitants of low latitudes mature earlier than those of colder countries do, and, doubtless, in Italy girls of fourteen, perhaps of fewer, years of age "are made already mothers." It is also true that, in exceptional cases, in our own time and country, children of tender years do suffer from an adolescent infatuation for members of the opposite sex, and to such an extent that sometimes they are driven to the desperate extremity of suicide; but such cases are, in the first class, merely physical incidents,—while, in the second, they are calamitous consequences of diseased, hysterical mental condition, and there is nothing more in the experience of either class of those victims than a superficial resemblance to the genuine tragedy of *Juliet*. No child of fourteen, whether of Italian, or English, or any other nationality, ever did, or ever could, possess the mental maturity, the independence, the strength of mind, and the profound capability alike of passionate love and fatal suffering revealed by Shakespeare's *Juliet*. She is, when first seen, a seeming girl: her womanhood is dormant; but she is not a child, and there is nothing in the least impossible or improbable, however unusual, in her sudden, complete, absolute love for *Romeo*. Marlowe's line, "Who ever loved that loved not at first sight," whether viewed as an inquiry or as a declaratory exclamation, has a feverish and extravagant sound, but love at first sight does, nevertheless, occur,—in England, as well as in the sun-kissed lands of the South. It is, I believe, an erroneous assumption which declares that the denizens of a tropical clime are, intrinsically, more passionate than natives of the temperate zone. That faith owes much to the melodious numbers of Byron and Moore. As often as I read the Balcony Scene of "Romeo and Juliet" I am more and more aware of its English atmosphere, and that those lovers are essentially English,—fine types of a steadfast yet intensely passionate and interesting race.

PLAYERS OF *JULIET*.—BRITISH STAGE.

On the British Stage more or less distinguished successors of Mrs. Cibber and Mrs. Bellamy, as *Juliet,* in the period from 1750 to 1800, were Miss Nossiter, Miss Pritchard, Mrs. Dancer, Maria Macklin, Isabella Hallam, Mrs. Robinson, Mrs. Atchmet, Mrs. Esten, Mrs. Jackson, Mrs. Siddons, Mrs. Jordan, and Mrs. Stephen Kemble. Miss Nossiter's first appearance as *Juliet* was made on October 10, 1753, at Covent Garden. The *Romeo* was Barry. The young actress (she was "in her teens") evinced uncommon sensibility. She was desperately enamoured of Barry, and as she was handsome, well educated, and attractive, Barry permitted himself to be, for a time, enamoured of her. The fact of their amatory intimacy was socially known, and the knowledge of it appears to have invigorated public interest in their performances. Tate Wilkinson, who saw them as *Romeo* and *Juliet,* wrote that Miss Nossiter "threw strokes in many passages that were not only genuine but forcible"; he neglects to describe them. This actress remained on the stage for a few seasons after her advent as *Juliet,* acted a few parts, the most conspicuous of them being Shakespeare's *Perdita* and Otway's *Belvidera* ("Venice Preserved"), and gained some popularity; but her dramatic powers were inconsiderable, and she soon languished into obscurity and died,—probably of a broken heart. It is mentioned of her that she had a wide mouth,—which, of course, is advantageous to a speaker, but that her voice was not melodious. It is also mentioned that she bequeathed to the all-fascinating Barry her property, amounting to £3,000,—which, presumably, was a comfort to him. He was, at the time of the death of Miss Nossiter, enamoured of Mrs. Dancer, who, widowed in 1759, became his wife. In acting he could "drown the stage with tears." It is quite possible for a human being, male or female, to possess a temperament of great sensibility, yet at the same time to be vain, sensual, selfish, and fickle.

Miss Pritchard, daughter of the renowned tragic actress Hannah Pritchard, acted *Juliet,* October 9, 1756, at Drury Lane, with Garrick as *Romeo,* her mother coöperating as *Lady Capulet.* The girl was a beauty, and as such, and also because of her exceptional dramatic talent, she was much admired. Her *Juliet* is nowhere particularly described. She remained only a few years on the stage, and she made no lasting impression. Mrs. Dancer (Ann Street), when associated with the Crow Street Theatre, Dublin, where her brilliant career began, acted *Juliet* (1759-'60), and in view of the ample contemporary testimony to her singular beauty and to her great ability, as shown in subsequent artistic achievements of the first order, it cannot be doubted that her personation was excellent. Barry, whose wife she eventually became, was the *Romeo.* Maria Macklin, daughter of stalwart old Charles, the famous restorer of Shakespeare's *Shylock,* acted *Juliet,* September 27, 1760, at Drury Lane, with David Ross as *Romeo.* Of this actress the inquirer learns that, while not handsome, she was "genteel in her figure and fashionable in her manners," of a good presence, and possessed of fine, piercing eyes and a melodious voice. She had been well educated, was a good singer, was expert in dancing, and evinced enough of dramatic talent to enable her to win considerable public favor. Miss Macklin had been for several years an actress before she essayed to act *Juliet,* and she was skilled in several lines of theatrical business, though not in gay characters; yet she attempted *Rosalind.* Her *Juliet* was praised. Isabella Hallam, afterward Mrs. Mattocks (wife of William Mattocks, an actor and manager at Liverpool), appeared as *Juliet,* April 10, 1760, at Covent Garden, for the benefit of a relative. She was then young,—according to one account only fifteen,—handsome, and talented. Her aptitude was for comedy, in which she became highly distinguished. Her tragic efforts were respectable. Mrs. Robinson (Mary Darby, 1758-1800) acted *Juliet,* December 10, 1776, at Drury Lane, making her first appearance on the stage, and winning admiration more for her beauty than her dramatic talent,—which, nevertheless, in time, became considerable. The *Romeo* was William Brereton. Mrs. Atchmet (Miss Egan) began her career in 1785, at the Crow Street Theatre, Dublin, acting *Imoinda,* in Arthur Murphy's tragedy of "The Grecian Daughter." John Jackson, the historian of the Scottish Stage, who saw the performance, "found her figure unexceptionable and her abilities promising." She, evidently, made good progress, for on September 14, 1789, she appeared in London, at Covent Garden, as *Juliet*,—Joseph George Holman being the *Romeo*,—and gave an effective performance. Mrs. Esten (Miss Bennett), after a novitiate at Bristol, Bath, and elsewhere in England, appeared at the Canongate Theatre, Edinburgh, January 19, 1790, acting *Juliet* in a manner that won enthusiastic admiration. That performance she supplemented, in the course of the season, with discriminative and able impersonations of more than twenty of the leading parts in standard drama,—ranging from *Desdemona* to *Lady Macbeth*. Her popularity was great. "She was adopted," says Jackson, "by the general voice, as the theatrical child of Scotland." Mrs. Esten, however, seems to have desired conquest of the English capital. She appeared at Covent Garden, September 20, 1790, as *Rosalind*, and with that theatre she remained for some time prominently connected. She acted *Juliet* there on September 26, 1792, and succeeded. Mrs. Siddons was in her thirty-fourth year when she played *Juliet*, and she had become too formidable in person and massive in style for the part of a loving girl. She was praised for her manner of humoring the petulance of the *Nurse*, and her adoring biographer, the poet Campbell, who defined

Juliet as "a shrewd and precociously strong-minded woman," ventures the conjecture that if she had assumed the part fourteen years earlier it then "would have completely suited the youthful loveliness of her intelligent physiognomy." Mrs. Jordan,—wholly unsuited to the part,—gave a few performances of *Juliet,* in the spring of 1795, at Drury Lane, at first (April 25) with William Brereton as *Romeo,* later with Wroughton. This actress, the soul of mirth, aspired to success in tragedy, but did not obtain it. Mrs. Stephen Kemble (Eliza Satchell), a pleasing actress, performed *Juliet,* in association with Elliston as *Romeo,* September 7, 1796, at the London Haymarket, and later at the Canongate Theatre, in Edinburgh, of which her husband became manager.

It would be tedious even to chronicle the numerous players of *Juliet* who graced the British Stage in the nineteenth century. Prominent names are those of Eliza O'Neill, 1814; Mrs. Bartley (Sarah Smith), and Lydia Kelly, 1815; Frances Maria Kelly, who had been taught by Macready, 1822; Miss Jarman, 1827; Miss Phillips, 1828; Fanny Kemble, 1829; Helena Faucit, 1836; Edith Heraud, 1851; Mrs. Arthur Stirling, 1851; Caroline Heath, 1859; Alice Marriott, 1864; Sarah Thorne, 1865; Kate Bateman, who had previously often played the part in America, 1865; Ellen Wallis, 1871; Milly Palmer, 1871; Ada Cavendish, 1873; Louise Hibbert, 1874.

The most popular of the *Juliets* which have been named was that of Eliza O'Neill (1791-1872), an Irish actress, remarkable for personal beauty and inordinate sensibility. Miss O'Neill's professional life lasted only five years (from 1814 to 1819), when she was married and retired. She was a realistic player, not an artist. She said of herself, to Fanny Kemble, that she "could shed tears by the bucketful," and, according to that friend, a close observer, she was neither powerful nor passionate. Her *Juliet,* however, was a perfect image of loveliness in distress, and it evoked prodigious sympathy—as loveliness in distress always will.

Fanny Kemble as *Juliet* was, in her day, thought to have excelled all competitors. Her victory was gained by great beauty and complete abandonment to emotion. "I did not return into myself till all was over," so she wrote, concerning her acting of *Juliet*. My memory of this famous person recalls only her readings, which often were deeply impressive,—one of the most significant of them, as indicative of the power of her imagination and the beauty of her vocalism, being the recital of a passage from Scott's "Marmion." Her great success on the stage must have been exclusively that of *personality,* for she has recorded of herself that she "never liked or honored" the art of acting, and she appears not to have studied it.

HELENA FAUCIT.

Helena Faucit (1819-1898), the latest of the old-time players of *Juliet,* gained and held the palm in England for many years. Miss Faucit was of opinion, which she has recorded in her book about "Some of Shakespeare's Female Characters," that in writing "Romeo and Juliet" the dramatist had "a far wider and deeper purpose than to show true love constant and triumphant throughout persistent evil fortune,"—the purpose, in fact, of inculcating "the lesson of amity and brotherly love" between the antagonistic families of *Capulet* and *Montague,* and, inferentially, all other hostile factions. That is an amiable fancy, but while the play contains much of that involuntary morality which pervades every true work of art there is nothing in it indicative of any sort of didactic design; and even if there were, the knowledge of that design would neither aid in perception of the characters nor guide in the impersonation of them. Shakespeare simply saw and seized the opportunity of making a great tragedy:

> "For never was a story of more woe
> Than this of Juliet and her Romeo."

ROMEO AND JULIET

Miss Faucit's careful analysis of the situations in which the lovers are placed shows her just and complete appreciation of the character of *Juliet,* and contemporary judges of her acting testify to the supreme merit of her performance. She first acted *Juliet* when she was a mere girl, appearing (1833) at the little theatre on Richmond Common,—so sadly associated with the last days of Edmund Kean,—and she made a formal and highly successful appearance in the part, at Covent Garden, January 5, 1836. Her great renown, however, was obtained in other and more important parts, such as *Imogen, Hermione,* and the exceedingly difficult parts of *Rosalind, Lady Macbeth,* and *Antigone.* Her presence was imposing, her voice clear, flexible, and mellow; she aimed at identification with every part that she assumed, but her method, in that respect, sometimes savored too much of the commonplace literality generally miscalled "realism" to allow fulfilment of her purpose. On the occasion of her first performance of *Juliet* she unconsciously crushed, in a convulsive grasp, the glass phial, supposed to contain the potion. "The fragments of glass," she says, mentioning this incident, "were eating their way into the tender palm, and the blood was trickling down in a little stream over my much admired dress,"—the customary white satin. Miss Faucit was then a novice, and such lack of artistic self-control was natural. Some players, however,—and Miss Faucit appears to have been one of them,—are temperamentally unable always to remember that acting is not nature, but the *imitation* of nature. On one occasion (recorded by herself) at Manchester, in 1871, this actress, at the end of the soliloquy which precedes *Juliet's* drinking of the potion, actually fainted from excess of fear and dread. George Vandenhoff, who had acted with Miss Faucit, bore this testimony to the quality of her acting: "Her expression of love is the most beautiful, confiding, truthful, self-abandoning in its tone that I have ever witnessed in any actress; it is intensely fascinating."

There have not been many important revivals of "Romeo and Juliet" on the British Stage since about 1850. The most memorable representatives of *Juliet*, in the period thus indicated, aside from those already described, were Stella Colas, 1863; Adelaide Neilson, 1865; Helena Modjeska, 1880, and Mary Anderson, 1884.

STELLA COLAS.

Stella Colas (Mme. Stella de Corvin) made her first appearance in England, June 24, 1863, at the Princess' Theatre, London, playing *Juliet*. Her performance attracted much attention and with the general public it was successful. Walter Montgomery coöperated with her, as *Romeo,* and George Vining, as *Mercutio.* Expert opinion of her acting was sharply divided. George Henry Lewes declared it to be "mob-acting," vehement, mediocre, conventional, "charming the eye and stunning the ear." Joseph Knight, writing about her in 1875, stated that "Stella Colas has not, in recent years, been surpassed in *Juliet.*" All judges agreed that she was exceptionally handsome. She possessed a strong voice and much force, volitive and physical. She was French, but had learned to speak English: her elocution was defective. It is remembered with pleasure that she participated, as *Juliet,* in the memorable performances that were given, April 23, 1864, at Stratford-upon-Avon, to celebrate the Tercentenary of the birth of Shakespeare,—John Nelson being the *Romeo.*

ADELAIDE NEILSON.

Whether it be true or not that *Juliet,* as drawn by Shakespeare, is an English girl, it was an English girl, Adelaide Neilson, who gave the amplest, the most passionate, enthralling personation of the character that a long remembrance of the Stage can recall. There was in circulation at one time a false story, declaring this actress to have been the daughter of a Spanish father and an English mother. She was, in fact, a native of Yorkshire, and her parents were English. She made her first appearance as *Juliet* in April, 1865, at Mrs. Thorne's theatre, Margate, and in the following July acted the same part at the New Royalty Theatre, London, thus beginning an ambitious, arduous, brilliant career, which was miserably and mournfully terminated by her sudden death, at Paris, in 1880. Her first appearance in America was made, November 18, 1872, at Booth's Theatre, as *Juliet,* in which character she gained immediate favor with the American audience, —a favor which, in several subsequent professional visits to this country, was augmented, and which was never lost. On the occasion of her advent at Booth's Theatre the fine scenery and appropriate dresses were again utilized which had originally been devised for the production of "Romeo and Juliet" effected by Edwin Booth when that house was opened, 1869.

Miss Neilson was, in every respect, exceptionally well suited to *Juliet.* Her person was slender and symmetrical. Her countenance was singularly expressive of commingled joy and latent melancholy. A slight irregularity of features imparted an air of piquancy to the strange beauty of her face. Her eyes were large, dark, lustrous, and radiant with inward light. Her mouth was large and expressive

From a Photograph by Sarony, N. Y.   Author's Collection

ADELAIDE NEILSON AS *JULIET*

"O, be some other name!
What's in a name? that which we call a rose
By any other name would smell as sweet!"

Act II., Sc. 2

of acute sensibility; her hair, originally chestnut brown, had been dyed to a golden tint; her voice was clear, sympathetic, various in tone, and deliciously musical; her every movement was unconsciously graceful; her temperament, though gentle, was intensely emotional, but in her acting the mind, invariably and rightly, controlled the feelings. Miss Neilson's *Juliet* was a being all truth, innocence, ardor, and loveliness, in whose aspect, nevertheless, there was something ominously suggestive of predestination to misery, herself meanwhile being pathetically unconscious of her doom. It was not so much what the actress said and did as what she *was* that permeated her performance of *Juliet* with this strange, touching quality, which saddened even while it enthralled; it was the personality of the woman, not only captivating the senses but powerfully affecting the imagination. All that she said and did, however, had been carefully considered. Nothing had been left to chance. She knew what she intended to do, and she knew how to do it— for which reason the personation was distinct, rounded, cumulative in effect, and free equally from tameness and extravagance. She had, as all actors of genius have, moments of sudden insight and electrical impulse, in which fine things are unpremeditatedly done, but she was, intrinsically, an artist, and over all that she said and did and seemed to be there was a dominance of artistic purpose which, without sacrifice of the glamour of poetry, made the poetic ideal an actual, natural human being.

The keynote of Miss Neilson's *Juliet* was struck in her solemn utterance of the words "Too early seen unknown, and known—*too late!*" and from that moment onward the magic of her passionate sincerity never faltered. Her identification with the character was complete. Her movement, in the minuet, was exquisitely graceful. Her startled, bewildered gaze, at *Romeo,* subtly but completely expressed the effect of first love. In saying "If he be married, my grave is like to be my wedding bed" there was a thrilling tremor of her voice that enhanced the pathos of the words, and as her riveted glance followed the vanishing *Romeo* she suddenly raised her left hand and kissed the spot that he, a moment earlier, had kissed, in parting from her. In the Balcony Scene, —surely the most truthful, delicious, and touching exposition ever made, in drama, of the feelings and conduct of youthful lovers, noble, innocent, and sincere,—her appearance was beautiful, her demeanor sweetly ingenuous, her feeling ardent yet restrained by a fine womanly instinct of reserve, which at the last gave way to the full sweep of irresistible passion. At the close of the scene, as she looked down on

Romeo, she impulsively snatched a handful of flowers from her girdle, pressed them eagerly to her lips, dropped them into the up-stretched hands of her lover, and darted into the chamber. I believe her to have invented this pretty and expressive stage business, which ever since has been customarily copied: I never saw any earlier actress do it, nor do I recall mention of any similar stage business in any of the records. The eagerness and restrained impatience and the alternation of girl-like archness and passionate impulse, in her management of *Juliet's* colloquy with the teasing *Nurse,* made that piquant passage exceedingly effective. It was in the Potion Scene and the Tomb Scene, however, that she exerted all her power, showing an intensity of feeling and an artistic control and employment of it possible only to an exceedingly deep nature and a great actress. I believe that if this richly gifted woman, who died at about the age of thirty-four, had lived ten years longer, she would, in her special field, have attained an eminence and exerted an influence commensurate with those of Mrs. Siddons and Charlotte Cushman.

156 SHAKESPEARE ON THE STAGE

AMERICAN STAGE.—EARLY REPRESENTATIONS.

The first performance of "Romeo and Juliet" that ever occurred in America was given in New York, at the Theatre in Nassau Street, on January 28, 1754, so that the tragedy has been current (1914) for one hundred and sixty years. *Romeo* was performed by ——— Rigby, an uncommonly able and versatile actor. Mrs. Lewis Hallam was the *Juliet,* and John Singleton, author as well as actor (there is extant a volume of poems by him), was the *Mercutio.* On January 11, 1762, at the theatre in Chapel, now Beekman, Street, the play was acted, with Lewis Hallam as *Romeo,* and his mother as *Juliet.* Mrs. Hallam had wedded a second husband, and was then Mrs. David Douglass. The mother and son had previously (1759) acted together, in Philadelphia, as *Romeo* and *Juliet.* At the John Street Theatre, on January 4, 1768, Lewis Hallam was the *Romeo,* while the *Juliet* was Margaret Cheer. At the same theatre, on October 31, 1791, Mrs. Henry, wife of the respected actor and manager John Henry, acted *Juliet,* with Lewis Hallam as *Romeo.* The brilliant John Hodgkinson played *Romeo,* on that stage, April 25, 1796, with Mrs. Johnson as *Juliet,* Lewis Hallam impersonating *Mercutio.* On September 11, 1797, at the theatre in Greenwich

ROMEO AND JULIET

Street, the *Romeo* was John Pollard Moreton, the *Juliet* the distinguished Mrs. Merry (Anne Brunton), esteemed by contemporary judges the most richly gifted and accomplished actress of her time in America. The cast on that occasion was remarkably strong. John Bernard, a capital actor (the author of "Retrospections of the Stage"), was the *Mercutio,* William Warren, the Elder, played *Friar Lawrence,* the droll comedian Francis Blissett played *Peter,* and Thomas Wignell was the *Tybalt.* Each of those players was, in his day, highly distinguished. On March 9, 1798, *Romeo* was acted by Thomas Abthorpe Cooper, *Juliet* by Mrs. Johnson, and *Mercutio* by Lewis Hallam. The lovely and exceptionally talented Fanny Kemble, then in the perfect bloom of her beauty, acted *Juliet* on October 1, 1832, at the Park Theatre (the first of the several New York playhouses which have borne that name), her father, Charles Kemble, acting *Romeo.* The showy and highly popular English actor James Robert Anderson acted *Romeo,* with Fanny Wallack as *Juliet,* at the old Broadway Theatre, on May 15, 1848, Lester Wallack, Fanny's cousin, being the *Mercutio.*

MANY ROMEOS.—FROM SNELLING POWELL TO EDWARD HUGH SOTHERN.

In the annals of the American Theatre many shining names are associated with the part of *Romeo*. Conspicuous among them are those of Snelling Powell, 1794; James Fennell, 1807; John Duff, 1810; James William Wallack, the Elder, 1819; Watkins Burroughs, 1824; William Augustus Conway, 1826; Frederick S. Hill, 1832; James Edward Murdoch, 1838; William Wheatley, 1843; James William Wallack, the Younger, 1850; Edward Eddy, 1854; Charles Fisher, 1856; Edwin Booth, 1857; Lawrence Barrett, 1858-'59; Frank Mayo, 1865; James W. Collier, 1867; W. F. Leggett, 1867; Joseph Wheelock, Sr., 1872; George Rignold, 1876; Eben Plympton, 1877; Samuel Piercy, 1880; Ernesto Rossi, 1881; J. B. Studley, 1882; Maurice Barrymore, 1883; Frederick Paulding, 1885; Kyrle Bellew, 1888; Robert Bruce Mantell, 1888; Robert D. Maclean, 1899; William Faversham, 1899, and Edward Hugh Sothern, 1904. Several of those actors played the part at earlier times than here mentioned, but those are the earliest obtainable dates of more or less notable ventures on our Stage, in *Romeo*.

The elder Wallack (1795-1864), founder of Wallack's Theatre, New York, was an accomplished

actor, in various branches of the vocation. He played
all sorts of parts, excelling more in comedy than in
tragedy, and attaining to perfection in romantic
melodrama,—as typified by *Don Cæsar de Bazan*
and *Massaroni, the Brigand*. His *Benedick, Don
Felix,* and *Rover* have not been surpassed. He came
to America, from the English Stage, in 1818, and
Romeo was one of the parts that he played in the
course of his first season in New York. His performance was warmly commended, for refinement,
noble bearing, and commingled passion and pathos.
Watkins Burroughs (1795-1869), also an English
actor, visited America (1824), prospered here, gained
popularity and a competent fortune, returned to
England, and retired from the stage. James
Edward Murdoch (1813-1893), whose professional
career began in 1829, and continued, intermittently,
till near the end of his days, was a brilliant comedian: his *Young Mirabel* (1857) was justly accounted
a marvel of ease, grace, buoyancy, elegance, and
impetuous action: but he adventured in tragedy and he
was admired both as *Hamlet* and *Romeo*. William
Wheatley (1816-1876) was an actor of the expansive,
sonorous, glittering order, essentially a comedian, and
his tragic exploits were merely utilitarian, containing
much show and little substance. Charles Fisher
(1816-1891) was much better suited to *Mercutio* than

to *Romeo*. He was one of the most versatile actors who have appeared in our time, but not a tragedian. Lawrence Barrett (1838-1891), whose *Romeo* I chanced to see for the first time at the Boston Museum, in the season of 1858-'59, was so distinctively intellectual as to be unsuited to the part, yet then and later he gave a performance of it which was admirable for its radically melancholy temperament, burning ardor, fine elocution, and pervasive poetic spirit. Collier (1834-1898), whom I recall as a genial comrade, was a follower of the style of Edwin Forrest, and in no way fitted for such a part as *Romeo,* but he was a handsome, manly fellow, and he acted well as *Rolando,* in "The Honeymoon"; *Appius,* in "Virginius," and *Landry Barbeau,* in "Fanchon." Particular comment as to each and every performer of *Romeo* would be a waste of words. No personation of that tragic lover given on the American Stage,—at least within the last half-century,—has aroused anything like the public interest and enthusiasm which appear to have attended the performances given by Garrick and Barry, in England. *Juliet* is the better part, and upon *Juliet* the vitality of the tragedy, as an acting play, mainly depends.

ROMEO AND JULIET

EDWIN BOOTH'S REVIVAL.

In the early morning of March 23, 1867, the Winter Garden Theatre, then under the management of Edwin Booth, burst into flames and, in a short time, was entirely consumed. John Howard Payne's tragical cento, "Brutus, or the Fall of Tarquin," had been performed on the previous night, and a spark from the thunderbolt which is used in that play is supposed to have lodged in the scenery, smouldered there, and finally started the conflagration. "Romeo and Juliet" had been announced for present revival, and preparation for that venture had been begun. Two years later, when Edwin Booth opened Booth's Theatre, February 3, 1869, he resumed his labor of theatrical management where it had been thus interrupted, and produced "Romeo and Juliet," presenting it in a magnificent setting, such as never before had been provided for the play, on the American Stage. The scenery, painted by Charles Witham and Henry Hillyard, admirably accomplished the purpose of sufficiently depicting the Verona and Mantua of the period of the play,— 1590-1600. Pictorial Italian streets, spacious, brilliant rooms, a luxuriant, almost tropical, garden, and the solemn, cypress-shaded precincts of the *Capulet* Tomb made up a pageantry of absorbing illusion, and swathed the tragic experiences of the ill-fated lovers in an atmosphere of afflicting reality. The emblematic scene with which the play begins,—that of the combat between the rival houses of *Capulet* and *Montague,*—was made superbly effective, occupying the whole large stage and involving a host of contestants. Each scenic picture seemed to surpass its predecessor, in brilliancy of contributory dramatic effect. The supreme scenes, however, were the Garden, by moonlight; *Juliet's* Chamber, and the Tomb.

Edwin Booth acted *Romeo*. Several features of the cast were exceptionally strong. Edwin Adams was the *Mercutio;* Mark Smith the *Friar Lawrence;* Harry Langdon the *Tybalt;* Fanny Morant, an excellent actress, the *Nurse*. A part customarily omitted, that of *Capulet's* old uncle, was, on this occasion, restored, and the venerable William C. Drummond assumed it. Miss Mary McVicker appeared as *Juliet*. Booth was superbly tragic in *Romeo's* killing of *Tybalt* and in the frantic passion of *Romeo's* collapse in the *Friar's* cell, and he was deeply pathetic in the Tomb Scene. A subtle and striking merit of his performance was its deft showing, at the outset, of the impulsive wildness of youth in its period of capricious fancy, vague longing, and turbulent desire. One notable peculiarity of Booth's

Romeo was that of personal appearance: he "made up" as a blond. Italians of fair complexion are unusual, and this was a novelty. In aspect the actor was perfect, and there were, in his performance, many right and splendid elements. The passion was artistically ardent, the suffering acute, the treatment poetic; but Booth never cared for the character of *Romeo,* and his presentment of it was fitful, not continuous,—lacking articulation of parts. At the essentially tragic moments it was thrilling; in other respects conventionally executive. Adams, an actor precisely suited to *Mercutio,* by appearance, personality, temperament, and style, gave a brilliant performance, particularly emphasizing the quality of comradeship. Adams was a good fellow, if ever a good fellow lived, and his manliness, kindness, joviality, buoyant humor, undertone of grave, sweet feeling, and his grace of manner, all shining through a thoroughly artistic treatment of the character, contributed to make his *Mercutio* a great success and truly the jewel of this production. Mark Smith (1829-1874), one of the best of stage "old men," whether serious or comic, was perfect as the ruminant, philosophical, kindly *Friar,*—dignified and benign in spirit and demeanor, and diffusive of a keen sense of that sober, kindly sympathy with the feelings of youth, and that solicitude as to its troubles and its welfare, which so much become the ripe maturity of a good man's mind. The *Juliet* of Mary McVicker was more notable for personal singularity than for either romantic aspect, poetic quality, or a finished artistic style. That actress was slight in person, a brunette, with flashing dark eyes that imparted remarkable animation to her countenance. She was imperious in mind, dictatorial in manner, of an impetuous spirit and a nervous, sensitive temperament. Her experience of acting was considerable, but her faculties of expression were limited. She did not possess either the appearance or the command of passion and of pathos that are essential to the representative of *Juliet*.

Booth's production of "Romeo and Juliet" held the stage for ten weeks and earned $60,000. Booth did not esteem his performance of *Romeo,* and after the play had run its course at Booth's Theatre he discarded the part and never played it again. In later days the comedian Edward A. Sothern, talking with him about the vicissitudes of professional experience, chanced to say:

"The worst performance ever seen was my *Armand Duval.*" In youth Sothern had acted that part in association with Matilda Heron as *Camille*. Booth puffed at his pipe for a moment, and then gravely inquired:

"The *worst?* Did you ever see my *Romeo?*"

It is an interesting fact that the play with which Booth's Theatre opened was also, by a singular chance, the play with which it was closed. Edwin Booth retired from management in 1873, and thereafter for several years the theatre experienced vicissitudes. Junius Brutus Booth managed it for a while; so did Messrs. Henry C. Jarrett and David Palmer; so did Augustin Daly; so did Dion Boucicault. It was finally closed on April 30, 1883, with a performance of "Romeo and Juliet," in which Helena Modjeska acted *Juliet,* Maurice Barrymore *Romeo,* and Frank Clements *Mercutio.*

VARIOUS NEW YORK PRODUCTIONS.

The example of Edwin Booth, in effecting (1869) his sumptuous presentment of "Romeo and Juliet," aroused a spirit of emulation, and at least twenty-five revivals of that tragedy were made on the New York Stage in the course of the next fifteen years,—those accomplished by Adelaide Neilson and Mary Anderson being the most important and the best. Marie Seebach (1837-18—), an eminent German actress, who came to America in the autumn of 1870, making a profound impression, especially by her beautiful impersonations of Goethe's *Gretchen (Mar-*

garet) and Schiller's *Maria Stuart,* acted *Juliet,* January 16, 1871, at the Stadt Theater, speaking her native language, and in that part, as in others,— among them *Adrienne, Deborah, Valerie, Jane Eyre,* and *Louisa Miller,*—she impressed and pleased by spontaneity of emotional power, poetic spirit, and exquisite delicacy of execution. Mme. Seebach (she was the wife of a German tenor singer named Niemann) was slender in person, elegant in manner, having an aquiline face, gray-blue eyes, silky, light brown hair, and a remarkably sweet voice, and her countenance expressively indicated a union of tenderness and strength. When she acted *Juliet* her associate, Mlle. Veneta, performed as *Romeo.* Agnes Booth (third wife of Junius Brutus Booth, Jr., elder brother of Edwin Booth) appeared as *Juliet,* February 21, 1874, at Booth's Theatre, of which her husband had assumed the management. This actress,—originally Marion Agnes Land, from Australia,—was a handsome blonde, of commanding appearance, unconsciously self-assertive manner, and vigorous executive faculty, and she showed herself better fitted to express the stormy resentment of *Queen Constance* than to realize the grace, tenderness, and passion of *Juliet.* In a production of the tragedy made at the same theatre, May 4, 1876, Sara Jewett was the *Juliet,* George Rignold the

Romeo, and Frederick C. P. Robinson the *Mercutio,*—none of those players being fitted for the responsibility thus assumed. Miss Jewett was a graceful, refined, pleasing *ingénue,* adequate to the expression of girlishness and sentiment, but deficient of strength. John McCullough appeared as *Romeo,* with Fanny Davenport as *Juliet,* acting in the Balcony Scene, April 19, 1877, at Booth's Theatre, both actors showing themselves to be out of place in such characters and such an atmosphere of amatory bewilderment and romantic feeling. A singular and unpleasing exhibition was made at that theatre, May 17, 1877, when George Rignold, taking a benefit, performed *Romeo,* having the coöperation, as *Juliet,* of a different actress in successive scenes of the tragedy. The female triflers in that freakish display were Fanny Davenport, Ada Dyas, Maude Granger, Marie Wainwright, Minnie Cummings, and Grace D'Urfrey. Frederick B. Warde acted *Mercutio.* On January 30, 1880, at the Grand Opera House, Ada Cavendish (1847-1895) acted *Juliet,* for the first time in New York. She was a beautiful woman, slender, lithe, graceful, having regular features, brilliant blue eyes, ruddy golden hair, and a musical voice, and, being of a sympathetic and impulsive temperament, her style was somewhat eccentric, from excess of feeling. *Juliet* was adopted into her repertory, September 26, 1873, when, at the Olympic Theatre, London, she played the part for the first time,—with Lionel Boyne as *Romeo*. She was exceptionally powerful when acting *Juliet* here, in the Potion Scene and the Tomb Scene,—evincing, in a marked degree, the prodigality of reckless emotional force for which her acting was, at all times, distinguished. Her *Romeo* was Samuel Piercey,—an actor of much ability and more promise, who prematurely died.

Ernesto Rossi (1829-1896), the most interesting of the various foreign actors who have visited America and endeavored to play Shakespearean parts, appeared in New York, as *Romeo,* in an Italian version of "Romeo and Juliet," at Booth's Theatre, November 1, 1881. Rossi was an accomplished actor, and no doubt his performance was creditable and pleasing in his youth, but when it was shown here his youth had long been past. A robust, elderly gentleman, obese and oleaginous, may be ever so earnest in his love, but the spectacle he presents, when under the influence of that distemper, is not edifying, nor does he in the least resemble Shakespeare's *Romeo*. Rossi's method was florid, but he was an absolute master of acting, his spirit was fervent, his action animated, his gesticulation apt and expressive, his attitudes pictorial. The best of his performance was its denotement of his comprehension of the change which is wrought by the pressure of grief, from youthful sentiment and sensuous ardor to manly maturity. His delivery of the Italian text was fluent, sometimes loquacious, and his execution of the duel with *Tybalt* was effective. As a whole, however, his *Romeo* was a dreary exhibition. There comes a time when an actor ought to lay aside the juvenile lovers. The same objection that *Mr. Pickwick* made against *Mr. Tupman's* appearance in a bandit's "green velvet jacket with a two inch tail" was valid against Signor Rossi's appearance in the person and dress of the love-lorn *Montague:* " 'Sir,' said Mr. Pickwick, 'you are too old,—too *old,* and *too fat!'* " In the version of the play used by the Italian actor, *Romeo,* in the last scene, was reanimated, and he lived long enough to explain to *Juliet* that he had swallowed poison because of the false report of her death.

On the occasion of a presentment of "Romeo and Juliet," June 26, 1883, at the Academy of Music, with selections from the opera on that theme by Berlioz, which were performed by an orchestra comprising sixty players, *Romeo* was undertaken by Signor A. Carrona, a flutist, while Louise Muldener appeared as *Juliet,* (she had acted it with Rossi, also), Hamilton Harris as *Mercutio,* and Louisa Eldridge as the *Nurse.*

Mantell first acted *Romeo* more than thirty years ago, at the Theatre Royal, Birmingham, to the *Juliet* of Ellen Wallis; he first acted it in America, in 1888, at Dayton, Ohio, with an obscure performer, named Fanny Gillette, of whom Augustus Pitou attempted to make a "star" actress; he has since played it in many different places in various associations, and he still sometimes appears in the part. He has always shown himself possessed of the feeling and the fire requisite for impersonation of the enraptured lover and the bereaved, dazed, distracted husband; but in his settled maturity of mind, experience, and condition he overweights the part, as other fine actors have done, particularly those of much tragic power. *Romeo,* of course, requires the perfect simulation of youth: Mantell, as *Romeo,* is surprisingly buoyant and full of dash and movement. His performance is best in the moment of the killing of *Tybalt,* in the conflict with *Paris,* at the entrance to the Tomb, and in the afflicting Death Scene. But Mantell's natural and best artistic powers are shown in *Othello, Brutus, Richelieu,* and *King John.* However, as long as the public support is given to an actor in any good part it would be unreasonable to expect him to discard it. The colossal Salvini insisted on appearing as *Hamlet:* Forrest went on for *Claude Melnotte:* Edwin Booth performed as *Benedick:* all the girls, from Julia Dean to Mary Anderson, thought themselves ordained to act *Lady Macbeth.*

MODJESKA AS *JULIET.*

Helena Modjeska first acted as *Juliet,* in 1866, at the Imperial Theatre, Warsaw, appearing in a Polish version of the tragedy, and coöperating with Boleslaw Ladnowski, a popular Polish actor, as *Romeo.* It was my valued privilege often to converse with Modjeska about acting, and she spoke to me freely of her performances. With reference to *Juliet* she mentioned the interesting fact that, in the work of preparation, she and Ladnowski rehearsed the Balcony Scene in the open air, in order there to produce and study the effect of voices expressing ardent passion in eager yet half-hushed tones. Her performance in Polish was much admired and commended. She first acted *Juliet* in English, in California, in 1877,—the year of her advent in New York. She was first seen in that city as *Juliet,* on November 1, acting in only the Balcony Scene: she appeared at the Academy of Music, on the occasion of a benefit for the Roman Catholic Orphan Asylum. Walter F. Burroughs played *Romeo.* That fragmentary essay was repeated, at the Fifth Avenue Theatre, January 11, 1878. It was not till the following autumn, October 12, 1878, that Modjeska effected her first New York production of the tragedy. This was well accomplished, at the Fifth Avenue Theatre, the *Romeo* being Frank Clements (1844-1886),—an actor of fine talent and much experience, who had, however, become somewhat languid and dispirited for this character,—and the *Mercutio* Frank Mordaunt, a heavy actor, better suited for *Lodovico* and *Baradas* than for any comedy part. Modjeska was fortunate as *Juliet*, by reason of the exquisite beauty of her face and person, the charm of her sympathetic temperament, and the refinement of her style: she had outgrown the part before she ever acted it in America. Her comprehension of it, however, was complete, and completely indicated. Her stage business was ingeniously devised and expertly used. The frenzy with which she hurled herself into a great chair, as the affrighted imagination of *Juliet* conjured up the *Ghost of Tybalt*, was electrical in its effect, and, indeed, her management of the Potion Scene was, in every particular, judicious and effective.

MARY ANDERSON'S REVIVAL.

Mary Anderson made her first appearance on the stage as *Juliet*, November 25, 1875, at Barney Macauley's theatre, Louisville, Kentucky. She was then only sixteen years old. Her performance, though crude and extravagant, was impassioned and sympathetic, and it was at once recognized as fraught with uncommon promise. Her first appearance in New York, September 19, 1877, at the Fifth Avenue Theatre, was made in that part, and she retained it in her repertory till nearly the end of her professional career (1889), continuously improving her impersonation, till it became one of the best and most famous known to the English-speaking world. The early productions of the tragedy in which she acted were merely conventional: at one time she, experimentally, used Garrick's arrangement of the last act: but in 1884, after having gained great public favor, both abroad and at home, she determined to present the play in an appropriate and suitably magnificent attire, and with that purpose in view she went to Verona, there to study Italian scenery, architecture, dresses and manners, and to obtain sketches that would serve as a basis for correct and picturesque stage setting. On her return to England she produced "Romeo and Juliet," November 1, 1884, at the Lyceum Theatre, London, in a scenic setting remarkable for its fidelity to Italian characteristics and for artistic splendor. Her adviser in the making of that production was the famous painter, Laurence Alma-Tadema, and by him the scenes and costumes (the latter designed by Lewis Wingfield) were supervised. The play, accordingly, was not treated as a vehicle for a pageant but as a work of poetic art.

An old civilization, the repose of massive towers, solidity and picturesque singularity of time-worn buildings, the strength and peace of aged, mossy trees, the cool gloom and awful splendor of ancient churches, the silence and mystery of dark cathedral crypts, the glimmering glory of moonlit summer nights, the climate of the South,—all those adjuncts are essential, in Shakespeare's scheme, as a background to the tragedy of "Romeo and Juliet," and for such a background his text makes ample provision. The opportunity thus provided had been improved by Henry Irving, in his rich revival of the play, in 1882, and it was now again improved by Miss Anderson. Scenery and dress, in the clothing of a play, should naturally express its character. They did so in this instance. In the painting of the seventeen scenes that were shown, the time, the place, the climate, the period of the year, the duration of the action, and the spirit of the story had been thoughtfully considered, and so a judicious design was accomplished of providing such illustration, and only such, as helped to make effective to the imagination as well as to the eyes a poetic picture, at once beautiful and terrible, of the passion and agony of life that is wrecked

From a Photograph by Sarony, N. Y.   Author's Collection

MARY ANDERSON AS *JULIET*

"What if this mixture do not work at all?"

by the fatality of circumstance and the precipitation of love. There is in Verona an ancient tower, visible from every part of the city and of its environment. This tower appears to be indicated in the text, by *Juliet:* "Oh, bid me leap, rather than marry Paris, from off the battlements of *yonder tower.*" Some editors, reasoning seemingly that because the speaker is indoors she could not refer to a tower not in sight, have changed "yonder" to "any." That tower was included in each exterior scene of Miss Anderson's production. The Public Square and the Churchyard, by O'Conor; the Grove of Sycamores, by Hawes Craven, and the *Friar's* Cell, by Bruce Smith, were, in particular, superb works of art. All the scenes were, in various ways, beautiful, being invested with an atmosphere so beguilingly poetic that the spectator who looked on them saw Verona itself, and, realizing Italy and golden joys, seemed to hear the rustling of leaves in the languorous air of Southern night, and the song of the nightingale, mourning in the dusky Italian woods.

Critical opinion relative to the production and the acting was, as usually it is, divided. The poet "Owen Meredith" (Robert, Earl of Lytton) thoughtfully expressed, in a discriminative published essay, the general sentiment of admiration. The prominent critic Clement Scott (1841-1904) affirmed that he had "never before seen 'Romeo and Juliet' rendered in such a listless and unimaginative fashion," and promulgated the interesting discovery,—illustrative of his sagacious perception,—that Miss Anderson's performance was "all trick, and artificial to the last degree," presenting a *Juliet* "modern, unideal, and exaggerative in every tender scene,—a *Juliet* who acts with her lips, not with her heart"; a personification "as far from *Juliet* as darkness from dawn"; and that deliverance was supplemented with the statement that "the play is a melodrama, as acted here, not a poem."

As a critical judgment on the inherent, essential quality of Miss Anderson's performance of *Juliet* and on her artistic method nothing could be more directly at variance with the truth than Mr. Scott's summary. It is possible, indeed probable, that, on the first sight of her *Juliet* at the Lyceum, Miss Anderson's performance suffered from the impedative effects of fatigue, anxiety, and strain: I was not present, and therefore cannot speak on that subject from personal observation: but, first and last, during a period of about twelve years, I saw Miss Anderson act *Juliet,* in many different places, under widely variant circumstances, about thirty-five times, and I carefully studied the development of her performance from its early crudeness to its later supremacy as a piece of tragic impersonation. In its maturity, viewed as a concrete achievement, apart from any particular occasion or any association of disturbing circumstances, considered in the light of what it revealed and with regard to the manner of its revelation, Miss Anderson's performance of *Juliet* was one of intrinsic charm, superlative beauty of artistic form, and great energy of passion and power of pathos; and, more than that of either Adelaide Neilson, Helena Modjeska, Ellen Terry, or any other actress whom I have ever seen in the part, it was saturated with the force and color of *tragedy*. Miss Anderson was supremely fortunate in her natural adaptability to the requirements for a great embodiment of *Juliet*. She possessed a tall and beautiful figure: her nature was sincere and her method in acting simple and direct: she was an incessant, studious worker; she possessed a gloriously sympathetic and copious voice; and, more than from anything that she did or seemed to be, her acting was triumphant because of what she was,—a good and noble woman. Her performance was notably exceptional in the felicity with which she harmonized the discordant elements in *Juliet,*—the combination of inexperienced, sweet, and winning girlishness with a woman's capacity to love and suffer. The felicity of her artistic method was particularly exhibited in the discriminative skill with which she marked the change from girl to woman, after *Juliet's* meeting with *Romeo*. Her expression of love, in the Balcony Scene, commingled tenderness with rapture, and yet with a gentle solicitude, sweet and touching. She was magnificent at such points as "Myself have power to die," and she reached the topmost height of pathos when she spoke, as no other actress within my knowledge has spoken, the despairing words,

"Is there no pity sitting in the clouds
That sees into the bottom of my grief?"

In her London revival of "Romeo and Juliet" Miss Anderson enlisted the professional coöperation of William Terriss, as *Romeo;* Herbert Standing, as *Mercutio;* Arthur Stirling, as *Friar Lawrence,* and Mrs. Stirling (who had once been a favorite *Juliet*), as the *Nurse*. The play was acted for 100 nights at the Lyceum, and subsequently in many cities of the British kingdom. In the autumn of 1885 Miss Anderson came to America, bringing her London production of "Romeo and Juliet," and also the production of "As You Like It" which she had effected, August 29, at Stratford-upon-Avon. Her dramatic company had been reorganized. Johnston Forbes-Robertson, succeeding William Terriss, had been engaged for leading business, and when, on November

12, at the Star Theatre,—a house long ago demolished,—"Romeo and Juliet" was presented, that fine actor appeared as *Romeo,* for the first time in America (he had made his first appearance on our Stage as *Orlando,* on October 12), Mrs. Billington as the *Nurse,* and Francis H. Macklin as *Mercutio.* Other actors than Robertson and Terriss who, at one time or another, performed as *Romeo* with Miss Anderson as *Juliet* were John Beresford Studley, Robert L. Downing, Edward J. Buckley, and Eben Plympton. The *Romeo* of Mr. Plympton was notable for enthusiasm, sustained identification, and physical vitality.

MARGARET MATHER AS *JULIET.*

An ambitious attempt to play *Juliet* was made in New York, October 13, 1885, at the Union Square Theatre, by Margaret Mather (1859-1898), an actress till that time practically unknown, though she had been for nearly eight years obscurely employed on the stage. The tragedy was produced, for the purpose of "starring" Miss Mather, by Mr. James M. Hill, of Chicago, since deceased, a genial speculator in popular "amusements," who believed, with *Bottom,* that Tragedy should not be permitted to fright the ladies. "A lion among ladies," says the immortal weaver, "is a most dreadful thing." In Mr. Hill's production, accordingly, the play,—arranged in six acts, sixteen scenes, and nine tableaux,—was considerately invested with the accessories of decorum and soothing domesticity. In the scene of the secret marriage of *Romeo* and *Juliet* two monks, moved, apparently, by springs, suddenly came out of the wall of *Friar Lawrence's* Cell and placed hassocks for the bride and groom to kneel on, while the service was in progress. *Juliet's* Bed-room,—the time of her nuptials being the middle of July, in a hot country,—was thoughtfully provided with a large fire of brightly blazing logs. On the morning appointed for her wedding a numerous company of young women entered her chamber, to awaken her with cheerful song, but, finding her dead, those accommodating vocalists placidly ranged themselves about the apartment and sang an appropriate and moving dirge. *Juliet's* Tomb, a huge, gilded structure, shaped like a glove-box interiorly illuminated, was exteriorly flooded with "moonlight," shed from a glaring "lime." And at the last, as a decent, orderly, becoming close to the spectacle of affliction, many friars thronged into the graveyard and sang the "Miserere,"—seeming to imply that *Romeo,* when on his way to the Tomb, had heedfully paused at the Abbey and bespoken ecclesiastical participation in the forthcoming obsequies. To enhance the effect of these imposing novelties Mr.

Hill furnished highly-colored scenery that shone like a brass coal-scuttle. As I viewed the spectacle I thought of an old play in which the comedian Burton was exceedingly droll, acting an ignorant parvenu, who, being asked whether, in the furnishing of his library, he wanted to have "all the old authors," exclaims, "No, not a damn' one of 'em! *All new!*"

Miss Mather showed no comprehension of *Juliet's* character or temperament. She was a small woman, slender in figure, having regular features, dark eyes, abundant dark hair, and a hard, unsympathetic voice. She had been laboriously trained, by George Edgar,—a good actor, descended from the respected comedian John Hogg (1770-1813), who flourished in the days of the old John Street Theatre,—and Edgar told me that he rehearsed her in the part of *Juliet* more than 500 times, and found that even then she did not understand it. Her notion of acting was to goad herself into a frenzy, to rage, storm, and "tear a passion to tatters." In *Juliet's* early scenes she was radically and obviously artificial, and therefore uninteresting. Acting, of course, is imitation,—but it must not seem to be so. Miss Mather could not, and did not successfully imitate the condition and conduct of a pure, innocent, ardent, ingenuous girl, enthralled by the irresistible passion of first love, but in the later scenes, when *Juliet* has become an agonized woman, tortured by contending emotions and distracted by unspeakable wretchedness, she evinced a capability of such excessive emotional demonstration as often stirs the enthusiasm of an audience. Her elocution was of the sing-song variety, and her method of action was mechanical and coarse. When the *Friar* offered the Potion to her she snatched the vial from his hand, emitting hysterical shrieks, and after she had swallowed the dose she collapsed in such a way as to roll down a short flight of steps and land on the stage level. She was, essentially, a commonplace person fortuitously placed in a prominent public position. Miss Mather, in her New York venture as *Juliet,* was associated with Frederick Paulding as *Romeo,* Milnes Levick as *Mercutio,* Henry A. Weaver as *Friar Lawrence,* Edwin Cleary as *Tybalt,* and Caroline Jamison as the *Nurse.* The play was kept on at the Union Square Theatre for twelve weeks and then was taken on a tour of the country. Miss Mather remained on the stage almost continuously till the time of her death. Among the parts in which she appeared were *Juliana, Leah, Pauline, Peg Woffington,* and *Imogen.* Her best performance was that of *Leah.* At one time the accomplished and popular Otis Skinner acted with her, as *Romeo* and as *Posthumus.* She was by birth a Canadian. Her maiden name was Finlayson. She began acting as Miss Bloomer, and later

ROMEO AND JULIET

adopted her mother's maiden name, Mather. She was twice married;—in 1887 to Emil Haberkorn, a musician; in 1892 to Gustav Pabst, a brewer, who divorced her, after she had beaten him with a horsewhip in the street, at Milwaukee. Miss Mather was an executive person, and her career was eccentric and instructive.

VARIOUS LATER PRODUCTIONS.

In the course of the thirty years prior to 1914 several revivals of "Romeo and Juliet" were made, most of which were unimportant. Alexander Salvini played *Romeo,* in the season of 1885-'86, with Viola Allen as *Juliet.* Daniel Edward Bandmann presented himself as *Romeo,* November 2, 1887, at the Third Avenue Theatre. That actor had, in his youth, played *Narcisse, Hamlet, Richelieu,* and other prominent parts, and he promised well, but the promise was not fulfilled. He was of a common strain, and as the glow of youth faded he became gross, ponderous, and repellent. His *Romeo* was all efflorescence. Mrs. Potter (wife of Mr. James Brown Potter, of Chicago, —maiden name Cora Urquhart) went on for *Juliet,* June 7, 1888, at the Grand Opera House,—Kyrle Bellew appearing as *Romeo.* Minna Gale (Mrs. Archibald C. Haynes), at the Broadway Theatre, January 17, 1891, performed *Juliet,*—Lawrence Barrett acting *Romeo*. Miss Gale had long been known in the part, having first played it, with Barrett, in Chicago, in 1885,—her first season on the stage. On March 3, 1896, a revival of "Romeo and Juliet" was effected at Daly's Theatre, with Mr. Bellew as *Romeo,* Mrs. Potter as *Juliet,* and William Redmund as *Mercutio.* Robert D. Maclean (Shepherd) appeared, April 10, 1899, at the Herald Square Theatre, as *Romeo,* in association with his wife, Odette Tyler, as *Juliet,* and Charles B. Hanford as *Mercutio.* Charles Frohman produced the tragedy, May 8, 1899, at the Empire Theatre, with William Faversham as *Romeo,* James Keteltas Hackett as *Mercutio,* and Maude Adams as *Juliet.* Eleanor Robson (now, 1914, Mrs. August Belmont) vainly undertook *Juliet,* May 25, 1903, at the Knickerbocker Theatre,—Bellew assisting, as *Romeo,* and Eben Plympton, as *Mercutio.*

Mr. Bellew's performance of *Romeo,* while never truly tragic or poetic, was more engaging when seen in 1888 than it was in later years, because he then still retained something of his pictorial youthful appearance, but his best acting of the part was shown when he played it at Daly's Theatre, in 1896, on which occasion the tragedy was carefully set and richly dressed. Mr. Bellew was an expert actor, but his conspicuous self-consciousness, self-complacency, and artificiality often vitiated his skilful art. His appearance in *Romeo* was prepossessing, and he indicated, though he did not make convincing, at first the love-lorn condition of the sentimentalist, and then the impetuosity of the reckless lover, infatuated by new-born passion. In the tragic passages,—the killing of *Tybalt,* the agony of the wretched husband, on learning of the decree of banishment, and the tearless despair and fatal grief that terminate in suicide,— he was shallow, feeble, and insignificant. Mr. Bellew and Mrs. Potter were out of place in tragedy. Mrs. Potter was a pretty woman, of the brunette type, not devoid of sensibility, pleasing in manner, costly in raiment, and qualified to shine in drawing-room entertainments. Mr. Bellew was, essentially, a light comedian, possessing aptitude for elegant types of comedy, such as *Charles Surface, Young Wilding, Young Marlowe,* and *Captain Absolute.* The best impersonation he ever gave on our Stage (he was an Englishman, the son of the Rev. John Montesquieu Bellew Higgin; he had his early career at home, and he came to America as leading juvenile for Lester Wallack, in 1885) was that of *Richard Voysin,* in an English adaptation of Henri Bernstein's "The Thief," produced by Charles Frohman, at the Lyceum Theatre, New York, in 1908. In that performance he evinced judgment, taste, authority, repose, and that complete control of faculties and resources which only ripe experience can bestow. William Redmund, an English actor, distinguished for sterling talent and versatility, expressed not only the frolicsome spirit and spontaneous buoyancy of *Mercutio,* but his dauntless mind, his generous heart, and the singularity of character which strangely seems to isolate him even from his boon companions,—that condition of exuberant fancy and extravagant hilarity which the Scotch call fey, meaning doomed, and which, perhaps, the poet intended as an omen of his untimely, lamentable death.

The revival effected by Maclean was notable chiefly because of the fact that he used the Cibber-Garrick alteration of the closing scene, which makes *Juliet* awaken before *Romeo* dies. The play was mounted and dressed in a conventional manner and it was mechanically acted. The players of the chief parts evinced the proficiency that comes of experience in saying words and doing "business,"—and evinced nothing else. Miss Tyler, an actress qualified to play such parts as *Nerissa,* in "The Merchant of Venice," and *Helen,* in "The Hunchback," was frivolous and insipid as *Juliet,* although she tried to be serious. All the salient characteristics of this player,—appearance, temperament, voice and demeanor,—signified a blithe, piquant, cheery personality, unsuitable to tragedy. Mr. Maclean's *Romeo* was a mature, robust, executive man of affairs, who, in becoming sentimental, became almost epicene, and whose denotement of passion and misery was obviously artificial and therefore futile,—eliciting no response of sympathy. Mr. Maclean is an actor of talent, who could be effective in sedate parts, such as *John Mildmay,* in "Still Waters Run Deep," but his temperament was seen to be at variance with the *Romeos* and *Hamlets,*—who are compounded of inordinate sensibility and tumultuous passion, or of distempered mind and lurid, haunted, agonized imagination. Mr. Hanford, who has, I believe, retired from the Stage, was a well-trained, competent actor. His professional career began in 1881 and continued for more than thirty years. His person and style made him more adaptable to heavy parts, such as *Mark Antony* and *Ingomar,* than to the buoyant *Mercutio.*

CHARLES FROHMAN'S PRODUCTION.

The presentment of "Romeo and Juliet" made by Charles Frohman was creditably ambitious in purpose and meritorious in the matter of costume and scenic attire. One detail of the setting was agreeably novel. The balcony was so placed that it overlooked a spacious garden, enclosed with a wall, in which, at the back, there was a massive iron gate. *Romeo* entered outside, crossing the opening, scaled the wall, and hid himself in the shrubbery. Then came *Benvolio* and *Mercutio* and played their scene in sight of the audience, but behind the iron lattice of the gate. It was a good device, obviating a change of scene.

The acting was, except in once instance, tame and tedious. Mrs. W. G. Jones (1829-1907) gave an excellent performance of the *Nurse,* making her precisely what she is in Shakespeare's text, garrulous, obsequious, kind, crafty, coarsely humorous, an incarnation of meanness, servility, and conceit. Mrs. Jones, in her day, had acted scores of parts, of every description, including both *Romeo* and *Juliet;* she was thoroughly accomplished in her art, and in Mr. Frohman's injudicious cast of this tragedy she proved the only satisfactory feature. William Faversham, an actor at that time wholly inexperienced in tragedy, proved inadequate to every requirement of the character of *Romeo,* but he acted earnestly and looked well. He has, since then, given considerable attention to the Shakespearean drama, having acted *Antony,* in "Julius Cæsar," and *Iago,* and has announced his purpose to appear in "Hamlet" and "King Henry VIII." In the disastrous season of 1913-'14 he revived "Romeo and Juliet,"—Miss Cecilia Loftus appearing with him, as *Juliet,*—but the adversity which thwarted his worthy enterprise, causing him temporarily to abandon Shakespeare, prevented the display of that production in New York, and I have not seen his later presentment of *Romeo*. Mr. Hackett embodied *Mercutio* as a jolly good fellow, a roisterer, shallow in feeling and metallic in style, but his delivery of the text was, in general, refreshing, by reason of his clear articulation: the Dream Speech, however, was, for some inscrutable reason, spoken mostly in a whisper.

Maude Adams, a clever and interesting actress in domestic or elfishly eccentric parts, showed herself unsuited to tragedy and wofully out of place as *Juliet,* giving a performance which ceased to be frivolous only when it became mildly hysterical. Shakespeare's *Juliet,* by her words and actions, shows herself to be superbly developed, of a vigorous mind, a passionate heart, a powerful imagination, and an imperious will, which, but that it is curbed by her sense of right and her womanly instinct of prudence, would overbear and demolish every restraint; and the dramatist has placed her in harrowing situations, and allotted for the expression of her feelings some of the most impetuous bursts of poetic frenzy that passion ever prompted or eloquence ever winged. Whether *Juliet* be considered fourteen or forty, it will make no difference as to the practical result, in acting. The representative of the character must be competent to realize it. *Juliet* cannot be effectually shown by either the precocious child or the priggish prude. The *Juliet* of Miss Adams was a mixture of both. The actress did not, even at the comparatively early age of twenty-seven, possess the exceptional physical beauty that would enable her to look like *Juliet,* nor did she evince the imagination, passion, personal force, vocal power, elocutionary art, or diversified professional skill that are essential for a true, or even for an acceptable, embodiment of that character. The performance was as flaccid in execution as it was mistaken and insipid in ideal. The Frohman production was quietly inurned after a brief tour, in the spring of 1899.

JULIA MARLOWE.—SOTHERN-MARLOWE.

Julia Marlowe appeared as *Juliet* in the course of her first season as a star,—that of 1887-'88,—and her first performance of the part in New York was given on December 12, 1887, at the Star Theatre. Joseph Haworth, an actor of signal ability and remarkable for devotion to his art, essayed *Romeo,* but not with success, and Charles Norris mistakenly undertook *Mercutio.* Miss Marlowe, then in her twen-

From a Photograph by White Courtesy of T. R. Smith, Esq.

JULIA MARLOWE AS JULIET

"*If he be married*
My grave is like to be my wedding bed."

Act I., Sc. 5

From a Photograph by White, N. Y. Author's Collection

EDWARD H. SOTHERN AS ROMEO

"*Is she a Capulet?*
O dear account! my life is my foe's debt."

Act I., Sc. 5

tieth year, was a tall, slender, handsome, interesting girl. Her acting of *Juliet* revealed an ardent temperament, much sensibility, dramatic talent, and careful training. The method of her art was indicative of uncommon self-control. In the earlier scenes of the play she sweetly expressed the sentiment of love, but neither then nor in the later scenes did she impart a convincing sense of its passion and power. At moments of *Juliet's* anguish she marred effects by concealing her face, sometimes with her hands, sometimes bending over furniture so that it could not be seen. She was inexperienced, unacquainted with grief, and her performance, while intelligent and full of promise, was crude. In the prodigality of her youthful, undeveloped powers she made use of the difficult, exacting colloquy between *Juliet* and the *Nurse* about the banishment of *Romeo,* which more judicious performers discreetly omit, and to which she proved unequal, as also she did to the frenzy of the Potion Scene and the anguish, horror, and desperation of the Tomb Scene. The promise of her early effort as *Juliet* was, however, amply and richly fulfilled in later years. Her performance underwent much change as a work of art, becoming spontaneously ardent in passion, in the scene of *Juliet's* interchange of vows with *Romeo;* profoundly affecting in its mingled ecstasy and solemnity, in the

Marriage Scene; piteous in the agony of the wife's parting from the husband who all too surely she feels is leaving her forever, and, in the tragic ordeal of the Potion Scene, tragically representative of the heroism of desperate resolve which is constant throughout a frenzy of dread and fear. No assumption of *Juliet* comparable with that of Miss Marlowe, at its best, has been seen on our Stage within the last twenty-five years. She is, however, and for some time has been, rather mature for this character.

In 1904 Julia Marlowe and Edward H. Sothern formed a professional alliance which has come to be known as the Sothern-Marlowe Combination, and on September 19, that year, they acted together, for the first time, appearing at the Illinois Theatre, Chicago, in "Romeo and Juliet." The production of the play,—which, by fortunate chance, I saw, on that occasion,—was creditable, as to scenery and dresses, but the stage management was, in several particulars, hurtfully negligent: for example, at the close of the street combat, in spite of the command, "Throw your mistemper'd weapons to the ground," not a weapon was dropped; in the Churchyard Scene *Romeo* killed *Paris* with a dagger, neither of the men bearing swords, though the text of Shakespeare (which was spoken) says:

"What mean these masterless and gory *swords*
To lie discolor'd by this place of peace?"

Mr. Sothern was executively skilful as *Romeo,* but in the tragic passages,—the killing of *Tybalt,* the colloquy with the *Friar* about the banishment, the killing of *Paris,* and the suicide in the Tomb,—while the right intention was indicated, the intended effect was not produced, and there was a lack of the magnetic tragic power which communicates emotion. This actor has found much favor with the public, in tragic as well as comic parts, and he merits respect and admiration for the zeal and resolute purpose which he has manifested in striving to make himself a thoroughly accomplished and efficient actor in every variety of character; but by temperament he is a comedian, and, while his tragic efforts are often, in some ways, effective, his comedy is intrinsically better than his tragedy. His *Romeo,* "both at the first and now, was and is" overshadowed by Miss Marlowe's *Juliet.* It should not be forgotten that *Juliet* is the better part, and that Miss Marlowe besides her natural advantages possessed that of sixteen years' experience in the tragedy. Other performers of *Romeo* associated with her as *Juliet* were Creston Clarke (1865-1910) and Robert Taber (1865-1904).

CHARACTER AND PLAYERS OF *MERCUTIO*.

The poet Dryden, in 1688, recorded a tradition which had lasted till his time, that Shakespeare had declared himself obliged to kill *Mercutio* in the Third Act of the play, lest *Mercutio* should "kill him,"—meaning that he felt himself unable to sustain beyond that point the exuberant spirits and effervescent brilliancy of that manly, genial, vital character. On this tradition Dr. Johnson sensibly remarks:

"*Mercutio's* wit, gayety, and courage will always procure for him friends that wish him a longer life; but his death is not precipitated; he has lived out the time allotted him in the construction of the play, nor do I doubt the ability of Shakespeare to have continued his existence."

There is no record of the first performer of *Mercutio*. The most dazzling personation of the part given on the early English Stage was that of Henry Woodward (1749), whose acting furnished a model for his successors. The memory of it long survived, and all the references made to it, in the old records, are warmly commendatory. Woodward's temperament singularly commingled gravity and gayety; his action was carelessly graceful, his person elegant. He possessed a fine voice, and his handsome face and vivacious demeanor enticed interest and prompted hilarity. He was the ideal comrade as *Mercutio,* and he lives in the dramatic chronicle as one of the most sympathetic and winning of actors. Notable embodiments of *Mercutio*, on the British Stage, subsequent to that of Woodward, were those of John Palmer, 1760; David Garrick, 1761; James William Dodd, 1768; William T. Lewis, 1777; John Bannister, 1796; Robert William Elliston, 1805; Frederick Edward Jones, 1809; Charles Kean, 1828; Charles Kemble, 1829; George Vandenhoff, 1843; Samuel Phelps, 1846; Walter Lacy, 1852; Frederick Augustus Everill, 1860; Johnston Forbes-Robertson, 1874; Charles Harcourt, 1878; William Terriss, 1882; and Charles F. Coghlan, 1897.

Palmer, uneducated, often careless and incorrect, was nevertheless held in high esteem as a comedian of versatile talent and broad range. He played *Touchstone* and *Dick Dowlas, Young Wilding,* and *Sir Toby Belch,* and he was the original *Joseph Surface.* I have not found particular account of his *Mercutio,* but I believe it fair to infer, from what is recorded of his acting in general, that it was robust in personality, gallant in bearing, rich in humor, and cordial in comradeship. Lewis, affable, kindly, and winning, revelled in the frolic of the part. Bannister's *Mercutio,* according to Leigh Hunt, was "not gay but jolly," exhibiting "not the elegant vivacity of the gentleman, but the boisterous mirth of the honest fellow,"—a distinction more nice than rational, relative to this character: even a gentleman can sometimes be exuberant in geniality and humor. Bannister was manly, genial, pathetic, and essentially natural. Garrick acted *Mercutio,* for the first time, April 6, 1761, at Drury Lane, and twice repeated the performance, in that season. His encomiasts only mention it, but it cannot be supposed that an actor of his consummate skill, both in tragedy and comedy, did not act it well. Dodd, superlative in beaus and coxcombs, is merely named as *Mercutio.* His style was nice, neat, exquisite, and it is not likely that he excelled in a part requiring sturdy vigor and sustained brilliancy. Boaden says of Dodd that "he was the paragon representative of all fatuity." Elliston's performance was exuberant with gay spirits, audacity of demeanor, sprightly speech, and vigorous action, but of that fine fibre of genius, that innate superiority of "one whom God hath made himself to mar" (so *Romeo* designates his friend), there was probably not even a suggestion. Jones made no special impression in the part. Charles Kean's humor was grim and caustic. Vandenhoff,—whom I had the good fortune to see in that part and many others,—was refined, elegant, spirited, and, in the Duel and Dying Scene, at first impetuous, then forlornly humorous, and touchingly pathetic. Lacy was a

ROMEO AND JULIET

showy, over-demonstrative actor, who excelled as *Goldfinch,* in "The Road to Ruin," not in *Mercutio.* Phelps, who discarded *Romeo* in 1843, retained *Mercutio* in his repertory as late as 1859, when he was fifty-five years old, and his acting of it was said to have been equal to that of Charles Kemble. Everill (1829-1900), one of the most accomplished all-round actors I have ever seen, acted *Mercutio,* in the course of his long association with the Theatre Royal, Manchester. Whether in grave mood or gay, his personality was winning. He was of a fine figure, his countenance was brightly expressive, his voice musical, his temperament one of much sensibility, his humor delicate, and his style marked by authority, distinction, and refinement. His performance of *Mercutio* must have been worthy to rank with the best that have been given. It was in Calvert's Manchester theatre also that the part was played by Forbes-Robertson.

On the American Stage *Mercutio* has been assumed by many players of distinction, among them being John Singleton, 1754; David Douglass, 1762; Lewis Hallam, 1796; John Bernard, 1797; Joseph Jefferson (the first of that name), 1810 (?); Edward Simpson, 1832; Lester Wallack, 1848; Charles Walter Couldock, 1850, and Edwin Adams, 1850. About sixty years ago, at the old Boston Museum, I saw with youthful delight the *Mercutio* of William Henry Smith (Sedley), and then and there obtained my first and lasting impression of the character as shown in action,—a character to be loved as well as admired,—which so delighted me that I adopted *Mercutio* as a pen-name, and for several years wrote theatrical commentary with that signature. Other esteemed actors of *Mercutio,* on our Stage, were Henry P. Grattan, William Wheatley, Charles Fisher, and the younger James William Wallack; but the best of them, within my remembrance, was Edward Loomis Davenport. That exceptionally versatile actor possessed exactly the affluent spirit, joyous, careless, breezy humor, generous, cheery mind, and kind heart which are *Mercutio's* attributes. His speaking of the Dream Speech was deliciously fluent and natural, and he was the incarnation of exultant audacity and freedom when he said:

"Men's eyes were made to look, and let them gaze;
I will not budge for no man's pleasure, I!"

FEMALE PLAYERS OF *ROMEO.*—ENGLISH STAGE.

The records of the old English Stage do not mention many women as performers of *Romeo.* Ellen Tree, who played the part in the autumn of 1829, at Covent Garden, in association with Fanny Kemble as

Juliet, seems to have made an exceptionally pleasing impression. The latter actress, in her "Records of a Girlhood," thus refers to this occurrence: "The only occasion on which I ever acted *Juliet* to a *Romeo* who looked the part was one when Miss Ellen Tree sustained it. . . . She looked beautiful and not unmanly; she was broad-shouldered as well as tall, and her long limbs had the fine proportions of the huntress Diana. . . . She fenced very well, and acquitted herself quite manfully in her duel with *Tybalt.*" Miss Kemble also relates that Miss Tree, as *Romeo,* wished to do, in the Tomb Scene, the stage business which Garrick had introduced and which had long been customary,—that of lifting *Juliet* from the bier and rushing with her down to the footlights: "This feat Miss Tree insisted upon attempting with me, and I as stoutly resisted all her entreaties to let her do so. . . . I said, at last, 'If you attempt to lift or carry me down the stage, I shall kick and scream till you set me down.'" The exploit, accordingly, was not attempted: Fanny probably feared a fall,—she was a heavy woman, though not large: why the fair Ellen should have wished to make use of such a piece of business is inexplicable. Garrick, of course, had a good reason for its introduction: in his day the lighting of the stage was bad, and he carried *Juliet* forward so as to act the last scene with her "in the focus," where they could be distinctly seen.

A representation of "Romeo and Juliet" which must have been interesting was given, in London, at the Marylebone Theatre, in the autumn of 1849, when Anna Cora Mowatt (1819-1870), called "the American Lily," was acting there. *Juliet* was played by Mrs. Mowatt, *Mercutio* by Davenport, and *Romeo* by Fanny Vining. Mrs. Mowatt long afterward wrote: "Miss Fanny Vining gave a fervid impersonation of the impassioned *Romeo;* nor did her sex destroy the illusion. I never knew the tragedy so popular with the public, and never had a *Romeo* whom I liked so well." As Mrs. E. L. Davenport that actress was long and deservedly popular on the American Stage, to which she came in 1855. One of Charlotte Cushman's presentments of *Romeo* was made, in London, at the Haymarket Theatre, April 23, 1854, in observance of Shakespeare's birthday,—*Juliet* being then acted by Ada Swanborough. Another English female *Romeo* was Margaret Leighton, who played the part in 1874, at Manchester. Esme Beringer appeared in London as *Romeo,* in 1896, and by some judges,— notably by the late Clement Scott,—was pronounced excellent. Mr. Scott wrote: "It was not a woman at all; it was a boy. . . . A more ideal *Romeo* has seldom been seen."

ROMEO AND JULIET

FEMALE PLAYERS OF *ROMEO*.—AMERICAN STAGE.

Among the female players who, on the American Stage, have appeared as *Romeo* were Mrs. Barry, 1827; Mrs. Barnes, 1833; Mrs. Lewis, 1836; Charlotte Cushman, 1837; Mrs. Shaw, 1840; Mrs. Wallack, 1842; Clara Ellis, 1846; Mrs. Hunt, 1847; Fanny Wallack, 1851; Susan Denin, 1854; Mrs. W. G. Jones, 1855; Mrs. Coleman Pope, 1857; Mme. Ponisi, 1857; and Mrs. Conway, 1859. In description of their performances the chronicles of our Theatre are comparatively barren. Mrs. Barry's *Romeo* seems to have been merely mechanical and to have made no impression. She was the first wife of Thomas Barry (1798-1876), long the much respected manager of the Boston Theatre. She came, with her husband, from England, and appeared in New York at the old Park Theatre, of which, at one time, he was stage-manager. Mrs. Barnes (Mary Greenhill, 1780-1864, wife of a favorite comedian of the time, John Barnes, 1781-1841) was a beautiful woman, and her acting, whether in tragedy or comedy, was greatly admired. She played *Romeo,* at the Richmond Hill Theatre, to the *Juliet* of Alexina Fisher (1822-1887), then a mere girl, but deemed to be a prodigy of talent. Mrs. Lewis, wife of Henry Lewis, low comedian, with whom she came from the London

Stage to the old Park Theatre, in 1835, was noted for a handsome person and uncommon versatility of dramatic talent. She acted several male characters of the highest order,—*Othello, Shylock, Richard the Third,* and *Virginius.* Her *Romeo* appears to have been one of the most creditable of the various attempts in that part. The fame of Charlotte Cushman as *Romeo* still glows in various printed pages of tribute, and doubtless her acting of the part was remarkable for tragic intensity.

Mrs. Shaw (1804(?)-1873), who became Mrs. Hamblin, fourth and last wife of the much-married T. S. Hamblin, was, if contemporary encomium can be fully trusted (often it cannot), another Mrs. Oldfield, possessing the "ravishing perfection" ascribed by Fielding to that renowned actress. Mrs. Shaw was accounted perfect alike in *Beatrice* and *Rosalind,* and beyond all female rivalry in *Hamlet* and *Romeo.* Mrs. Jones, efficient in all kinds of parts, a favorite at the old Bowery Theatre as long ago as 1850, and within comparatively recent years rightly esteemed one of the best "old women" on the stage, acted *Romeo,* about 1855, with Mrs. Farren as *Juliet,*—the latter an actress whom I recall as charming in many youthful heroines, at the old Boston Museum, about sixty years ago. Mrs. Wallack, wife of J. W. Wallack, the Younger, a tall, stately, commanding woman, eminently capable in tragedy, first played *Romeo* in 1851, appearing at the Marylebone Theatre, London, with Mrs. Arthur Stirling as *Juliet;* later, in Philadelphia, she repeated the performance, to the *Juliet* of Melinda Jones. Clara Ellis, who came from London, was for a short time employed at the Park Theatre, where she made her first appearance, September 2, 1844, as *Desdemona*, to the *Othello* of James R. Anderson. She is described as uncommonly tall and not graceful,—an intelligent, useful actress, but nothing more. The *Juliet* with whom she played *Romeo* was Mrs. Crisp, —wife of the Irish comedian William Henry Crisp,— an actress better suited to comedy than to tragedy. There is no account of Miss Ellis's *Romeo*. Mrs. Hunt (Louisa Lane, 1820-1897) became, in 1850, Mrs. John Drew, Sr., and under that name she is remembered as the wonderful *Mrs. Malaprop* of Joseph Jefferson's "star company." Her performance of *Romeo* was given, January 26, 1847, at the old Park Theatre, with Ada Stetson as *Juliet*.

Fanny Wallack (1822-1856), daughter of Henry Wallack and cousin to Lester Wallack, was a beauty, and a fine actress, particularly in comedy. She played *Romeo,* with Mrs. Mowatt as *Juliet*. Fanny Wallack also acted *Juliet,* appearing at the Bowery Theatre, August 16, 1852, with Edward Eddy as

Romeo. Susan Denin, an actress of uncommon ability, acting at the Bowery Theatre, played *Romeo,* August 22, 1854, to the *Juliet* of Miss Woodward. The *Romeo* of Mrs. Coleman Pope attracted some favor when shown at the Academy of Music, January 16, 1857, in association with an attempt to play *Juliet* made by Mrs. Dennis McMahon, an amateur actress of social repute. Mme. Ponisi (Elizabeth Hansom, 1818-1899), an English actress, who came to America in 1850 and was long distinguished on our Stage, played *Romeo,* in 1851, at the old Broadway Theatre. Her range of characters extended from *Lady Teazle* to *Lady Macbeth.* She was a dark, handsome woman, and no doubt she looked well as *Romeo.* Mrs. Conway (Sarah E. Crocker, 1834-1875) was the wife of Frederick Bartlett Conway, an actor of much versatility and of humorously eccentric character, and was deservedly eminent in her profession. She played *Romeo,* April 23, 1859, at the Metropolitan Theatre, with Jean Davenport (Mrs. Lander) as *Juliet.* Both players were highly accomplished. Of the actresses of *Romeo* here noted, only three were of American birth,—Miss Cushman, Susan Denin, and Mrs. Conway.

ROMEO AND JULIET

CHARLOTTE CUSHMAN AS *ROMEO*.

Charlotte Cushman, who liked to represent male characters, early assumed the part of *Romeo,* and her performance elicited, in England, fervent admiration for which it is not easy to account. She acted the part for the first time on April 23, 1837, at the old National Theatre, New York. That theatre, built in 1834-'35, and at one time known as the Italian Opera House, was unlucky, almost from the beginning. It stood at the northwest corner of Leonard and Church streets. The Italian Opera failed in it. The management of it changed hands several times. It saw its best days when managed by the elder Wallack, who opened it in the autumn of 1837 and conducted it for two years. It was burnt down in 1839, and, having been rebuilt, was again burnt down, in 1841,—and it ceased to exist. James H. Hackett was manager of it in 1837, when Charlotte Cushman acted in it, and it was by way of observing Shakespeare's birthday that he brought her out as *Romeo.* She was then in her twenty-first year. The performance attracted no special attention, and it was not till after she had appeared in London and made a brilliant hit,—as *Bianca,* in "Fazio," February 14, 1845, at the Princess' Theatre,—that her *Romeo* became celebrated. One of her biographers, Emma

Stebbens, mentions that after the close of her first season in London, while residing in a cottage at Bayswater, in that capital, "she and her sister Susan studied 'Romeo and Juliet' together," and adds that "they afterward went for a few nights to Southampton, where they made their first essay in this performance." Later, continuing her narrative, she says that Miss Cushman began her second engagement in London,—this time at the Haymarket Theatre,—on December 30, 1845, "when the sisters made their first appearance together," in this tragedy: that statement, however, is true only as to London: they had, in fact, long before that time, played *Romeo and Juliet* together in America. The novelty of their presentment of the tragedy in the British capital was enhanced by the fact that they insisted, against opposition in the theatre, on having it acted "according to the original version of Shakespeare, instead of the ordinary acting play with which the company were familiar." Susan Cushman (18—-1859) was not then a novice. She made her first appearance on the stage at the old Park Theatre, New York, June 8, 1839, in association with her sister, acting the part of *Laura,* in "The Genoese," and subsequently they made tours and acted together in various plays. In 1848, on her marriage to Dr. James Sheridan Musprat, Susan Cushman retired from the Theatre.

ROMEO AND JULIET

She was a handsome woman, which Charlotte was not.

"Romeo and Juliet," as revived by the Cushman sisters at the Haymarket, was performed twenty-seven consecutive times, and subsequently Charlotte and Susan were exceedingly prosperous with it, in a long tour of the provincial cities of Great Britain. They presented the play according to the text of Shakespeare. The ardor of the commendation then lavished on the performance is signified by the following extracts from "The London Times," which recorded the performance as "one of her greatest successes," particularly noted, as pinnacles of its excellence, the "passionate breathings of love that rendered the interviews with *Juliet* so remarkable," the acting of the Balcony Scene, "an inspiration, an impetuous outpouring of devotion, here and there tempered by the opposite quality of shrinking reverence," "the indignation with which *Romeo* rushed on *Tybalt,* after the death of *Mercutio,*" "the grief in *Friar Lawrence's* cell, when *Romeo* set forth the sorrows of his banishment in tones of ever-increasing anguish, till at last it reached its culminating point, and he dashed himself on the ground with real despair" and "took the house by storm."

"The *Romeo* of Miss Cushman is far superior to any *Romeo* we have ever had. The distinction is not one of degree, it is one of kind. For a long time *Romeo* has been a convention. Miss Cushman's *Romeo* is a living, breathing, animated, ardent human being. The memory of play-goers will call up *Romeo* as a collection of speeches delivered with more or less eloquence, not as an individual. Miss Cushman has given the vivifying spark whereby the fragments are knit together and become an organized entirety."

The dramatist Sheridan Knowles, with the Gallic effervescence characteristic of him, wrote:

"I witnessed with astonishment the *Romeo* of Miss Cushman. . . . I was not prepared for such a triumph of pure genius. You recollect, perhaps, Kean's Third Act of *Othello*. Did you ever expect to see anything like it again? I never did, and yet I saw as great a thing in *Romeo's* scene with the *Friar*, after the sentence of banishment—quite as great! It was a scene of top-most passion; not simulated passion,—no such thing; real, palpably real: the geniune heart-storm was on,—on in its wildest fitfulness of fury: and I listened and gazed and held my breath, while my blood ran hot and cold. . . . There is no trick in Miss Cushman's performance: no thought, no interest, no feeling, seems to actuate her, except what might be looked for in *Romeo* himself, were *Romeo* reality."

There can be no doubt that Miss Cushman's impersonation of *Romeo* was pictorial, passionate, and, in the great tragic moments, powerful and effective: she was a masculine woman and a wonderful actress: but I entirely disbelieve that her performance deserved the praise that was lavished on it, in England. It elicited no such encomium in America; and if at any time she actually indulged in the "real, palpably real" passion discerned by the fervid Knowles she departed widely from her invariable custom as a dramatic artist during the quarter of a century and more that I saw and closely studied her acting,— for her control and direction of herself as a public performer were intellectual and complete. That veteran theatrical recorder the late Douglas Taylor (1830-1913) mentioned her *Romeo* as merely "acceptable." The accomplished actor George Vandenhoff, her sincere admirer and friend, who acted with her, and who was a judicious critic of acting, writing in his "Diary,"—"Leaves from an Actor's Note Book," 1860,—makes a reference to the performance which is no less instructive than interesting:

"*April, 1843.*—Passing through Philadelphia, played my second engagement, five nights, at the Walnut Street Theatre, and on one night for Marshall's (manager) benefit; on which occasion Charlotte Cushman played *Romeo*, for the first time, I believe [Error: she had acted the part six years earlier: see *ante*]. I was the *Mercutio*. I lent her a hat, cloak, and sword for the second dress, and believe I may take credit for having given her some useful hints for the killing of *Tybalt* and *Paris*, which she executes in such masculine and effective style—the only good points in this *hybrid* performance of hers. She looks neither man nor woman in the part,—or both,—and her passion is equally epicene in form. Whatever her talent in other parts, I never yet heard any human being that had seen her *Romeo* who did not speak of it with a painful expression of countenance, "more in sorrow than in anger." *Romeo* requires a man, to feel his passion and to express his despair. A woman, in attempting it, unsexes herself, to no purpose except to destroy all interest in the play and all sympathy for the ill-fated pair."

John Coleman (1832-1904), who knew her well, often saw her, and acted in this tragedy with her, wrote, 1903:

"Curiosity and Miss Cushman's fine form attracted attention to her *Romeo*, but it was by no means the abnormal performance described by Mr. Sheridan Knowles and other indiscreet adulators; it was simply the effort of a monstrously clever woman,—but it was not *Romeo*. Certain passages were powerful and passionate—notably the death of *Tybalt*, a dexterous and splendid *coup de théâtre*. Then her Banishment Scene 'struck fiery off indeed' through the feebleness of her sister's attempt in the previous scene. This lady's *Juliet* was about as puerile an effort as I have ever seen. Its most conspicuous feature was its costume and its corsetage, both of which were notably mediæval and appropriate, and at a time when shoulder-of-mutton sleeves, *décolleté* necks, short waists, and huge bunchy petticoats were *à la mode*, singularly novel and becoming."

When Miss Cushman acted at the old National Theatre as *Romeo,* the *Juliet* was the beautiful Mrs. Flynn (Matilda Twibill, 1814-1851), and the *Mercutio* was J. W. Wallack, the Younger. On May 13, 1850, at the Astor Place Opera House, Miss Cush-

From an Old Print   *Author's Collection*

CHARLOTTE CUSHMAN AS *ROMEO*: SUSAN CUSHMAN AS *JULIET*

"I must be gone and live, or stay and die."

ACT III., Sc. 5

man, as *Romeo,* was associated with Fanny Kemble, as *Juliet,* and that sterling actor Charles Walter Couldock, as *Mercutio.* At Niblo's Garden, June 22, 1858, she acted *Romeo,* to the *Juliet* of the lovely Mary Devlin (1840-1863), first wife of Edwin Booth (to whom she was married in 1860). Miss Cushman again acted *Romeo,* in the autumn of 1860, at the Winter Garden Theatre, Mrs. D. P. Bowers (1830-1895) being the *Juliet.* Mrs. Bowers (Elizabeth Crocker) was highly and worthily distinguished in her day, and by persons who recall what her acting was, at its best, she is remembered as indeed a great actress. Miss Cushman's male characters, it is of interest to observe, were,—besides *Romeo,*—*Hamlet, Cardinal Wolsey, Claude Melnotte, Montaldo,* in the tragedy of "The Genoese," by Epes Sargent; *Patrick,* in John O'Keefe's farce of "The Poor Soldier," originally called "The Shamrock"; *Count Bellino,* in Henry R. Bishop's "The Devil's Bridge"; *Gossamer Gadfly* and *Edwin Vere Gadfly,* the twins, in the farce of "The Brothers," and *Paul,* in John Baldwin Buckstone's "The Pet of the Petticoats." She also assumed several male characters in Opera. Her complete repertory comprised 311 parts.

THE CONSUMMATE TRAGEDY OF LOVE.

Among the many qualities which have insured immortality to the works of Shakespeare no one is more conspicuous than the *actuality* of his characters. Notwithstanding remoteness of time and place, antique garb, idealized condition, and versified and therefore artificial form of speech, those characters are, for the reader or spectator who truly knows them, as real as actual acquaintances, and the sympathies and antipathies which they excite are as intense as those resultant from contact with living persons. Nowhere is that fact more strikingly exemplified than in the tragedy of "Romeo and Juliet." It is not true that "all the world loves a lover"; many a lover, whether male or female, in life or on the stage, is tedious to intelligent observation: but to all persons capable of understanding the passion of youthful love the tragedy of "Romeo and Juliet" comes home with an afflicting sense of present actuality. It is not difficult to discern the cause of that effect. Morning and midnight touch their lips in this truthful, pathetic play. No one who has had youth can think of it without remembering a sacred time when the flowers were sweeter than now and the winds were softer, and in the hush of the night there was a celestial mystery, and the stars seemed friends, and the affairs of other human beings were remote and trivial. Then one pair of eyes was worshipped, and one voice was all there is of music, and life was exalted into sanctity. That time can never be called back. In the turmoil of practical worldly affairs memory can scarcely realize that it ever existed. But Shakespeare knew it, and he could surcharge his mind with its spirit, and he has poured that spirit through the current of his exquisite poem of love, disappointment, and hopeless grief. Sometimes, whether in reading those scenes or in viewing them, the world-worn dreamer feels a sudden throb of pain and seems to hear, as if in his heart, a distant, mournful voice speaking words of a half-forgotten language. Not to all persons comes that subtle message; but the nature is not to be envied which, under the stress of this tragedy, is not made more sympathetic with the terrible earnestness of true love, more tender toward youth, more wishful to sweeten and prolong its period of romance, and to shield it from contact with the dreary selfishness and commonplace of the world; nor is that nature enviable which is not touched by the awful closing picture of love's calamity and ruin. Never were passion, anguish, and death so enshrined as under the starless sky that bends over the broken tomb of the *Capulets,* while the cold night wind moans around it, and dark branches wave above the white, still faces of those true lovers who have died for love. Never was there a sadder spectacle, yet never did a spectacle so sad present at last a sense of relief so sweet, so absolute, so holy. I know not how many times I have witnessed that tragedy, nor how often I have mused over it in the printed page; but for me the feeling most often inspired by it is the feeling so beautifully expressed by the sad words of Swinburne, hopeless, yet full of comfort:

> "From too much love of living,
> From hope and fear set free,
> We thank with brief thanksgiving
> Whatever gods there be
> That no life lives forever;
> That dead men rise up never;
> That even the weariest river
> Winds somewhere safe to sea!"

III.

AS YOU LIKE IT.

> *"When as I talk of Rosalind*
> *The god from coyness waxeth kind,*
> *And seems in self-same frame to fly,*
> *Because he loves as well as I."*
> —Thomas Lodge.

IN THE FOREST OF ARDEN.

In Shakespeare's youthful days the Forest of Arden was close at his hand, and no doubt he often wandered in it and knew it well. It covered a large tract of country in Warwickshire, extending from the west bank of the Avon six or eight miles northwest to Stratford, and while that region is cleared now, beautifully cultivated, sprinkled with trim villages and lovely manors, and diversified with many appellations, the general name of Arden cleaves to it still. Many of its great trees, indeed, sturdy and splendid at a vast age, remain in flourishing luxuriance, to indicate what it was; and if you stand upon the hill near Beaudesert Church,—where once the banners of Peter de Montfort floated from his battlements,—and gaze over the adjacent plains, your eyes will rest upon one of the sweetest landscapes in all the delicious realm that environs the heart of England. It is idle to suppose that Shakespeare was unacquainted with that old woodland and the storied places round about it—with Wroxall Abbey, and the moated grange of Baddesley Clinton, and all the historic spots associated with the wars of King Henry the Third, the dark fate of handsome Sir Piers Gaveston, Earl of Cornwall, and the romantic traditions of the great house of Warwick. From his boyhood this region must have been his field of exploration and adventure and must have been haunted for him with stately shapes and glorious visions. His mother's name was Mary Arden; and we may reasonably be sure that with her name, to him beautiful and sacred, he always associated the freedom and the splendor of that romantic forest. When therefore we read his exquisite comedy of "As You Like It," and observe, as we cannot help observing, that every flower that blooms, every leaf that trembles, and every breeze that murmurs in it is redolent of his native Warwickshire, we are naturally disinclined to surround a purely ideal and fanciful conception with the accessories of literal France, or to endure an iron-bound conventionality of treatment in the illustration of it.

TRUE SCENE OF THE ACTION.

There are a few French names in the comedy, and in its first scene *Oliver* designates *Orlando* as "the stubbornest young fellow of France"; but later we meet with the serpent and the lioness, indigenous to the jungles of Africa and Asia, and as inappropriate to France as to England. The story upon which, to a considerable extent, the play was founded,—Thomas Lodge's novel of "Rosalynd,"—is French in its location and its persons, but Shakespeare, in his use of that novel, has played havoc equally with the geography and the nomenclature. His scene is anywhere—and nowhere; but if in this play the wings of his imagination do brush against the solid ground at all it is against that haunted woodland of Arden which waved its sweet green boughs around his English home. "As You Like It" is an English pastoral comedy, through and through, and therefore it should be dressed in English pastoral robes,—with such genial though discreet license as poetic fancy might prompt and approve,—and it should be acted under such greenwood trees as bloom in the vale of the Red Horse, where Shakespeare lived and loved. Planché will have it,—since Shakespeare has introduced possibly French dukes into his play, whereas in the novel those potentates are French kings,—

that the action must be supposed to occur in France, and to occur at a time when yet independent duchies existed in that country; and that time he declares must not be later than the reign of King Louis the Twelfth (1498-1515), who married Anne of Brittany and so incorporated into the royal dominions the last existing fief to the crown. It must be a French garb of the preceding reign, says that learned antiquarian and rose of heraldry,—the reign of King Charles the Eighth (1470-1498); and that will be picturesque and appropriate. In that way at once this lawless, lilting, drifting fiction is brought within the precise lines of fact and duly provided with a local habitation. A distinct purpose and a definite plan, of course, there must be, when a play is to be acted: only it should be allowed that in dealing with this exceptionally vagrant fabric the imagination ought to be permitted to have a free rein. "As You Like It" is a comedy which in a peculiar and unusual degree requires imagination; and not only in those who present it but in those who see it performed.

SPIRIT OF THE PLAY.

The composition of this comedy occurred at a specially interesting period of Shakespeare's life. He was in his thirty-fifth year. He had written all but one ("King Henry VIII.") of his English historical plays; he had written eight out of his fourteen comedies; he had written "Romeo and Juliet"; while his great tragedies of "Hamlet" and "Julius Cæsar" were close at hand and must have been much in his thoughts: the first draft of "Hamlet," indeed, may have been written long before his thirty-fifth year. Imagination had obtained full possession of him by this time, and he was looking at life with a comprehensive vision and writing about it with an imperial affluence of freedom, feeling, and power. No work of art was ever yet created by anybody without labor, but the proportion of effort differs in different cases, and surely no quality is more conspicuous in "As You Like It" than that of spontaneity. The piece is exceptional for its graceful fluency. It must have been written easily, in a happy, dream-like, careless mood, half revery and half frolic. There is much wise philosophy in it, veiled with playfulness; there is much in it of the poetry which with Shakespeare was incidental and natural; and here and there it is lightly touched with the pensive melancholy of a mind that has become somewhat disenchanted with the world: but its predominant tone is sprightly, and we may be sure that Shakespeare was at ease in its creation, and we can discern in it much of his temperament and perhaps of his habitual mental attitude,—which, apparently, was that of benign, humorous, half-pitying, half-playful tolerance toward human nature and human life. He seems to have thrown aside all restraint when writing this play and to have allowed his fancies to take care of themselves. The persons who figure in "As You Like It" are, in some measure, shadowy. They are at once real and unreal. They lay hold of experience, but their grasp is frail. The loves of *Orlando* and *Rosalind* are not the loves of *Romeo* and *Juliet*. The musings of *Jaques* are not the corrosive reflections of *Hamlet*. The waggish drollery of *Touchstone* is not the pathetic levity of the *Fool* in "King Lear." The drift, the substance, the significance is "as you like it,"—as you may please to find it; grave or gay, according to the eyes with which you look and the heart with which you feel. Those persons, entangled with incidents that are mostly impossible, drift under green leaves, amid the mossy trunks of slumberous trees, in dells that are musical with bird-songs and running water and resonant with the echoes of the huntsman's horn; and while the fragrant wind blows on their faces and the wild deer dash away at their approach they play their parts in a sweetly fantastic story of fortune's vicissitudes and love's delays such as never could literally have happened in the actual world, but which the great poet, in his own wonderful way, has made tributary to an exposition of the strongest contrasts that the vicissitudes of human life can afford. There is one obvious lesson to be deduced from this understanding of the subject: the reader or the spectator who would fully enjoy "As You Like It" must accept it in the mood in which it was conceived. He knows that lions do not range in French or English forests, and that *Rosalind,* though in man's apparel, would at once be recognized by the eyes of love. Yet to those and to all discrepancies he is, and must be, blind. He even can assent to the spectacle of *Jaques* stretched beside the brawling stream at the foot of the antique oak, speaking his sermons upon human weakness, folly, and injustice, with nobody for an audience. He feels himself set free from the world of hard facts. He is in Arden,—and the less fool he!

DATE OF COMPOSITION, AND SOURCE OF THE PLOT.

"As You Like It" is not mentioned by Meres, whose book, "Palladis Tamia," 1598, names twelve of Shakespeare's plays as then existent, and in Act III., sc. 5, of the comedy a line is quoted from Marlowe's poem of "Hero and Leander,"—"Whoever lov'd that lov'd not at first sight?"—also first published in that year. The inference is warranted that this play was not composed earlier than 1598. The date of its composition has been variously set, all the way from 1598 to 1607, but it has not been positively determined. An entry in the Stationers' Register, August 4 (presumably 1600), names the comedy, with the memorandum "to be stayed,"—that is, not to be published without further and satisfactory authority. It was first printed in the Folio of 1623. Minor variations of the First Folio text of it appear in that of the Second Folio, 1632, but, essentially, the two texts are in agreement. Richard Grant White remarks, as to the text of "As You Like It," that "few of its corruptions are due to any other cause than the lack of proof-reading." Some of those corruptions, however, are flagrant and clearly perceptible,—for example, that in the speech which makes *Rosalind* declare that some of her solicitude is "for my child's father," when, obviously, the text should be "my father's child," that is, herself. White, at first, approved the old, wrong reading, but ultimately he reversed his judgment and corrected his error. Upon the whole the text of the comedy, as it stands in the Folio, is a pure one.

The antiquated metrical story, Coke's "Tale of Gamelyn," which antedates Chaucer, was the precursor of Lodge's novel of "Rosalynd, or Euphues' Golden Legacye," published in 1590, and that novel, by one of Shakespeare's contemporaries, was in turn the precursor of "As You Like It." Shakespeare followed the novel in his use of incidents and conduct of plot, but he has transfigured it by his investiture of the characters with new and often exalted personality and by his poetical expression and embellishment of them. He furthermore invented and introduced *Jaques, Touchstone, Audrey,* and *Martext.* The Epilogue is considered to be spurious, at least in part. It shows itself to have been designed with a view to its being spoken by the boy or man who, in Shakespeare's time, and later, played *Rosalind,*—for the speaker of it is made to say, "If I were *a woman,* I would kiss as many of you as had beards that pleased me," etc. It is a feeble composition, by whomsoever it was written. For use on the modern stage the language of it is slightly altered. W. W. Lloyd surmised that there *may* have existed an earlier play, based on the novel of "Rosalynd," and Furness seems inclined to adopt that view; but there is no known reason for its acceptance.

SHAKESPEARE'S MOOD AND INSPIRATION.

It has often been urged that the necessity of providing occupation for a dramatic company and of furnishing a novelty to win the public attention and support is a sufficient motive, or impulse, or inspiration for the making of a good play, and the believers in that doctrine usually cite the example of Shakespeare to substantiate it—an example by which their theory is not in the least supported. Shakespeare was an actor and a theatrical manager as well as a dramatist, and he wrote and worked, as other men do, for a subsistence. No person acquainted with the subject doubts or disputes those facts. There is not anything derogatory to genius, poetic or other, in its possessor's endeavor to profit and live by the use of it. "The laborer is worthy of his hire,"—just as much if he works with a pen as though he worked instead with a pick. But merely professional necessity or the desire of gain does not, never did, and never will inspire any artist to "fine issues." Shakespeare was a poet, and it is beyond rational dispute that his mind, however practically thrifty it may have been in some moods, operated, in its artistic expression, from a far grander inherent propensity, a far nobler impulse, a far loftier intellectual purpose than that which actuates mere commercial enterprise. Shakespeare's greater plays tax to the utmost limit the best powers of the best actors, and, generally, they contain more material, and that of a higher order, than the average public has ever comprehended or ever will comprehend. If indeed Shakespeare wrote his plays simply to fit the company engaged at the Globe Theatre and the Blackfriars,—in both of which he owned an interest and at both of which the same company performed,—or if he wrote them simply to please the passing caprice of the time, he must have had a marvellous dramatic company in his view, and he must have been aware of a still more marvellous community to be addressed. Either this or, for commercial purposes, assuredly he made needless exertions, since he has over-freighted his text with every sort of mental and spiritual wealth and beauty.

The affluence of mentality in the comedy of "As You Like It,"—consisting in the quaint whimsicality of its humor, the complex quality of its chief characters, the airy, delicate, evanescent poetry of its atmosphere, the sequestration of its scene, and the fantastic caprice and indolent drift of its incidents,—has always rendered it a difficult play for actors to treat in a perfectly adequate, complete manner, has always kept it rather remote from general appreciation, and has made it a cause of some perplexity to the critical mind. The truth is that Shakespeare, out of the necessities of his nature, and not merely out of those of worldly circumstance, while laboring for the Stage, wrote for a larger theatre than ever was comprised within four walls, and in accordance,—whether consciously or not,—with higher laws of expression than those that govern a theatrical manager, in the matter of demand and supply, in dealing with the public. He was not a photographer; he was an artist. He did not merely copy life; he transfigured it and idealized it. The great creations of his dramatic genius are not actual men and women of the every-day world; they are representative types of human nature, and there is always a deeper meaning in them than the obvious one that appears upon the surface. For this reason they inspire incessant interest, and hence it is that the field of Shakespearean study can never be exhausted.

In "As You Like It" Shakespeare's mood, while happy and frolicsome, is also whimsical, satirical, full of banter, covertly wise but outwardly fantastic. He fools you to the top of your bent. He is willing that you should take the play in earnest if you like to do so, but all the while he smiles at your credulity. He will end it rationally, in the matter of doing "poetic justice"; but in the meanwhile he has turned everything upside down and he is making merry over the spectacle. Such incidents as the radical conversion of the wicked *Duke* by the good hermit and the instantaneous regeneration of the malignant *Oliver* by his brother's single act of generosity are sufficiently typical of this poetic pleasantry. The most sonorous and apparently the most searching observations upon human experience are put into the mouth of *Jaques;* but *Jaques* is perhaps the least sane and substantial of the representative persons in the comedy,—being an epicurean in sentiment and a wayward cynic, whose remarks, although quite true as far as they go, and quaintly felicitous in manner, really contain no deep truth and no final wisdom, but are alike fragile and fantastic; as any one can see who will, for a test, set them beside either of the four great soliloquies in *Hamlet,* or beside the principal speeches of *Ulysses,* in "Troilus and Cressida." The wisest man in the play is the professed fool, *Touchstone,*—by whom and by the old servant *Adam* the only manifestations are made of the highest of human virtues, self-sacrifice: for even as *Adam* devotes all to *Orlando* so does *Touchstone* devote all to *Celia.* No special stress was laid on the lover. He is handsome, manly, ingenuous, and brave, and he serves his purpose; but it is evident that Shakespeare loved *Rosalind,* since in drawing her he ceases to jest. *Rosalind* is not merely the heroine of an impossible courtship in a visionary forest; she is the typical perfection of enchanting womanhood. She is everything that man loves in woman. She is neither an angel nor a fairy. She is flesh and blood; and while her mind and accomplishments are noble and her attributes of character poetical, she is depicted in absolute harmony with that significant line, wrapping truth with a jest, in Shakespeare's one hundred and thirtieth sonnet:

"My mistress, when she walks, treads on the ground."

Amid the sprightly caprice, the tantalizing banter, the drift and whirl of fantastic incidents, and the glancing lights of folly and wisdom which constitute this comedy the luxuriant, sumptuous, dazzling, entrancing figure of *Rosalind* stands out clear and firm in the warm light of its own surpassing loveliness: and this is the personality that has from time to time brought "As You Like It" upon the stage, and, temporarily at least, has kept it there.

EARLY PERFORMANCES.—SHAKESPEARE IN ECLIPSE.

Nothing is positively known as to the first production of "As You Like It," or as to presentments of it on the early English Stage. There is a tradition, first recorded by the biographer and antiquarian William Oldys (1687-1761), to the effect that Shakespeare's brother Gilbert,—born in 1566, and said to have been living as late as the reign of King Charles the Second, in which case he would have been at least ninety-four years old,—had been heard to declare, in his age, that when a young man he visited London and saw performances of his brother Wil-

AS YOU LIKE IT

liam's plays, and that he remembered having seen William acting a feeble old man,—presumably, *Adam,* in this comedy. The words of Oldys are:

"This opportunity of consulting the poet's brother made the actors greedily inquisitive into every little circumstance, more especially in Shakespeare's dramatic character, which his brother could relate of him. But he, it seems, was so stricken in years, and possibly his memory so weakened by infirmities (which might make him the easier pass for a man of weak intellects), that he could give them but little light into their inquiries; and all that could be recollected from him of his brother Will, in that station, was the faint, general, and almost lost idea he had of having seen him act a part in one of his own comedies, wherein, being to impersonate a decrepit old man, he wore a long beard and appeared to be so weak and drooping and unable to walk that he was forced to be supported and carried by another person to a table at which he was seated, among some company who were eating, and one of them sung a song."

The tradition is one of dubious authenticity, but if credited it would warrant belief that Shakespeare himself participated in the early representations of "As You Like It." Conjecture, furthermore, might assign the leading parts in the play to professional associates of his ("my fellowes," as he calls them, in his Will), whose lines of business are discernible in such authentic records as have survived of those theatrical times. But the process of conjecture, while tempting, is useless. There is a statement, of recent origin, that "As You Like It" was acted, by Shakespeare and his companions of the Globe company, before King James the First, and under the patronage of William Herbert, Earl of Pembroke, at Wilton House,—the beautiful country seat of the earls of Pembroke, in Wiltshire,—on December 2, 1603, but it lacks confirmation. King James and his court were at Wilton, for several weeks, toward the end of that year, while the plague was raging in London, and theatrical performances were given in His Majesty's presence: *some* play was acted before him on December 2, and, on the next day, the players were paid £30, "by way of His Majesty's reward"; but there is no definite record of a presentment of "As You Like It" at that time and place, or anywhere else, until about 140 years after the comedy was written and, presumably, first acted.

At the time of Shakespeare's death (1616) two movements had already begun which, gathering power and momentum as the years rolled on, have done much to shape the dubious, shifting, political condition of the world of to-day. One of these was a movement in favor of government by the many; the other was a movement against the Roman Catholic Church. Both prevailed in the establishment of the Commonwealth, and one of the first institutions that went down under them was the British Drama. Shakespeare was an exceedingly popular author during his lifetime, and his works must have been in request for a considerable time after his death, because the First Folio, 1623, was succeeded by another in 1632; but soon after that date theatres and plays began to drop out of the public view. The fecundity of play-writers between Shakespeare's theatrical advent, 1588, and the year 1640 must indeed have been abundant, since out of nearly or quite six hundred plays that were printed in England before the Restoration, only fifty-eight are believed to have existed before Shakespeare began to write. The others, therefore, must have been made during and after his immediate time. But the war between King Charles the First and his Parliament put an end to that dramatic epoch; and presently, when the Puritans prevailed, they authorized by law, 1647, the destruction of theatres and the public flagellation of actors. There is a great darkness over that period of theatrical history. Soon after the Restoration, indeed, the Third Folio of Shakespeare's works made its appearance (1663-1664), containing six if not seven plays that were spurious, and in 1685 came the Fourth Folio; yet all the while Shakespeare seems to have been banished from the stage, and in general from contemporary knowledge.

232 SHAKESPEARE ON THE STAGE

Dryden mangled his lovely comedy of "The Tempest" (1670) and his noble tragedy of "Antony and Cleopatra" (1678), and sapiently referred to his manner as "out of date." Not till the period of Queen Anne did the Shakespeare revival begin, and even then it was languid: but it began,—and little by little the plays of the great master made their way back to their rightful preëminence.

EIGHTEENTH CENTURY PRESENTMENTS.—FROM MRS. PRITCHARD TO MRS. SIDDONS.

After its career at the Globe Theatre (and whether that was long or short is unknown), "As You Like It" seems to have sunk into abeyance and to have remained for a long time unused. A worthless alteration of it, called "Love in a Forest," by Charles Johnson (1679-1748),—a lawyer, of the Middle Temple, mentioned by Pope, in a note to "The Dunciad," as "a martyr of obesity,"—was produced at Drury Lane, January 9, 1723, was acted six times, and in the same year was published. Colley Cibber appeared in it, as *Jaques,* Wilks as *Orlando,* and Mrs. Booth (Hester Santlow) as *Rosalind.* The part of *Touchstone* was omitted, together with several other parts, and Shakespeare's text of "As You Like It" was interspersed with extracts from some of his other

AS YOU LIKE IT

plays. Downes, in his little but exceedingly valuable book, the "Roscius Anglicanus," which, in a cursory manner, tells the story of the English Stage from about 1660 to about 1706, makes no mention of this comedy. It may have been revived after the Restoration, but there is no record of it in that period, and the learned and careful Genest is of opinion that Shakespeare's play, in its original form, was not acted in England, at any time after King Charles the Second came to the throne, till December 20, 1740. On that date, however, it was acted at Drury Lane, with a cast of exceptional strength, Mrs. Pritchard being the *Rosalind,* Mrs. Clive the *Celia,* Mrs. Egerton the *Audrey,* Quin the *Jaques,* Thomas Chapman the *Touchstone,* William Milward the *Orlando,* Mills the *Banished Duke,* and Edward Berry the *Adam.* It was repeated about twenty-five times before the close of that season, 1740-'41. It maintained itself in some degree of public favor, and on the London Stage, within the next sixty years, more than twenty special productions of it, with numerous repetitions, were accomplished: it has not, however, at any time been an exceptionally popular play, either in England or America.

Among the rivals or successors to Mrs. Pritchard as *Rosalind,* down to 1800, were Peg Woffington, 1741; Miss Macklin, 1754-'55; Mrs. Dancer (Mrs.

Barry, Mrs. Crawford), 1767; Mrs. Bulkley, 1771; Miss Younge (later Mrs. Pope), 1774; Mrs. Robinson, 1780; Miss Fordsham, 1783; Mrs. Siddons, 1785; Mrs. Wells, 1786; Mrs. Jordan, 1787; Mrs. Goodall, 1788; Miss Wallis, 1789; and Miss Biggs, 1799. Mrs. Woffington acted *Rosalind* for the first time, October 16, 1741, at Drury Lane,—Mrs. Clive appearing with her as *Celia,* Macklin as *Touchstone,* and Theophilus Cibber as *Jaques.* Her performance was brilliant and her success great. To the end of her career she was warmly admired in this part, and she appears to have been, with the possible exception of Mrs. Jordan, the best *Rosalind* of the eighteenth century. It was in that character she was last seen on the stage, May 3, 1757, at Covent Garden, when, while trying to speak the Epilogue, she suffered a nervous collapse and was carried from the scene: she never played again, although she somewhat improved in health, and lingered, at her home, in Teddington, for three years: this beautiful woman and wonderful actress died, in London,—at a house in Queen Square, Westminster, where she was temporarily lodging,—on March 13, 1760, of apoplexy, aged only thirty-nine. Mrs. Dancer (Mrs. Barry, Mrs. Crawford, to whom, because of her successive names, reference is likely to become confused) first played the part in London, October 22, 1767, the fine comedian

Thomas King, on that occasion, acting *Touchstone* for the first time. The *Orlando* was Palmer, the *Jaques* Love (James Dance), the *Celia* Mrs. Baddeley. By some critics Mrs. Dancer's *Rosalind* was considered better than that of either Mrs. Woffington or Mrs. Pritchard. The versatile ability of Mrs. Dancer was extraordinary. She is described as of fair complexion, having regular features and light, auburn hair, being a little above the middle size, well formed, graceful and spirited in manner, of great sensibility, and exceedingly attractive. She is accredited with having said, "I play Tragedy to please the public, Comedy to please myself." The veteran journalist, John Taylor (17—-1832), in his "Records of My Life," published in 1832-'33, mentions her several times, and enthusiastically declares:

"Mrs. Dancer's *Rosalind* was the most perfect representation of the character that I ever witnessed. It was tender, animated, and playful to the highest degree. She gave the 'Cuckoo Song' with admirable humor."

The "Cuckoo Song," "When daisies pied and violets blue," taken from "Love's Labor's Lost," of which comedy it is the conclusion, appears to have been first used in "As You Like It" in 1740 or 1747, when it was sung by Mrs. Clive, as *Celia:* thereafter it was frequently sung by the players either of *Celia* or *Rosa-*

lind. Mrs. Mattocks sang it, when acting *Celia,* in 1775, and Mrs. Wilson in 1789. One authority says that Mrs. Clive first sang it when acting *Rosalind,* but I believe there is no authentic record that she ever played the part. She could not have been Shakespeare's *Rosalind,* for the reason that her style, while exceedingly comic, was also exceedingly broad. Mrs. Clive was born in 1711, began acting in 1728, left the stage in 1769, and died in 1785. She was deemed by her contemporaries "a great comic genius." "I shall as soon expect," says Davies, "to see another Butler, Rabelais, or Swift, as a[nother] Clive." Dr. Johnson said that he had never seen Clive equalled for sprightliness of humor, and added, "she was a better romp than any I ever saw in nature." Mrs. Robinson ("Perdita") acted *Rosalind* in her last season on the stage, and was considered charming. The writings of that actress, verse and prose, indicate imagination and the capability of deep feeling. It is significant of her merit that she was admired by Coleridge, Wolcot, and Sir Joshua Reynolds, among many other persons of discernment and intellectual authority. Her *Rosalind* was less esteemed than her *Juliet.*

AS YOU LIKE IT

MRS. SIDDONS AND MRS. JORDAN.

Mrs. Siddons first acted *Rosalind* when she was about twenty-two years old (1777), at York. Her first performance of it in London occurred on April 30, 1785, at Drury Lane. Campbell says, "I somewhat grudgingly confess my belief that her performance of it [*Rosalind*], though not a failure, seems to have been equally short of a triumph." Anna Seward the poet,—so much esteemed and so well commemorated by Sir Walter Scott,—a clever woman, who ardently admired her, wrote that "though her smile is as enchanting as her frown is magnificent, as her tears are irresistible, yet the playful scintillations of colloquial wit, which most strongly mark that character [*Rosalind*], suit not the Siddonian form and countenance." It was as the *Princess* that Mrs. Siddons pleased,—as this same friendly observer remarked,—"when she resumed her original character, and exchanged comic spirit for dignified tenderness." Her close friend and chief biographer, Campbell, while claiming that "it appears she played the part admirably in some particulars," noted that *"Rosalind's* character has a gay and feathery lightness of spirits which one can easily imagine more difficult for Mrs. Siddons to assume than the tragic meekness of *Desdemona."* Charles Young, the actor, in a letter to

Campbell wrote: "Her *Rosalind* wanted neither playfulness nor feminine softness, but it was totally without archness,—not because she did not properly conceive it; but how could such a countenance be *arch?*" How, indeed! The judgment of Genest is explicit and explanatory:

"Mrs. Siddons contrived a dress for *Rosalind* which was neither male nor female. For this she was ridiculed in the papers, and very deservedly. She had it entirely at her option to act *Rosalind* or not to act *Rosalind;* but when she determined to act the part it was her duty to dress it properly. Mrs. Siddons did not add to her reputation by her performance of *Rosalind*, and when Mrs. Jordan had played the character few persons wished to see Mrs. Siddons in it."

Mrs. Abington, long afterward, in a conversation with the veteran Henry Crabb Robinson (June 16, 1811), mentioned that effort by the great tragic actress, saying: "Early in life Mrs. Siddons was anxious to succeed in comedy, and played *Rosalind* before I retired"; and Robinson ingenuously adds: "Mrs. Siddons she praised, though not with the warmth of a genuine admirer."

Mrs. Jordan first acted *Rosalind,* April 13, 1787, at Drury Lane. She was then in her twenty-fifth year, had been on the stage since girlhood, and had already delighted the London public with *Peggy*

Thrift, Hypolita,—a part of which she was very fond, —*Priscilla Tomboy,* and *Viola,* and, though at first not very warmly welcomed in the capital, had become exceedingly popular. Her success as *Rosalind* was immediate and brilliant. Judicious observers seem to have felt that the part had not been acted in such a winning manner since the days of the incomparable Woffington. "The elastic step, the artless action, the sincere laugh, and the juicy tones of her clear and melodious voice" (so the biographer and novelist John Galt, writing in 1831, named her salient charms) were all, we may be sure, delightful attributes of that performance. "Her *Rosalind,*" says Oxberry, "was exquisite." Mrs. Jordan herself seems to have taken a different view, since, long afterward, in the greenroom at Covent Garden, on a night when she was playing *Rosalind,* she said to John Taylor: "If the public had any taste, how could they bear me in the part which I play to-night, and which is far above my habits and pretensions!" Her disparagement of her *Rosalind* was probably honestly made, at the moment: I have known many actors speak in a similar way, at times, of their best performances: but there is no reason to believe it warranted. Hazlitt's testimony avers of Mrs. Jordan that

"Her face, her tones, her manner, were irresistible. Her smile had the effect of sunshine, and her laugh did one good to hear it. Her voice was eloquence itself: it seemed as if her heart was always at her mouth. She was all gayety, openness, and good nature. She rioted in her fine spirits, and gave more pleasure than any other actress, because she had the greatest spirit of enjoyment in herself."

Boaden, clinging to his idolatry of Mrs. Siddons, and, as it were, viewing Mrs. Jordan's *Rosalind* "with one auspicious and one dropping eye," says that "she somewhat divided the town, and the lovers of the sentimental and the humorous were arranged under the standards of Siddons and Jordan"; but ultimately he is constrained to reflect, since "the natural buoyancy of *Rosalind* is incessant and her wit inexhaustible," that, if Shakespeare were to decide, Mrs. Jordan would be preferred in the part; because, he concludes, that "beside the adaptation of her figure to the moonish youth, I can have no doubt that her peculiar *animal spirits* rendered her the truer *Rosalind*."

LATER REVIVALS.—BRITISH STAGE.

No fewer than sixty notable revivals of "As You Like It" were made on the British Stage in the nineteenth century. Among the many actresses who performed *Rosalind* were Miss Duncan, 1804; Miss

From an Old Print   *Author's Collection*

John Fawcett, the Younger (1769-1837), a versatile comedian, the original *Caleb Quotem* and *Dr. Pangloss,* rich in humor and a fine singer, was deemed nearly the equal of "Tom" King as *Touchstone.* This picture, while not indicative of the character, shows the Costume used in his time when playing the part.

Smith, 1805; Mrs. H. Johnson, 1810; Mrs. Egerton, 1811; Sally Booth, 1816; Mme. Vestris, 1825; Lydia Foote, 1830; Ellen Tree, 1833; Mrs. Yates, 1835; Helena Faucit, 1839; Mrs. Nisbett, 1842; Charlotte Cushman, 1845; Fanny Cooper (Mrs. T. H. Lacy), 1847; Isabella Glyn (Mrs. E. S. Dallas), 1848; Julia Bennett (Mrs. Jacob Barrow), 1850; Jean Davenport (Mrs. Lander), 1851; Mrs. J. W. Wallack, 1854; Mrs. Charles Young (Mrs. Herman Vezin), 1857; Amy Sedgwick (Mrs. Goostry), 1859; Alice Marriott (Mrs. Robert Edgar), 1861; Mary Provost (Mrs. Samuel Colville), 1861; Carlotta Leclercq, 1862; Mrs. Scott-Siddons, 1867; Mrs. Wybert Rousby, 1871; Mrs. Kendal, 1871; Adelaide Neilson, 1871; Ada Cavendish, 1878; Marie Litton, 1880; Miss Wallis, 1881; Mrs. Langtry, 1882; Eleanour Calhoun, 1882; Ada Rehan, 1890; Mrs. Patrick Campbell (Mrs. Cornwallis West), 1891; and Julia Neilson, 1896. Mary Anderson acted *Rosalind,* for the first time on any stage, August 29, 1885, producing the comedy in the Shakespeare Memorial Theatre, Stratford-upon-Avon, for the benefit of that institution. Ada Rehan, as *Rosalind,* with the coöperation of Augustin Daly's dramatic company, also acted at Stratford, for the benefit of the Memorial Theatre, August 26, 1897; arrangements had been made for a performance in the open air, on the lawn of the theatre grounds, beside the Avon, and it was there begun, but a heavy rain compelled players and auditors to take refuge in the theatre, and it was continued and finished on the stage. Comment on all the presentments of *Rosalind* thus made would be tedious and useless. Some of them were given by actresses better fitted for tragedy than comedy. Most of them followed the same general course, as to purpose of merriment and as to stage business. Those that judgment has pronounced representative are here duly considered.

Miss Duncan had founded her style on that of Eliza Farren, who called her, as a child actress, "the Little Wonder." She became distinguished, playing many parts of the first importance. Boaden said that, in some respects, she surpassed her model, having more force though less delicacy, a finer figure, but a less interesting personality. She excelled in singing and in dancing, as well as in acting. This actress made her first appearance, October 8, 1804, at Drury Lane, as *Lady Teazle*. About 1812 she became Mrs. Davison, and a few years later she retired from the stage. Miss Smith (1783-1850), who acted *Rosalind* in John Philip Kemble's revival of the comedy, at Covent Garden, in 1805, became, in 1814, Mrs. Bartley, and at that time was deemed a rival to Mrs. Siddons. The cast with which the comedy was pro-

duced was truly remarkable: *Jaques,* J. P. Kemble;
Orlando, Charles Kemble; *Touchstone,* Fawcett;
Adam, W. Murray; *Oliver,* Brunton; *William,*
Blanchard; *Audrey,* Mrs. Mattocks,—a comedian of
the first order, who, more than thirty years earlier,
1774, had acted *Rosalind* and won ample admiration.
Incledon, the superb singer,—of whom the reader is
told that, although he was ignorant of music, he never
was heard to sing out of tune,—participated, as
Amiens, and sang the songs which are so delightful
and so essential in this delicious play. The acting copy
then used was one that Kemble had made: he published
it in 1810. On November 22, that year, he again revived
"As You Like It," with the same cast as before,
except that Mrs. H. Johnson played *Rosalind.*
Kemble made stage versions of twenty-one of Shakespeare's plays, freely cutting the text and, in some
cases, introducing new names or characters. Garrick
had considerably altered some of those plays, but
Kemble, as an adapter, exercised a much greater
license. His version of "The Comedy of Errors" is
entitled, "Oh, It's Impossible." In his play-book of
"As You Like It" the speeches of the *First Lord,*
Act II., sc. 1, of the original, are given to *Jaques,*
and Kemble spoke them, whenever he played the
part,—of which he was accounted an excellent representative. His example, in the use of those speeches,

has been followed, and the custom of the modern stage has been to give them to *Jaques.*

Ellen Tree first acted *Rosalind,* November 2, 1833, at Drury Lane, London, and it was as *Rosalind* that she made her first appearance in America, at the old Park Theatre, New York, December 12, 1836, in her thirty-first year. Ireland, who saw all her performances at that time, declares that "in *Viola, Rosalind, Beatrice,* and *Portia* she was inimitably great." Buoyancy, vivacity, sweetness, and elegance are the qualities ascribed to her, as the representative of *Rosalind.* On the occasion of her first personation of the part in London Macready acted *Jaques,* J. Cooper *Orlando,* and Harley *Touchstone:* when she acted it, in a celebrated revival at the Haymarket, September 13, 1839, Phelps acted *Jaques,* Priscilla Horton,—afterward Mrs. German Reed,—was the *Celia,* Cooper again the *Orlando,* and *Touchstone* was assumed by Buckstone.

In characters which are essentially feminine,—that is to say, gentle, tender, sweet, and winning,—Ellen Tree was ardently and unreservedly admired, alike in America and England. George Vandenhoff wrote that "in a certain line of tragedy she displayed great concentration of passion, a subdued intensity, a suppressed fire, that seemed to burn her up and gnaw her heart"; but the consensus of contemporary critical opinion approved her comedy rather than her tragedy, and especially her gayety and her pathos. Her reading was admirable: she conveyed the full meaning of every word she spoke. Her laugh was musical and irresistibly stimulative of merriment. She could incarnate gayety. Those who heard her exclaim, as *Rosalind,* "Alas, the day! What shall I do with my doublet and hose?" were charmed by her artless confusion and natural loveliness. It is significant of her spirit and her style that, even in acting the satirical *Beatrice,* she suffused the performance with a winning, womanly charm. Her *Rosalind,* undoubtedly, was a beautiful impersonation. In witnessing (1865) her portrayal of *Mrs. Oakley,* I saw that, in comedy, she was a consummate artist.

Helena Faucit acted *Rosalind* for the first time on March 18, 1839, at Covent Garden, pleasing her audience but not her critics,—the latter expressing dissatisfaction because she had not made "the traditional points." The part was not attractive to her, at first, but she was obliged to play it, in deference to the command of Macready, who had selected it for her benefit performance. "In my first girlhood studies of Shakespeare,"—so she wrote,—"this play ["As You Like It"] had no share." In later years *Rosalind* became a special favorite with her; she often acted the part, and her personation of it was accepted and extolled as incomparable. In her book about

"Some of Shakespeare's Female Characters" there is a minute, discriminative, and sympathetic analysis of it. She retained the part in her repertory to the end of her professional career: her last performance of it in London was given, April 23, 1875, at Drury Lane, in aid of the fund for building the Shakespeare Memorial Theatre, at Stratford-upon-Avon. She participated in the ceremonies incident to the laying of the corner-stone of that edifice, April 23, 1877, and she acted, as *Beatrice,* in the dedicatory performance which occurred there, April 23, 1879. Her last appearance on the stage was made as *Rosalind,* when, on October 2, 1879, she emerged from retirement and acted at the Theatre Royal, Manchester, for the benefit of the widow and children of the lamented actor and manager, Charles Calvert.

Helena Faucit, the child of actors and early habituated to theatrical associations, was a woman of histrionic genius, personal beauty, and individual charm. Her range of parts was wide,—from *Lady Macbeth* to *Pauline,* in "The Lady of Lyons"; from *Antigone* to *Imogen,* from *Beatrice* to *Juliet,* and from *Queen Constance* to *Rosalind.* She was a woman of gentle mind, innate refinement, and considerable force of character. She possessed an almost febrile sensibility, and she somewhat lacked the poise and self-control which are imperatively necessary to a complete artist;

she, nevertheless, mistakenly prided herself on her capability of artistic finish. She expended much care and thought on the minutiæ of her stage business. She was prone to import into Shakespeare's plays subtle over-refinements of meaning which they do not contain, and which would be a defect if present, and she was one of the performers who, in semi-hysteric spectators, create emotional disturbance by "acting from the heart," that is, by surrender to "real feeling." She understood the character of *Rosalind*, and her performance of it was supremely good, —one reason being that, in acting *this* part, after she had fully developed her performance of it, she customarily and completely controlled her feelings and exactly accomplished a definite and right design. "No one can study this play," ["As You Like It"] she wrote, "without seeing that through the guise of the brilliant-witted boy Shakespeare meant the charm of the high-hearted woman, strong, tender, delicate, to make itself felt." That is exactly true, and the practical observance of that truth made her *Rosalind* a perfect performance. "I do not think I ever altered the main outlines of my first conception," she wrote, in another place.

The essential qualities of Miss Faucit's *Rosalind* were innate nobility, purity of mind, acute sensibility, a joyous temperament, sustained, consistent identification with the character, and womanly loveliness. At her best she pleased the most critical judgment and cast a spell over every order of mind. In Macready's eyes she was a perfect *Rosalind*. George Fletcher wrote that she infused "into the part of *Rosalind* all the tender, though lovely, grace which the poet has made its principal attribute and most exquisite attraction, breathing the soul of elegance, wit, and feeling through that noble forest pastoral." Another keen observer, Geraldine Endsor Jewsbury, the novelist, particularly commended Miss Faucit's manner of saying "I do take thee, Orlando, for my husband" as "exquisite," adding "and must have strangely puzzled any mortal *Orlando*." Henry Irving wrote (1879), "If Kean's interpretation of Shakespeare was like reading him by flashes of lightning, Mrs. Martin's reading is by the broad light of the sun. A more brilliant and exquisite conception of *Rosalind* never entered into the imagination of man." It is significant that these three eminently critical observers,—persons of widely different mind, experience, and taste,—all use the same word to signify their impressions of this performance,—"exquisite." Irving's commendation of Miss Faucit affords one more striking commentary on Ellen Terry's amiable intimation as to her great co-laborer in the dramatic art, that he never admired any actor but himself.

Miss Faucit richly deserved respect and admiration, but the encomium lavished upon her was at times extravagant. John Coleman, who, in youth, acted with her, provided the following tribute:

"In *Rosalind* she was Jove's own page. Beauty of face and form were combined with those rarer gifts,—beauty of mind and purity of soul, which make the owner omnipotent. 'More than common tall,' and perfectly balanced from head to heel, the short waist and long and superbly moulded lower limbs [why not legs?] which go with the Grecian type of beauty harmonized perfectly with the sloping and majestic shoulders, the virginal bust, and the arms lost to the Venus of Milo. Then her face was the face of Artemis herself, while her eyes of Aphrodisian gray varied in color and expression with every mood, as they glittered through their long, dark lashes. Her voice, with its infinite varieties of tremulous minors and full flushed, resonant crescendos, was 'an alarm to love'! I protest, the bare recollection makes music now in my memory!"

Thomas De Quincey wrote:

"He who has seen the Coliseum by moonlight, the Bay of Naples by sunset, the Battlefield of Waterloo by daybreak, and Helen Faucit in *Antigone*, has only to thank God and die, since nothing else remains worth living for!"

Macready, who evinced a strong partiality for this comedy, first acted in it, appearing as *Jaques*, January 11, 1820, at Covent Garden. He was then a member of the dramatic company under the direction of Henry Harris,—who, as active manager, had succeeded his father, the veteran Thomas Harris, in 1809. *Rosalind* was assumed by "a Young Lady," of whose acting there is no mention. In allusion to his part in this revival Macready wrote, in his "Diary": "*Jaques* is one of those real varieties of mind with which it is a pleasure, in representation, to identify one's self." Long afterward, when he had become manager of Drury Lane, he presented the comedy, in a magnificent manner, October 1, 1842. The scenery was painted by Stanfield. The cast was remarkably strong. J. R. Anderson was the *Orlando,* John Ryder the *Banished Duke,* Phelps the *Adam,* Robert Keeley the *Touchstone,* Mrs. Nisbett the *Rosalind,* Mrs. Sterling the *Celia.* Macready again acted *Jaques,* a character to which his peculiar style must have been singularly appropriate. The stage version of the play then employed was one that he had himself studiously and judiciously made. It was a happy device of his to introduce, in the pastoral scenes, the delicate tinkle of sheep-bells, heard from afar, as if a flock were somewhere straying and feeding, in pastures incident to the Forest of Arden. Phelps, in later years, told his friend and biographer, John Coleman, that this revival of the comedy by Macready was "the most superb production of 'As You Like It' the world has ever seen or ever will see"; and, speaking of Mrs. Nisbett, the veteran said:

"Not having seen her *ye* don't know what beauty is. Her voice was liquid music. Her laugh—there never was such a laugh! 'Her eyes, living crystals, lamps lit with light divine!' Her gorgeous neck and shoulders—her superbly symmetrical limbs, her grace, her taste, her nameless but irresistible charm. . . . *Ye* may rave about Helen Faucit's *Rosalind*, but *ye* never saw the Nisbett."

That rapturous deliverance,—somewhat in the vein of *Sir Anthony Absolute's* description of *Lydia Languish*,—glances at a woman whose portraits show her to have been very beautiful. She was the daughter of Captain Macnamara, who is supposed to have suggested to Thackeray the immortal *Costigan*, and she is said to have been the original of *Miss Fotheringay*, in his novel of "Pendennis." Macready's comment on the manner in which the comedy was acted when he thus produced it is in sharp contrast with that of Phelps:

"The only shortcoming in the whole performance," he said to Lady Pollock, "was the *Rosalind* of Mrs. Nisbett, a charming actress in many characters, but not equal to that. She was not disagreeable, but she was inadequate."

Mrs. Nisbett's *Rosalind*, according to the testimony of one of her auditors, Westland Marston, "was much like her *Beatrice*. Gay, mischievous, it carried one away by its exhilarating animal spirits, which never sank into coarseness."

VARIOUS PERFORMANCES OF *ROSALIND*.

Fanny Kemble's repertory did not include *Rosalind,* but in her latter years, when she gave public Readings, she sometimes rendered scenes from "As You Like It," and in that way signified her ideal of the character, which was true and fine. She possessed a strong mind and poetic insight, and,—however hard, selfish, and tyrannical she became, in her age,— a naturally kind heart and good taste. Her domestic experience had not been of a kind to foster gentleness of disposition. Isabella Glyn (Mrs. E. S. Dallas, 1823-1889), tall, dark, and handsome, could have looked like *Rosalind* in her youth, and may have been able to play the part, but when she visited America, in 1870 and 1879, she was suited only for tragic characters, or what are called "heavies,"—such as *Queen Margaret,* in "King Richard III."; *Emilia,* in "Othello," and *Bianca,* in Webster's "The Duchess of Malfi." On the English Stage she had a distinguished career, beginning about 1848. She acted *Rosalind* in that year, at York. I have found no description of the performance. In America she gave Readings. Mrs. Charles Young (Mrs. Herman Vezin), as *Rosalind,* gave a performance which was called charming, but which contemporary criticism did not commend. She was, however, an actress of fine ability, versatile and accomplished, but better fitted for tragedy than comedy. Alice Marriott was another of the female tragedians, and much too heavy for *Rosalind*. Amy Sedgwick failed in the part. Mrs. Rousby was a beauty, and her acting evinced sensibility and refinement, but her *Rosalind* was insignificant. Mrs. Kendal,—one of the most intellectual women I have had the good fortune to meet, and one of the most thoroughly accomplished actresses who have appeared in our time,—often played the part, in England, but was not accounted successful in it. Eleanour Calhoun, now Princess Lazarovitch, was remarkable for refinement, grace, and many accomplishments, but the impression that she made as *Rosalind* was dubious and faint.

AMERICAN STAGE.—EARLY REPRESENTATIONS.

The first representation of "As You Like It" given in America occurred at the John Street Theatre, New York,—"the paltry wooden theatre," as Dunlap contemptuously calls it,—on July 14, 1786, with Mrs. Kenna as *Rosalind*. That actress, with her husband and son, both actors, had arrived from England in the previous May, and joined "the old American company," managed by Lewis Hallam and John Henry, and then acting sometimes in Philadelphia and sometimes in New York. Ireland records that "Mrs. Kenna was an actress of respectable ability, whose talents were neutralized by the companionship of a husband and son who proved to be greatly disliked by the audience." There is no specific account of her acting as *Rosalind*. On June 21, 1796, at the same theatre, the comedy was again performed, under the same management (that of Hallam and Henry), with a notable cast, the beautiful Mrs. Johnson acting *Rosalind,* in association with Hodgkinson as *Jaques,* Hallam as *Touchstone,* Cleveland as *Orlando,* Mrs. Cleveland as *Celia,* and Mrs. Brett as *Audre*y. Joseph Jefferson, grandfather of our Joseph (*Rip Van Winkle*), enacted *Le Beau*. Hodgkinson was, at that time, considered the most brilliant general actor on the American Stage. Jefferson had not yet achieved the great eminence to which he subsequently attained. Mr. and Mrs. Cleveland were "useful and genteel, young and handsome." Hallam, father of the Lewis Hallam who later became the prime favorite of his day in the theatre, was a good comedian.

The opening of the Park Theatre,—a specially important event in American theatrical history,—was effected January 29, 1798, with a production of "As You Like It," and "a musical entertainment," called "The Purse; or American Tar." The managers of "The New Theatre," as it was then and for some time afterward designated, were Hodgkinson and Dunlap. The cast of the comedy, on the opening night, included Mrs. Johnson as *Rosalind,* John E. Martin as *Orlando,* Hodgkinson as *Jaques,* Hallam as *Touchstone,* John Johnson as *Adam,* and Mrs. Broadhurst as *Celia.* The theatre appears to have been stormed by a multitude, on this occasion. Many persons entered without paying for admission. In theatrical parlance, the house would hold $1,700: the receipts were $1,232, though the house was full "and hundreds were turned away" (Dunlap). The next mention of "As You Like It," in the story of the New York Stage, records the first appearance in America of Ellen Tree, who (1836) made an instant conquest of the delighted public. At the old Bowery Theatre, September 20, 1841, Mrs. Shaw played *Rosalind,* for the first time, and in October, 1849, at the old Broadway Theatre, she repeated that performance: it is probable that she acted the part several times in the course of the intervening eight years, but I have found no record of the fact. A "Life" of that actress, with particular description of what she was and what she did, in her profession, is greatly to be desired. She must have been a wonder. Ireland, who often saw her, says that "rarely have so many charms of figure, face, and mind been united in one individual. . . . Gayety sat like a crown upon her brow." It is recorded of this actress that she could not easily compose her countenance so as to appear to be serious. One of her most brilliant personations was that of the sparkling *Constance,* in Knowles's comedy of "The Love Chase,"—of which part she was the original representative in America, at the Park Theatre, New York, January 13, 1838. Being exceptionally beautiful and possessing an exuberantly joyous temperament and a deliciously melodious voice, she must have been admirably fitted for *Rosalind.*

Charlotte Cushman, whose first presentment of *Rosalind* appears to have been the one made in London, soon after her advent there, in 1845, acted the part, at the Astor Place Opera House, New York, January 8, 1850, appearing for the benefit of the American Dramatic Fund Association. The cast was remarkable: *Jaques,* Hamblin; *Orlando,* Humphrey Bland; *Touchstone,* Burton; *Adam,* Chippendale; *Le Beau,* George Jordan; *Celia,* Mrs. Abbott; *Audrey,* Mrs. John Gilbert. Miss Cushman entered heartily into the mirth of *Rosalind* and into her spirit of adventure; sustained perfectly the humorous colloquies with *Orlando,* and at times was not,—as, indeed, she could not be,—devoid of tender feeling. A peculiar artistic merit of her performance was that she made the woman inexperienced, and at first ill at ease, in the wearing of male attire. Her raillery was piquant and effective. She lacked, however, the personal beauty indispensable to the character, and she lacked the peculiar distinction of *Rosalind,*—which is not power, not majesty, not masculinity, but a quality of enchanting womanhood. Miss Cushman possessed abundant humor, and she knew the art of acting, but her proper field was tragedy or melodrama, and the *Rosalinds* and *Violas* were not for her. In England her performance was much applauded and commended.

Mrs. Mowatt, whose career as an actress began, June 13, 1845, at the old Park Theatre, with a performance of Bulwer's *Pauline,* and ended, December 16, 1854, at Niblo's Garden, with a performance of Mrs. Lovell's *Parthenia,* acted *Rosalind* for the first time when in England (1847 to 1851), and subsequently in New York. Bayle Bernard, certainly an experienced observer, wrote of this actress: "It is in *Beatrice* and *Rosalind* that she must be witnessed to be esteemed: equalled by some in art, and surpassed in force by many, she alone has the poetic fervor which imparts to them their truth, and makes our laughter ever ready to tremble into tears." Allowance must often be made for the superfluity of enthusiasm: carefully analytic perception, severely correct judgment, and the capacity of fervently keen appreciation are seldom combined: several actresses on the London Stage contemporary with Mrs. Mowatt (Helena Faucit, Mrs. Nisbett, Ellen Tree, and Mrs. Warner, for example) were remarkable for "poetic fervor": there can, however, be no doubt that Mrs. Mowatt was a delicate and lovely performer of *Rosalind.* She was a little slip of a woman, above the medium height, but, at the time of her visit to England, weighing "less than ninety pounds,"—as she has herself recorded,—and she was talented, charming, and exceptionally accomplished. Laura Keene, a glittering beauty, of high, imperious temper, whose art was as bright as polished steel, and as cold, performed *Rosalind,* in a production of "As You Like It," made by the elder Wallack, at Wallack's Lyceum, June 8, 1853. The play was acted seven times. Wallack played *Jaques.* Lester Wallack was the *Orlando,* Walcot the *Touchstone,* Blake the *Adam,* Mrs. Conover,—who became the wife of the excellent and beloved James H. Stoddart,—the *Celia,* and Mrs. Brougham the *Audrey.* Laura Keene again appeared as *Rosalind,* November 18, 1856, when she opened Laura Keene's New Theatre, at No. 622 Broadway, presenting the play with an uncommonly good cast: *Orlando,* George Jordan; *Jaques,* G. K. Dickinson; *Touchstone,* Charles

Wheatleigh; *Celia,* Mrs. Stoddart; *Audrey,* Mrs. Grattan. At Burton's Metropolitan Theatre, afterward the Winter Garden, Julia Bennett Barrow acted *Rosalind,* January 29, 1857, with Belton as *Orlando,* Fisher as *Jaques,* and Burton as *Touchstone.* Belton had come from Canada. I first saw him on the Boston Stage,—an earnest, pictorial, dashing actor; one of the many of whom no particular record remains.

LATER AMERICAN REVIVALS.—AUGUSTIN DALY'S PRODUCTIONS.

On the American Stage, within the fifty-four years since 1860, "As You Like It" has been more frequently performed than it was, on either side of the Atlantic, in the course of the preceding sixty years. Many fine casts of the play might be cited, not only from the records of the Stage in New York, but from those of the Stage in Boston, Philadelphia, and some other cities. Under the management of Augustin Daly the comedy was presented many times, and in many places. It was always a special favorite with that manager, and the most brilliant success ever gained with it, on the American—or, perhaps, on any—Stage, was gained under his sympathetic, wise, and able direction. Daly's first season as a theatrical manager, which began, August 16, 1869, when he opened the Fifth Avenue Theatre, in West Twenty-fourth Street, continued till July 9, 1870, and in the course of it he presented twenty-five plays,—"Twelfth Night," "As You Like It," and "Much Ado About Nothing" being among them. His dramatic company, of thirty-three members, included E. L. Davenport, George Holland, William Davidge, James Lewis, George Clarke, Daniel H. Harkins, Mrs. G. H. Gilbert, Fanny Davenport, Agnes Ethel, Clara Jennings, Lina Edwin, Mrs. Chanfrau, Mrs. Marie Wilkins, and Mrs. Scott-Siddons,—the last-named actress having been specially engaged for the Shakespearean revivals. She was then in the bloom of her beauty, and was an object of much public attention. She made her first appearance on the London Stage, April 8, 1867, at the Haymarket Theatre, playing *Rosalind,* and her performance elicited warm critical approbation. She gave a reading of "As You Like it," October 26, 1868, at Steinway Hall, New York, and for the first time in America she acted *Rosalind,* November 14, following, at the Boston Museum. Her first performance of the part in New York occurred, November 30, 1868, under Daly's management, at the New York Theatre,—the house which he temporarily occupied and for some time conducted, after the burning of his first Fifth

Avenue Theatre. In the revival of "As You Like It" which he made in 1869 Mrs. Scott-Siddons acted *Rosalind* on October 18, 20, and 23, with the *Celia* of Clara Jennings,—who, in turn, acted *Rosalind* on October 19, 21, and 22, with the *Celia* of Mrs. Scott-Siddons. Davidge played *Touchstone*, Harkins *Jaques*, and George Clarke *Orlando*. The name of Clara Jennings had been, for about two years prior to the giving of those alternate performances under Daly's direction, prominently associated with *Rosalind*, and she was well adapted, both by temperament and culture, to play that and kindred parts, an essential quality of which is sweet, tender, sprightly womanhood: Mrs. Jennings was long connected with Lester Wallack's dramatic company, at Wallack's Theatre, where she distinguished herself by many fine achievements in the vein of high comedy. Mrs. Scott-Siddons gave an unequal performance of *Rosalind*, but she was bright, interesting, and at her best in *Rosalind's* first Forest Scene with *Orlando* and that of the mock marriage. She was both true and lovely in her showing of *Rosalind's* changing moods,— her gladness in the presence of her lover, her joyous, artfully veiled exultation in him and in her love for him and his for her, and in her tantalizing, sweetly mischievous assumptions of mocking levity. The blissful vitality and gracious ardor of springtime womanhood shone through her acting, in those scenes: there she burst the shackles of inexperience and sparkled into freedom.

Daly made an elaborate revival of the comedy, November 18, 1876, at the Fifth Avenue Theatre, Fanny Davenport playing *Rosalind,* with Charles Coghlan as *Orlando,* William Davidge as *Touchstone,* and Charles Fisher as *Jaques.* Miss Davenport had played the part on a previous occasion, May 24, that year, at the same theatre, her father, E. L. Davenport, acting *Jaques* and Lawrence Barrett *Orlando.* The revival now made was judicious and tasteful: the scenic pictures, especially those of the Forest of Arden, were beautiful: leafy vistas in the woodlands were shown, suffused with continuously changing light, the hues of dawn and the glowing colors of sunset, fading into dark. The costumes were rich and handsome, and it was seen that scrupulous care had been taken to make them accordant to the fashions of the assumed period of the play,—about 1490, in France, in the reign of King Charles the Eighth. In loveliness of picture and completeness of accessories the spectacle presented was one of ample luxury. The incidental music was sympathetically executed and with delicious effect.

The acting was, in general, prosy, but it was earnest in spirit and usually correct in mechanism,

and as the stage direction was in every way efficient
the performance moved smoothly, being at no point
either hurried or slurred. In Miss Davenport's
Rosalind there was abundant frolic, but no undertone of deep feeling. For poetic conceptions of
character the dramatic artist must be born, not merely
made. The superb mentality, rich womanhood,—
sensuous, yet spiritual,—child-like ingenuousness,
radiance of glee, like the sparkle of rippling water
beneath the summer sunshine, and the passionate,
affectionate heart of *Rosalind* Miss Davenport did
not indicate, and, apparently, had not comprehended.
She was first a buxom beauty and then a saucy boy,—
and she was particularly clever in the maintenance of
her assumption of boyhood. Her mischievous, tantalizing coquetry was skilful, and in the singing of the
"Cuckoo Song" her neat execution and arch demeanor were charming. In speaking she sometimes
marred the text by excessively rapid enunciation and
the clipping off of sentences with a nasal twang. Her
ideal of *Rosalind* was meagre, her personation devoid
of poetry. This actress was at her best in melodrama
and in comedy parts of a gay and dashing order.
She was remarkably handsome.

Coghlan, as *Orlando,* presented a kind of rural
Hamlet, mooning in the woods, as listless as idleness,
and lethargic to the verge of sleep. He had often

played the part, and been highly commended for it, and his performance still occupies a traditional eminence; yet his personation was not above the level of mediocrity. It was laborious, and the art of it was not well concealed. The pervasive air of it was that of nonchalance. The actor not only seemed to be condescending to the part but allowing observation to perceive that he knew he was doing so. Yet there were fine points in his performance,—for Coghlan was a superb comedian, when he chose to be, and he could not help being correct and splendid at times. His figure was tall and manly, his manner elegant, his voice golden; his delivery of the text was fluent, musical, and marked by perfect appreciation of every shade of meaning. He was particularly felicitous in conveying the humor that lurks in certain delicate inflections of voice when uttering playful banter and mild sarcasm. In *Orlando's* colloquy with *Jaques,* when they meet in the Forest, his demeanor and speech were charming. The best moment of his performance was that of his truthful, touching expression of amazed, bewildered surrender of *Orlando's* heart to *Rosalind:* but, as a whole, the assumption was vitiated by lack of joyous buoyancy and passionate fervor. The *Jaques* of Fisher gave no sign, either in the facial expression or in the demeanor, of the experience to which that kindly cynic so significantly alludes,—the irreparable wreck of a life that cannot be repaired. The voice had no sound of sadness in it,—and *Jaques,* though never lugubrious, sometimes gay, always whimsical, is not without a touch of pathos, latent and remote, but actual. Fisher was an actor of great and various talent, but his *Jaques* was not one of his representative performances.

Daly's great and memorable successes in the revival of Shakespeare's plays were not gained in the early years of his theatrical management, and it was not until after he had established Daly's Theatre where it now stands, and enlisted the services of Ada Rehan, that he accomplished a perfect production of the beautiful comedy of "As You Like It." That achievement, however, he did accomplish when, on December 17, 1889, he produced the play at his theatre, investing it with a scenic attire completely and practically harmonious with its vernal bloom, and, for the first time, presenting Miss Rehan as *Rosalind.* His purpose was to delight. Every tone and tint of melancholy was rigorously excluded, equally from the performance and from the picture. The old theory which mingled pensive sadness with buoyant gayety in the interpretation of the comedy was abandoned. That theory is based in part on the fact that the theme is life in exile; in part on *Orlando's* allusion to "the shade of melancholy boughs"; in part on the mournful cadence of "Blow, blow, thou winter wind"; in part on the assumption that *Jaques,*—one of the most prominent of the implicated figures,—is a gloomy misanthrope, and in part on an exaggerated estimate of the character of *Rosalind.* Those denotements, considered apart from the context, prompt the solemn mind to a sombre view of Shakespeare's design, and in accordance with that view it has been maintained that, with all its glittering vitality, "As You Like It" is a mournful play. Yet, in fact, the comedy is essentially cheerful. The exiles are as merry as gypsies. *Orlando* is only hungry when he remarks on the "melancholy boughs." The plaintive sigh of the winter wind is only a stray note of pensive regret, much intensified by Dr. Arne's delicious but sorrowful music. *Jaques* is not in any sense a *Hamlet,* for he takes delight in his contemplative rumination and in his faculty of cynical satire; and *Rosalind,* while pure, sweet, and lovely, is a creature of flesh and blood, neither made of the clouds nor resident in them, but bent on enjoying, within the limit of right conduct, whatever physical as well as sentimental comfort there is to be enjoyed in her earthly state. In a word, the atmosphere of the comedy is happiness, nor is that fact invalidated by the consideration that Shakespeare's mood, when he wrote it, was tinged

ADA REHAN AS *ROSALIND*

"Odds my little life,
"I think she means to tangle my eyes, too!"

ACT III., Sc. 5

with a depth of thought which, while humorous, did not cease to be grave.

As the comedy is intrinsically a happy one the investiture of it ought to be bright and joyous. Daly made it so. The lovely scenery suggested the poet Browning's glowing aspiration, "Oh, to be in England, now that April's there!" Even the time of the "old and antique" incidental music was quickened, to harmonize with the abounding, rejuvenating spirit that controlled in the representation,—the spirit of bud and blossom, velvet verdure, golden sunshine, fragrant breezes, and ecstatic human vitality.

In the original play there are twenty-five speaking parts. In Daly's stage version all of them were retained, except *Sir Oliver Martext* and the *Second Lord*. The speeches descriptive of *Jaques,* when moralizing, alone, as he supposes, in the Forest,—speeches which, according to ridiculous old custom, had been spoken by *Jaques* himself,—were restored to the *First Lord*. (Macready, acting *Jaques,* was the first to make this restoration.) The two *Pages* were retained, with the song that they sing, for *Touchstone,* and that pretty episode of whim and vocalism was permitted to have its rightful effect, in further exemplification of the quaintness of the *Jester's* eccentric, facetious, lovable character. Various lines of the original text which usually are excluded were restored, and a few good emendations were adopted,—such as that (suggested by Farmer) which took the line, "With bills on their necks," from *Rosalind* and gave it to *Le Beau,* and such also as the rearrangement of incidents in the Fifth Act. The Second Act was effectively ended with the touching song, "Blow, blow, thou winter wind." All the music was included that the author meant should be used. The woodlands had been painted in the colors of spring and early summer, and, obviously, with remembrance of the gentle, soothing beauty of rural England,—though the scene was, as usual, laid in France. By skilful blending of set pieces with panorama the effect was secured of boundless extent and luxuriance in the breezy clearing and sun-dappled glades of the fanciful sylvan refuge that Shakespeare depicted while memories of the Warwickshire Forest of Arden floated in his mind.

The character of *Rosalind* has, by some writers, been deemed impracticable for the stage,—elusive, scarcely to be comprehended, never really to be represented. With the exception of *Lady Macbeth* no one of Shakespeare's women has been so much in controversy as *Rosalind.* An ideal that may be grand but certainly is vague has possessed some critical minds, together with the fixed and comfortable conviction that it cannot be realized. It is true that, in the long stage history of the comedy, comparatively few actresses have proved entirely adequate to the part of *Rosalind,* and that there are serious difficulties in the way of giving a thoroughly true and right performance of it; but those difficulties do not arise from any obscurity in the character, and those players who have fallen short in it have done so because of their personal deficiencies. Lodge's story of "Rosalynde," a wild girl frolicking in the woods, suggested to Shakespeare the image of delicious womanhood that he has created—the genuine, unconventional woman whom all true-hearted, right-minded men adore. *Rosalind,* while veritably human, is not "of the earth earthy." It is to *Celia* that the dramatist has given a slightly carnal bent: *Celia* is fine, but not of the rare strain of *Rosalind.* Force, coquetry, mirth, and mischief are constituents of *Celia's* character: the charm of *Rosalind* is a refined gypsy charm. She is young, handsome, pure, noble, and, beneath a sparkling outside of nimble wit, smiling levity, and amiably satirical banter, she veils a passionate temperament, sensitive to every good impulse and every lovely influence. The reason why she has not been, and is not, more often embodied in a wholly competent manner is that her enchanting quality is something that cannot merely be assumed,—it must be possessed; it must exist in the fibre of the individual, and its expression must be, as in that case it naturally would be, spontaneous.

Rosalind is the exquisite embodiment of that springtime vigor, freshness, and loveliness which make the essential soul of "As You Like It," and therefore *Rosalind* is the comedy, and when the comedy is acted the representative of *Rosalind* must stand forth as its most conspicuous and important figure. Shakespeare is not trifling in his portraiture of that enchanting woman. She was, in his imagination, intended to be spiritually pure, intellectually brilliant, physically beautiful, temperamentally ardent and tender,—the incarnation of glowing health and captivating personal charm. Her distinctive superficial attribute is piquant sprightliness, but beneath that she has a deep heart, and the freedom of her conduct and the exuberance of her wit flow out of her sincerity and innocence. She has not the half-mournful sweetness of *Viola,* nor the self-centred composure of *Portia,* nor the tragic intensity of *Imogen:* she is the type of a fervent, happy woman, loving dearly and wishful to be loved, and ultimately exultant in the ecstatic consciousness that her natural wish has accomplished its aim. There are persons who appear to resent that they possess bodies, and there are some who seem ashamed of their emotions. Not so *Rosalind.* She rejoices in her physical life, her heart is full of tenderness, and what her heart feels her tongue must speak.

In that way the character was comprehended by Ada Rehan, and in that way she embodied it, charming the observer by the copious, prodigal exuberance of her sweetness and her brilliancy. Miss Rehan exerted that charm because she could not help doing so, and the method of her art was the fluent method of natural grace. She did not try to be anything more than a woman. She did not grope after abstract meanings. She dashed merrily into the woodland frolic; and the image of sprightly womanhood that she embodied was sweetly reckless, because absolutely innocent as well as ardently impetuous. The performance was marked by incessant movement, and yet it did not become monotonous or insincere, because it was continuously fraught with suggestiveness of the bounteous nature beneath it. Those courtship passages, wherein the "boy" plays the woman, drag wearily when *Rosalind* is not the actual woman of Shakespeare's conception. In Miss Rehan's portrayal they ran with the sparkle of the brook in springtime. Her spirit was in the personation, a spirit brimming over with affluence equally of feeling and of mirth. *Rosalind* is not one of the cold, experimental women who stop short with wishing, not to love, but to experiment by making men love them; she is herself a lover, and the crowning ecstasy of her life arrives in that golden hour when at length she is sure of *Orlando's* fidelity. Few emotions that women feel are of a more sacred character than the one that must be experienced and conveyed by the representative of this heroine. Miss Rehan rose naturally to the height of the character and sustained herself easily at that poise. The three essential dramatic conditions of *Rosalind,*—the woman, the woman playing the boy, and the "boy" playing the woman,—could not be more exactly discriminated than they were by her, and throughout them all the refinement of the personality was not for an instant frayed or warped by even the least tone of that involuntary coarseness which, under such conditions, excitement develops in a vulgar nature. The innate delicacy of Miss Rehan's embodiment was a principal and decisive ingredient of its captivation: the spectator of her momentary perplexity, through feminine modesty, on the score of her "doubtlet and hose," was aware of contact with a nature radically good,—a nature of which sincerity was a cardinal virtue and to which meanness was impossible. Furthermore, that delicacy was found to be perfectly compatible with brilliant, incessant sprightliness. Throughout the First Act, at court Miss Rehan made *Rosalind* interesting by simple loveliness and by a bearing that was invested more with the superiority of genius or of original character than with the distinction of royal manner; yet that distinction was not wholly omitted. Her personal fitness for the part was proved in nobility of stature and presence, in opulence of essentially feminine charms, and in sympathetic voice and limpid melody of speech. The situation was not used merely as a preparation for assuming male attire. There was ample revelation in it of the sweetness, passion, and buoyancy of *Rosalind's* nature, and Miss Rehan, in the scene of the wrestling, gave a touching expression of the bewildered tremor naturally incident to the first love of a girl's heart. Later, when *Rosalind* emerges in her state of liberty and not of banishment in the Forest of Arden, the gleeful spirits of the actress soon began to irradiate the performance, and from that time onward the inspiriting glow of happy-hearted raillery never flagged. The relief that *Rosalind* experiences, as soon as she knows that she is beloved by *Orlando,* liberates her into a tumult of pleasure, and that condition is expressed in Shakespeare's text by incessant frolic. In order, however, that the mood may not become monotonous or insipid, *Rosalind* is implicated in the episode of *Silvius* and *Phebe,* which is a case of unreciprocated passion, while still another phase of the universal susceptibility is provided in the betrothal of *Touchstone* and *Audrey.*

Miss Rehan, in this performance, showed herself to be one of the most proficient artists that have appeared in our time—producing in art the perfect effect of nature. No performer within contemporary knowledge has acted a poetic part with more flexibility, or spoken blank verse with more fluency of natural utterance, or delivered prose speeches with a nicer perception of the melody inherent in our language. It is not easy to perceive by what principle Shakespeare was governed in making those alternations of prose and verse that constitute the text of "As You Like It," but *Rosalind's* words, as they were delivered by Miss Rehan, merged into one uniform current of melody, so that no listener remembered that the text is composite. Throughout *Rosalind's* scenes with *Orlando* the variety of her limpid elocution, combined with incessant animation of capricious demeanor, sustained the impersonation in a clear light of sparkling piquancy. In *Rosalind's* rebuke of *Phebe*,—whose subsequent speech to *Silvius* is such an ample and delicious description of her person,—the jocular humor and bubbling glee of the actress reached their height, and when she spoke the Epilogue, which she did with zest and finish that gave point and glitter to that inadequate tag, she finally vindicated her rank among the great comedians of the nineteenth century.

In one of his latest presentments of "As You Like It" Daly used a scene, based on a photograph by Mr. Greatbach, of Birmingham, England, showing a glade in the only existing remnant of the old Forest of Arden,—a wooded region, lying at Parkington, about midway between Birmingham and Coventry. It made a lovely picture. By some ingenious device which I did not understand and neglected to inquire into, a wonderful effect of perspective was created; the spectator seemed to be gazing, under cathedral-like arches of trees, down long vistas in the very forest that Shakespeare must have known. No person familiar with Warwickshire and "As You Like It" can harbor a doubt of the source of the poet's foliage, color, and atmosphere, when he drew the matchless pastoral scenes of that comedy. It was inevitable that, in writing those scenes, he should have depicted the delicious scenery of his native Warwickshire. In the original play, as distinguished from the stage versions, there are twenty-two scenes, but there is not a single stage direction in any one of them which restricts the locality to any particular country.

When Miss Rehan first acted *Rosalind* her chief associates in the comedy were John Drew, as *Orlando;* Henrietta Crosman, as *Celia;* Charles Wheatleigh, as the *Banished Duke;* George Clarke, as *Jaques;*

James Lewis, as *Touchstone;* Charles Fisher, as *Adam,* and Charles Leclercq, as *Corin.* Drew's *Orlando* was a sturdy, vigorous youth, a little given to grimace, mechanically correct and proficient, not convincing in his ardor, and over-satisfied at once with himself and his circumstances. Lewis was dry, quaint, and tart as *Touchstone,* but not suggestive of the gentle nature of that wise *Fool.* Fisher, whose life was then drawing to its close, made his reappearance as *Adam* after a long absence from the stage, and was pathetically affecting in his simple, manly portrayal of the sweet, loyal, "good old man." George Clarke's embodiment of *Jaques,* though it was a little marred by obvious artifice and over-elaborate elocution in the difficult Seven Ages Speech, showed just and complete comprehension, presenting an amiable cynic and an interesting type of "humorous sadness," such as the text requires, and a memorable image of ripe thought, formidable presence, and quaintly erratic character. It was a definite, direct, authoritative performance; it had whimsical mind, mellowed by "gained experience," and it had the exceptional merit of seeming to drift into the fanciful fabric of a dream-land comedy rather than to walk upon the earth.

In subsequent revivals of "As You Like It," under Daly's management, Miss Rehan was associated, successively, with John Craig, Frank Worthing, and Charles Richman, as *Orlando;* Herbert Gresham and Sidney Herbert, as *Touchstone;* Tyrone Power and William F. Owen, as *Corin;* and Edwin Varrey, as *Adam.* Varrey was one of the best of men and an extraordinarily fine all-round actor, one who could play everything and who played nothing ill. He moved his audience to enthusiasm by the lovely simplicity and deep feeling of his reverend and pathetic embodiment of *Adam.* In Miss Rehan's presentations of the comedy after Daly's death (1899) George Clarke acted *Jaques,* Wilfred Clarke, son of John Sleeper Clarke, *Touchstone,* and White Whittlesey *Orlando.*

Gresham denoted the mind and caustic wit of *Touchstone,* and he gave a brilliant, bold performance, successfully aiming to elicit the mirth, rather than the ruminant, whimsical drollery, of the part. Sidney Herbert lacked mellowness and meditative pleasantry, but his personation was clear-cut in form, delightful with drollery, fluent and effective in delivery, and continuously animated and sparkling in style. An actor who passes with ease,—as Herbert has done,—from *Shylock* to *Touchstone,* and from old *Crabtree,* in "The School for Scandal," to *Zambault,* the detective officer, in "The Thief," and is competent in such a wide range of parts, is an actor richly entitled to critical admiration.

Orlando is generally regarded by actors as "a feeder" and, accordingly, few actors like the part: indeed, it is possible that *Rosalind* sees more in *Orlando* than has ever been seen by anybody else,—for the gaze of love pierces deep. Though not a part of the first order, it is, however, an extremely difficult one to impersonate truly and it requires not only a fine nature in the man but fine art in the actor. The youngest son of old *Sir Rowland* must be sensitive, alert, impetuous, and ardent. He needs, above all things, vitality and romantic glamour, and the representative of him must never lag. He can philosophize,—"chewing the cud of sweet and bitter fancy," but *Orlando* is not supine: he is a perplexed and doubtful lover, and he does not submissively accept his trials. Worthing lacked the physique to "look successfully," in the wrestling with *Charles,* but his performance combined the attributes of simplicity, grace, sentiment, tender feeling, and gentle humor, and over it all there was a charm of aristocratic elegance. Richman's performance of *Orlando* was bland and dignified; he had a fine figure, a pleasing, eager, kindly countenance, an amiable voice, and a youthful, yet manly, bearing. He did not display lightness, grace, passion, exaltation, or much sensibility.

A notable feature of Daly's revivals,—one which,

generally passed, in the representation, with the matter-of-course, incidental effect that is exactly right, but which, in stage representation, is most difficult of attainment,—was the wrestling, before *Duke Frederick*. The occasion, plainly, was that of festival: the scene was brightly lighted, gay with many colors, and crowded not only with the *Duke's* attendant courtiers, ladies, and pages, but also with yeomen and peasants, men and women, from the countryside, come in to see "the bony priser of the humorous duke" wrestle for his credit. A sense of fiercely eager strain seemed diffused among the crowd, natural in a concourse of persons excited by the rough and brutal sport, and by the pitiful condition of "the poor old man's" three sons, defeated and injured. Hobart Bosworth, a good actor, who played *Charles,* was a large man, of commanding presence, an athlete and a trained wrestler. In the conflict with *Orlando* he denoted exceedingly well the savage animosity naturally enkindled in a coarse, animal person by *Oliver's* mendacious warning. Twice, after the contestants had come to grips, *Charles* seemed about to throw *Orlando,* whom he hurled from him with terrific force, but who, each time, desperately recovered himself. Then, as though maddened by his failure instantly to conquer the "young gallant," the *Wrestler,* like a maddened bull, rushed upon his adversary, who, stepping suddenly forward, in the very instant of the contact of their bodies, whirled upon his heel, reaching over his own shoulder, grasped *Charles* about the neck, and, using as an aid the momentum of that swiftly rushing attack, heaved his body aloft and seemed to dash it upon the ground, with killing force. The feat was, in reality, performed by Bosworth, using *Orlando's* shoulder to pivot upon; the effect was appalling.

THE MUSIC OF "AS YOU LIKE IT."

Shakespeare fully appreciated the value of music, in association with drama. There are songs in "Hamlet," "Othello," "King Lear," and "Antony and Cleopatra." There are passages in "Macbeth" obviously designed to be chanted. There is music in the Masquerade Scene in "Romeo and Juliet," and in the tent of *Brutus,* just before the *Ghost of Cæsar* invades the deep of night. There is use of song in "King Henry IV." and "King Henry VIII." The comedies abound with music. "The Tempest" and "A Midsummer Night's Dream" are exceptionally rich in strains that must be sung; and songs also occur in "The Two Gentlemen of Verona," "The Merry Wives of Windsor," "All's Well That Ends Well," "Much Ado About Nothing," "Love's Labor's

Lost," "Measure for Measure," "The Merchant of Venice," "The Taming of the Shrew," "The Winter's Tale," "Cymbeline," "Twelfth Night," and "As You Like It." Music has been conjoined with other plays of Shakespeare: there are no fewer than 350 pieces of music set to words from his plays and poems: but with the plays here mentioned it was associated by his own hand.

In "As You Like It" the songs are: "Under the greenwood tree" (Act III., sc. 5); "Blow, blow, thou winter wind" (Act II., sc. 7); "What shall he have that killed the deer?" (Act IV., sc. 8); "It was a lover and his lass" (Act V., sc. 3); and the verses allotted to *Hymen* (Act V., sc. 4), "Then is there mirth in heaven," and "Wedding is great Juno's crown." The verses of *Hymen*, together with all that relates to that personage, are usually omitted in the representation of this comedy. In Daly's arrangement of the play *Hymen* participated, and those rhymes were retained. The music for "Under the greenwood tree" and for "Blow, blow, thou winter wind" was written by Dr. Thomas Augustine Arne (1710-1778), and delicious it is. The air for "What shall he have that killed the deer?" was composed by Sir Henry Rowley Bishop (1780-1855). The lovely melodies for "It was a lover and his lass" and the two songs of *Hymen* were written by William

Linley (1771-1835). All the music was delightfully performed, and what with good acting, good scenery, and good music, the lovely comedy was, for the first time in many years, presented substantially as Shakespeare wrote it,—in the glad light of springtime and in one continuous picture of sylvan beauty. The only objectionable incident that I recall, of Daly's later revival, was the introduction of "descriptive music," performed by the orchestra, incidental to the delivery of the Seven Ages Speech. That was a serious blemish.

The "Cuckoo Song," customarily used in this play, was not used by Daly. That song, "When daisies pied and violets blue," occurring at the close of "Love's Labor's Lost" (Act V., sc. 2), appears to have been first introduced into the performance of "As You Like It" about 1747-'50, at Drury Lane, and to have been sung by Kitty Clive, acting *Rosalind*. The place of its insertion was in Act IV., sc. 1., immediately after the words, spoken by *Rosalind,* in colloquy with *Orlando:* "O, that woman that cannot make her fault her husband's occasion, let her never nurse her child herself, for she will breed it like a fool." This subject is clouded with doubt. When Garrick revived "As You Like It," November 2, 1747, at Drury Lane, the *Rosalind* was Mrs. Woffington, and Kitty Clive played *Celia.* Mrs. Woffington's voice was harsh, she was not a singer, and there is no record that the song was then used. Mrs. Pritchard acted *Rosalind,* at the same theatre, in the same season. I have found no mention of Kitty Clive as *Rosalind,* yet she may have acted the part, and probably did, on an odd occasion of necessity, some time in the period named. She played *Celia* many times, and perhaps it was as *Celia* that she sang the "Cuckoo Song." " It was the wish of Mrs. Clive's life to act female parts of importance" (Davies). She even appeared as *Ophelia,* in which she was bad, and as *Portia,* which she made ridiculous. She would not have hesitated at *Rosalind.* At Drury Lane, in 1767, Mrs. Dancer sang the "Cuckoo Song," acting *Rosalind.* At Covent Garden, in 1775, Mrs. Mattocks sang it, acting *Celia.* It is possible that, in the many years of stage usage, the song was sometimes assigned to the one part and sometimes to the other, according to the capability of the actress for singing. The purpose of introducing it was, probably, to enhance and coarsen coquetry and piquant banter. The first and second stanzas are sprightly and felicitous. The music, by Dr. Arne, is expressive and such as haunts remembrance.

284 SHAKESPEARE ON THE STAGE

VARIOUS PRODUCTIONS AND PLAYERS.—1871 TO 1885.

Rose Evans, an intelligent, clever little person, who had been well trained for the stage, went on for *Rosalind,* May 2, 1871, at Niblo's Garden, where E. L. Davenport,—who acted *Jaques,*—was then playing a star engagement, and although she proved incompetent for the part she made a pleasing personal impression. Her *Rosalind* was not at all that of Shakespeare, because it was devoid of airiness, variety, brilliancy, and especially of that blending of arch, piquant humor and passionate tenderness which is the soul of the character. *Orlando* was acted by Charles R. Thorne, Jr.,—a manly, pictorial actor, whose early death was a serious bereavement to our Stage. An English pugilist, "Jem" Mace, was presented as *Charles, the Wrestler.*

Adelaide Neilson's performance of *Rosalind,* in New York, occurred at Booth's Theatre, December 2, 1872. It was artistically competent, and, by reason of the player's personal charms, interesting and attractive; but it was not then, nor did it become, one of her distinctively characteristic, representative personations. It ripened, in repetition,—as, of course, her acting in general did,—and when last seen here, in the season of 1879-'80, it was much superior, as to spontaneity of action and warmth of feeling, to what it had been; but it remained always a little labored. It possessed, however, the charm of mingled sweetness, archness, and dazzling joy, and, in particular, it was made sympathetic by the rich, lingering, caressing, tender tones of a voice of deliciously musical quality. Many judges of acting admired it, and by some it has been highly extolled. In my esteem it was ever second to her *Viola*,—as to which the observer might well exclaim,

> "Of Nature's gifts thou may'st with lilies boast,
> And with the half-blown rose!"

Carlotta Leclercq first appeared as *Rosalind,* February 10, 1862, at the Princess' Theatre, London, and it was as *Rosalind* that she made her first appearance in America, at Booth's Theatre, New York, March 25, 1872. She was then, apparently, in middle age, and having been continuously on the stage since childhood she was an accomplished performer. Charles Fechter brought her to America, and she participated here, in various plays, in association with that erratic actor. She was a handsome, buxom woman, rather mature for *Rosalind,* and her assumption of girlishness, while expert, was not either persuasive or enticing. Her bearing, as the aggrieved and resentful *Princess,* was dignified, and her expression of feeling, in the rejoinder to *Duke Frederick,* was earnest and pathetic. In the Forest scenes with *Orlando* she gracefully indicated the fluctuations between woman-like reserve or maiden coyness and the ardor of impulsive love. Her luxuriant figure and her expressive face,—beaming with joy and kindness,—were pleasing to the eye, and her clear enunciation, in the easy delivery of the text, was pleasing to the ear. Miss Leclercq could act in French as well as in English. On April 23, 1872, at Bryant's Opera House, New York, she personated *Madame Lery,* in "Un Caprice," by Alfred de Musset, acting, in French, for the benefit of the French manager, M. Juignet, who had long labored to establish a French Theatre in that city. Her beauty, intelligence, sensibility, and precise method, and her capability of simulating the many and ever-varying moods of capricious feminine feeling, combined with natural dramatic talent and much experience, made her a capital general actress; and if she had possessed the attribute of spiritual refinement,—of which she was conspicuously deficient,—and if her voice had been more pure and sweet and more simply used, she would have ranked among the finest comedy players of her time. She died in 1895. Her *Rosalind* was commendable, not superior. The setting of the comedy, at Booth's Theatre, was rich and effective, judicious attention having been given to the woodland scenes, which were fine. The acting, in general, was weak and wooden. Robert Pateman, a boisterous low comedian, divested *Touchstone* of both quaintness and whimsicality; Daniel Wilmarth Waller, a good tragic actor, out of place as *Jaques,* deprived that character of every vestige of its intrinsic, peculiar, "most humorous sadness"; and George W. Wilson made the *Banished Duke,*—one of the kindliest of Shakespeare's minor sketches of character,—hard, metallic, and heavy, whereas he should be sweet-tempered, urbane, gentle, and interesting.

Ada Cavendish appeared as *Rosalind,* which part she had never acted anywhere before, on May 19, 1879, at Wallack's Theatre, and gave a personation of the dashing order, frolicsome and mischievous, with but a slight undertone of sentiment, and no indication of deep feeling. The part was not sympathetic to her. She was of a fine figure, exceptionally handsome, and her assumption of caprice and utterance of banter were spirited and effective. She was better suited to *Beatrice* than to *Rosalind.* The conspicuous successes of that fine actress were gained in characters of a passionate, impetuous nature, touched with eccentricity, such as *Mercy Merrick* and *Miss Gwilt,* in plays based on novels by Wilkie Collins. She lacked the poise essential for *Rosalind,* and her rapid, vehement, sometimes indiscriminate, delivery was not suited to the part.

Rose Coghlan acted *Rosalind* for the first time in a production of "As You Like It" made by Lester Wallack, at Wallack's Theatre, September 30, 1880. She was twenty-eight years old at that time, and in the rich bloom of her Irish beauty. Her performance of *Rosalind,* often repeated in later years, was agreeably piquant, but neither poetical in spirit nor flexible in style, and it lacked refinement. Her voice, which she knew how to use, was strong and melodious, and in the Forest scenes of the comedy, attired in a garb of slate-colored cloth and leather, with a red cap, she was a bewitching figure.

Wallack's production of the play was tasteful and pleasing, much to the credit of John Gilbert's stage direction. An effect of morning twilight, broadening into dawn and then the light of day,—introduced at the beginning of the scene in which *Orlando* comes, to hang his verses on the trees, and *Touchstone* and *Corin* dispute about philosophy,—was, at that period, novel, and it was beautiful. The *Jaques* of Osmond Tearle impressed by its authority and by correct, even, exquisitely smooth elocution: he was a remarkably fine speaker: but as a personation,—the interpretation of a pronounced type of mental idiosyncrasy,—it was abortive, and merely a specimen of respectable acting.

Henry M. Pitt, as *Orlando,* pleased by intrinsic manliness, earnest feeling, and a specially clear and effective delivery. William Elton, as *Touchstone,* evinced neither the quaintness, sapience, satiric drollery, kindly feeling, nor quizzical manner of the eccentric *Jester,* but, as is the way of the conventional low comedian, presented simply "the clownish fool"; that phrase, used by *Rosalind,* is merely a designation, not a definition.

These three actors, Tearle, Pitt, and Elton, all English, made their first appearance on the American Stage in this revival of "As You Like It." Elton returned to England. Pitt, an actor of rare talent, had a long career on our Stage, but eventually he declined into obscurity, and, oppressed by penury, lapsed into melancholia, and committed suicide. He was the son of Charles Pitt, whom I saw more than fifty years ago, as *Duke Aranza,* in "The Honeymoon,"—of which part he gave a striking performance, not to be forgotten. Tearle became a prosperous manager, in Australia.

Mrs. Langtry acted *Rosalind,* for the first time in America, on November 13, 1882, at Wallack's Theatre, New York. She had first assumed the part on the preceding September 23, at the Imperial Theatre, London, with Frank Cooper as *Orlando* and J. G. Graeme as *Jaques.* The performance was not, in a high sense, successful, and it never became so. Mrs. Langtry portrayed the character not as a complex web of thought, passion, sentiment, and archly simulated coquetry, but as that of a merry, rather unrefined girl who, having put on the garments of a boy disposed for frolic, is romping in the woods, and whose business is to be as mischievous as possible. Her movement was almost incessant; her face was invariably joyous and sparkling; not the slightest suggestion was given of the underlying seriousness and substantial fibre of the character, or of the experience of "one out of suits with fortune"; her tones were those of mockery and her demeanor was that of mischievous trifling. Saucy merriment was the spirit of the performance, and sport was its best result. Those observers who discern nothing deeper than that in *Rosalind* were satisfied with Mrs. Langtry's assumption, as soon as time and practice had enabled her to perfect her execution of it. Her nature was bright and sweet, not deep; she was handsome, with clear, level-gazing, eager, gray eyes and a firm, square chin; she had youth, ambition, and courage; she wore the male attire with jaunty assurance and dainty grace, modestly, yet with a pretty and pleasing swagger. I have seldom seen as charming a woman in the part,—or as weak a performance of it, judged by the standard of Shakespeare's play.

From a Photograph by Lafayette, London   *Author's Collection*

LILLIE LANGTRY AS ROSALIND

"What would you say to me now, an I were your very very Rosalind?"

Act III., Sc. 5

Helena Modjeska, after having played the part several times "on the road," acted *Rosalind* for the first time in New York, December 11, 1882. She was a lovely woman and a great actress, greater, it ever seemed to me, in serious romantic drama than in comedy. When first seen here (she came out as *Adrienne Lecouvreur*) she was a slender, lithe creature, exceedingly vital, animated by intense nervous energy, and the melancholy loveliness of her countenance, the exquisite refinement of her personality, the sweetness of her temperament, the grace of her manner, the music of her voice,—a voice the pathetic tremor of which could suddenly stir the tears of the listener,—and therewithal the beauty of her art, combined in the manifestation of a well-nigh unmatchable capability to charm. She thoroughly comprehended *Rosalind,* but it was natural and involuntary for her to present, as certainly she did, the serious, more than the brilliant, aspect of the character. There was, in her demeanor, a tender gravity, sweet and winning; her mirth was subdued and gentle, not exuberant, yet not devoid of spirit. The imperial beauties of the performance were profound sincerity of feeling; intrinsic royalty of condition; and invariable elegance of bearing, movement, and gesture. The remonstrative, defensive, almost defiant, rejoinder of the *Princess,* addressed to the usurper, *Duke Frederick,* was superbly spoken and in her most characteristic style. In the colloquy that *Rosalind* has with *Orlando,* immediately before the occurrence of the wrestling, her manner was over mature, almost amusingly maternal, but her keen, swift, all-embracing, rapturous glance, at first sight of him,—a glance that was a visual caress, lighting up her countenance with pleasure and kindness,—was wonderfully expressive and captivating. She manifested, with subtle, consummate skill, the woman's inexperience in pretending to be a man. Her behavior in the scene of *Rosalind's* first meeting with *Orlando* in the Forest was delightfully significant of passionate enjoyment of his presence, yet it was delicately tempered with modesty and coyness. The quality that the personation lacked was an over-flowing, never-ending, still-beginning, *physical vigor,*—an ecstatic exultation in life and love. In her later years her performance of *Rosalind* sometimes seemed more like a disquisition than an impersonation; but, at its best, it was one of the most charming embodiments of the part that have adorned the modern stage. Modjeska loved both the comedy and the character, and her presentments of them gave abundant, ennobling pleasure to thousands of auditors. I treasure the remembrance of her as one of the most noble and gracious figures of the Stage in her time, and also as a dear friend. Her great representative personations were *Adrienne, Mary Stuart,* and the complete transfiguration that she effected of *Camille.* Her own favorite, among Shakespeare's heroines, was *Rosalind:* critical judgment of acting preferred her personations of *Portia* and *Isabella.*

MARY ANDERSON'S REVIVAL.

Mary Anderson produced "As You Like It" and acted *Rosalind,* for the first time, August 29, 1885, at the Shakespeare Memorial Theatre, in Stratford-upon-Avon. Her first presentment of the comedy in America occurred, October 12, 1885, at the Star Theatre, New York. It was my good fortune to see both performances, and later to witness many repetitions of *Rosalind* by this fine actress. The Stratford production was made by her for the benefit of the Shakespeare Memorial; the net profit exceeded £100, and Miss Anderson, by reason of her gift, became one of the life-governors of that institution. The occasion was one of festival; the residents of Stratford and many visitors united in making it so, and I found the old town,—usually quiet,—joyously excited over the announcement that Miss Anderson would there make her first venture in the part of *Rosalind.* Many of the shop-windows in High Street and Bridge Street displayed portraits of her, in character. All available rooms in the two principal hotels, the Red Horse and the Shakespeare, had been engaged by her manager, the late Henry E. Abbey, for the accommodation of her dramatic company. Every reserved seat in the Memorial Theatre had been sold. Provision had been made for the running of special trains between Stratford, Leamington, and Warwick, on the night of the performance. American travellers were numerous in the town. The press of London and of New York had sent representatives. The weather was fine. All circumstances were auspicious of success, and on the night of trial there was no disappointment. A more distinguished and judicious audience than the one that assembled in the Memorial Theatre to welcome Miss Anderson has seldom been seen, and when at last she came on as *Rosalind* it greeted her with such continuous tumult of applause that several minutes passed before her resonant, sympathetic voice could pour out its music on the eager throng and the action of the play could proceed. Her triumph was complete. She was recalled many times before the final curtain fell, and was cheered with an enthusiasm unusual in England.

Rosalind, when first we meet her, has reached the period of a girl's development when, unconsciously to herself, love has become a necessity. Her merry question to *Celia,* "What think you of falling in love?" is more than playful; it is the involuntary denotement of her tenderly passionate heart, which longs for an object to love and for reciprocal affection, and she is disturbed by this emotion, without knowing why. She also is, secretly, saddened because of the misfortune of her father, in exile, and because of her uncle's aversion,—a dislike which her womanlike intuition could not have failed to divine,—and she assumes a blithe manner, essentially natural to her, but not now entirely genuine: "I show more mirth than I am mistress of." Miss Anderson clearly denoted *Rosalind's* condition, in this respect, and gained instant sympathy. Her appearance was superb. Tall, regal, beautiful, clad in a rich robe of flowered gold, cheerful in demeanor, yet earnest by reason of a sweet, thoughtful gravity, she looked the veritable *Princess,* and was indeed the incarnation of the exuberant physical vitality, finely poised intellect, and affectionate, sensitive temperament of *Rosalind.* The change from pensive abstraction to arch levity, in the opening talk with *Celia,* was made with winning grace. On first seeing *Orlando* she became eagerly attentive, and after their colloquy, as she turned away, saying "Pray heaven I be deceived in you!" her backward look upon him, intense, wondering, and spontaneously indicative of incipient fondness, clearly told that love would soon be in full possession of her heart. At the climax of the wrestling the pretty business was introduced of giving to the victor a wreath of laurel,—a custom long prevalent at court games in Europe. The usual practice is for *Rosalind* to hang a gold chain around *Orlando's* neck. In this case *Rosalind,* after the wreath had been given to him, slowly dropped the chain into his extended left hand,—slowly, gently, with a lingering grasp of it, as though she would caress the hand into which it fell,—while he, already charmed and won by her radiant, gracious beauty, allowed the victor's wreath to drop unheeded to the ground. The manner and tone with which she said "Sir, you have wrestled well, and overthrown—*more than your enemies,*" the last four words being half-murmured to herself, were bewitching, in the commixture of earnest candor and demure reserve. Her delivery of the rejoinder to the splenetic *Duke Frederick,*—speeches which combine dignified resentment, grieved expostulation, righteous anger, and stern, almost defiant, rebuke,—was fraught with intense feeling, and her sudden, considerate repression of censure of the *Duke,* at thought of the presence of his daughter, *Celia,* whom *Rosalind* dearly loves, was a delicate stroke of art, and indicative of the highest courtesy. In the making of the plot of adventurous exile her glowing spirits, eager self-reliance, and merry humor disclosed themselves with delicious freedom, and the exit, with *Celia* and *Touchstone,* was made in a burst of gladness.

It is not till *Rosalind* has put on her boy's dress and escaped into the joyous freedom of the woods that her exultant spirit and her lovely power of innocent allurement are fully shown. The dress worn by Miss Anderson comprised russet doublet and hose,—the sleeves of the doublet being slashed with white puffs; long boots; a shapely velvet hat; a dark red mantle, thrown carelessly round the body and negligently carried; a kirtle-axe for the thigh, and a boar-spear for the right hand; and never was raiment worn with more bewitching grace. The rustic scenes set for Arden were beautiful. In the first of them a soft sunset light streamed through the trees, and you could almost hear the low murmur of the brook and the notes of birds, calling their mates to rest. The song of the *Duke's* foresters, returning from the chase, was faintly heard, at distance, dying away in the shadowy glades. It was thus toward the end of day that *Rosalind, Celia,* and *Touchstone* came wandering into the Forest, almost worn out with fatigue and listless with long endurance. The scene, with its episode of the love-lorn *Silvius* and the sapient *Corin,* does not require much action, but deft artistic touches were made in it by Miss Anderson,—expressive, by turns, of her sense of humor and her sensibility,—at "Doublet and hose ought to show itself courageous to petticoat," and at "Alas, poor shepherd, searching of thy wound, I have by hard adventure found my own"; but the excellence of her acting here (and this quality pervaded the whole impersonation) was its impartment of a sense of innate aristocracy, the natural attribute of a woman noble in soul as well as in birth. She rounded and closed this passage, in an expressive exit, with an assumption of spirit and strength, human, tender, almost pathetic, in its conveyance of cheer and encouragement to the weary companions of her pilgrimage.

When *Rosalind* is next seen a few days may be supposed to have passed. There is no more fatigue now, and there will be no more real trouble. It is bright daylight, and the adventurous youth, as assumed by Miss Anderson, came rambling through the Forest, singing as he strode. The song "When daisies pied and violets blue" has usually been introduced at a late point of the representation of "As You Like It," as a musical feature and a vocal exploit. Miss Anderson, possessing a magnificent voice, and being a fine singer, might have made it a musical feature of the first order, had she been minded to do so, but she wisely and tastefully used it as a minor embellishment. Her voice, sweetly melodious and deeply sympathetic,—the grandest woman voice heard in her day from the dramatic stage,—was audible before she entered. When she came into view she was sauntering, and the song was negligently continued by her till she had noticed *Orlando's* paper, hanging on a tree, and had taken it down and glanced, with an air of momentary bewilderment, at its contents. The felicity of this business is obvious. Her surprise was only momentary,—for she made *Rosalind* almost instantly cognizant, by intuition, of the source of the versified tribute; and during the subsequent colloquy with *Celia* her bearing was that of a delighted lover who guards her delicious secret beneath an assumption of indifference, and only waits to be told what she is already enraptured to know. The start, at "What shall I do with my doublet and hose?" was made with precipitate confusion, in the sudden remembrance of an awkward predicament which the tumult of her pleasure had thitherto caused her to forget. Throughout the ensuing scene with *Orlando* she was natural and delightful, alike with the exuberance of her delight and the incessant felicity with which she denoted the tenderness that it only half conceals. At the question,—archly uttered but seriously meant,—"Are you so much in love as your rhymes speak?" her pretty action of pressing her hand to her bosom, where those rhymes were hidden, was aptly and sweetly expressive; and when *Orlando*, turning away from his questioner, answered, sadly, "Neither rhyme nor reason can express how much!" her acted caress,—nearly detected by him, and giving her the pretext for an arch transition from passionate rapture to demure gravity,—became charmingly illuminative of *Rosalind's* nature. The Reproof Scene, with *Silvius* and *Phebe,* was carried with a good assumption of manly swagger and with a pleasing variety of intonation and of dramatic embellishment, in the use of the text. Amid all her glee she contrived to invest the scene of the mock marriage with a delicious sentiment, the sweet ecstasy of triumphant love. In the Swoon Scene she was easily victorious, using those means of serious expression which were so entirely at her command. There was a true and touching note of pathos in her voice when she murmured those simple words of weakness and grief, "I would I were at home": and when at last this beautiful *Rosalind,* clad in spotless white and dazzling in the superb beauty of her auspicious youth, stood forth to part the tangled skeins of the plot and so terminate the play, it seemed, for an instant, as if a spirit had lighted on the earth. I thought of what the great magician himself has said:

From a Photograph.   *Collection of Evert Jansen Wendell, Esq.*

MARY ANDERSON AS ROSALIND

"To have seen much and to have nothing, is to have rich eyes and poor hands."

Act IV., Sc. 1

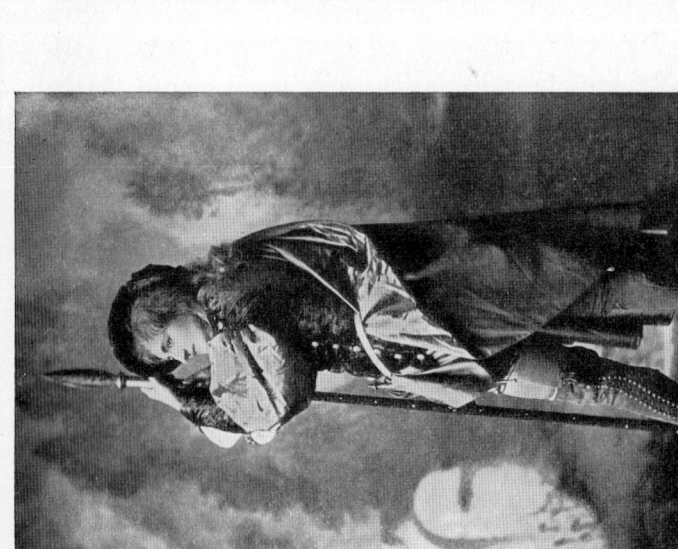

From a Photograph.   *Collection of David Belasco, Esq.*

HELENA MODJESKA AS ROSALIND

"Alas, poor shepherd! searching of thy wound, I have by hard adventure found mine own!"

Act II., Sc. 4

AS YOU LIKE IT

"Women will love her, that she is more worth
Than any man; men that she is
The rarest of all women."

Miss Anderson used a stage version of the comedy made by herself, on the basis of the one generally employed. It afforded no new feature of special importance, and it adhered to the wrong custom of assigning the speeches of the *First Lord,*—descriptive of *Jaques,* when soliloquizing at the brook-side,—to *Jaques* himself. The part of *Touchstone* was curtailed, part of the colloquy of the shepherds was discarded, and *Hymen* and his verses were excised. Charles Edward Flower, of Stratford,—that public-spirited citizen and devotee of Shakespeare who gave the Shakespeare Memorial grounds to the Borough,—observing that there was, among Miss Anderson's stage properties, an artificial Oriental palm-tree, intended for use in the comedy, called her attention to the fact that there is a variety of tree, called the "palm," growing along the banks of the Avon and abundant in Warwickshire, to which, and not to the Oriental palm, the allusion in the text of the play refers: "For look here what I found on a palm tree": Act III., sc. 2. The artificial palm-tree, accordingly, was not included in any Forest Scene. In her first production of "As You Like It" and throughout the subsequent season Miss Anderson was associated with Johnston Forbes-Robertson as *Orlando,* Francis H. Macklin as *Jaques,* J. G. Taylor as *Touchstone,* and Kenneth Black as *Adam.* Miss Anderson sometimes spoke the Epilogue, but, generally, omitted it, and she closed the performance with a dance.

It was acutely remarked by Boaden, when commenting on the *Rosalind* of Mrs. Siddons, that "she closed her brilliant raillery upon others with a smothered sigh for her own condition." That aspect of the part had been perceived by Miss Anderson. She displayed spontaneous enjoyment of exuberant physical vitality, a little subdued by stress of restrained emotion. Her performance of *Rosalind* has only once, within my observation, been excelled. Ada Rehan's personation surpassed it in spontaneity, and, through the Forest scenes, in exuberance of joy and in cumulative vigor of execution: indeed, Miss Rehan's *Rosalind* was, as Mrs. Clive said of Mrs. Siddons, "all Nature and daylight,"—the best that has been seen within the last sixty years.

LATER REVIVALS.—1885 TO 1914.

Since the presentment of "As You Like It" made by Miss Anderson in 1885, no exceptionally important revival of the comedy has been effected on the American Stage, except the one so brilliantly accomplished by Augustin Daly, in 1889, which has already been considered. The play has been several times revived, and several notable performances have been given, particularly of *Rosalind, Jaques,* and *Touchstone.* The part of *Rosalind* has been assumed by, among others, Adelaide Moore, Margaret Mather, Marie Wainwright, Julia Marlowe, Minna Gale, Alberta Gallatin, Julia Arthur, Henrietta Crosman, Margaret Anglin, and Viola Allen. Miss Wainwright, acting at the Star Theatre, January 7, 1889, presented *Rosalind* as a sensuous, vivacious coquette. Louis James, appearing with her, as *Orlando,* acted that part in a negligently graceful manner, with the precision of a practised old player, not wasting emotion and not neglecting any opportunity for the exercise of the faculty of playful humor for which he was distinguished. Julia Marlowe, who had acted *Rosalind* "on the road," first played the part in New York, January 27, 1889, at the Fifth Avenue Theatre, and was personally interesting in it, but not distinguished. She has often since appeared as *Rosalind* and always has pleased, by reason of her beauty, sensibility, demure, ingenuous demeanor, and the wistful, dreamy, half-melancholy aspect which helps to make her so completely the ideal of a serious romantic heroine; but she never has seemed to identify herself with the character, or much to care for it. Her conspicuous associates on the New York Stage were Eben Plympton as *Orlando;* Milnes Levick as *Jaques;* W. H. Crompton as *Touchstone;* and Charles Leslie Allen as *Adam.* Plympton's *Orlando* was earnest, sincere, and in the wooing of the supposed *Rosalind* spirited, graceful, and touching. Milnes Levick was sepulchral and monotonous as *Jaques,* more suggestive of the churchyard gloom and Hessian boots of *Mr. Haller,* in "The Stranger," than of the quaint, ruminant, half-quizzical, half-cynical philosopher of Arden. Mr. Crompton's amusing sapience and his easy denotement of the gentle spirit which makes the best of everything made him interesting as *Touchstone.* Mr. Allen, long known on our Stage as one of the most competent of eccentric comedians and "old men," was duly dignified, venerable, and pathetic, as *Adam,* not forgetting that the part is that of a vigorous, not a decrepit, veteran. "Remember," said Fanny Kemble, addressing her cousin Henry, after seeing him act the part, "that *Adam* is a virile old man,—not a sack of potatoes!"

In a later revival of "As You Like It," effected at the Academy of Music, March 21, 1910, Miss Marlowe played *Rosalind,* in association with E. H. Sothern as *Jaques,*—a part he had not before assumed in the metropolis. His performance was notable only as exemplifying a rigid and unpleasing use of the method which is miscalled "natural," and which is, in fact, prosy and tiresome. He wore a beard which, practically, hid his face, and also he wore a heavily draped head-dress, which dwarfed his stature. The effect that he thus sought was, apparently, "correctness" of make-up and costume,—a merit praiseworthy in itself, but of secondary value, as compared with the effect to be obtained by acting. Sothern's delivery of the text was, of course, intelligent, but it was mechanical and spiritless. The speeches descriptive of *Jaques,* by the *First Lord,* were omitted. Miss Marlowe's presentment of *Rosalind* on this occasion, though more definite than it had previously been, was less pleasing. The personal charm of the actress was still potent, but her simulation of coquetry was transparently artificial, and of the deep heart of *Rosalind* she gave but a faint indication. The cast included Frederick Lewis, as *Orlando;* Albert S. Howson, as *Touchstone;* William Harris, as *Adam;* and Norah Lamison as *Celia.*

Julia Arthur (Ida Lewis, Mrs. Benjamin P. Cheney), an actress qualified by considerable experience, appeared as *Rosalind,* for the first time on any stage, November 28, 1898, at Wallack's Theatre, and gave a respectable but in no way distinguished performance. Her beauty, graceful behavior, and clarity of spirit made her acting agreeable and attractive, but her ideal of *Rosalind* was indistinct and her expression of it crude and ineffective. She seemed to be acquainted with some of the traditional stage business of the part, her delivery was fluent, her use of raillery piquant, and her elocution, while often careless in the prose passages, was sometimes pleasingly melodious in the verse. In the Forest scenes she evinced sympathy with their free, careless spirit, and in her demeanor and action there was a romantic quality. Her personation lacked innate distinction and deep feeling, and was neither brilliant nor tender. There was no intimation in it that *Rosalind* loves "at first sight"; the manner of the award of the chain,—which is a love-token,—to *Orlando* was perfunctory, and there was no suggestion of latent ardor in the Forest dialogues. *Rosalind* is not a *Juliet,* but she is passionate. The current of destiny for both of those lovers starts in much the same way,—only, with *Rosalind,* it runs to happiness, not misery: and *Rosalind* is not personified unless she is made intellectual, noble, ardent, and tender, however vivacious and mischievous in her tantalizing frolic, or however capricious and mischievous in her assumption of levity. The use of the word "work" seems objectionable as applied to the art of acting, but if ever a dramatic encounter was devised that exacts *work* it is that of

Rosalind and *Orlando,* in the Forest of Arden; and, all the while, the stream of mingled ingredients,—passion, exultation, glee, and banter,—must flow as smoothly as the brook that sings beside them or the breeze that whispers in the branches over their heads. In Miss Arthur's revival of the play the best performance was that of the *Banished Duke,* by Edwin Holt, a capable and experienced actor, thoroughly in earnest. There was a tinge of quaintness in Robert McWade's *Touchstone,* but nothing more.

A BAD READING.

In the colloquy between *Rosalind* and *Celia,* Act 1., sc. 3, after the wrestling, Miss Arthur used one of the erroneous First Folio readings, making *Rosalind,* in reply to *Celia's* question, "Is all this for your father?" say, "No, some of it is for my *child's father."* I knew Miss Arthur to be an intelligent and refined person, and therefore I supposed this reading to be accidental, not intentional, and in commenting on the performance, at the time, mentioned it as an error due to nervousness, not bad-taste,—thereby incurring a liberal allowance of what Disraeli happily characterized as "the hare-brained chatter of irresponsible frivolity," in the newspaper press. The main-spring of that chatter was Mr. Norman Hapgood, a clever but ill-balanced, crotchety, mischievous writer, who recently has gained bad distinction by making havoc of the once respectable periodical "Harper's Weekly." The purport of it was that I had shown ignorance of Shakespeare in general and the First Folio and "As You Like It" in particular—an aspersion which, in view of my life-long study and varied work as an adapter of Shakespeare's plays (including "As You Like It") to the modern stage, incidentally examining every available text, I do not care to answer.

This matter is inconsiderable, but a correct reading of Shakespeare's words is important, especially where it vitally affects an ideal of character, and such a reading has been diligently sought by many editors and commentators. Every Shakespeare scholar concedes the obvious facts that the proof-reading of the First Folio was not well done and that the book contains many errors. The reading of the line in question, "some of it is for my *child's father*," has been approved,—injudiciously, beyond reasonable question,—by one or two editors of authority, but common-sense is against them, and so is the weight of critical judgment. The bad reading, not only indelicate but senseless, was, obviously, a compositor's blunder,—one of the many that the Folio contains. The first editor to correct it was Nicholas Rowe, to whose labor all students are much indebted, and this particular emendation by Rowe was approved by Pope, Dr. Johnson, Charles Knight (usually an almost fanatical devotee of the text of the First Folio), Coleridge, Collier, Keightley, Dyce, Richard Grant White (in his latest edition), Hudson, Flower, and Rolfe. Keightley's note reads: "Rowe properly read, 'father's child.' Sense, taste, and delicacy alike commend this simple and natural transposition. Some editors, however, think otherwise." Dyce's note reads: "The Folio has, '—— for my childes father'; which could only have been right if *Celia's* question had been, 'But is all this for your *child?*'" The only other way in which to convey sense out of the Folio misprint of *Rosalind's* words would be for *Celia* coarsely to lay the emphasis "Is all this for *your* father?"

Furness, declining "to discuss this passage," remarks that "it is well, in this, and all similar cases . . . to bear in mind that modes of thought and speech, as well as of manners, shift and change from age to age, as widely as do the costumes, and that every age must be measured by its own standard"; and he quotes Moberly as declaring that "Shakespeare would have smiled" at Rowe's emendation. He *might* have smiled, —and then again, he might not. The standard of taste in the time of Queen Elizabeth and King James the First was low and vulgar. Shakespeare could be coarse, and sometimes he was, but as contrasted with other writers of his day he was uncommonly pure. It is, however, a specious and misleading practice which tries to palliate vulgarity and justify obvious blunders in Shakespeare's text by citing the gross influence of the age in which he lived. His writings amply prove that he could resist all such influence. When he set out to depict a refined, delicate woman he did not put into her mouth the language of a flippant vulgarian or a prurient wanton. If he drew *Doll Tearsheet,* he also drew *Miranda, Isabella,* and *Desdemona.* The reader will remember that there is a word (frequent in the discourse of Shakespeare's time and frequent in the usage of to-day) which *Desdemona* finds it almost impossible to utter, and when at last she forces it from her lips, she adds, "It doth abhor me, now I speak the word." *Rosalind* is neither less pure nor less fastidious than *Desdemona.* To make *Rosalind* within a few moments of first seeing *Orlando,* while yet her love for him is incipient and she is half-perplexed at her own emotions, refer to him as the father, in her gross desire, of a child that she is yet to bear is instantly to vitiate a lovely ideal of womanhood and to evince entire ignorance of human nature: the effect of sudden and true love, on a fine mind, is to idealize and exalt, not to vulgarize and degrade. *Rosalind,* though not equal to *Viola* in poetically spiritualized quality, *is,* incontestably, fine, and she is incapable of such a speech as this Folio reading would assign to her. It is the necessity of a true ideal of *Rosalind,* not prudish application of "modern standards" to Shakespeare's text, that requires insistence on this point. Even *Celia* could not, almost in the moment of *Rosalind's* first meeting with *Orlando,* make such an intimation as the Folio reading conveys,—and it is not forgotten that, later in the comedy, *Celia* utters an equivoke which, even by the standard of Shakespeare's time, must have been deemed downright vulgar in its sportive levity.

HENRIETTA CROSMAN.

The production of "As You Like It" made by Henrietta Crosman, February 27, 1901, at the Republic Theatre, New York, was creditable to her judgment and taste, and her personation of *Rosalind* was mechanically competent. Her qualifications for the part were a slender, lithe, boy-like figure, a handsome face, a blithe temperament, cheery spirits, physical alacrity, aptitude for playful banter, and artistic skill to indicate sentiment masked by levity. She also possessed the advantage of familiarity with Ada Rehan's splendid performance of *Rosalind,* having acted *Celia* with her, in Daly's revival of the comedy, in 1899. Her ideal was good; her expression of it finical. The acting was fluent, brisk, and dashing, but it was hard, the glitter of it being that of ice. The personality lacked distinction; the presentment of it lacked spontaneity. There was no exuberance in the glee and no warmth in the feeling, though the intention of both was visible. The vocalism was metallic, the general effect that of monotony. A subtle and felicitous novelty in Miss Crosman's stage business was *Rosalind's* perception of the "love at first sight" between *Celia* and *Oliver,* in the scene that closes Act IV. This was deftly done, by attentive gaze and rapidly changing facial expression, and was neat and effective,—the suggestion having been derived from *Rosalind's* subsequent statement to *Orlando:* "Your brother and my sister no sooner met but they looked; no sooner looked but they loved." "I know not," wrote Dr. Johnson, "how the ladies will approve the facility with which *Rosalind* and *Celia* give away their hearts." That they do give them away precipitately is certain, and it is also certain that each perceives the precipitation of the other, and a little wonders at it. Even the headlong *Orlando* somewhat marvels at the suddenness of his brother's passion,—his own, of course, being entirely natural! But let us remember that these are all human lovers in fairy-land and the Forest of Arden. The chief associates of Miss Crosman when she appeared in New York as *Rosalind* were Barton Hill, who was duly dignified, gentle, and philosophic as the *Banished Duke,* and John Malone,—a student, a scholar, and a good actor "of the old school,"—who played *Jaques* according to the ponderous, gloomy stage tradition which adheres to that part. I remember he asked the opinion of a friend, in The Players, who had seen the performance, "What do you think of my *Jaques?*" and received for reply: "Well, John, I think it only needs *three silver handles down each side* to be complete!" That implication is applicable to many presentments of *Jaques* that have shed Milton's "dim, religious light" upon the stage.

MARGARET ANGLIN'S REVIVAL.

Margaret Anglin first produced "As You Like It," July 23, 1898, at the Royal Opera House, Yarmouth, Nova Scotia: her first presentment of it in New York occurred, March 16, 1914, at the Hudson Theatre. Her prompt book of the comedy, made by herself, comprises twelve scenes, and the representation shows six different places, namely: *Oliver's* Orchard; a Hallway in *Oliver's* House; a Lawn before the Palace of *Duke Frederick;* the Edge of the Forest; the Heart of the Forest; and, Another Part of the Forest. The action is, as usual, located in France. Miss Anglin's version of the play does not materially differ from others long familiar to the Stage. A peculiarity of it is pedantic adoption of some manifestly erroneous Folio readings, such as "O Jupiter, how *merry* are my spirits!" instead of "how *weary* are my spirits!"—an absurd reading, which the context shows to be wrong, and which, obviously, came of a compositor's blunder. It is not scholarship to adopt misprints as the true text of Shakespeare. The setting of the play, under Miss Anglin's direction, was, in one respect, appropriate, being bright in color, but the scenery, particularly that of the Forest, was ordinary and insignificant, lacking all charm of rural character and poetic atmosphere. The acting, in general, was earnest, but it was not, excepting in one instance, in any respect brilliant, or even interesting.

Miss Anglin assumed *Rosalind,* a part for the true performance of which she lacks not only the necessary personal beauty, but the sensibility of temperament, the melody of voice, the enchantment of personality, and the competent capability of poetical artistic expression which are imperatively essential, and her personation, accordingly, while it signified careful study, intelligence of ideal, and facility of executive method, was merely the mechanical achievement of an experienced actress. The best part of it was the spirited tone and demeanor in the raillery. The speech beginning "Say the day, without the ever!" was exceedingly well spoken. Miss Anglin has shown useful talent for light comedy, and has proved herself amply proficient in plays relative to contemporary life, but while no doubt she understands and admires the poetic heroines of Shakespeare, she is unsuited for them, in person and in style. Her signal ability, worthy ambition, and devoted fidelity to her art have long been recognized, with sympathy and respect. It would be indeed pleasant to extol her efforts in the Shakespearean drama, but thus far (1914) no occasion has been provided by her for anything more than qualified praise. Her *Rosalind,* while radically defective, is the best of her Shakespearean impersonations. The chief associates of this actress, in the performance of "As You Like It," were Fuller Mellish, as *Jaques;* Pedro de Cordoba, as *Orlando;* Sidney Greenstreet, as *Touchstone;* E. Y. Backus, as the *Banished Duke;* and Ruth Holt Boucicault, as *Celia.* The *Orlando* was neither poetic nor romantic, but it was manly and intelligent. The *Touchstone* was silly, vacuous, vulgar, and offensive, and beneath criticism. The *Jaques* was a fine work of art, and indeed the only memorable feature of this revival.

Mr. Mellish rose to the occasion. His performance was simple, direct, consistent, sustained, and deeply impressive. He evinced a perfect comprehension of the character of *Jaques,* and he made his ideal known and felt. His aspect, demeanor, and voice conveyed to apprehension the ample experience through which this cynical eccentric has lived,—the aggregate of vicissitude, trial, and suffering, in the long backward of the Past. There was in the face the sadness of a man world-worn and weary, yet there was no gloom of despondency. *Jaques* is philosophic, and Mr. Mellish made him so,—wise, ruminant, tolerant, quizzical,—observant of human doings, but isolated. The complete ease of this actor,—his absolute identification with the character, and his continuous, flexible, subtly appreciative, rightly expressive delivery of the text,—the freedom and fluency which concur to make acting seem natural,—caused a delightful effect. He uttered the Seven Ages Speech, standing beneath a tree, at the side, peeling an apple, and speaking as if to himself, becoming more and more intent on the train of thought, and regardless of the foresters clustered near him; despite a slight touch of the "pipes and whistles" of senility, a beautiful exploit in elocution and an admirable piece of dramatic art. His management of the colloquy with *Touchstone* concerning "the Seventh Cause" was, likewise, exceed-

MARGARET ANGLIN AS ROSALIND
"*I could find it in my heart to disgrace my man's apparel, and cry like a woman!*"
ACT II., SC. 4

FULLER MELLISH AS JAQUES
"*Rosalind is your love's name?*"
ACT III., SC. 2

From Photographs by White, N. Y.

Author's Collection

ingly felicitous, showing, in face, voice, and manner, the natural delight of a cynic in the oddity and the satiric humor of a kindred spirit, and the eager wish to keep him talking and to listen to his subtle ridicule of human folly. Since the time of Davenport I have not seen a better impersonation of *Jaques*. Nothing else need detain attention in Miss Anglin's production of "As You Like It."

JAQUES AND HIS PLAYERS.

Jaques is a conspicuous eccentricity. He seems to be a good man, spoiled. He has been a libertine. He has been saddened by much and hard experience. He has learned the vanity of everything. He is tired of the world. His mind is warped. Yet, though given to "sullen fits," he is neither gloomy nor bitter. His melancholy is humorous,—that is, not comic, but full of humors or moods. Life to him is a humdrum spectacle, vapid and pitiful, over which he moralizes, grimly tolerant, playfully caustic, sadly happy in his ability to "suck melancholy out of a song," and, apparently, cynicism from anything. He is alone; he craves no sympathy; yet he wins affection. I have found him one of the most deeply interesting of Shakespeare's characters. He remains in the Forest, an exile, communing with the "convertite," *Duke*

Frederick, when his companions have returned to the comforts and pleasures of the Court; and fanciful conjecture dwells pleased on the nature of his life in that dreamland from which he never emerges.

Edward L. Davenport made the part his own,—an impressive incarnation of substantial, eccentric character, half-cynical, half-playful, affecting by reason of involuntary pathos, sometimes suggestive of abstraction and lonely dignity, always consistent and charming in philosophical humor. In substance, solidity, and reality Davenport excelled all players of *Jaques* that ever I have seen.

Charles Coghlan (1889) indicated a clear ideal, spoke the text with complete appreciation of its meaning, and enforced that meaning with excellent by-play. The background,—the indication of what *Jaques* has experienced,—was denoted by him, and the effect of all that *Jaques* sees and hears was expressed in his face, voice, and demeanor. His delivery of the speech about the Seven Ages was beautiful: he refrained entirely from mimicking the "pipes and whistles" of senility. A picture of Coghlan's *Jaques,* as he appeared while listening to *Orlando's* narrative, in the Woodland Scene, would show the veritable *Jaques* of Shakespeare. Many actors of this part are content to indicate a world-wearied philosopher, and to invest him

AS YOU LIKE IT

with gloom, a saturnine aspect, and the quality of caustic humor,—and there to stop; and they are heavy and tedious. Coghlan made him continually vital and interesting.

On the English Stage the first recorded performance of *Jaques* is that given by Colley Cibber, at Drury Lane, when the alteration of the comedy was produced there, January 9, 1723, under the title of "Love in a Forest." Among Cibber's successors in the part, after the restoration of the original play,—effected December 20, 1740, at Drury Lane, when James Quin acted *Jaques,*—were Richard Ryan, 1742; Isaac Sparks, 1747; James Love (Dance), 1767; Matthew Clarke, 1771; Thomas Jefferson (the founder of the Jefferson Family of actors), 1774; Spranger Barry, 1775; John Henderson, 1779; Robert Bensley, 1783; John Palmer, 1785; F. Aicken, 1786; Richard Wroughton, 1788; George Frederick Cooke, 1802; —————— Raymond, 1804; Charles Mayne Young, 1814; J. Prescott Warde, 1830; Edward William Elton (true name Elt), 1833; Samuel Phelps, 1839; Charles John Kean, 1842; John M. Vandenhoff, 1845; James William Wallack, 1854; Barry Sullivan, 1855; Henry Howe (Hutchinson), 1856; John Ryder, 1862; Thomas Swinbourne, 1866; James Robert Anderson, and Thomas C. King, 1871; Herman Vezin, 1875; William Creswick, 1875; J. G. Grahame, 1882; John

H. Barnes, 1883; Arthur Stirling, 1888, and Oscar Asche, 1907.

In the few productions of "As You Like It" that were made in the early days of the American Stage,—occurring exclusively in Philadelphia, Boston, New York, and Baltimore,—*Jaques* was impersonated by ———— Chalmers, 1794; ———— Hipworth, and also John E. Harwood, 1794-'95, and John Hodgkinson, 1796. Other actors, in their day celebrated on our Stage, who played the part were Thomas Abthorpe Cooper, 1827; Thomas Sowerby Hamblin, 1841; Charles Walter Couldock, 1849; George K. Dickinson, 1856, and Charles Kemble Mason, 1866.

It does not appear that either Quin or Henderson made any particular mark as *Jaques*. The custom of the old-time actors was to make him grim, sombre, and didactic. Leigh Hunt says that, as played by Cooke, he was "merely a grave scoffer," and Cooke, no doubt, possessed the stage tradition of the part. The elder Jefferson was one of the many disciples of Garrick, whose style he copied, and probably he played *Jaques* exceedingly well. He played many parts, excelling in kings and tyrants. I have traced him in more than sixty characters, but have found no description of his *Jaques*. Young, in his cold, severe style, and with his fine figure, dignified carriage, grave temperament, and sweetly sympathetic voice, must have been an excellent *Jaques*. Phelps is credited with having shown a distinctively original ideal of the part, but precisely what it was I have not been able to discover: his personation is described as quaint and dry, and also as diverting: it caused frequent laughter. Anderson was stately in demeanor, deliberate in speech, heavy and prosy,—a designation equally applicable to Creswick. J. M. Vandenhoff, who acted *Jaques,* in association with his daughter, Charlotte Vandenhoff, as *Rosalind,* and Gustavus V. Brooke, as *Orlando,* at Manchester, England, 1845, was deemed exceptionally good: he was an imitator of Macready,—and Brooke was, avowedly, an imitator of him. Hodgkinson, whose versatility is said to have been amazing, but whose temperament seems to have been essentially blithe, may have played *Jaques* in a superior manner, but his performance is not described. Cooper should have been superb in it, if all is true that is recorded of his impressive presence and intellectual character, but his acting in this part, like that of Hodgkinson, is not critically noticed. Couldock, whom I remember in many characters as an actor of great force and versatility, was merely gloomy as *Jaques.*

TOUCHSTONE AND HIS PLAYERS.

Throughout the First Folio text of "As You Like It" the speeches of *Touchstone* and his entrances and exits are specified by the designation *Clown,* except that, in Act II., sc. 4, the original stage direction is: " Enter *Rosaline* for *Ganymede, Celia* for *Aliena,* and *Clown,* alias *Touchstone."* Theobald, in his second edition of "The Works of Shakespeare," was the first editor to change the designation of *"Clown,"* in the First Act, to that of *Touchstone,* and that change was right. Some authorities, however, do not think so,—finding "an inconsistency" between the *Clown* of the First Act and the *Clown,* alias *Touchstone,* of the other four acts; which inconsistency they feel must be rectified. Furness, inclining to the opinion that Shakespeare's "As You Like It" was not based directly on Lodge's "Rosalynd," but on "some pale, colorless drama which had been tried and failed, but whose dramatic capabilities Shakespeare's keen eye detected," thought that "these two clowns *cannot* be one and the same: the true *Touchstone* we meet for the first time in the Forest of Arden." That is an assumption, resting on nothing more authoritative than a Shakespeare lover's dissatisfaction with what he fancifully deemed defective in the early delineation of a favorite character. The learned and gentle

AS YOU LIKE IT 323

Furness himself wrote: "The chiefest objection to this [assumption] lies in the uncritical method which is herein implied, whereby we ascribe whatever is good to Shakespeare, and whatever is less good to some one else." There is no more reason for using that "uncritical method" in the analysis of this play and character than in that of any other;—in fact there is no reason at all for using it. The introduction of two *Clowns* in one play would have caused confusion and vexation, and therefore would have been destructive.

It does not appear to have occurred to any other commentator that *possibly Touchstone* is a name *assumed* by the *Clown*. *Rosalind* assumes the name of *Ganymede, Celia* that of *Aliena:* why should not the *Clown* have followed their example, and assumed the name of *Touchstone?* The likelihood that he did so seems favored—certainly it is not lessened,—by the First Folio stage direction, in Shakespeare's words, "Enter . . . *Clown,* alias *Touchstone.*" I do not recall any other similar instance of the use of the word *alias* in the works of Shakespeare. It is, perhaps, also significant that throughout the play the speeches of the "alias *Touchstone"* are never designated by that name, but always by the contraction, *Clo.,* exactly as the speeches of *"Ganymede"* and *"Aliena"* are designated, respectively, by the contractions *Ros.* and *Cel.* If the fooling of *Touchstone,* in the First Act, is somewhat heavy and "laid on with a trowel," it nevertheless is consistent *in kind* with his fooling in the later scenes. The wit, even of an allowed Fool, cannot always be "excellent jests, fire new from the mint,"—nor could even Shakespeare (so deplorably addicted to the making of bad puns) always write at his best. The speech "Thus men may grow wiser every day! It is the first time that ever I heard breaking of ribs was sport for ladies!" is very *Touchstone,* to the letter. The speeches "By my knavery, if I had it," and "Why, if thou never wast at court," are in the same vein. Furness says, "This clown [Act I., sc. 2] *Rosalind* threatens with the whip—would she ever have thus menaced *Touchstone?*" Such a "threat" would be but inconclusive evidence on the point in question,—namely, whether there are *two* Clowns or Fools in this play, or only *one,*—and it is inadmissible, for the reason that no such "threat" is made. *Celia,* not *Rosalind,* warns *Touchstone* (she does not threaten him) of the danger of gibing at one whom "old Frederick," her father, loves, saying, "Speak no more of him; you'll be whipped for taxation, one of these days." That is a speech of kindness, not of harshness, and it indicates the natural solicitude of *Celia* for the quaint *Jester* whom she loves, and of whom she says, "He'll go along o'er the wide world with me; leave me alone to woo him."

AS YOU LIKE IT

The editorial trifling which has sought to justify the error in the Folio whereby *Celia's* speech is given to *Rosalind* is too trivial for patience to endure or for judgment to expound. It is sufficient to observe here that Furness, naturally, approves of Theobald's obviously right correction, restoring the speech to *Celia*.

It is not known who was the first player of *Touchstone*. Fleay says that "the introduction [into "As You Like It"] of a *fool proper,* in place of a *comic clown,* such as is found in all the anterior comedies, confirms this statement [that the date of the production is 1599]: the 'fools' only occur in plays subsequent to Kempe's leaving the company." William Kempe (the original *Dogberry* and *Peter*) left the Lord Chamberlain's company in 1598 and, if Fleay's assumption is correct, he was not the original performer of *Touchstone*,—who is "a Fool proper"; and the first of that kind. Kempe's place, probably, was taken by Thomas Pope, and he may have been the original *Touchstone*. Since the restoration of the comedy to the English Stage, 1740, when *Touchstone* was assumed by Thomas Chapman, many distinguished names have been associated with the part, among them Charles Macklin, 1741; John Collins, 1756; Edward Shuter, 1762; Thomas King, 1767; George Alexander Steevens, 1771; John Quick, 1779; John

Edwin, 1783; John Palmer, 1788; Robert Keeley, 1830; Benjamin Webster, and John Pritt Harley, 1833; John Baldwin Buckstone, 1837; Henry Compton, 1845; ―――― Scharf, 1847; Henry Widdicombe, 1862; John Ryder, Frederick Everill, and Stanislaus Calhaem, 1871; J. G. Taylor, 1875; Arthur Cecil, 1877; Lionel Brough, 1880; Charles Groves, 1883; John Hare, 1885; William MacIntosh, 1888; George W. Weir, 1901; and Courtice Pounds, 1907.

On the American Stage conspicuous representatives of *Touchstone,* aside from others previously mentioned, were Lewis Hallam, who was the original on our Stage, 1796; William Warren, 1849; William Evans Burton, 1850; Charles Walcot, Sr., 1853; Charles Wheatleigh, 1856; Vining Bowers, 1870; William F. Owen, 1882; and Wilfred Clarke, 1889.

The quizzical humor of *Touchstone* is the overflow of a wise mind and a kind heart. Commentary, gathering volume in the passage of years and fortified by continuous repetition, has ascribed to that character various attributes which studious observation fails to discover, and in that way it has come to be regarded as a much more important and effective part than, in reality, it is. But it certainly is quaint, attractive, and even lovable. *Touchstone* wins by his fidelity, his good-nature, his ready mirth, his indifference to the caprices of Fortune, his philosophic habit of making the best of everything. There is no selfishness in him, and no conceit. The last scene is very difficult for an actor of *Touchstone,* because of the vivacity with which it requires to be played and the extremely tricky nature of the Quarrel Speech.

Thomas Chapman (——-1747) was celebrated for the excellence of his acting in all the *Clowns* or *Fools* in Shakespeare's plays, and particularly for his personation of *Touchstone.* This actor was one of those naturally comic persons who consider themselves specially capable of being tragic. He was delightfully humorous, but insisted on appearing in tragedy, —in which he was noisy and absurd. He managed for a time the little theatre at Richmond. Dunlap says he was excellent in "fops and fantastics" and particularly commends his *Marplot,* in "The Busybody,"—"in which he excited as much good laughter as ever shook a merry audience." Genest wrote that "his dry and voluble expression of the sarcastic humor of *Touchstone* has been equalled by nobody but King."

The pleasing eccentricity of *Touchstone,* his blithe humor, and his kindly spirit,—for, while satirical, he is gentle and wins affection,—will always endear him, alike to readers and auditors. It is impossible minutely to specify the particular quality of each and every performance of the part of which there is mention in the old and widely scattered records of the Stage, and perhaps it will suffice here to say that those actors who have specifically excelled in expressing quaint, whimsical, droll, sweet-tempered characters, have, naturally, succeeded in making *Touchstone* distinctive and delightful. One reason for the uncommonly high and somewhat disproportionate esteem in which the part is held, in the Theatre, undoubtedly is the fact that so many actors of the first order have played it. Thomas King, for example, who rivalled Garrick in comedy, was deemed perfection as *Touchstone;* and of King's rare qualifications, physical and mental, it is abundantly significant that he was the original representative of *Sir Peter Teazle* and of *Lord Ogleby,* and approved by both Sheridan and Colman. On the modern stage, in England, that exquisite artist John Hare has afforded another instance of the devotion of the finest talent to an exposition of *Touchstone* so rich in humor, so sweet in spirit, and so artistic in finish that it was declared incomparable; Hare is one of the few actors who can combine minute realism with poetic quality. On the American Stage the elder Charles Walcot, almost or quite forgotten now, made *Touchstone* conspicuously charming, by reason of the keen intellectuality, lurking beneath drollery, with which he suffused a delightfully fluent performance, his natural oddity,—which was unique,—and the facile

AS YOU LIKE IT

method of his art, which created a complete illusion. That great comedian William Warren likewise applied his wonderful faculty of impersonation to the character of *Touchstone,* and provided a memorable image of quizzical sapience, commingled with dry humor, playful satire, and kindly feeling. William Davidge also bestowed more than common care upon the part, and his *Touchstone* was highly valued by the critical judgment of his day. The embodiment, I remember, was bold and vigorous, rather than odd or recessive, for the reason that the personality of the actor was sturdy and rugged; he acted with authority and gained his effects by command rather than by enticement. His method was precise: every detail had been considered, but the total result was seeming spontaneity. The humor of his *Touchstone* was more ebullient than quaint, but it was rich and exhilarating, and lacked only a little in geniality. Davidge was one of the best of men, but his experience, while it had not embittered him, had made him somewhat cynical.

ORLANDO AND HIS PLAYERS.

John Philip Kemble played *Orlando* on several occasions, notably on the night, April 13, 1787, when Mrs. Jordan appeared as *Rosalind,* for the first time in London, and practically wrested that part from

Kemble's great sister, Mrs. Siddons. He did not excel as a lover, but he was by no means deficient in such parts: a piece of verse, by John Taylor, entitled "The Stage," contains these lines about Kemble, which are informingly suggestive of the quality of his acting in amatory characters:

> "When merely tender he appears too cold,
> Or, rather, fashioned in too rough a mould;
> Not fitted love in softer forms to wear,
> But stung with pride or madd'ning in despair,
> As when the lost *Octavian's* murmurs flow,
> In full luxuriance of romantic woe;
> Yet where *Orlando* cheers despairing age,
> Or the sweet wiles of *Rosalind* engage,
> We own that manly graces finely blend
> The tender lover and the soothing friend."

Orlando is a type of youthful manhood, resolute, but not obtrusively self-assertive, matured by some experience of adversity and harshness, gentle in temperament, noble in nature, courageous, instinctively gracious in manner, ardent in feeling, romantic and peculiarly winning by reason of half-wistful, half-playful humor. Among the best representatives of the part whom I remember were Walter Montgomery and Johnston Forbes-Robertson. Montgomery (his true name was Richard Tomlinson, and he told me that he was born in Brooklyn, when that place was called Gowanus) was so precisely suited to the part of *Orlando* that, in the acting, he seemed to live it, and, while he lived it, he filled the stage with sunshine. This remarkable actor (1827-1871) played many of the greatest parts in the Drama, ranging from *Othello* and *Hamlet* to *King Louis the Eleventh* and *Sir Giles Overreach,* and won popularity in England and Australia as well as in America; he died, in London, September 1, by suicide. The specific merits of Forbes-Robertson's *Orlando* were truth of ideal, sincerity, charm of personality, grace of manner, deep feeling, manly tenderness in the scenes with old *Adam,* impetuosity in the meeting with the exiles, nonchalant humor in the colloquy with *Jaques,* good-natured, kindly, half-amused, half-perplexed toleration of the winsome boy who would be taken for *Rosalind,* and, throughout the impersonation, his air of fine breeding and his perfect taste.

Other performers of *Orlando,* on the English Stage, were William Milward, 1740; ———— Hale, 1742; ———— Blakes, 1747; John Palmer, 1767; William Smith, 1771; W. T. Lewis, 1775; John Bannister, 1783; William Brereton, 1785; Joseph George Holman, 1789; ———— Barrymore, 1799; R. W. Elliston, 1804; Charles Kemble, 1805; W. A. Conway, 1814; F. Vining, 1825; J. R. Anderson, 1838; Henry Marston, 1847; Alfred Wiggin, 1854; William Farren, 1856; Frederick C. P. Robinson, 1857; Herman Vezin, 1860; William H. Kendal, 1867; Wybert Rousby, 1871; J. B. Howard, 1871; H. B. Conway, 1876; William Terriss, 1879; Kyrle Bellew, 1880; Luigi Leblache, 1881; George Alexander, 1883; F. R. Benson, 1901, and Henry Ainley, 1906.

On the American Stage actors of *Orlando,* other than those already mentioned, were ———— Moreton (true name, John Pollard), 1794; ———— Taylor, 1794; ———— Cleveland, 1796; John E. Martin, 1798; Humphrey Bland, 1850; Lester Wallack, 1853; and George Jordan, 1856.

COSTUME.

Particular consideration of the dressing of this comedy, in all its parts, would require more space than I can here allot to it, but a few general remarks are required and they may be found useful. If the period of the action of "As You Like It" is assumed to be that of the reign of King Charles the Eighth of France (1470-1498), and the scene somewhere in that country, the proper dresses for *Rosalind, Celia,* and the ladies of the Court of *Duke Frederick* would comprise,—with reasonable variations to suit individual peculiarities,—"gowns of silk velvet and cloth of gold, rich embroideries in Venice gold, chiefly of the net and pine-apple pattern; deep trimmings of fur or velvet to collars, cuffs, and skirts" of dresses (E. W. Godwin). The dresses would be low at the throat, with short waists, rather full over the hips, with full sleeves, caught in at the wrists, and with long "over-sleeves" depending from the shoulder as low as to the knee, or even lower. The ladies might wear high, conical shaped hats, with "scarfs or veils depending from the peaks." Godwin, a trustworthy authority on Costume, sensibly remarks,—and every manager and actor in selecting costumes for any play might well be guided by his opinion,—that "The more we know of the costume of the past, the more satisfied we are that we can avoid, *if we choose,* those curiosities of dress where the ludicrous is predominant, and which, by causing untimely laughter, interfere sadly with the dramatic action."

Duke Frederick would wear trunks, tights, and a long gown, reaching to the ankles or even dragging upon the ground; belted at the waist; and, probably, both a pouch, dependent from his girdle, and a dagger or a short sword. The gown, open from the waist upward, would disclose a rich doublet, and the edges of the opening of the gown would be trimmed with fur. The *Duke's* shoes would be of leather, and pointed, with toes from "two inches to three quarters of a yard in length," and he would wear a hat made of cloth, circular in shape, with a crown of cloth hanging down on one side, or with long feather plumes. The dress of a *Forester* would be a leather jerkin, a short cloak, trunk hose or short pantaloons, all of russet color or dark green, except the jerkin, and top-boots: the collar of the cloak might be lined with yellow or red. *Rosalind's* Forest dress should be a modification of this, blended with the garb of a shepherd, such as would make her appearance specially attractive, and such as would be reasonably suggestive of disguise. It would be rank absurdity to attempt (as Richard Grant White recommended) to present *Rosalind* in a disguise that would deceive an audience and thus make absolutely credible the deception practised by her upon her father, *Orlando, Jaques,* and others. White would have *Rosalind* arrayed in "a doublet or short jacket, with close sleeves, fitting tight to the body, and coming down only to the hip or a very little below it"; with trunk hose laced to that doublet with silken points, those trunk hose "stuffed out about the waist and the upper thigh with bombast, or what was called cotton-wool," so as to "make it impossible to tell, so far as shape was concerned, whether the wearer was of the male or female sex," and with "loose boots of tawny leather and almost meeting the puffed and bombasted trunk hose. To complete this costume in character she should wear a coarse russet cloak, and a black felt hat, with a narrow brim and slightly conical crown, on the band of which she might put a short feather and around it might wear a light gold chain or ribbon and medal. Thus disguised," and, as White also wished, with her face stained with umber, and "her hair tied up in love knots, after the fashion of young military dandies of that time," *Rosalind* might have defied her lover's eye or her father's. She might, indeed!

The application of such silly, prosy literalness to the treatment of *Rosalind's* "disguise" exhibits a surprising density of perception of this entirely fanciful subject. The effective disguise of *Rosalind* must be granted as a basic premise, along with all the other impossibilities and absurdities of the play: we are in Arden!—and in Arden all things are possible and are accepted as credible, as long as they are lovely and charming. Judged by the test of probability, this play would not "hold water" at any point. The "disguise" of *Rosalind,* as a matter of fact, is no disguise at all, and it cannot be made so. Not one woman in ten thousand (and certainly *Rosalind* is not the one!) can, in male attire, conceal her sex. Besides the shape of the body (which White recommends to be padded out with "bombast"), the shape of the limbs, the hands, fingers, and nails, the size and carriage of the head, the quality of the hair, the expression of the face, the eyes, and, above all, the quality of the voice, would disclose her sex. Even in the present time, with the aid of modern chemistry applied to cosmetics, it is not easy to color the countenance so that, under the direct rays of natural light, it will deceive attentive scrutiny. *Rosalind,* furthermore, is not a detective officer, expert in "make-up"; she is a gently nurtured lady, a court beauty, and she would indeed soon have reason to be "more clamorous than a parrot against rain" if she were to expose her fair face, smeared with umber, to the burning sun and wind: is it not enough, ladies, to have your skin burnt till it peels, without having *umber* rubbed on the sore, inflamed surface? But it would be a waste of time further to discuss this notion of *Rosalind's* "disguise": the part might better be given back to the "boy" actors, and played as it was when Shakespeare saw it, than to be so treated.

Douce says of *Touchstone* that "His dress should be a parti-colored garment. He should occasionally carry a bauble in his hand and wear ape's ears to his hood, which is, probably, the head-dress intended by Shakespeare, there being no allusion whatever to a cock's head or comb."

CURIOSITIES.

In July and August, 1880, Mme. Modjeska and a party of friends, one of whom was Johnston Forbes-Robertson, passed a little time at the fishing village of Cadgwith, near Lizard Point, Cornwall, England, where, incidentally, Mme. Modjeska was asked, by the Rev. Mr. Jackson, Rector of the parish, to give a performance in the open air, for the benefit of a local charity. This she consented to do, and, on a night in August, in the grounds of the Rectory, under an almost full moon, she and Robertson played two scenes from "Romeo and Juliet," acting on a platform erected among trees. The attendance was large and the effect of the performance was considered fine. An enthusiastic spectator wrote a glowing account of the incident and sent it to Edmund Yates's London newspaper, "The World," in which it was published, and it was widely read. Among the readers of that article was Lady Archibald Campbell, a devotee of the Drama and specially interested in amateur theatrical performances. After some correspondence with Robertson, Lady Campbell arranged an out-door representation of "As You Like It," in which, I believe, professional as well as amateur performers participated, and in which she assumed the part of *Orlando*. An open-air presentment of the comedy was, later, given under the direction of the artist and antiquarian Edward W. Godwin, and still later the plan was adopted by "Ben" Greet. Thus the casual acting of scenes from "Romeo and Juliet," in a rectory garden in a remote Cornish village, led to the many so-called "Pastoral Performances" of "As You Like It," and other plays, which, since, have occurred in America as well as in England and elsewhere.

"As You Like It" is not better adapted to outdoor representation than are several other of Shakespeare's plays, notably "A Midsummer Night's Dream" and "The Tempest" (in the latter all the scenes are exterior, except the glimpses of *Prospero's Cave*), but its presentment out-of-doors, while always much less effective than a good performance of it given in a proper theatre, is, when discreetly directed, interesting as a curiosity. The first of such eccentric displays of "As You Like It" given in America occurred, August 8, 1887, on the lawn of the Masconomo House at Manchester-by-the-Sea, Massachusetts. That hotel, a summer resort, was built, in 1878, by Junius Brutus Booth, Jr., and at the time of the open-air performance here mentioned it was managed by Agnes Booth, his widow (Mrs. John B. Schoeffel), now deceased, who acted in it as *Audrey*. An auditorium was made by enclosing, under canvas, a central tract of the lawn, about 100 feet square, and in this were ranged seats for upwards of 1,200 persons. The "stage," showing the Forest of Arden, was constructed by walling in, with cedar branches, a grove of about 100 trees, many of which, full grown, were transplanted for the occasion. No canvas was used in the tract reserved for the play. At the back there was a dense copse, which marked the southern boundary of the lawn. The scene was veritably sylvan and prettily effective. The day was calm and still, and the performance, which was largely attended, gave much pleasure and was generally considered a successful novelty. The costumes were loaned by Miss Rose Coghlan, who acted *Rosalind*. Frank Mayo played *Jaques* and his personation was admirable, —true in the quality of character displayed, discreet and various in elocution, and impressively suggestive of a rich background of thought and experience.

One of the most continuous and insistent endeavors of the Stage has been to allure profitable public notice by the ever potent device of novelty, and one of the oldest expedients employed with a view to imparting "novelty" to theatrical exhibitions is the assumption of male characters and costumes by women. The first regular appearance of women as actors, on the English-speaking Stage, occurred in 1660-'61, and, about 1672, "the *actresses* in the King's Theatre, to vary the amusements of the house, represented 'Marriage-a-la-

Mode' in men's dresses" (Scott's "Life of Dryden").
"As You Like It" has, in the same way, been utilized
for "novel" presentation of this kind. It was acted,
at Palmer's Theatre, New York, November 21 (afternoon), 1894, by a company exclusively of women.
Mary Shaw performed as *Rosalind;* Emma Field as
Celia; Maude Banks as *Orlando;* Mrs. E. A. Eberle
as the *Banished Duke;* Mrs. Chambers-Ketchum as
Adam; Kate Davis as *Touchstone;* and Mme. Fanny
Janauschek as *Jaques.* The only notable performance was that given by Mme. Janauschek. She was a
large, formidable woman, sufficiently massive in person
and method to make possible an acceptable assumption
of masculinity; her voice was copious and powerful,
she possessed histrionic genius, and she was a consummate artist. She did not much exert herself as *Jaques,*
and I do not recall that she ever acted the part
again. Her personation was marked by authority,
distinction, and a pleasing atmosphere of singularity;
and,—notwithstanding her imperfect pronunciation of
the English language, the principal speeches were
intelligently and impressively delivered. The representation, as a whole, was indeed a curiosity.

In almost every representation of "As You Like It"
which I have seen, and in every one of which I have
read, there has been a discord, arising from the
inexorable fact that the play is ideal and fanciful,

AS YOU LIKE IT 341

in various ways distinctly at variance with probability, even possibility, while the players are necessitated to make the action seem to be real. Lower in imagination and nearer to human sympathy than "The Tempest" and "A Midsummer Night's Dream,"—those representative poetic fantasies,—"As You Like It" is almost as elusive of the actor's grasp as either of them, and quite as difficult to maintain in a perfect poise of illusion. The first and last acts are, comparatively, easy to manage: it is in the intermediate sylvan scenes that the poet has sounded his strange, wild, ruefully glad note, which no common medium can catch and transmit. Players of uncommonly fine intelligence, feeling, and artistic faculty alone can do justice to this fine comedy. The heart that beats in it is that which Wordsworth so happily designates:

> "The heart that every hour runs wild,
> Yet never once has gone astray."

IV.

KING LEAR.

"A poor old king, with sorrow for my crown,
Throned upon straw, and mantled with the wind,—
For pity, my own tears have made me blind
That I might never see my children's frown;
And may be madness, like a friend, has thrown
A folded fillet over my dark mind,
So that unkindly speech may sound for kind,—
Albeit I know not.—I am childish grown—
And have not gold to purchase wit withal—
I that have once maintain'd most royal state—
A very bankrupt now that may not call
My child, my child—all-beggar'd save in tears,
Wherewith I daily weep an old man's fate,
Foolish—and blind—and overcome with years!"
—Thomas Hood.

THE OLD STORY OF KING LEAR.

The story of "King Lear" is ancient. It occurs in various forms, largely that of verse, in old English writings. It is found in the "Historia Brutonum," by Geoffrey of Monmouth (1110-1154); the "Brut," by the thirteenth-century Worcestershire monk Layamon; the "Concordances of Histories," by Robert Fabyan (1450-1512); the "Chronicles of England, Scotland, and Ireland" (1557), by Raphael Holinshed

KING LEAR 343

(———-c.1580); that part of Thomas Sackville's "The Mirror for Magistrates" which was written by John Higgins, one of his assistants, and published in 1574; and "Albion's England" (1586), by William Warner (1558-1609). It also is told by Spenser, in fifty-four lines of the Tenth Canto of "The Faerie Queene" (1590-1594). With at least one of those works, that of Holinshed, Shakespeare is known to have been familiar, and it is not impossible that he was acquainted with some of the others. His tragedy of "King Lear," however, while, obviously, based, to some extent, on the story as told by Holinshed, was, to a larger extent, based on an earlier play, by an unknown author. That earlier play is extant, and the fact that Shakespeare was indebted to it is established by comparison of the two compositions.

"KING LEIR."—THE OLD PLAYS.

The first mention of a piece of writing on the subject of King Lear which appears in the Registers of The Stationers' Company is made under date of May 8, 1594, in these words:

> "Edward White. Entered also for his Copy, under the hands of both the Wardens, a Book entitled 'The Most Famous Chronicle History of Leir, King of England, and His Three Daughters.'"

No copy of this "book" has been found, and whether it was a narrative or a play is unknown.

The next entry alluding to this subject is made under date of May 8, 1605, to

> "Simon Stafford. Entered for his Copy, under the hands of the Wardens, a Book called 'The Tragical History of King Leir and His Three Daughters,' etc. *As it was lately acted.*"

(On the title page of the book [printed for John Wright, London, 1605] this play is called "The *True* Chronicle History of King Leir, and his Three Daughters, Gonorill, Ragan, and Cordilla," and the assertion is thereon made that it is printed "As it hath been *divers and sundry times lately* acted" [Capell].)

Then follows this entry, to

> "John Wright. Entered for his Copy, by assignment from Simon Stafford, and by consent of Master Leake, 'The Tragical History of King Leir, and His Three Daughters,' Provided, that Simon Stafford shall have the printing of this book."

This latter "book" was the old play that appears to have prompted Shakespeare to write his tragedy. When, where, or by whom it "was lately acted" is not known, but a record exists, made, apparently, on the authority of Philip Henslowe's "Diary," of the presentment of a drama on the subject of King Lear, at the Rose Theatre, Southwark, on April 6, 1593, the actors being "the Queen's Men and Lord Sussex's together." That, possibly, was the actual first production of "King Lear" upon the stage. Furness wished to believe that those two old plays were identical. Halliwell-Phillips intimated the opinion that the former, which is lost, "bore, probably, more affinity to Shakespeare's drama." The same learned editor also remarked that "some of the incidents" of Shakespeare's tragedy "were adopted from one *or more* older dramas on the same legend."

SHAKESPEARE'S "KING LEAR."

Shakespeare's "King Lear" was first published in 1608. The entry of it in the Stationers' Registers appears under date of November 26, 1607. The publisher was Nathaniel Butter, who brought out two editions of it, in quarto form, in the same year. It is not known and cannot be determined which of those quartos was the first. The title page of one of them says, "Printed for Nathaniel Butter, and are to be sold at his shop in Paul's Churchyard, at the sign of the Pied Bull, near St. Austin's Gate."

The title page of the other contains the specification "Printed for Nathaniel Butter." The typographical composition of the Pied Bull quarto is defective. Halliwell-Phillips, who investigated the matter, with his customary scrupulous care, says that in the twelve known copies of it no two are exactly alike. It was long supposed, because of this confusion, that *three* quarto editions of the tragedy were published by Butter. This is affirmed by Collier, who infers "the extreme popularity" of the play. The error was perceived and exposed by Aldis and Wright. After 1608 "King Lear" was not again published till 1623, when it appeared in the precious First Folio, in which it stands eighth in the division of Tragedies, occupying pages 283 to 309, inclusive, of that division. There are fifty lines in the Folio print which are not in either of the quartos, and there are 220 lines in the quartos which are not in the Folio. It is not supposed that any of those lines are spurious. It is not known by whom the text of the Folio was prepared for publication. The printer's copy was furnished by Heminge and Condell, Shakespeare's fellow actors and friends, who were the owners of the plays and who, presumably, delivered to the press the versions of them which had been used in the theatre. The best text of "King Lear," that which stands in the authoritative library editions of

Shakespeare, is an eclectic one, suitably combining those of the quartos and the Folio.

It should be observed that while Shakespeare was indebted to Holinshed's "Chronicles" and to an earlier drama for some of the materials of his tragedy, he departed widely from those precedents, introduced new characters, invented a new final catastrophe, and vitalized the whole fabric of narrative and action with the fire of tragic passion and the glow of poetry. In Holinshed's version of the story and in the earlier "King Leir," which follows that authority, the cruel, ingrate daughters are discomfited, there is no mention of madness, and the *King* is restored to his throne.

By some authorities it is maintained that Shakespeare was acquainted with a Ballad on the story of King Lear, the date of which has not been ascertained, in which the *King* is declared to have been driven "mad." Those authorities consider that the Ballad followed Holinshed's "Chronicles" but preceded Shakespeare's play, and that the dramatist was indebted to it for the intimation of *King Lear's* madness,—the theme which he has exploited with such tremendous power. Bishop Percy included that Ballad in his "Reliques of Ancient English Poetry" (1765), remarking: "Here is found the hint of *Lear's* madness, which the old chronicles do not mention." The "hint" occurs in this stanza:

> "And calling to remembrance then
>   His younger daughter's words
> That said, the duty of a child
>   Was all that love affords:
> But doubting to repair to her
>   Whom he had banish'd so
> Grew frantic mad; for in his mind
>   He bore the wounds of woe."

Other authorities maintain that the Ballad followed Shakespeare's play, and was, in a measure, based on it. Halliwell-Phillipps, recording that the most ancient known copy of the ballad is one contained in a book called "The Golden Garland of Princely Pleasures and Delicate Delights," states that the earliest known copy of that book with which he was acquainted was one of the third edition, dated 1620; and he declares: "it is all but impossible that it could have been published before the appearance of Shakespeare's tragedy." Various Shakespeare scholars, Ritson, Dowden, and Furness among them, concur in that opinion. The question is, mainly, one of date, and it remains unsettled.

Ritson, affirming that "the performance and celebrity of Shakespeare's play might have set the ballad-maker at work, and furnished him the circumstance of *Lear's* madness, of which there is no hint either in the histories or the old play," also states that "the writer of the ballad *does not appear to have read*"

Shakespeare's play. This is singular reasoning, since, while it assumes that the performance and celebrity of Shakespeare's play may have prompted "the ballad-maker" to make his ballad, it intimates that instead of deriving material from the imputed source of his inspiration he went to Holinshed's "Chronicles." *Why* should it be supposed that a writer inspired by Shakespeare's tragedy resorted to Holinshed's histories?

It is notable that "the ballad-maker" spells the *King's* name *Leir,* and designates the *King of France* by the name *Aganippus,* thus making use of details which it is impossible would have been used by a "servile" writer, prompted by "a recollection of Shakespeare's play,"—as Halliwell-Phillipps believed "the ballad-maker" to have been. Dr. Johnson's opinion on this subject was expressed in these explicit words: "The writer of the ballad added something to the history, which is proof that he would have added more if it had occurred to his mind, *and more must have occurred* if he had seen Shakespeare."

The names of the fiends mentioned by *Edgar,* Act IV., sc. 1, appear to have been taken by the poet from a contemporary book, by Samuel Harsnett (1561-1631), Archbishop of York from 1628 till his death, entitled "Declaration of Egregious Popish Impostures to withdraw Her Majesty's subjects from their

Allegiance." That part of Shakespeare's play which relates to the wretched experience of *Glo'ster* may have been suggested to the poet by passages in the romance of "Arcadia" (1590-1593), by Sir Philip Sidney (1554-1586), relative to "the pitiful state and story of the Paphlagonian unkind *King* and his kind son"; but that material the dramatist varied and invigorated by his unique treatment of it. In Sidney's romance the *King of Paphlagonia* (the precursor of *Glo'ster*) is reinstated in his sovereignty, and his oppugnant sons are reconciled. In Shakespeare's "King Lear" the culmination is entirely tragic,— misery and ruin, relieved only by death.

FIRST PERFORMANCE.—RICHARD BURBAGE.

The date of the first recorded representation of Shakespeare's "King Lear" is specified in the entry of the play in the Stationers' Registers, that entry being dated November 26, 1607, and containing the words, "as it was played before the King's Majesty, at Whitehall, upon Saint Stephen's night, at Christmas *last,* by his majesty's servants, playing usually at the Globe, on Bankside." In effect that statement is repeated on the title page of the Pied Bull quarto. St. Stephen's night is December 26. The King was James the First. The date of the performance given

KING LEAR

before him was December 26, 1606. It is improbable that an untried play would have been selected for presentation at Court, and it is reasonable to suppose that "King Lear" had been successfully acted, at the Globe Theatre, in the summer of 1606,—then being produced for the first time. Richard Burbage was the leading actor at the Globe Theatre, and the same testimony which declares him to have been the original performer of *Hamlet, King Richard the Third, Othello,* and other Shakespearean parts, is adduced to show that he was the original performer of *King Lear*. A part of that testimony is the "Elegy upon Burbage," believed to have been written soon after his death (1619), which contains these lines:

"Thy stature small, but every thought and mood
Might thoroughly, from thy face, be understood;
And his whole action he could change with ease
From ancient *Lear* to youthful *Pericles*."

THOMAS BETTERTON.

In the interval between the dramatic regnancy of Burbage and that of Betterton,—a period of about sixty years,—the tragedy appears to have been neglected, but at some time between 1662 and 1665, the precise date being unknown,—Downes implies 1663,—it was produced by Sir William Davenant, at Lincoln's Inn Fields, and, according to that recorder, "as Mr. Shakespeare wrote it, before it was altered by Mr. Tate." Betterton was a member of the company and he may have appeared as *King Lear,* in that production: in 1663 he was twenty-eight years of age, and he had been then only two, or perhaps three, years on the stage, and, possibly, the part was assigned to an older and more experienced actor: it is not positively known by whom it was then played. Betterton, however, did act *King Lear* when Tate's alteration of Shakespeare's tragedy was first represented (1681) at Dorset Garden. There is no account of his performance. He was then forty-six years old and in the prime of his powers, but the old writers who express enthusiastic admiration of his acting in other parts,—*Hamlet, Macbeth, Othello,* and *Brutus,*—are silent as to his *King Lear.* Cibber, in particular, does not mention it, but he declares that "genius, which Nature only gives, was so strong in Betterton that it shone out in every speech and motion of him." Rowe, the first editor of Shakespeare, who saw him often, affirmed "he has studied Shakespeare so well and is so much master of him that whatever part of his he performs he does it as if it had been written on purpose for him, and that the author had exactly conceited it as he plays it." His performance must have been commendable, but, as remarked by Davies (1783), "It is in vain to talk of Betterton's *Lear,* for we know nothing of it."

Genest, with characteristic asperity, rebukes Davies for making this statement, declaring that "Downes expressly mentions *Lear* as *one of* Betterton's best parts." That is not true, or, if it is, I have not been able, in a careful reading of the "Roscius Anglicanus," to find Downes's "express" mention. The old Prompter does, in his high-flown way, pay tribute to Betterton, saying "There needs nothing to speak his Fame more than the following parts," and appending a list of sixteen parts (and plays), one of them being *King Lear.* It can, no doubt, rightly be assumed that Downes would have selected for specification only Betterton's "best parts," or some of them, as significant of his title to renown, but it cannot rightly be said that, in furnishing his list, "Downes *expressly mentions Lear* as one of Betterton's best parts." The statement of Davies remains authentic. Betterton acted Tate's *King Lear,* but there is no *proof* that he acted Shakespeare's, and no known writer has told us *how* he acted Tate's.

GEORGE POWELL.

George Powell (1658-1714), who appears to have been an actor of extraordinary ability, in both comedy and tragedy, acted *King Lear,* November 30, 1710, at Drury Lane. This talented man marred his fortune and ruined himself by inebriety. He was, however, much admired, and the records of him make it manifest that he signally excelled in characters of acute sensibility and scenes of pathos. Genest expresses the impression that he needed only industry and sobriety to have made him, next to Betterton, the first actor of his time. He was uncommonly popular with members of his profession,—a significant fact. Addison wrote of him, in "The Spectator": "He is excellently formed for a Tragedian, and, when he pleases, deserves the admiration of the best judges." Powell was a dramatist as well as an actor: he wrote four plays,—"Alphonso, King of Naples," "A Very Good Wife," "The Treacherous Brothers," and "The Impostor Defeated." His personation of *King Lear* is praised, but not particularly described. He likewise acted *Edgar,* in this tragedy, and his performance is declared to have been excellent. *George* Powell is not to be confounded with *William* Powell, a performer of later date, not a descendant or relative, who also was distinguished, and who also acted *King Lear.*

BARTON BOOTH.

Barton Booth (1681-1733), poet and scholar as well as actor, and certainly a man of genius, first appeared as *King Lear* on October 29, 1715, at Drury Lane. Booth had acted with Betterton, whom he admired and revered, and of whom his imitation, when he chose to give it, was considered perfect. But Booth's style was his own. On being asked why he did not, on the stage, play the whole of a part in the manner of Betterton, he answered, "The *whole* is too much for me: I shall be content with taking from this great exemplar what I think best suited to my general powers." He could have acted *King Lear* in the manner of Betterton, but it does not appear that he did so. Davies, who had seen Booth, but not Betterton, says that Booth "stole what he could from Betterton and fitted it to his own powers." Booth's performance of *King Lear* is nowhere minutely described, but somewhere it is designated as "sorrowing, not roaring." Davies, descanting on Garrick's *King Lear,* recalls that of Booth, and says that Booth was more rapid than Garrick in speaking the imprecation on *Goneril,* that "his fire was ardent and his feelings were remarkably energetic, but they were not attended with those strugglings of parental affection and those powerful emotions of conflicting passions so visible in [Garrick's] every look, action, and attitude." Theophilus Cibber, writing of Booth, declares that in *King Lear* "his madness is hardly to be described: never did pity or terror more vehemently possess an audience than by his judicious and powerful execution of that part."

BOHEME AND QUIN.

Anthony Boheme, who seems to have been an actor of superior talent but of whom the record is meagre, appeared as *King Lear* October 29, 1715, at Lincoln's Inn Fields. He is said to have been, at first, a sailor, afterward a performer at Fairs. From an obscure beginning he made his way to distinction, but his career was brief. His performance of *King Lear* was commended by Macklin, whose recorded judgments of acting are usually marked by uncommon good sense. Davies mentions Boheme as an original actor, not an imitator. His person was large, his face expressive, his bearing authoritative. His *King Lear* appears to have been characterized by venerable aspect, majestic demeanor, suitable action, and a vocalism equally powerful and harmonious. Benjamin Victor says, of Boheme, that "the natural musical, piercing tones of his voice, particularly adapted to grief and distress, must have touched the heart of every feeling auditor too forcibly ever to be forgot." The same recorder states that "in some scenes in *King Lear,* though he wanted judgment to mark and support the fine variety of that character, he has surprised many a critic with his powers, in the distressful passages."

James Quin, who had acted with Boheme, as *Glo'ster,* giving an excellent performance, succeeded him as *King Lear,* March 8, 1739, at Drury Lane, but did not equal him. Murphy says that Quin was "admired in the character," adding, however, that "to express a quick succession of passions was not his talent." All that is known of Quin indicates that, while capable of bluff geniality and generous conduct, he was a hard, arrogant, overbearing man, deficient of sensibility and tenderness, but possessed of a discriminative sense of character, and coarsely humorous. Davies testifies that "Quin, in characters of singular humor and dignified folly, of blunt and boisterous demeanor, of treacherous art, contemptuous spleen, and even of pleasing gravity, had no equal," and also that he was "an excellent speaker"; but, with reference to his *Lear,* records a distinctly adverse judgment, saying that "Quin felt neither the tender nor the violent emotions of the soul, and therefore should not have hazarded his reputation in a part for which Nature unfitted him." Boheme and Quin performed in Tate's version of the tragedy, which, indeed, from the time of its first presentment (1681) held the stage for more than a century and a half.

DAVID GARRICK.

It can be inferred from the discriminative comparison of Booth and Garrick (already quoted), by Davies,—an eye-witness, an experienced actor, and an observer qualified to judge,—that Garrick, when impersonating *King Lear,* completely concealed the art of the actor and conveyed a convincing sense of being identified with the man,—the agonized father as well as the outraged King. Davies also declares that "Garrick rendered the curse so terribly affecting to the audience that during his utterance of it they seemed to shrink from it as from a blast of lightning." Before speaking the curse Garrick stood, rigid and silent for a moment, as if paralyzed with amazement and horror at his daughter's repellent behavior; then,—throwing away a crutch, which he carried in that scene, and kneeling upon one knee,—clasped his outstretched hands, looked upward, invoking the heavens, and began to speak, in a strained, choked, breaking, thrilling voice, which caused a tremendous effect.

In forming his *King Lear* Garrick profited by visiting an insane asylum and observing the demeanor and conduct of insane persons, and also, after his first appearance in the part, he profited by the counsel he received from old Charles Macklin, and from a clever, dissipated man-about-town, Dr. Barrowby, whose

From an Old Print   *Author's Collection*

DAVID GARRICK AS *KING LEAR*

*"Let the great gods,
That keep this dreadful pother o'er our heads,
Find out their enemies now!"*

Act III., Sc. 2

criticisms he had solicited and whose suggestions he carried into effect. After again seeing the performance Macklin commended it, in terms which, for him,—a truthful, blunt man, incapable of flattery,— were enthusiastic. Garrick's delivery of the curse, he said, seemed to electrify the audience with horror. Also he noticed that the words "Kill—kill—kill!" were uttered in a way to express the uttermost of frenzy, and that the pathos of the acting, in the scene of the recognition of *Cordelia,* was irresistible: "In short," Macklin concluded, "the little dog made it a *chef d'œuvre,*—and so it remained to the end of his life."

The acting of Garrick when depicting the madness of *Lear,* evidently, was perfect. "He had no sudden starts,"—so wrote the biographer Arthur Murphy,— "no violent gesticulations; his movements were slow and feeble; misery was depicted in his countenance; he moved his head in the most desolate manner; his eyes were fixed, or if they turned to any one near him, he made a pause and fixed his look on the person after much delay, his features at the same time telling what he was going to say before he uttered a word. During the whole time he presented a sight of woe and misery and a total alienation of mind from every idea but that of his unkind daughters."

John Bannister,—an actor acquainted with all the artifices of the vocation,—told the poet Rogers that he happened to be behind the scenes at Drury Lane one night when Garrick was acting *King Lear,* and that the tones in which Garrick uttered the words, "O fool, I shall *go mad,*" "absolutely thrilled him." In using the exclamation, "O fool," etc., the actor's intention must have been to make the wretched *King* refer to himself,—as a distracted man often does. Garrick at first used Tate's version of the play, but later (1756) somewhat changed it, introducing more of the original than Tate had retained; he always excluded the part of the *Fool,* though he once dubiously entertained a purpose of restoring that character to its place in the play and assigning it to Woodward, who (says Davies) "promised to be very chaste in his coloring, and not to counteract the agonies of *Lear";* but the purpose was abandoned.

SPRANGER BARRY.

Spranger Barry (1719-1777) first acted *King Lear* in 1744, at the Smock Alley Theatre, Dublin, but he did not play the part in London till 1756, when, on February 26, he appeared in it at Covent Garden. He had then been twelve years an actor and ten years on the London Stage, and in the popular esteem had established himself as a successful rival to Garrick. He possessed the signal personal advantages of a manly figure, a handsome face, and a copious and sympathetic voice: "never was heard such a voice," said Mrs. Abington, long afterward, speaking to Henry Crabb Robinson. According to contemporary testimony, Barry was a man of excessive sensibility and ardent feeling, by which, in acting, he was sometimes overcome. He excelled in the expression of the amatory emotions, and for that reason was much admired by females. His performance of *Romeo* was generally preferred to that of any other actor of his time, and he was enthusiastically commended for the passionate ardor of his *Othello*. His manner and tone, in saying, "No, not much moved" were deemed the perfection of pathos. To certain requirements of *Romeo* and *Othello* he was, temperamentally and physically, better suited than Garrick was, and there is no question that, in them, he excelled his rival not only in popular esteem but in artistic merit: on the other hand there is no room for doubt that Garrick possessed a more authoritative personality, a more comprehensive and potent imagination, more various and brilliant capability of dramatic expression, more of both tragic and comic power, and far more intellect. Barry was five feet, eleven inches in height, an expert dancer and fencer, and therefore lofty and easy in bearing and movement. Garrick was lower in stature and slighter in frame, but his figure was symmetrical, his demeanor noble and graceful, and his personality singularly attractive; he possessed wonderfully brilliant dark eyes and a superlatively expressive countenance, and he managed his clear, melodious voice so thoroughly well that it seemed of vast volume and unlimited scope. He was an impersonator, not a declaimer. "On the stage," says Goldsmith, in the well-known lines called "Retaliation," "he was natural, simple, affecting." Barry, as *King Lear,* was venerable, impressive, and at moments pathetic, but he was unequal to the mad scenes, and as a whole the part eluded his grasp. In all the accounts of the rivalry between Barry and Garrick, in this character, an epigram makes its appearance, which was written by an attached friend of the actor's, ——— Berenger, but of which the authorship has sometimes been imputed to Garrick himself, who was prone to that form of composition and who habitually made expert use of the press:

> "The town has found out different ways
> To praise the different *Lears:*
> To Barry they give loud huzzas!
> To Garrick—only tears."

Theophilus Cibber, a person unfriendly to Garrick, but a shrewd observer of theatrical affairs in the Garrick period, critically commenting on that epigram, questioned the truth of it, saying:

" . . . 'Tis as certain that Garrick has had other applause besides tears, as 'tis true Barry, besides loud huzzas, has never failed to draw tears from many of his spectators. Were it injurious to the Author of this Epigram to suppose he was a little hurt by Barry's success? Though it may be difficult to say who was the Author, yet to guess who was hurt most by Barry's applause cannot be a very hard matter to guess. Permit me, therefore, to deliver to you a reply to the forementioned Epigram. I believe it may fairly stand by the other, and is not the less poignant for its truth:

'Critics attend,—and judge the rival *Lears;*
Whilst each commands applause, and each your tears:
Then own this truth: Well he performs his part
Who touches,—even Garrick to the heart!' "

There is no doubt that, notwithstanding his preeminent superiority, Garrick was sometimes a little "touched" by the success of some of his contemporaries, but there is also no doubt that he had no occasion to distress himself about the applause bestowed on Barry, in this contest. The most informing of the epigrams which were inspired by the rivalry of those two great actors in *King Lear* is this:

"A King—nay, *every inch a King!*
Such Barry doth appear:
But Garrick's quite a different thing,
He's—every inch KING LEAR!"

William Smith, one of the best actors of the Garrick era, who also was one of the best men of that time, finely educated, of sober judgment and of irreproachable life, and whose testimony, therefore, is of the greatest value, wrote as follows, about Garrick and Barry, in a letter to his friend, the veteran journalist John Taylor:

"Of Garrick and Barry, where *love* was the burthen or rather support of the scene, Barry was at least equal to Roscius. *Romeo, Castalio, Varaves,* and *Jaffier* were *his own.* In the more commanding passions, where the brain forced its workings through the magic power of the eye, Garrick was beyond comparison in *everything;* but Barry next to him. . . . As to Garrick, my utmost ambition as an actor was to be thought worthy to hold up his train. . . . As a man I admired, loved, and honored him. His merits were great, his benevolence and generosity, though disputed by some, were, to *my certain knowledge,* diffusive and abundant. In bargains, perhaps he was keen—but punctual. *Fiat justitia.* . . . My embers will a little warm when I think of his departed spirit."

Taylor himself accords that "after seeing Garrick, Barry's *Lear* appeared to me cold and tame in comparison." Barry recognized the general superiority of Garrick as an actor. The latter having decided to act *Evander,* in Arthur Murphy's "The Grecian Daughter," which part Murphy had promised to Barry, it became necessary for the author to notify Barry of Garrick's determination and to excuse himself for not fulfilling his promise regarding the part of *Evander.* "Let him perform it," said Barry, interrupting Murphy's apology; "he will soon be tired and resign it to me, and *I* shall be able to perform it much better for his example." In the event, however, Garrick finally decided *not* to act *Evander,* and it was played by Barry without the benefit of his example.— "Roscius" elected to say Farewell to the Stage in comedy, and made his last professional appearance as *Don Felix,* in "The Wonder." The last serious part he acted was *King Lear.*

HENRY MOSSOP.

Henry Mossop (1729-1773), an actor of great ability, as signified by much and earnest contemporary encomium of his acting as *Zanga, Coriolanus, Cassius,* and *King John,* had his career mostly on the Dublin Stage, though for several seasons, 1751-1754, he was a member of Garrick's company, at Drury Lane. He acted *King Lear,* about 1769, at the Crow Street Theatre, Dublin. His performance, as a whole, was deemed unequal and inadequate, but special points in it were cordially commended. There was irresistible pathos in his delivery of the recognition speech, "Pray, do not mock me." One writer, who saw and heard him, says: "The awful, tremulous depth with which he uttered the rational gleams of moral reflection which break through the clouds of *Lear's* madness seemed to harmonize with the storm, increased the sublimity of the scene, and appeared to lift the poet above even his great height, and almost dispelled all idea of fiction." Mossop's figure was imposing, his countenance severe in expression, his voice strong, copious, and beautifully modulated. He could not act the lover, but he was supreme in scenes of terror. His egregious vanity, haughty, repellent manner, and injudicious management of his affairs militated against him, and he died, in extreme penury, of a broken heart. His grave is near old Chelsea Church, London,—probably under what is now the street, which has encroached on the churchyard. Years ago, when last I saw the neighborhood, I asked the sexton of that church whether he had ever heard of Mossop. "No," he replied; "he doesn't live in this parish."

ALTERATIONS OF SHAKESPEARE'S "KING LEAR."
TATE.—COLMAN.—GARRICK.—KEMBLE.

Much effort has been made, first and last, to justify or excuse what Charles Knight, with felicitous contempt, designates "the Tatefication of Shakespeare." Nahum Tate (1652-1715) mangled Shakespeare's "King Richard II." and "Coriolanus" as well as his "King Lear," but the botch that he made of "King Lear" (1681) may well be deemed the chief of his literary sins. An editor takes no unwarrantable liberty who re-arranges, for a stage amply provided with scenic appurtenances, a play that was written for a stage practically destitute of such accessories, or who abridges, with deference to a rightful public preference for directness and lucidity, a play which, however meritorious, is either prolix or obscure. Old plays, by whomsoever written, must, necessarily, in the adaptation of them to the modern stage, be subjected to some changes. There is, for example, no longer any need of an explanatory Chorus, or of a passage descriptive of the scene of action, and a cultivated audience will not,—certainly should not,— tolerate horrible business or vulgar words. Some modification of the language and the business of even Shakespeare's stupendous tragedy of "King Lear" is essential in the present day, and perhaps it was expedient in Tate's day, but Tate made such radical alterations in the play, and so jumbled and degraded the text of Shakespeare with a farrago of his own composition, that he despoiled the original of its power, deprived it of its grandeur, effaced much of its pathos, and, ultimately, destroyed its terrific tragic significance.

It does not signify that even such a critic as Dr. Johnson could approve of the flummery of Tate: the sage, sensible as he was, sometimes gave way to the caprice of sentiment: nor can any reader who understands and appreciates Shakespeare's tragedy sympathize with the dismay and solicitude of Johnson's friend Thomas Davies, who shuddered at the thought of "depriving an audience, almost exhausted with the feeling of so many terrible scenes, of the inexpressible delight which they enjoyed when the *King* cried out, 'Old Lear shall be a king again!'" Neither will Arthur Murphy's amiable conviction,—that "the play as altered by Tate will always be most agreeable to an audience, as the circumstances of *Lear's* restoration and the virtuous *Edgar's* alliance with the amiable *Cordelia* must always call forth those gushing tears which are swelled and ennobled by a virtuous joy,"— persuade such readers that a rickety, paltry love-story should be injected into the portrayal of the terrific experience of *King Lear*. Tate's alteration of the tragedy is indefensible on any ground whatever, and it only affords an astonishing example of stupidity, presumption, and conceit. The fact that it kept its place on the stage for so long a time,—about 160 years,—is explicable only by consideration of the stability of custom, particularly in England; the habitual timidity of theatrical managers relative to the institution of needful innovations and improvements, and the commanding dramatic genius of great actors, such as Betterton, Booth, Garrick, Barry, and

KING LEAR

Henderson, who permitted the weight of their authority to be used in the exploitation of it. The splendid passages of Shakespeare's play which Tate retained must have counted for something,—even though mobbled up with his contemptible "rectifications" and "new-modellings,"—and the magnificent acting with which, from time to time, those passages were illustrated would, infallibly, have served to hide defects and to beguile the judgment of a public not prone to critical analysis or competent to make it.

The first performance of Tate's alteration was given at Lincoln's Inn Fields, in the year 1681, and that version, published in quarto in 1687, contains the cast of parts, as follows, with which it was then performed:

King Lear, ... Mr. Betterton.
Glo'ster, ... Mr. Gillo.
Kent, ... Mr. Wiltshire.
Edgar, ... Mr. Smith.
Bastard (Edmund), ... Mr. Jo. Williams.
Cornwall, ... Mr. Norris.
Albany, ... Mr. Bowman.
Gentleman Usher, ... Mr. Jevon.
Goneril, ... Mrs. Shadwell.
Regan, ... Lady Slingsby.
Cordelia, ... Mrs. Barry.

The following letter, by way of Dedication, is prefixed to Tate's play, as published:

"To my Esteemed Friend, *Thomas Boteler*, Esq.:

"Sir, you have a natural right to this piece, since by your advice I attempted the revival of it with alterations. Nothing but the power of your persuasions, and my zeal for all the remains of SHAKESPEARE could have wrought me to so bold an undertaking. I found that the new-modelling of this story would force me sometimes on the difficult task of making the chiefest persons speak something like their character, on matter whereof I had no ground in my author. *Lear's* real and *Edgar's* pretended madness have so much of *extravagant Nature* (I know not how else to express it) as could never have started but from our SHAKESPEARE's creating fancy. The images and language are so odd and surprising, and yet so agreeable and proper, that whilst we grant that none but SHAKESPEARE could have formed such conceptions, yet we are satisfied that they were the only things in the world that ought to be said on those occasions. I found the whole to answer your account of it, a heap of jewels, unstrung and unpolished, yet so dazzling in their disorder, that I soon perceived I had seized a treasure. 'Twas my good fortune to light on one expedient to rectify what was wanting in the regularity and probability of the tale, which was to run through the whole, as *Love* betwixt *Edgar* and *Cordelia*, that never changed a word with each other in the original. This renders *Cordelia's* indifference, and her father's passion in the first scene probable [!!!]. It likewise gives countenance to *Edgar's* disguise, making that a generous design that was before a poor shift to save his life. The distress of the story is evidently heightened by it, and it particularly gave occasion of a new scene or two of more success (perhaps) than merit. This method necessarily threw me on making the tale conclude in a success to the innocent distressed persons; otherwise I must have incumbered the stage with dead bodies, which conduct makes

KING LEAR

many tragedies conclude with unseasonable jests. Yet was I wract with no small fears for so bold a change, till I found it well received by my audience; and if this will not satisfy the Reader, I can produce an authority that questionless will. *'Neither is it of so trivial an undertaking to make a tragedy end happily, for 'tis more difficult to save than 'tis to kill: the dagger and cup of poison are always in readiness; but to bring the action to the last extremity, and then by probable means to recover all, will require the art and judgment of a writer, and cost him many a pang in the performance.'*

<small>Mr. Dryden's Pref. to "The Spanish Friar."</small>

"I have one thing more to apologize for, which is that I have used less quaintness of expression, even in the newest parts of this play. I confess 'twas design in me, partly to comply with my author's style, to make the scenes of a piece, and partly to give it some resemblance of the time and persons here represented. This, Sir, I submit wholly to you, who are both a judge and master of style. Nature had exempted you before you went abroad from the morose saturnine humor of our country, and you brought home the refinedness of travel without the affectation. Many faults I see in the following pages, and question not but you will discover more; yet I will presume so far on your friendship as to make the whole a present to you, and subscribe myself,

"*Your obliged friend and humble servant,*

"N. Tate."

The smug complacency of that ebullition of dulness could not readily be surpassed. Addison, in "The Spectator," No. 40, April 16, 1711, makes pertinent comment on the impropriety of vitiating the effect of genuine Tragedy by providing it with a "happy ending":

"The English writers of Tragedy are possessed with a notion that when they represent a virtuous or innocent person in distress they ought not to leave him till they have delivered him out of his troubles, or made him triumph over his enemies. This error they have been led into by a ridiculous doctrine in modern Criticism, that they are obliged to make an equal distribution of rewards and punishments, and an impartial execution of Poetical Justice. Who were the first that established this rule I know not; but I am sure it has no foundation in Nature, in Reason, or in the Practice of the Ancients. We find that Good and Evil happen alike to all men on this side the grave: and as the principal design of Tragedy is to raise commiseration and terror in the minds of the audience, we shall defeat this great end, if we always make Virtue and Innocence happy and successful. . . . 'King Lear' is an admirable tragedy, . . . as Shakespeare wrote it; but as it is reformed according to the chimerical notion of Poetical Justice, in my humble opinion it has lost half its beauty."

The mild protest of Addison was disregarded. The leading actors of the period continued to perform Tate's play. Garrick, indeed, who had acted in it in his first season on the London Stage, and who long continued to use it, made a few changes in it, and restored a little of the original which had been omitted, producing his slightly amended version, October 28, 1756, at Drury Lane, and repeating his much admired performance of *King Lear,*—in association with the *Cordelia* of the handsome and excellent Mrs. Davies. George Colman, the Elder, made a considerable alteration of it, restoring much of Shakespeare's text, but not eliminating all of Tate's fustian. Colman's version was produced, February 20, 1768, at Covent Garden, and in the same year was published. The cast of parts, when it was first presented, included William Powell, as *King Lear;* William Smith, as *Edgar;* Robert Bensley, as *Edmund;* Matthew Clarke, as *Kent;* Mrs. Yates, as *Cordelia;* Mrs. Stephens, as *Goneril;* and Mrs. Du Bellamy, as *Regan.* Colman omitted the character of the *Fool,* as Tate and Garrick had done. John Philip Kemble altered the Tate-Colman alteration, but without improving it; indeed, he rather marred than mended it. The Kemble version was presented by him, February 27, 1809, at Covent Garden, printed copies of it being sold in the theatre. Kemble had, previously, January 21, 1788, at the same house, acted *King Lear* in the Tate jumble,—Mrs. Siddons playing *Cordelia;* and he had again acted the part in a presentment made at Drury Lane, January 3, 1801. Tate's "miserable debilitation and disfigurement of Shakespeare's sublime tragedy" (Macready), slightly varied, held its place on the British Stage and served the professional occasions of all Kemble's immediate successors,—including Junius Brutus Booth, Edmund Kean, John M.

Vandenhoff, and Macready himself, who presented it at Swansea, in 1833, then acting *King Lear* for the first time. Later Macready made an acting version of the play for his own use, and on May 23, 1834, produced it in London, acting *King Lear* for the first time in that city. He used only the text of Shakespeare, though excluding the *Fool:* it was not till January 25, 1838, when he had assumed management of Covent Garden, that, in a splendid production of "King Lear" which he then effected, the character of the *Fool* was restored, Priscilla Horton (afterward Mrs. German Reed) playing the part, and succeeding in it.

The analytical account, by Genest, of the alterations of Shakespeare's tragedy made by Tate, Colman, and Garrick is particularly interesting and instructive, and an essential part of the Stage History of the play; in the belief that it will be useful to many students to whom Genest's scarce and costly "Account" is not accessible I reproduce it here.

FIRST ACT.

"Tate opens with *Edmund's* soliloquy; this is not bad, but why make unnecessary changes? The following short scene with *Kent* and *Glo'ster*, Tate alters much for the worse. Next enter *Edgar* and *Cordelia:* this is by far the best of the love scenes, as being the shortest. When *Lear* enters, Tate makes

KING LEAR

many little alterations much for the worse,—in particular *Lear* tells *Cordelia*,

> '. . . Now, minion, I perceive
> The truth of what has been suggested to us;
> Thy fondness for the rebel son of Glo'ster.'"

[Genest neglects to specify that, in Tate, when the play begins, *Glo'ster* has already been convinced of *Edgar's* treason.]

"The ensuing scene between *Goneril* and *Regan* Tate omits: Colman retains it, as it tends to elucidate what follows: but *Edgar* and *Cordelia* are Tate's peculiar care, and after the *King's* departure we have another love scene. When *Cordelia* goes out *Edmund* enters and recommends his brother to seek his safety in flight, as their father is mortally offended at him, *Edgar*, however, is so wrapped up in the thoughts of *Cordelia*, that he hardly hears what the other says to him: the scene between *Edmund* and *Glo'ster* Tate has mangled shamefully. In the grand scene when *Lear* returns, Tate has judiciously transposed the Curse to the end,—in which he is followed by Colman.

"In the original play *Glo'ster* says 'the King is confined to exhibition.' Dr. Johnson tells us this means allowance, and in this sense it is still used in the Universities; but the proper signification of it is to be met with, in a note, page 83, of the Amsterdam edition of 'Cyprian': it is a law term and means the necessaries of life,—'exhibere *sonat vitæ necessaria suppeditare.*' Exhibition was not become obsolete in 1678,— it is twice used in 'The Man of Newmarket.'

SECOND ACT.

"In the short scene between *Edgar* and *Edmund*, both Tate and Colman alter a line or two for the worse; and when

Glo'ster comes on, Tate curtails and alters without reason. Tate mutilates the scenes between *Kent*, and *Oswald, the Steward*, whom he politely changes into a *Gentleman Usher*. When *Regan* enters she says of *Edmund*,

'A charming youth and worth my farther thought.'

Next comes *Edgar's* soliloquy, in which Tate inserts,

'. . . How easy now
'Twere to defeat the malice of my trail,
And leave my griefs on my sword's reeking point;
But Love detains me from Death's peaceful cell,
Still whispering me Cordelia's in distress:

. . . .

Who knows but the *white* minute yet may come
When Edgar may do service to Cordelia?'

"This is vastly more heroic in *Edgar* than merely preserving his life in compliance with the first law of Nature. In the next scene *Kent* tells *Lear* that *Regan* is within, at a masque; I feel myself infinitely indebted to Tate for this piece of information, as, till I read his play, I used to think that no dramatic exhibitions or masques were known in England, till many hundred years after the time in which *Lear* is supposed to have lived [such strictures as this about "masques" are idle, the plays of Shakespeare, and especially this one, abounding in worse anachronisms]. Davies is mistaken in saying that Tate omits 'Age is unnecessary' &c.,—he only mutilates and alters. Tate properly retains

'. . . Strike her young bones,
You taking airs, with lameness!'

as also *Lear's* proposition to return to *Goneril* with fifty knights, both of which Colman omits. Tate inserts, in the fine concluding scene, some of his own lines, particularly,

KING LEAR

'Blood! fire! here—Leprosies and bluest Plagues!
Room, room for Hell to belch her horrors up,
And drench the Circes in a stream of fire;
Hark, how th' Infernals echo to my rage
Their whips and snakes!'

THIRD ACT.

"When *Lear* enters both Tate and Colman make some unnecessary changes, especially Tate,—who, in the following scenes, favors us with a great deal of his own poetry. First *Edmund* has a soliloquy; then two Servants enter and deliver two love-letters to him from *Goneril* and *Regan:* the short scene between *Edmund* and *Glo'ster*, Tate has altered shamefully for the worse: when *Glo'ster* is going off, Tate makes *Cordelia* enter: she solicits his assistance for *Lear*, which he promises; then she determines to put herself into a disguise, and with her confidante go in search of the *King* herself; *Edmund*, overhearing this, resolves to take advantage of her unprotected situation; thus Tate, not content with bringing forward *Edmund's* intrigue with *Regan*, which Shakespeare keeps in the background, here makes him plan a scheme for ravishing *Cordelia*,—he was determined to prove him 'rough and lecherous': this scheme, however, *Edmund* seems totally to forget afterwards; it does not even occur to him, when *Cordelia* is a prisoner and in his power,—but perhaps (as Wycherley says on a similar occasion) he had no more China at that time.

"Tate properly consolidates the two scenes between *Lear* and *Edgar*, and transposes judiciously enough, but puts in some weak lines of his own. Both Tate and Colman change Saint Withold to Swithin; such alterations, though of no importance, are wrong, as being unnecessary. Tate makes *Edgar* distressed at seeing the situation of the *King*, which is very generous in him, as *Lear* had, in open court, proclaimed him a rebel to his father. Then comes Tate's grand scene, in which *Cordelia* is attacked by two *Ruffians* in the pay of *Edmund*, and rescued by *Edgar;* by the bye, it seems a little ungallant in *Edgar* to leave *Cordelia* afterwards, more particularly as his sole motive for preserving his own life was for the sake of being of service to her.

'And angels visit my Cordelia's dreams.'

This is improper, as the characters are heathens; the impropriety, however, is such as Shakespeare is frequently guilty of—and once in this play:

'What, did my father's *God-son* seek your life?'

—this Tate omits—Colman retains it. When the scene changes to *Glo'ster's* Castle, Shakespeare sends *Edmund* off the stage, in attendance on *Goneril* and with a message to *Albany;* Tate, on the contrary, makes *Regan* say to him, aside,

'The Grotto, Sir, within the lower grove,
　　Has privacy to suit a mourner's thought.
Edmund: And there I may expect a comforter? Ha, madam?
Regan:　What may happen, sir, I know not,
　　But 'twas a friend's advice.'

"When *Glo'ster's* eyes are put out, *Regan* says,

'Read, and save the Cambrian prince a labor;
If thy eyes fail thee, call for spectacles.'

"*Glo'ster* concludes the act with a long soliloquy, by Tate.

FOURTH ACT.

"Tate opens with a grotto, in which *Edmund* and *Regan* are said to be 'amorously seated, listening to music.' He drops

KING LEAR 379

Goneril's note, which *Regan* finds. In the next scene, when *Glo'ster* enters led by an old man, Tate alters and adds without reason: then enter *Kent* and *Cordelia:* in this scene some few lines only are Shakespeare's, and they are taken from another place: the rest of the scene is contemptible to the last degree. The scene in *Albany's* Palace Tate mutilates shamefully; the scene between *Kent* and a *Gentleman,* Tate omits and Colman retains; the scene between *Cordelia* and the *Physician,* Tate omits; Colman retains it, with the addition of some unimportant lines by Tate from Act Third. *Edgar* and *Glo'ster* enter, and then *Lear,* mad; this scene, in both alterations, differs but little from the original. Tate and Colman both omit the most essential part of *Oswald's* dying speech—absurdly, as, if he had said nothing about the letters, it would hardly have occurred to *Edgar* to search his pockets. The scene between *Cordelia,* the *Physician,* and *Lear,* Tate adulterates with several lines of his own, which Colman retains. Tate ends the act as in Shakespeare: Colman opens the Fifth Act with this scene.

FIFTH ACT.

"This act is materially altered from the original. Tate makes *Goneril* tell us of her design to poison *Regan;* he alters *Edmund's* solioquy and adds to it; he also furnishes *Glo'ster* with a soliloquy of sixteen lines, part of which Colman retains. When *Lear* and *Cordelia* are brought in prisoners, Tate transposes what they should say to another place: *Edgar* enters disguised and challenges *Edmund;* in this particular, and in the following scene between *Lear, Kent,* and *Cordelia,* Colman copies Tate: *Albany,* &c., enter: then *Edgar* comes on, armed, and fights with *Edmund:* here Tate makes considerable additions; when *Edmund* is dying, *Goneril* and *Regan* pull caps for him, and he consoles himself in his last moments with his success in love:

> 'Who wou'd not choose, like me to yield his breath,
> T'have rival queens contend for him in death?'

"Colman retains some of Tate's lines in this scene, but rejects by far the greater part. Both Tate and Colman mutilate Shakespeare sadly in this scene. *Lear* is next discovered asleep, with his head on *Cordelia's* lap: a *Captain* and *Officers* enter (four at least in number), with a view to murder them; *Lear*, though turned of fourscore, snatches a partisan and strikes down two of them, the rest turn upon him; *Edgar* and *Albany* enter, then *Kent*, and lastly *Glo'ster*,—and they are all as happy and jolly as heart could wish, instead of Shakespeare's tragical catastrophe. Colman follows Tate in a considerable degree, but *Lear*, of course, does not give *Cordelia* to *Edgar*. Tate, having altered the last part of the play so materially, was obliged to new write it, which he has done in a style as unlike Shakespeare as possible; he has, however, retained as much of the original as his plan would admit of.

"Thus it appears that Tate considered himself as authorized not only to omit, alter, and mutilate the text at pleasure, but also to change the plot and insert as much of his own poetry as he liked. He has, properly [! ! ! !], omitted the character of the *Fool*, and he sometimes transposes with effect; in other respects his alteration is an execrable one. His additions are contemptible, and his happy catastrophe injudicious.

"The delicate nerves of Dr. Johnson were so shocked at *Lear's* bringing in *Cordelia* dead in his arms, that he doubts whether he ever endured to read the last scenes of this play a second time, till he undertook to revise them as an editor: he inclines to the happy catastrophe, and says that in this case the public has decided: to this Steevens replies, that he should rather have said, that the managers of the Theatres Royal have decided, and that the public has been obliged to acquiesce in their decision. The altered play has the upper gallery on its side; the original drama was patronized by Addison.

'Victrix causa Diis *placuit, sed victa* Catoni.'

"If a happy catastrophe were indispensably necessary, it might have been brought about without the gross absurdity of making 'a poor, infirm, and weak old man' disarm one ruffian and strike down two. *Edmund's* revocation of his order for the death of *Lear* and *Cordelia* might have come in time, instead of being too late, and *Lear* might have 'killed the slave that was just going to hang her.'

"Colman's object was to *restore Shakespeare* (Murphy says 'Colman, with an unhallowed hand, defaced the Tragedy of "King Lear" ': if Murphy had taken the trouble to look into Colman's alteration he would not have made this silly remark.)—and this he has done, in the first four acts, which he has altered very judiciously, only he has omitted some few lines of the original, that should have been retained; and retained some few of Tate's, that should have been omitted. Of his Fifth Act the less is said, the more it will be to his credit.

" 'The Dramatic Censor,' in 1770, wishes some able critic, Mr. Garrick for instance, would undertake a third alteration. Garrick, on October 28, 1756, brought forward 'King Lear,' with restorations. His alteration of this tragedy probably did not differ materially from 'King Lear' as printed by Bell in 1773 or 1774, from the Prompt Book of Drury Lane. Let us briefly examine what this able critic has done. A great deal of Tate's own stuff is omitted: many of the scenes that Tate had altered for the worse, are restored, as by Colman; but the love scenes (all but one) are studiously retained, as also *Edmund's* design on *Cordelia*, and her being rescued by *Edgar*, her supplications to *Glo'ster*, in the Third Act, and the scene in the fourth, between *Kent, Glo'ster, Edgar*, and *Cordelia*. The mention of the *Duke of Cambray* (whom Shakespeare never dreamt of) is omitted from one scene and retained in another. *Edmund's* soliloquy, with the two *Servants* and the two letters, is omitted, but *Regan's* assignation in the grotto is retained. *Glo'ster* leaps from the cliff as in the original: *Oswald's* dying speech is properly restored; *Glos'ter's* two soliloquies are retained, and, in Act Fifth, Tate is chiefly followed, but when *Edgar* and *Edmund* fight, the scene differs but little from Colman's.

"That Colman's alteration was not successful; and that the love scenes still retain their place on the stage, is not wonderful: *non tam bene cum rebus humanis agitur, ut meliora pluribus placeant:* many frequenters of the theatre cannot distinguish between Tate and Shakespeare, even some managers do not always discriminate; and it may be questioned whether the generality of performers would not prefer acting *Edgar* and *Cordelia* as altered by Tate than as written by Shakespeare,—though certainly an actor can hardly be condemned to pronounce more insipid lines than those of Tate."

Genest's approval of the omission of the *Fool* and his seeming propitiatory notion of "a happy catastrophe" to the tragic story are not consistent with his customary sound judgment and refreshing common sense. The *Fool* is essential to the accomplishment of the enthralling effect upon the feelings which, obviously, the dramatist intended to cause.

His presence, in company with the extruded and wretched *King,* and his intimations, direct and indirect, of the old man's folly in making himself subordinate and dependent, materially enhance a poignant realization of the hapless outcast's miserable plight, and so they deepen the pathos of his lamentable experience. The nature of the *Fool,*—who is sketched rather than fully drawn,—can be apprehended from two significant facts, that he pines with secret grief because of the unjust and cruel banishment of *Cordelia,* and, following the poor old *King* into the night and tempest, "labors to outjest his heart-struck injuries." He is a supreme type of fidelity, pathetic in his affectionate devotion and in his wistful commingling of humor with sadness. As to the notion of "a happy catastrophe" to the story, such an ending is contemptible, and, however devised, it would remain so, because equally false to Nature and to Art. Tate might have perceived a warning in the very words of Dryden which he quoted as a justification, since they declare that it is the use of *"probable* means to recover all," when a writer has brought the action to the last extremity, which is the test of his judgment and art. The means used by Tate "to recover all" in "King Lear" are worse than improbable; they are preposterous, and his style is as bad as his invention: here are specimens of it:

GLOS'TER:
"Fly, Edmund, seek him out; wind me unto him,
That I may bite the traitor's heart, and fold
His bleeding entrails on my vengeful arm."

CORDELIA:
"Or, what if it be worse?
As 'tis too probable, this furious night
Has pierc'd his tender body, the bleak winds
And cold rain chill'd, or lightning struck him dead;
If it be so, your promise is discharged,
And I have only one poor boon to beg,—
That you'd convey me to his breathless trunk,
With my torn robes to wrap his hoary head,
With my torn hair to bind his hands and feet,
Then with a show'r of tears
To wash his clay-smear'd cheeks, and die beside him."

VARIOUS PERFORMERS.—BRITISH STAGE.

Robert Wilks (1666-1732) played *King Lear*, in Tate's version, about 1711, at Drury Lane, but not with conspicuous success. All the recorded testimony shows that he was one of the most accomplished and versatile actors that have ever graced the Stage, and also one of the worthiest and most generous of men. He acted tragic parts,—*Othello* and *Hamlet*, among them,—and his performances were finely intelligent; but he was best in comedy and, indeed, as a

KING LEAR

comedian, surpassed all competitors. His personation of *King Lear* seems to have been regarded with indifference. He excelled in the part of *Edgar,* in this tragedy, marking with pathetic effect *Poor Tom's* alternation between sanity and assumed madness. Davies, who saw him, records that for many years he pleased the public in this character. John Mills (1678-1736), a correct and useful actor, played *King Lear,* January 11, 1729, at Drury Lane. His person was large, his countenance inexpressive, his demeanor dignified. He acted many kinds of parts, all of them in a creditable manner. His *King Lear* was merely respectable. He is recorded as a good representative of *Edmund.* It is related of him that once, when he was performing as *Macbeth,* a tired auditor suddenly interrupted the proceedings, addressing Powell,—who had come on, late in the play,—with the earnest request, "For God's sake, George, give us a speech, and let me go home." Mills had a theatrical career of forty years, and is commended for sobriety (a virtue, in his time, often "more honor'd in the breach than the observance") and for diligence. He lived and died much respected. The handsome and gallant West Digges went on for *King Lear,* at the Smock Alley Theatre, Dublin, in 1749, and gave a tolerable imitation of Garrick in that part. Dennis Delane gave a somewhat similar performance of the *King,* at Drury

Lane, in 1750. William Powell (1735-1769), who
had the good fortune to be instructed by Garrick,
made his first appearance in 1763, at Drury Lane, and
speedily gained public favor. He performed *King
Lear,* for the first time, January 2, 1765, at Drury
Lane, and his effort seems to have been highly commendable. He was an imitator of Garrick. His chief
talent was shown in his felicitous expression of tender
feeling. He was a partner with the elder George
Colman in the management of Covent Garden Theatre,
and he acted *King Lear,* at that house, when Colman's
arrangement of the tragedy was first produced. His
grave is in Bristol, and his monument bears an inscription written by Colman. John Henderson (1747-1785) first played *King Lear,* January 20, 1773, at
Bath, and after he went to the London Stage, in 1777,
he repeated his performance, at Covent Garden. His
acting of this part, however, made no memorable
impression; it is not anywhere particularly described.
Henderson was not, even by ardent admirers, esteemed
successful in pathetic characters, or adapted to them.
John Taylor said that his "face and person were
not fitted for tragedy," and that he was "the best
general actor since the days of Garrick, but wanted
the ease and variety of that great and unrivalled
master of his art." There is no doubt that Henderson was one of the truly great actors,—in *Shylock,*

Iago, Falstaff, and *Sir Pertinax Macsycophant.* His comic powers were extraordinary; *Falstaff* was one of his most successful performances, and his recital of Cowper's "John Gilpin's Ride" "rendered a tale, hardly known, popular all over the kingdom." As an actor he was thoughtful, studious, original, and scrupulously and minutely careful about the details and finish of his performances. He was exceptionally heedless regarding costume. The elder Farren attempted *King Lear,* May 6, 1786, at Covent Garden, Miss Brunton acting with him, as *Cordelia.* Her performance was fine; his creditable. Alexander Pope (1763-1835) acted *King Lear,* for the first time, January 6, 1794, at Covent Garden, Mrs. Esten playing *Cordelia,*—her first appearance in the part. Pope was handsome, in rather an effeminate style, possessed a melodious, sympathetic voice, and particularly excelled in the representation of pathetic characters. He was, however, notably versatile,—for he played *Iago* and *Iachimo* as well as *Beverley* and *Kent.* His *King Lear* is not commemorated. He, probably, lacked power, authority, and distinction, but, in the scene of the recognition of *Cordelia,* was effective. Charles Mayne Young's personation, first seen March 30, 1829, at Drury Lane, was deemed respectable. Macready said of Young that he was an actor of great ability, that he had genius but neglected it, being too easily satisfied with applause. Gustavus V. Brooke, who, in essential particulars, rivalled Edwin Forrest, acted *King Lear,* July 9, 1855, for the first time on any stage, at the Theatre Royal, Sydney, New South Wales, Australia, and, remembering his astonishing resources of physical power, vocal energy, and sympathetic emotion, it is easy to believe that he excelled in the bursts of passion and the moments of pathos. Charles Calvert's *King Lear,*—Manchester, 1867,—was accounted exceptionally good. Wybert Rousby, who played the part in London, in 1873, is remembered as correct, artistic, and effective.

JOHN PHILIP KEMBLE.

John Philip Kemble (1757-1823), when he acted *King Lear,* in Tate's version of the tragedy, January 21, 1788, was seen by Boaden, who wrote, long afterward, in his account of Kemble's life:

"I have seen him since, in the character, but he never again achieved the excellence of that night. Subsequently he was too elaborately aged, and quenched with infirmity the insane fire of the injured father. The curse, as he then uttered it, harrowed up the soul: the gathering himself together, with the hands convulsively clasped, the increasing fervor and rapidity, and the suffocation of the convulsive words, all evinced consummate skill and original invention. The countenance, too, was finely made up."

The poet Campbell, in his "Valedictory Stanzas," addressed to the actor, which were read, by Charles Mayne Young, at a Farewell Dinner given, in honor of Kemble, June 27, 1817, at the Freemasons' Tavern, London, made this felicitous reference to his personation of *King Lear:*

> "High were the task—too high—
>   Ye conscious bosoms here!
> In words to paint your memory
>   Of Kemble and of *Lear;*
>   But who forgets that white discrownèd head,
>   Those bursts of Reason's half-extinguish'd glare,
>   Those tears upon *Cordelia's* bosom shed,
>   In doubt more touching than despair,
> If 'twas reality he felt?
>   Had Shakespeare's self amidst you been,
> Friends, he had seen you melt,
>   And triumph'd to have seen."

Those tributes signify the quality of the esteem in which Kemble's acting of this part was held by his contemporaries. Sir Walter Scott, one of his most intimate friends, and a close observer of his art, declared him to be "a great artist, who shows too much of his machinery," a performer who was "best in those characters in which there is a predominant tinge of some overmastering passion, or acquired habit of acting and speaking, coloring the whole man,"—and referred to his *King Lear* as being "inferior in spirit and truth." Kemble's supreme excellence was shown in his personations of *Hamlet, Brutus, Cato, Penruddock,* and *Coriolanus.* Oxberry, generally a harsh censor, affirmed that he had "left no equal" in *King Lear,* adding: "All his personations were like finished pictures; you might gaze at any point and discover no deficiency; it was perfectly correct, and it only wanted that magic coloring that we all feel and cannot describe." Emotional fervor, in acting, will sometimes induce sympathetic agitation in the spectator's nervous system; but it is well, I believe, that criticism of acting should generally be incredulous as to all vague notions of something "grand, gloomy, and peculiar" which everybody feels but nobody can describe. Where great effects are caused in acting it is lack of acute attention or calm judgment or disability to think which prevents clear perception of the means by which they are effected, and precise statement of those means. Kemble, evidently, was an actor of the highest order, one who imitated nature by means of judicious art, and did not vulgarize his imitation by realism. He probably was unequal, as all fine actors are, but there seems no room for doubt that his *King Lear,* at its best and in those scenes where the character of Shakespeare emerges, was a masterpiece. It is a pity that he acted

KING LEAR

in Tate's play, but Tate's play does contain passages of the original in which an actor can show his quality.

GEORGE FREDERICK COOKE.

Cooke (1756-1812) declared to a brother actor William Francis (1757-1826) that, in his younger days, the greatest popularity he ever acquired was gained in sympathetic characters and by the use of his pathetic powers. Contemporary accounts of his acting, however, extoll him chiefly in such parts as *King Richard the Third, Sir Giles Overreach, Shylock, Kitely,* and *Iago,*—all wicked and detestable men,—and as *Sir Pertinax Macsycophant,* and *Falstaff*. Admiration, indeed, to some extent, followed all his performances, for he was an original and exceptionally interesting person; but he led a hard life, he was a drunkard, he was at times crazy, and although he possessed a fine mind and was a great actor it is more than probable that his early tenderness of feeling was blunted and his capability of expressing the softer and finer emotions marred, if not destroyed, by habitual inebriety. I have not found any really convincing cordial praise of his performance of *King Lear*. He first acted the part in 1792, in Liverpool, and he acted it for the first time in London, January 8, 1802, at Covent Garden, but he did not then make a strong impression. The estimate of this actor, long ago expressed, is probably sound;—that he played only a few parts well, but, in those parts which he did play well, was incomparable. It is significant of his excellence that Edmund Kean admired and imitated him,—founding his style upon that of the elder tragedian.

Cooke records that he saw both Garrick and Barry as *King Lear:* it was in his youth, because Garrick retired in 1776, and Barry died in 1777: he must have profited by study of those actors, but he was not an imitator. John Howard Payne said of him: "He always presented himself to me in the light of a *discoverer,* one with whom it seemed that every action and every look emanated entirely from himself; one who appeared never to have had a model." John Galt wrote that "vastness of power" was a predominant quality of his acting. That would have helped him in *King Lear.* With his commanding figure, expressive features, dark, fiery eyes, copious voice, and prodigious physical force, he must have been a dread image of frenzy when uttering the curse on *Goneril,* or when rushing through the midnight tempest on the wide and desolate heath: he certainly was a master of the art of theatrical effect: but that he elicited the natural grandeur, the paternal emotion, and the pathos of *King Lear* is doubtful. Dunlap, whose "Memoir" of him is largely devoted to "the pints he swallowed" (Byron), wrote: "I never shall forget the effect produced upon me by his tottering limbs, while sinking on his knee to pronounce the terrible curse on his unnatural daughters, or by the passage itself as he gave it." Almost every actor of *King Lear*, if possessed of real ability, has been effective in the Curse Scene. It is in the Mad Scenes, the scene of the recognition of *Cordelia*, and the Death Scene that the actor must bear the supreme test of his ability to act this part. "For the part of *Lear*," says Galt, "however judicious his conception, his physical powers were of too coarse a texture." Genest curtly remarks that *"Lear* was not one of Cooke's good parts."

JUNIUS BRUTUS BOOTH AND EDMUND KEAN.

The elder Booth appeared as *King Lear*, April 13, 1820, at Covent Garden. He was at that time only twenty-four years old, and he was fulfilling an engagement at the Coburg Theatre, one of the minor theatres in London, but permission was obtained from the manager, ——— Glossop, that he should perform at the more important theatre. The venture was proposed by Harris, of Covent Garden, who meanly wished to oppose Booth to Kean, then performing, with much success, at Drury Lane. The tragedy had not, for ten years, been presented, because of the mental derangement of King George the Third, but the death of that sovereign, January 29, 1820, had operated to remove the restriction placed upon it, and the managers of the patent theatres,—in which the right to produce Shakespeare's plays was exclusively vested,—promptly bethought themselves of its possible utility. Glossop, who could not touch Shakespeare, brought out "Lear of Private Life," a play based on a story called "Father and Daughter," by the beautiful and talented Mrs. Opie (Amelia Alderson, 1769-1853), engaging Booth to act the leading part in it, *Fitzarden,* the father (in the story his name is *Fitzhenry*), on three nights a week, being the off nights of his engagement at Covent Garden. Booth's performance of *King Lear* was disregarded by the public, and he then acted the part only three times; his associates in the tragedy were Charles Kemble, as *Edgar;* John Fawcett, as *Kent;* Daniel Egerton, as *Glo'ster,* and Sally Booth, as *Cordelia.* At the Coburg Booth was more fortunate than at Covent Garden: "Lear of Private Life,"—in which a father, who has gone mad because of his daughter's disgrace, presently recovers his reason, recognizes her, and dies in her arms,—pleased the public, and Booth acted *Fitzarden* fifty-three times. Meanwhile, at Drury Lane, "King Lear"

KING LEAR

was produced, April 24, eleven days after the Covent Garden revival, and Kean acted the *King*. Macready, who saw the performance, says that the tragedy "was brought out with 'dress, scenery, and machinery,' all new: a great display was attempted by what the playbills called 'a Land Storm,' intended to represent the overflowing of a river, bearing down rocks and trees in its course; but as a scenic effect it was a noisy failure, and as an illustration of Shakespeare's text, which tells us 'for many miles about there's scarce a bush,' a ludicrous blunder." The players who coöperated with Kean, on that occasion, were Alexander Rae, as *Edgar;* T. S. Hamblin, as *Edmund;* Dowton, as *Kent; Holland,* as *Glo'ster;* Mrs. W. West (Miss Cooke, an actress of great talent and beauty), as *Cordelia;* Mrs. Glover, as *Goneril,* and Mrs. Egerton, as *Regan*. The play was represented twenty-eight times. On February 10, 1823, "King Lear" was again presented at Drury Lane, with Kean as the *King,* with a considerably altered cast, and with the original Fifth Act of Shakespeare's tragedy restored,—by Elliston.

Hazlitt says of Kean, as *King Lear,* that "he drivelled and looked vacant, and moved his lips so as not to be heard, and did nothing." Dana, the old poet, says "there was a childish, feeble gladness in the eye and a half-piteous smile about the mouth, at times, which one could scarce look upon without tears." Lewes wrote of him: "He was not a flexible genius. . . . His miming power, although admirable within a certain range, was singularly limited. . . . He was tricky and flashy in style. . . . He was incomparably the greatest actor I have seen. . . . He had many and serious defects." When a writer descants on the wonderful art of an actor as "miming power" it can be assumed that he is thinking more about his own importance than he is about the duty of intelligence and justice in criticism. Lewes must have seen singularly inapt actors, if one whom he deemed to be "tricky and flashy in style" was "incomparably the greatest" that he ever saw. Washington Irving wrote of Kean: "He is either very good or very bad,—*I* think decidedly the latter." Scott, who admired, though not without judicious reservation, John Philip Kemble, and the Kemble School, described him as "a two-penny tear-mouth." The incorrectness of such estimates cannot be doubted. Take him for all in all,—making allowance for the injury done to his health, his mind, his moral nature, and his acting by inebriety and reckless behavior, admitting that he was uneven and fitful and that (like every other human being) he had distinct limitations, —the incontestable fact remains that Edmund Kean was a man of wonderful genius, fascinating personality, a devoted, if not continuous, student of his art, and one of the greatest actors that ever lived.

WILLIAM CHARLES MACREADY.

When, in 1820, Harris, of Covent Garden, hearing that "King Lear" was in preparation at Drury Lane and would be presented with Kean as the *King,* determined to forestall that production by a precipitate revival of the play at his own theatre, he assigned the part of *King Lear* to Macready, who then was acting under his management. Macready, who disapproved of this *"ruse* of antagonism," and thought that it would be injudicious for him to venture before the public in that grand character without thorough preparation, declined to attempt the *King,* but expressed his willingness to act any other part in the play. Harris thereupon cast him for *Edmund,* and, as already described, engaged J. B. Booth to undertake *King Lear.* The experiment was made, and it failed. Not till thirteen years later, August 29, 1833, at Swansea, did Macready attempt *King Lear,* and his performance then was given in the old Tate distortion of the original. He has himself recorded the result of his endeavor: "Acted *Lear.* How? I scarcely know. Certainly not well, not so well as I rehearsed it; crude, fictitious voice, no point,—in short, a failure. To succeed in it I must strain every nerve of thought, or triumph is hopeless." Later he was prompted, on reading a newspaper article on the subject, by John Forster, to consider "the prudence and practicability" of presenting the tragedy according to Shakespeare,—that is to say, as nearly as possible in its original form, and his "Diary" shows that he deeply pondered on this subject, and that he studied the play with scrupulous attention. As a result of his thought and study, the opportunity arriving (it was the occasion of his benefit), he presented the tragedy, May 23, 1834, at Covent Garden, using only the text of Shakespeare, but excluding the character of the *Fool*. His wise and commendable venture was attended with success, and his *King Lear*, retained in his repertory throughout his professional life, became, in time, the greatest of his impersonations, with the exception of *Macbeth:* in his own estimation it was the best. On February 2, 1838, at Covent Garden,—of which theatre he was then the manager,—he effected a grand revival of the tragedy, and on that occasion he restored the character of the *Fool*.

It seems strange that a thoughtful student of the subject should not have perceived at once the dramatic value of that character, which is used by Shakespeare to accentuate the pathos of *King Lear's* miserable condition, and which fully accomplishes that purpose.

WILLIAM C. MACREADY AS *KING LEAR*, AND HELENA FAUCIT AS *CORDELIA*

"Why should a dog, a horse, a rat, have life,
And thou no breath at all?"

Act V., Sc. 3

KING LEAR

Macready's doubt and hesitancy as to this matter, and also the consideration which finally prevailed with him, are thus specified in his "Diary":

"My opinion of the introduction of the *Fool* is that, like many such terrible contrasts in poetry and painting, in acting representation it will fail of effect; it will either weary and annoy or distract the spectator. I have no hope of it, and think that at the last we shall be obliged to dispense with it. . . . Speaking to Willmott and Bartley about the part of the *Fool* in 'Lear,' and mentioning my apprehension that, with Meadows, we should be obliged to omit the part, I described the sort of fragile, hectic, beautiful-faced, half-idiot-looking boy that he should be, and stated my belief that it never could be acted. Bartley observed that a woman should play it. I caught at the idea, and instantly exclaimed: 'Miss P. Horton is the very person!' I was delighted at the thought."

To a man more than eighty years old, and that man *King Lear*,—made older yet, and almost isolated by excruciating anguish, so that everything appears to him disproportionate,—a person past boyhood might, nevertheless, seem to be a "boy." There is nothing boyish in either the thoughts or the words of the *Fool;* he pines for his "young mistress," gone into France; all his talk is that of a man; he may be, constitutionally, an odd, eccentric being—he is a professional and "allowed fool,"—but his *folly* is assumed. He is not "half-idiotic"; and, assuredly, a "half-idiot-looking boy"—or man—could not be "beautiful-faced."

Macready's reasoning about the character of the *King* was, however, more sensible than his reasoning about that of the *Fool*. He contended that the language of *King Lear* "never betrays *imbecility* of mind or body," and that the *vigor* rather than the *feebleness* of old age is characteristic of him: "the towering range of thought with which his mind dilates, identifying the heavens themselves with his griefs, and the power of conceiving such vast imaginings, would," he wrote, "seem incompatible with a tottering, trembling frame." His personation was grounded in this idea. He embodied the *King* as aged, but vigorous. His step alone denoted the weight of years. His movements and gestures were large and free. His demeanor and delivery were imperious. His use of voice was exceptionally felicitous. His spirit was consistently, and almost continuously, passionate. Toward the close of the speech of dismissal to *Cordelia,*—"The barbarous Scythian," etc., his voice trembled and broke, as with an access of emotion at the thought of banishing his favorite child, but "then, to the end of the sentence, it hardened to inflexibility." "The bow is bent and drawn; make from the shaft" was ejaculated in a tone of warning and implied menace. In the speeches immediately subsequent there was "a mingling of amazement, scorn, and convulsive rage." The Curse on *Goneril* was not thundered, but uttered with terrible, "still intensity," and there was a breaking "change from wrath to agony" on the words

> "That *she* may feel
> How sharper than a serpent's tooth it is
> To have a thankless child!"

In the final scene with *Goneril* and *Regan* his intensity and screaming vehemence greatly exceeded even the power of the first Curse. He "developed the insanity of the old *King* very gradually" (Lady Pollock), and therein, as it seems to me,—for reasons assigned later,—he pursued a mistaken course. His plan contemplated depiction of the madness of the *King* as induced by the harsh and vile ingratitude of his "dog-hearted daughters" (old *Kent* wrongs even the wolf-hound and the cur to call them so!), and as entirely consequent on cruel ill-treatment of him, received at their hands. The cause of madness was thus shown to be the afflicting excitement of his feelings, together with a gradual exhaustion of his physical strength, through exposure to the tempest,—whereas, in fact, the *King's* wildness in what are called "the mad scenes," is supervenient on a long anterior condition, and is precipitated by his daughters' conduct. In the first part of the Storm Scene *King Lear,* as played by Macready, still retained some power of self-control; in the latter part of it, when *Edgar,* pretending to be a madman, emerges from the hovel, he became wholly insane. "The recurrence to a fixed idea, in his obstinate and, at last, passionate asseveration that *Edgar's* 'unkind daughters' were the cause of his affliction, might, in its air of penetration and good faith, have been set down in the diagnosis of a physician" (Marston). As to his acting in the scene of the *King's* recognition of his daughter Lady Pollock says: "Who that has heard can ever forget the storm of sighs and tears which shook the audience when the old man woke from his dream of madness, to fall upon *Cordelia's* neck with the unrestrained emotion of his great age! To the horror of the first acts this appeal to a softer sympathy came as a relief which was an actual necessity." In tenderness Macready was supreme.

The acting of Macready was, in his time, and has been almost ever since, among devotees of the Stage and essayists on Dramatic Art, the cause of the same kind of controversy as that which still alternately seethes and murmurs around the well remembered acting of Henry Irving. In Edmund Kean a considerable critical authority glorified a man of Genius: in Macready the same authority recognized a man of Talent. The prevalent notion was, and it still is, that the regnant quality of Genius is delirium, while the regnant quality of Talent is sobriety: that Genius works by *inspiration,* while Talent works by *study,*— the one producing the vital effect of Nature, the other producing only the chill effect of Art. Cooke, Kean, and Booth, all three more or less crazy, were, according to this theory, men of Genius: Kemble, Macready, and Young, all three sane, temperate, and studious, were actors of Talent. So the tale ran, and so it still runs. The truth, meanwhile, is that in every branch of Art,—and particularly in that of Acting, which is the imitation of nature and not nature itself,—delirium is a fault, not a merit, and sometimes an exceedingly obnoxious fault. William Charles Macready, weighing all the evidence which survives, both for and against him, was just as much an actor of genius as either Cooke, Kean, or Booth,—and *their* genius is unquestioned, but they won their victories in spite of their defects, not because of them. Macready read and studied and thought, in order that he might minutely comprehend and fully interpret. He did not try to make his audience 'read Shakespeare by flashes of lightning,' but he did try to make them read Shakespeare by daylight, and to understand what they read. He did not indulge in convulsions or aim to cause spasms. He was a great actor; and so, in our day, was Henry Irving, who also read and studied and thought, in order that he might act in an intelligent and comprehensible manner, who did not believe frenzy to be the inspiration of genius, and who never, as a true and right dramatic artist, did anything that he had not intended to do, or said anything that he did not perfectly understand. Macready, like all other actors, had his limitations: he played some parts better than he played others; there were some parts that eluded him: but he treated Acting as a great Art, and he greatly excelled in it.

THE CHARACTERS, AND THE PLAY.

The constituents of the personality of *King Lear* are not obscure: he is clearly drawn: the character, nevertheless, has been designated as "incredible," and the tragedy,—particularly with reference to its opening, which exhibits the basis of its action,—as "impossible." Such mistaken opinions can have proceeded only from a wrong assumption of the state of the old man's mind at the beginning of the play. *King Lear,* when we first see him, is not sane, nor has he been sane, for a considerable antecedent time. His plan of dividing his kingdom amongst his three daughters and dwelling with the youngest of them ("I lov'd her most," he says, "and *thought to set my rest on her kind nursery*") is a mad scheme,—the infallible spring of strife and internecine warfare, impossible of adoption by a sound mind, but entirely natural to tainted wits; and, though the self-interest of the most powerful of the *King's* nobles, *Albany* and *Cornwall,* and of their spouses, *Goneril* and *Regan,* makes them acquiescent in their sovereign's folly, that folly is clearly perceived. One friend bluntly tells the *King* that his behavior is *madness:*

"Be Kent unmannerly,
When Lear is mad! What wouldst thou do, old man?
Think'st thou that duty shall have dread to speak
When power to flattery bows? To plainness honor's bound
When majesty *falls to folly!*"

The conduct of the *King* in the scene of the abdication, impossible to a sane man, is perfectly natural to *King Lear.* In his doting paternal fondness and his greedy desire of filial affection, he adjures his daughter *Goneril* to speak her love for him, in order "that we *our largest bounty may extend* where nature doth with merit challenge";—yet he has already made division of his kingdom, and he proceeds to reward, successively, the protesting *Goneril* and *Regan* with the exact one third he previously had assigned to them! His treatment of *Cordelia* is not only unjust, cruel, and odious, but such as, by a rational man, however ill-tempered or angry, would be impossible. *Cordelia* is a sweet and gentle girl, his cherished favorite, under whose care he has intended to place himself during the closing years of life: there can be no question of his love for her or of her love for him, and of her truth and tenderness he must, for years, have had ample knowledge: yet, upon the instant, when she fails in mere verbal protestation, this "old, kind father," intense beyond parallel in his passionate paternal feeling, casts her off, dowered with his *curse,* abhorrent to him, and level in his thoughts with creatures the most horrid to imagination:

> "He that makes his generation messes
> To gorge his appetite, shall to my bosom
> Be as well neighbor'd, pitied, and reliev'd,
> As thou my sometime-daughter!"

He declares she had better "not been born than not to have pleas'd me better," and proclaims her to be the object of his intensest *hate,*—"A *wretch* whom Nature is asham'd almost to acknowledge hers!"

All this is impossible to sanity, but it jumps exactly with the over-excitability and extreme violence of the senile mania of which the *King* is a victim. The *King of France,* hearing the old man's burst of invective, is, naturally, amazed, and he expresses his astonishment precisely as any observer would, who was unaware of the monarch's already vitiated mental condition:

> "This is most strange,
> That she, *who even but now* was your *best object*,
> *Most best, most dear'st*, should in *this trice of time*
> Commit a thing so monstrous, to dismantle
> So many folds of favor. Sure, her offence
> Must be of such unnatural degree,
> That monsters it, or your fore-vouch'd affection
> Fall'n into taint: which to believe of her,
> Must be a faith that reason, without miracle,
> Shall never plant in me."

The *King's* state of alienation, furthermore, appears distinctly in his banishment of *Kent* and in the insane fury of his edict threatening the present death of a man whom he has long known for a loving and devoted friend and defender. *Goneril's* testimony, likewise, is significant, given, as it is, when she is not seeking personal benefit through falsehood, but speaks in all sincerity: "You see how *full of changes* his age is; *the observation we have made of it hath not been little:* he always loved our sister most; and with what *poor judgment* he hath now cast her off *appears too grossly.* . . . *The best and soundest of his time hath been but rash."*

King Lear, when first we see him, is very old, "four score and upward," not decrepit, but beginning to break, though not yet outwardly broken. He is like some majestic tower, massive, venerable; some grand, surviving monument of long past years, seeming a part of the adamant on which it rests, but, actually, so worn and frayed that it is ready to totter and crumble at a touch. His original nature is felt to have been one that combined goodness and simplicity; but he has been long a King, ruling over a semi-barbarous people; he has maintained a despotic sway; has, necessarily, been a warrior and a conqueror, and has never known what it is to be subjected to the discipline of self-denial. His will has been his law. His temper, naturally imperious, is one that will brook no restraint, and as he has grown old he has become more and more self-centred, self-willed, imperative, overbearing, and inflexible. Were it not that he is naturally virtuous, kind, noble, a supremely grand being, he would be intolerable: and this nature, so great and yet so weak,—since it cannot govern itself,—has been slowly vitiated by the encroachment of mental decay. At the outset the condition of the *King* is that of subjective emotional excitement. The slightest opposition to his will, even if it be no more than a semblance of dissent, is sufficient to stir his wrath. A mere word of respectful entreaty appears to him to be insufferably audacious. A loving remonstrance makes him fierce. An open protest against his injustice awakens his fury. "Out of my sight!" he screams, when his true friend, *Kent,* who loves him, fondly and bravely strives to curb his madly foolish conduct, and he would draw his sword and slay his faithful servant, on the instant, were it not that he is prevented. Throughout the whole first scene his demeanor and his talk are irrational. His final speech to *Kent* fairly throbs with the passion of insane egotism:

> "Since thou hast sought to make us break our vow,
> (Which we durst never yet) and with strain'd pride
> To come betwixt our sentence and our power
> (Which nor our nature nor our place can bear)
> Our potency made good, take thy reward," etc.

His distemper, it is evident, will increase. He will be exacting, impatient, irritable, capricious, at times violent, at times gentle, and under stress and strain he will become delirious and then collapse. His reason is unsettled. But, all the while, there lingers around him the glory of what he once has been.

It is not until *King Lear* has been smitten with affliction, struck down and shattered, that the true quality of his nature is fully revealed,—the original greatness of his mind, the tenderness of his heart, the vast scope of his imagination. Then, eventually, his egotism is dissipated; then, even in his abject condition of disordered reason, he perceives the sorrowful state of man, the vanity of mundane things, the duty of power toward weakness, the obligations of humanity: "Oh, I have ta'en too little thought of this." It is in the capability of entirely and exactly comprehending and displaying the true nature of *King Lear* that the actor shows,—if he can show it at all,—his fitness and power to play this part. A clear comprehension of the original man is imperative. All his life *King Lear* has been, intrinsically, a great person; not royal merely by lineage, but royal by nature. He was born to the purple. He is like the mountain that rears itself in the plain. He is an image of lonely grandeur, and the fall of his mind and sovereignty is like the terrific downward rush of the avalanche, that sweeps everything before it into a chaos of ruin. He is not a common man grown old,—the petty justice of a country town, enfeebled by weight of years and made, by domestic misfortune, "a lunatic, lean-witted fool." It is not an old *Capulet* or an old *Brabantio* who is mad, in this terribly afflicting tragedy; it is old *King Lear;* it is a born monarch of mankind, whom "sharp-toothed unkindness" has, in his weakening age and incipient decay, "struck, serpent-like, upon the very heart"; and when that awful figure of ruined majesty rushes, with streaming hair and blazing eyes, across the thunder-blasted heath, raving amid the tumult of the tempest, the spectacle thrills our souls, not alone with afflicting sense of the agony into which the poor old *King* has fallen, but of the lost estate of colossal grandeur from which he fell. We see this august and splendid person torn from all the moorings of life and love, and driven forth upon the gale-swept ocean-wastes of misery, but it is less because of what he suffers than because of what he is that we pity, love, reverence, and deplore him. The best elements of our human nature are felt to be combined in this ravaged figure of shattered royalty,—once so glorious, now so abject and woful,—and so his anguish comes home to us with a keen perception of its personal significance. There are many denotements of this sympathetic humanity which is the fascination of the character of *King Lear*. It links to him the heart-strings of the sweet, tender, and true *Cordelia*. It holds the love, loyalty, and compassion of the wronged, persecuted, wretched *Edgar*. It enchains the fealty and abiding affection of *Glo'ster:* "if I die for it, as no less is threatened me, the King, my old master, must be relieved." It inspires the beautiful devotion of the helpless but faithful *Fool*. It commands the pity and the mercy of conquering *Albany*. It inspires the life-long, adamantine, loving fidelity of the good, wise, honest, manly *Kent*. Nothing, indeed, in all the play is more decisively illuminative of the grand character of *King Lear*,—of what he has been and what essentially he is,—than the passionate, affectionate fidelity of this unswerving follower of the dethroned and outcast sovereign, this true man, who, "from the first of difference and decay," follows his sad steps, and will not be parted from him, even at the brink of the grave:

> "I have a journey, sir, shortly to go;
> My master calls me—I must not say no."

In the element of action, always the most essential quality of a play, "King Lear" ranks with "Othello" and "Macbeth." Coleridge remarks that " 'Lear' combines length with rapidity,—like the hurricane and the whirlpool, absorbing while it advances." In the main the construction of it is exceptionally skilful. There are, indeed, many changes of scene, and for the modern stage cuts and a few transpositions are essential. There is one serious defect in the play, and that is the glaring improbability of the conduct of *Glo'ster* and his son *Edgar,* in the matter of the early severance of their relations. The father and son love each other and are dwelling together in perfect amity. *Edmund, Glo'ster's* illegitimate son, who has been absent from home "nine years," returns, and being desirous of supplanting his natural brother, *Edgar,* as heir to the paternal estates and title, tells their father that *Edgar* intends to murder him, and produces a forged letter in proof of his preposterous yarn—a document which *Glo'ster,* with absurd credulity, instantly accepts as conclusive: yet *Glo'ster* knows that his two sons are living close to each other and are

KING LEAR 413

in daily contact and most unlikely to communicate with one another by the epistolary method, and also must know, since he possesses common sense, that the person to be benefited by his repudiation of *Edgar* is the very person whose story is calculated to cause it. *Edmund* subsequently finds *Edgar* even precipitately ready to believe that his loving father has been envenomed against him and purposes to have him murdered, and, at *Edmund's* instigation, he incontinently takes refuge in flight. "A credulous father," exclaims *Edmund,* "and a brother noble, on whose foolish honesty my practices ride easy." They do, indeed!—far too easy for credence. The whole scheme is preposterous. A few words between *Edgar* and *Glo'ster* would have blown it away. *Edgar,* as a character, is virtuous and amiable, but mentally he is insignificant: on the other hand, as an acting part he is showy and effective, because provided with the opportunity of simulating madness, under exceedingly pictorial circumstances. *Edmund,* a sort of miniature *Iago,* and an industrious promoter of the action, is much the better part. Actors, however, do not generally so esteem it, and as a rule "the leading man" insists on playing *Edgar.*

An exceedingly difficult passage in the tragedy is that in which *Edgar* leads the blind *Glo'ster* to the supposed edge of the Cliff of Dover, and the poor old man hurls himself forward, and after striking the ground is persuaded that he has fallen to the beach, far below. It would be difficult to find an actor capable of impersonating *Glo'ster*, in that scene, and in arranging this play for the stage I should cut the passage out. In "The Edwin Booth Prompt Book" of "King Lear," edited by me, and published in 1878, Booth prescribes that as *Glo'ster* is about to leap from the supposed cliff *Edgar* shall catch him, exclaiming "Hold, who comes here?" and then that *King Lear* shall enter, fantastically dressed with wild flowers. As the passage stands in Shakespeare's text, the representation of it can be made credible and effective only by ingenious treatment. If it be assumed that *Glo'ster*, whose eyes have lately been brutally torn out, is fevered and half-delirious, so that he does not truly know what is going on, and if the scene is acted in accordance with that assumption, a rational effect might ensue: otherwise the incident is absurd and, in the acting, goes for nothing.

The sturdy, magnanimous character of *Kent* has been many times nobly represented. It is one that appeals directly to the sense of manliness and at once enlists sympathy. No record exists as to its first representative. In Garrick's production of the tragedy *Kent* was assumed by Winstone, whose person was large, whose features were harsh, and whose voice was

KING LEAR

loud. Davies commends his "manly boldness," but intimates that he was deficient of sympathy. Bransby, who succeeded Winstone, seems to have given a better performance: he was "spirited without being boisterous, and blunt without vulgarity." Other good players of *Kent,* in the olden time, were Luke Sparks, Thomas Davies, and John Pritt Harley.

William Smith was the first performer of *Edgar,* in Tate's version of "King Lear," 1681. He was a man of commanding presence and fine talent. George Powell succeeded him as *Edgar.* Wilks was elegant in demeanor and highly spirited in the delivery of *Edgar's* challenge to *Edmund.* Ryan was manly and effective in the same dramatic passage, and Ryan had learned from Powell, on whom, in youth, he attended. Havard and also Samuel Reddish were conspicuously successful in this character. When Henderson, in London, first acted *King Lear,* 1779, the *Edgar* was Webster, the *Edmund* John Palmer. In Kemble's revival of the play, 1788, Wroughton acted *Edgar* and Barrymore acted *Edmund.* When Alexander Pope ventured in *King Lear,* January 6, 1794, the *Edgar* was Holman. In a later time the part was made prominent by the brilliant and graceful Charles Kemble. In August, 1820, at Drury Lane, the elder Booth acted *Edgar,* to the *King Lear* of Edmund Kean. On March 1, 1811, at the Park Theatre, New

York, John Howard Payne, taking a benefit, performed *Edgar,* to the *King Lear* of George Frederick Cooke.

The "historical period" of "King Lear" is the year of the world 3105. Mention of the "architecture" and "costume" of that period in what we now call Britain prompts remembrance of the terse chapter in Irish history, about "Snakes in Ireland":—"There are no snakes in Ireland." The tragedy admits of being dressed in accordance with the customs of a much later time than that of the fabulous story of which it is the chief medium. The architectural accessories which are used in the representation of it should be of a rough, dusky, grim character,—massive columns, huge structures of stone,—all suffused with an atmosphere of antiquity, wild, strange, romantic; derived without any consideration of "historical correctness," but made subservient to the creation of a weird, gloomy, haunted effect. Sir Walter Scott wrote: "In the time in which Lear is supposed to have lived the British were, probably, painted and tattooed. . . . As the poet, carrying back his scene into remote days, retains still, to a certain extent, the manners and sentiments of his own period, so it is sufficient for the purpose of costume if everything be avoided which can recall modern associations, and as much of the antique be assumed as will at once harmonize with the purpose of the exhibition, and in so far awaken recollection of the days of yore as to give an air of truth to the scene." Godwin would elect "the early Celtic period," or a time at least 100 to 400 years B.C., as the era in which "King Lear" should be placed, for representation. In Shakespeare's day the tragedy, we can feel sure, was dressed in such garments as were then commonly worn, with some consideration of the different ranks in social life. At the time of the Restoration, and long afterward, the plays of Shakespeare were dressed either as they had been dressed in Shakespeare's day, or in raiment of the contemporaneous period. Garrick, as *King Lear,* wore a dress of the Georgian era: a loose, white shirt; knee-breeches; long, close-fitting silk stockings, which were drawn up over the knees of the breeches; a scarlet surcoat, reaching almost to the knees, and adorned at the wrists with white ruffles, heavily trimmed, along the front and bottom edges, with white ermine; a long, flowing white scarf, fastened at the throat with a jewelled clasp; and low-cut shoes: and he carried, in early scenes of the play, a crutch or cane. He did not, as some other actors of the part had done,—and as, indeed, was customary,—wear a full-bottomed wig: his wig was a "tie," and, in the tempest scenes and the latter part of the play, the hair of it was loose and dishevelled: his face was clean shaven—as were the faces of all the old performers of *King Lear:* Macready was the first actor to wear a beard when playing this part. There was no pretence, in the Theatre of Garrick's day, any more than there had been in that of Betterton, of dressing the characters in "King Lear" in even a remote semblance of such habiliments as were worn in ancient British times. The subsidiary parts were attired in garb as inappropriate as that of Garrick's *King Lear.* Indeed, the mis-dressing of Shakespeare's plays persisted, even in leading theatres, to a much later time than that of Garrick. John Pritt Harley, for example, one of the best of the secondary actors of the Kemble-Kean period, who appeared as *Kent,* in "King Lear," wore a military uniform, comprising a close-fitting red coat, the sleeves of which were slashed, to show white "puffs," and also were ornamented with gold-braid; a short cloak, with a wide collar, trimmed with white; knee breeches and top boots; a profuse, curly wig, tied at the back with ribbon; and a black cocked hat, garnished in front with a large bow: this *Kent* also was armed with a heavy cavalry-sword, of the time of King George the Third!

Shakespeare, as he pictured to himself the daughters of *King Lear,* undoubtedly saw them in rich apparel and, probably, of the fashion which a princess of his own day approved. That his fancied costume for those persons was rich is indicated by his text, for the `King` says, to *Goneril,* Act II., sc. 4:

> "Thou art a lady.
> If only to go warm were gorgeous,
> Why, Nature needs not *what thou gorgeous wear'st*
> Which scarcely keeps thee warm."

The characters of those daughters are simple: *Goneril* and *Regan* are cruel, fierce, treacherous, wanton, devilish,—the veritable incarnations of duplicity and ferocity. *Goneril* is a little more fiendish in spirit than *Regan,* but no more so in conduct. To me they seem more like wickedly beautiful reptiles than like women: but, though exceptional, they are examples of entirely possible human depravity. *Cordelia* is young, beautiful, affectionate, reticent, faithful, and not without executive faculty and courage; but she neither says nor does anything to justify the extravagant adulation of the many commentators, from Anne Jameson onward, who have celebrated her as a marvel of all excellence. She is described, in Act IV., sc. 3, as displaying those emotions which any good, sensitive, loving child might feel, and which, certainly, in *Cordelia,* are indicative of a generous nature, considering the cruelly harsh treatment to which she has been subjected by her father. Her responses to the *King,* in the First Scene, do not indicate much inclination to humor the vagaries of her parent. Some commentators have described, in *Cordelia's* fate, a punishment for a filial fault! Persons interested in twaddle of that sort can find an abundance of it. *Cordelia* is absent from the stage from the First Scene of Act I. until the Fourth Scene of Act. IV. She participates in only four scenes of the tragedy, as written by Shakespeare, and in one of them she merely appears. She speaks, altogether, less than one hundred full lines. Ellen Terry described the part, after acting it, as "wee, but fine," and that description denotes it. The famous old-time actresses whose names are associated with *Cordelia* performed only the ridiculous heroine devised by Tate. All of them, —Mrs. Barry, Mrs. Cibber, Mrs. Bracegirdle, Mrs. Woffington, and the rest,—dressed the *Princess* in garments such as were worn by the fine ladies of their respective periods; and singular indeed her appearance must have been, in a long, tight waist, a high ruff, and a wide-skirted hoop! Not until Kemble's time was any considerable effort made to effect a radical reform in the use of costume, and Kemble's well-meant endeavors did not accomplish much, aside from pointing the way. According to all the old records, the most profoundly pathetic and soulful impersonation of *Cordelia* ever given on the English Stage was that of Mrs. Cibber: she must have been indeed marvellous, to have created such an enduring effect with such material.

SAMUEL PHELPS.

Phelps produced "King Lear," "from the original text," November 5, 1845, at Sadler's Wells Theatre, himself acting the *King,* with Henry Marston as *Edgar,* George Bennett as *Edmund,* A. Younge as *Kent,* H. Mellon as *Glo'ster,* Scharf as the *Fool,* and Miss Cooper as *Cordelia.* His version of the play adhered to the text of the First Folio and to the division and sequence of the scenes as they therein appear, restored the *Fool,* and made no alterations, and only a "few inevitable omissions." Careful attention was bestowed upon minute details as well as upon the most commanding features of the tragedy. The scenery and the dressing, though the former, especially at the opening, was meagre, were commended by contemporary judges as "in that ideal and simple style . . . which befits an altogether fabulous period." John A. Heraud, who highly extols Phelps's performance, complained that "the storm into which poor *Lear* is turned out . . . is too naturally rendered— it is not imitation, but realization." That objection seems more captious than judicial, and probably the audience at the Wells did not find a "too natural storm" any deterrent to enjoyment of the acting,—which was specially admired for "the intelligence and energy" of the several actors in coöperating to show the *King* "not the one engrossing object, . . . but the centre of a group of varied characters, each possessing marked distinctive features and exercising an agency either for good or evil." Special praise was accorded to Scharf, for his "clear conception of the nature and importance of the *Fool,* laboring to out-jest *Lear's* 'heart-struck injuries,' and his careful and characteristic impersonation." Scharf was the first *man* to act the *Fool* on the modern English Stage: for many years after Macready's restoration of the part it was assumed by women. Phelps's production of "King Lear" was the most rounded and complete that had been given in England, and it is doubtful whether, in thoroughness, it has been surpassed. In Phelps's performance of the *King* the emphasis was laid on the *pathos* of the part: "as a piece of *pathetic* acting [it] is unrivalled. Mr. Phelps never forgets the father—never seeks to surprise, but contents himself with exciting pity for the wrongs that the outraged parent suffers" (Heraud). At the beginning, Phelps depicted the *King* as extremely infirm with age. As he was led in and assisted to his seat his hands trembled, his head wavered, and his whole demeanor indicated a weakened body, in which the

KING LEAR

stricken mind was weakly working. This element was excessive in the personation, because it could not be maintained through the following scenes, which are prohibitive of such treatment: but Phelps, no doubt, intended the revivification to be that of the semi-delirium of insanity, the last flash of the expiring flame; and, thus shown, the treatment could not have been ineffective. The gradations of change through which the mind of the father passes, from tenderness toward *Cordelia* to surprise, resentment, and burning wrath, were delicately traced. The Curse on *Goneril* was spoken with deficient vehemence, the sense of the pitiful weakness of the *King* obscuring the denotements of passion and terror. The Curse in the Second Act lacked variety and intensity: "it was decidedly inferior to that of Macready." Phelps, however, was specially fine in his utterance of

"No, you unnatural hags!
I will have such revenges on you both,
That all the world shall—I will do such things,—
What they are, yet I know not; but they shall be
The terrors of the earth!"

"There was *a fearful beauty* in some of his bursts of passionate anger." In the first scene with *Kent* and *Edgar* he seemed lost in self-absorption, as though oblivious of everything but the overwhelming agony that "bound him for ever to his woes and his wrong."

Royalty, inherent and persistent through all vicissitudes, is a fundamental necessity of the nature which must stand back of any true impersonation of *King Lear,* and royalty is a quality in which Phelps,—sturdy, honest, curt, and gruff,—was lacking. He was at his best in the closing scenes, where, according to a recorder in "The Court Journal," there was, in his performance, "a greater depth, simplicity, and unity of purpose, and a more perfect embodiment of that purpose, than even in the great performance of Macready himself." Professor Morley (who significantly noted that, in the earlier scenes, Phelps failed sufficiently to contrast "the royal state with the abject misery"), writing in "The Examiner" of June 1, 1861, paid him this cordial and informing tribute:

"But from the time that *Lear* enters with his robes washed almost colorless by the rain, a feeble old man, weary and witless, after his night's wandering under the storm, everything is exquisitely done, the story being read wholly with regard to its pathos, not to its terror. The king is utterly lost in the father. The wound to the heart has struck, as no hurt to the dignity of royal robes can strike a man. Majesty has been contemned in its rags. Humanity lives to assert itself. The quiet broken spirit, the strayed wits, the tender nursing and rocking of the body of *Cordelia* in the closing scene; the faint interest in all but her by whose love *Lear's* broken heart was held together; the tenderness with which he lays her down, as for an instant, while he lifts his hands to the throat in which the last convulsive throe of death is rising; his quiet death, with his eyes, his pointing hands, and his last words directed to her lips, are exquisitely touching."

CHARLES JOHN KEAN.

Charles Kean (1811-1868) produced "King Lear," April 17, 1858, at the Princess' Theatre, London, and for the first time assumed the character of the *King*. The version that he presented was one made by himself, in which the text of Shakespeare was intelligently condensed,—a few allowable transpositions being skilfully made,—and from which certain coarse and offensive lines were excluded: the incident of the extrusion of *Glos'ter's* eyes, which is barbaric and horrible, was only mentioned. The stage-setting was faithfully representative of some aspects of England in "the early Saxon age." The cast included Kate Terry, as *Cordelia;* Caroline Heath, as *Goneril;* Eleanor Bufton (Mrs. Arthur Swanborough), as *Regan;* John Ryder, as *Edgar;* Walter Lacy, as *Edmund;* and John Cooper, as *Kent*. The part of the *Fool* was made specially pictorial and pathetic by Miss Poole (Mrs. Dickons), who sang some of the bits of verse allotted to that character, and whose singing was delicious.

Charles Kean's personation of *King Lear,*—which

I saw in New York, September 13, 1865,—at the house which had been opened as Brougham's Lyceum, and which, when Kean acted there, was called the Broadway,—was, at that time, fine in many particulars, and, reflecting on descriptions I have read of what it was when first presented and on what it was when I first saw it, I discover that he strictly adhered to the ideal which he had early formed,—that of the injured, afflicted, suffering father, driven mad by the cruelty of his elder daughters, *Goneril* and *Regan;* by remorse for his injustice toward his younger daughter, *Cordelia,* and by exposure to the rigors of a terrible storm. He made no effort to depict *King Lear* as a crumbling Hercules, and,—as with Phelps, —it was more the heart-broken parent than the discrowned, discarded, and despised monarch that he aimed to represent. In the opening scene he gave no intimation of madness, present or impending: he was a capricious, imperious, choleric old man, rash, impetuous, bent on having his own way, easily moved to anger, and, when angry, fierce and reckless; he rapidly recovered from his indignation against *Cordelia* and *Kent;* in the scene at *Albany's* Palace, in which the *King* enters, as from the hunt, he carried a boar-spear, was eager and rapid, and exclaimed "Let me not stay a jot for dinner!" much as a bluff, hearty, good-natured country Squire might do. It

was not till after the repulse by *Goneril* that he began
to manifest the wavering mind, the latent sense of
folly, the presence of remorse. He delivered the
adjuration "Hear, Nature, hear!" beginning solemnly
and speaking in a fervid whisper, which gradually
changed into a gasping, choking outcry. His business was the simultaneous action of throwing away
the spear and falling upon his knees. With the
Curse Speech he closed Act I. In the scene before
Glo'ster's Castle he put forth all his strength, and
his simulation of frenzy was made effective by
intensity. He was variously abject and forlorn in
the scenes of madness, his method of treating them
being marked by absolute simplicity. My remembrance is that he did not discriminate as to the phenomena of lunacy, but, while faithfully portraying
the wretched condition of the outcast *King,* left those
scenes to cause, by their intrinsic pathos, the sense of
misery and desolation with which they are so terribly
freighted. His finest acting was done in the scene of
the recognition of *Cordelia,* when the broken old man
feebly recovers his reason.

HENRY IRVING.

Irving acted *King Lear,* for the first time, November 10, 1892, at the Lyceum Theatre, London. He mounted and dressed the play in a style which, judging from all accounts, has never been equalled. The historic period in which he laid the action was soon after the evacuation of Britain by the Romans, and therefore centuries later than the fabulous period of the ancient British King. The scenery, painted by Hawes Craven and Joseph Harker, must have been beautiful: "Notwithstanding all that has been said and written of the revivals of the past, we do not believe,"—so wrote Clement Scott,—"that the English Stage has ever seen 'King Lear' mounted and set in such a splendid frame or colored with such artistic taste." Ellen Terry played *Cordelia,* William Terriss *Edgar,* Ada Dyas *Goneril,* Maud Milton *Regan,* and William Haviland the *Fool.* That revival of the tragedy achieved the longest "run" ever obtained for "King Lear,"—seventy-two consecutive performances.

To my profound and lasting regret, I never saw Irving as *King Lear*. His performance was generally accounted a failure, though *why* it should have been so accounted is not entirely clear, for it pleased his audiences, and it elicited considerable critical commendation. The dissatisfaction which was expressed by some judges seems to have proceeded from the fact that Irving did not fulfil a commonplace, popular, erroneous ideal of *King Lear,* which would have him

From a Drawing by J. Bernard Partridge

HENRY IRVING AS *KING LEAR*

"Hence, and avoid my sight!
So be my grave my peace, as here I give
Her father's heart from her!"

Act I., Sc. 1

represented as a barbaric chieftain, huge and boisterous. One sapient censor of Irving's personation indicated the presence of this ideal in his mind by his remark that "those early moods of unrestrained fury . . . are meet for men of *brawn and lung.*" The paradox of acting,—manifestation of great strength by a broken old man,—*is* displayed in *King Lear;* but the strength is that of frenzy reanimating a body originally of exceptional muscular power, but no longer normally vital. "Brawn and lung" are useful, sometimes, in acting, but their possession will not insure a great embodiment of *King Lear,* nor does the lack of them form an insurmountable obstacle to such an embodiment. "The best thing I ever did," Irving said to me, at the old Plaza Hotel, New York, in one of the many conversations we had regarding his acting, "was my performance of *King Lear.* They would not have it," he added, "but it was my greatest work. All around that play there is an awful atmosphere of danger—mystery—omen—whispering in corners—plotting by night—something terrible impending. My performance was *psychological,* and I know it was right. I wish *you* had seen it." I wish I had! From all that he said to me, and from all that I know of the play and the actor, I believe that if he were alive now, to act *King Lear,* his personation would receive public indorsement of his high estimate of it: the blacksmith ideal of that character is not as highly esteemed as once it was.

The statement has been recorded, by Walter Herries Pollock, quoting, as authority for it, Frank Tyars,—a good actor, for many years a member of Irving's theatrical company,—that Irving "definitely adopted" a change in his conception of the character of *King Lear,* in the interval between "his arrival at the theatre, to dress, and the rise of the curtain on the first night of the production"; and Mr. Pollock believes that this, alleged, change of conception "fully accounts for the strangely hesitating touch which was noticeable in Irving's treatment of the earlier scenes, on that night, and which never wholly disappeared afterward."

Irving's original conception and that which he adopted after the "change" are not specified. The notion emitted by Mr. Tyars is, to me, utterly preposterous. I often talked with Irving about the character of *King Lear,* both before and after he acted the part, and I never perceived any alteration in his views of it. He may have altered some technical expedients of expression, some stage business, at the last moment; but that he radically changed his "conception" within the period of about one hour is incredible. It is contrary to all the laws of the

KING LEAR

mind; and the notion of Henry Irving, under the tremendous stress of approaching his first performance of this terribly exacting part, while dressing and making up for it, confiding to Frank Tyars his sudden intention to alter his conception,—even if it had been possible for him to make such alteration,—is fantastic. Ellen Terry spoke to me slightingly of the performance: in her "Diary" she recorded, immediately after it had ended, "H. was just marvellous, but indistinct from nervousness. T[erriss] spoke out, but who cared! Haviland was very good. . . . I was rather good to-night. It is a *wee* part, but fine."

A minute, elaborate, thorough analysis of Irving's impersonation of *King Lear* would make an exceedingly interesting and instructive chapter in the history of the Theatre, and would be of great value to all actors who might hereafter undertake to play the part. It is much to be desired that some English writer familiar with this subject would do this work. I can think of no one more competent to execute the task than Walter Herries Pollock, who was one of Irving's intimate friends, one whom he greatly liked and respected, and who, during many years, observed his career and closely and carefully studied his acting.

That Irving did not at any time after his first venture revive the tragedy of "King Lear" may have been due to the fact that the costly scenery he had provided for it was consumed in the fire, February 18, 1898, which destroyed all the material he had accumulated for the stage settings of no fewer than forty plays,—one of the several disasters which clouded the latter years of that great actor's life.

AMERICAN STAGE.—EARLY REPRESENTATIONS.

In the early days of the American Stage "King Lear" was seldom presented. The first performance of it given in America occurred, January 14, 1754, at the Theatre in Nassau Street,—mentioned by Ireland as "the first building in New York erected for dramatic representation": it was opened September 17, 1753, and closed March 18, 1754. The performer of *King Lear,* on that notable occasion, was ——— Malone, a useful member of Hallam's American Company, who played all sorts of parts but seems to have been better in comedy than in tragedy. No record of his *King Lear* survives. The parts were cast as follows:

King Lear	Mr. Malone.
Kent	Lewis Hallam, Sr.
Glo'ster	Mr. Bell.
Cornwall	Mr. Miller.
Edgar	Mr. Singleton.
Edmund	Mr. Clarkson.
Albany	Mr. Adcock.

KING LEAR

Burgundy	Mr. Hulett.
Usher	Mr. Rigsby.
Cordelia	Mrs. Hallam.
Goneril	Mrs. Becceley.
Regan	Mrs. Adcock.
Aranthe	Mrs. Rigby.

Aranthe is the name given by Tate to the *confidante* whom he provided for *Cordelia*. The Hallam mentioned in this cast was the elder Lewis Hallam: the Mrs. Hallam was his wife, a woman of uncommon talent and beauty: both had gained professional experience and reputation at Goodman's Fields Theatre, London. Hallam was accounted a fine comedian and was deemed especially proficient in playing old men: his performance of *King Lear,* presumably, was one of respectable utility. He died, in 1756, at Jamaica, and his widow eventually became the wife of a brother actor and manager, David Douglass. Hallam's son, Lewis Hallam the second, played *King Lear,* at the John Street Theatre, January 25, 1768, and again on March 27, 1795, and also he participated in the first performance of the tragedy ever given in Philadelphia,—September 28, 1759, at a theatre built and managed by David Douglass, at a place called Society Hill. This was the cast:

King Lear	Mr. Harman.
Glo'ster	Mr. Scott.
Kent	Mr. Tomlinson.

Edgar	Mr. Hallam.
Edmund	Mr. Reed.
Cornwall	Mr. Horne.
Albany	Mr. Morris.
Burgundy	David Douglass.
Usher	Mr. Allyn.
Goneril	Mrs. Love.
Regan	Mrs. Harman.
Cordelia	Mrs. Douglass.

"King Lear" was not popular in those days: indeed, it never has been a popular play, and revivals of it have been effected only at long intervals. The version invariably used on the early American Stage was that of Tate, with, later, more or less of the Garrick and Kemble modifications, and Shakespeare's tragedy, according to the original text, was never acted in America until Macready presented it, September 27, 1844, at the Park Theatre, New York. Among the performers of *King Lear,* in the early days of our Theatre, in New York, Philadelphia, Baltimore, and other places on the Atlantic seaboard, were William Warren, the Elder, about 1805; Thomas Abthorpe Cooper, 1809; James Fennell, 1810; George Frederick Cooke, 1811; Edmund Kean, 1820 (at the Anthony Street Theatre, N. Y., December 13); Junius Brutus Booth, 1821; and Edwin Forrest, 1826. Fennell, fine in *Othello* and *Zanga,* made no distinctive impression as *King Lear.* Warren was the

KING LEAR 435

Falstaff of his day, and an accomplished "all round" actor: he was the worst dresser of his time. I have found no emphatic tribute to his performances in tragedy. Cooper (1776-1849), who ranks with the great actors of the period, was only "indifferent good" in *King Lear*. He acted the part, February, 1824, at the Park Theatre, where he and William Augustus Conway were jointly filling an engagement, but his performance was ineffective, and contemporary critical opinion was adverse to it. Conway acted *Edgar*. The first American actor who truly distinguished himself as *King Lear* was Edwin Forrest.

JUNIUS BRUTUS BOOTH.

The elder Booth first acted *King Lear* in America, at the theatre in Richmond, Virginia, in the summer of 1821, and thereafter he repeated his performance, from time to time, in many American cities, throughout the whole of his eccentric career,—always appearing in the old Tate version, modified as has been described. His impersonation was fragmentary,—like that of Edmund Kean,—and for that reason impressive only at points. He was grand in declaring the *King's* purpose to "resume" his royal "shape," and he was supremely pathetic in the scene of the *King's* recognition of his daughter,—his delivery of the line, "If you have poison for me I will drink it" being indescribably touching. He treated the madness of *King Lear* as episodical and transient,—a method which is incorrect: the conduct of the *King* is partly crazy at the beginning, and his "restoration" is but temporary. The *Physician* warns *Cordelia,* saying:

> ". . . the great rage,
> You see, is kill'd in him; and yet 'tis danger
> To make him even o'er the time he has lost."

And the ultimate irrational condition of the poor, broken old man is indicated in his words to *Cordelia,* in the Camp Scene, Act V., sc. 3, original,—the most pathetic passage in the whole tragedy,—always omitted, even in modern representation:

> "Come, let's away to prison.
> We two alone will sing like birds i' the cage:
> When thou dost ask me blessing, I'll kneel down
> And ask of thee forgiveness. So we'll live,
> And pray, and sing, and tell old tales, and laugh
> At gilded butterflies, and hear poor rogues
> Talk of court news; and we'll talk with them too,
> Who loses and who wins; who 's in, who 's out;
> And take upon 's the mystery of things,
> As if we were God's spies; and we'll wear out,
> In a wall'd prison, packs and sects of great ones
> That ebb and flow by the moon."

But the elder Booth, unlike Edmund Kean, never gave the last act according to Shakespeare.

KING LEAR

EDWIN FORREST.

Edwin Forrest (1806-1872) first played *King Lear*, December 27, 1826, at the Bowery Theatre, New York, appearing in the version of the tragedy then customarily used, which was Tate's medley, as slightly amended by Garrick. Among his associates in that presentation were Mrs. Duff, as *Cordelia;* John Duff, as *Edmund;* and T. S. Hamblin, as *Edgar.* Forrest was then only twenty years and some months old and had been only about six years on the stage, yet he gave a performance which seems to have surprised some observers, by its power and its use of pathos. The part of *King Lear* early became a favorite with him, and it so remained throughout his life. In a letter, toward the end of his days, he wrote: "For forty years I have studied and acted *Lear.* I have studied the part in the street, on the stage, in lunatic asylums all over the world, and I hold that, next to God, Shakespeare comprehended the mind of man." That piously extravagant deliverance exhibits ardent devotion to the poet, and it seems singular that, possessed by such a profound feeling of reverence, Forrest should have exercised his powers, as he did throughout the whole of his professional career, in the exhibition of a mangled and partly spurious version of Shakespeare's sublime tragedy. In his early years, as an itinerant stock-star, it probably was imperative that he should perform in the accepted stage version of "King Lear," because that, and no other, was known to the various stock companies with which he was obliged to act; but he never entirely discarded Tate's contemptible hash of the original play. While, however, he spoke, as *King Lear,* a considerable number of lines not written by Shakespeare, he retained the closing scene, and ended the piece with the death of the *King,* beside the dead *Cordelia.* His authorized stage version includes not only pieces of Tate's inflated verse but several of his absurd "new modellings";—the lascivious epistolary solicitation of *Edmund* by *Goneril* and *Regan; Edmund's* announcement of his purpose to outrage *Cordelia; Cordelia's* intercession with *Glo'ster,* to rescue the *King;* the message of *Glo'ster* to Tate's improvised nobleman, the *Duke of Cambray;* and a part of the love business between *Edgar* and *Cordelia,—Edgar* making a tender of his affection (Act I., sc. 3) and *Cordelia* replying "study to forget your passion," and then remarking, as she makes her exit:

> "But if his love be fixed, such constant flame
> As warms my breast, if such I find his passion,
> My heart as grateful to his truth shall be,
> And cold Cordelia prove as kind as he."

From a Steel Engraving   *Author's Collection*

EDWIN FORREST AS *KING LEAR*

*"Ay, every inch a king:
When I do stare, see how the subject quakes."*

Act IV., Sc. 6

This terminates the love affair, warm *Edgar* seeing no more of "cold Cordelia" till, at the last, he composedly beholds her corpse, when she is cold indeed. Another of Tate's gems, that Forrest's reverence for Shakespeare did not deter him from preserving, is this speech, which he, as the *King,* addressed to *Cordelia,* Act I., sc. 1:

" 'Tis said that I am chol'ric. Judge me, gods,
  Is there not cause? Now, minion, I perceive
  The truth of what has been suggested to us,
  Thy fondness for the rebel son of Glo'ster.
  And oh! take heed, rash girl, lest we comply
  With thy fond wishes, which thou wilt too late
  Repent!"

These illustrations of Forrest's professional acumen and Shakespearean scholarship are derived from a literal transcript of his "Prompt Book of 'King Lear'" made by the Prompter, J. H. Browne, the stage directions and business being carefully written in, "with the kind permission of the eminent tragedian." This interesting theatrical relic, now in my library, was given to me by my friend Robert Mantell,—himself the best representative of *King Lear* now on the American Stage.

I first saw Forrest as *King Lear* more than sixty years ago, on the Boston Stage, and thereafter, till near the time of his death, in 1872, I saw and studied many repetitions of the performance: It was always massive and powerful; in the physical sense, for a long time too powerful,—the animal element predominating over the mental and spiritual; but it was tremendously effective. Forrest was never indefinite. In all his acting clarity of design was conspicuous, and strength of person went hand in hand with strength of purpose. He knew his intention and he possessed absolute control of the means needful for its fulfilment. He was never weakened by self-distrust. He never wavered. Adamantine authority, inflexible repose, explicit intent, directness of execution, and physical magnetism were his principal implements, and he used them freely and finely. His figure was commanding, his voice copious and resonant. He was a man of prodigious individuality, an egotist of the most positive type. The beauties of his acting were much upon the surface; the defects of it were largely those of his character. In the vigorous maturity of his professional life his *King Lear* was little more than an exhibition of himself; an exceedingly strong and resolute man, assuming, not very convincingly, the appearance of being old, and imitating, cleverly but not pathetically, the condition of madness. In his latter years he had become much changed. Thought, study, observation, experience, and the silent discipline of time, had, in a measure, chastened his egotistical spirit and refined his art. Misfortune, sickness, and suffering had done their work on him, as they do on others. The last times I saw him as *King Lear* he played the part as it should be played, and was like the breaking and then broken old man that *King Lear* is. The demeanor was royal; the mind vacillant, yet imperious; the portrayal of madness pathetic; and above all, there was in the performance a spiritual quality such as it had never before revealed. The method remained, what it had been, that of realism: the ancient snort was heard, in the Curse Scene, and the wretched *King,* in his senile debility, was made to drool upon his beard: but the acting completely conveyed a sense of the fact and the significance of human suffering, and it gained the involuntary tribute of tears. It was not so much the despised and degraded sovereign or the discarded, heart-broken father, that Forrest represented, as it was the *wretched, desolate man,* abject and piteous. The intrinsic grandeur of *King Lear's* mind and the great tenderness of his heart become manifest in his overthrow. The shattered fragments of the column indicate its original magnificence. No actor can truly impersonate *King Lear* unless he knows and feels (as Forrest in his latter years did) the vanity and mutability of the things of this world. In the Mad Scenes of this tragedy the deepest deep of sad experience is sounded and the topmost height of pathos is reached. Forrest, toward the end of his career, illumined those scenes in such a manner as to enthrall and satisfy the imagination and deeply affect the feelings. The desolation of a strong mind blasted by misery and enfeebled by physical decay, and an affectionate heart broken by injustice and submerged by grief, looked out at his eyes and spoke in his voice.

All the actors of *King Lear* on the early English Stage, from Garrick onward, made an exceptional point, in delivering the *King's* answer to *Regan,* when she has told him to return to *Goneril,*—the speech beginning, "Ask her forgiveness?" Sarcasm was mingled with resentment and indignation. The *King,* in mock supplication, when he said "Dear daughter, I confess that I am old," knelt,—as the text prescribes. Garrick clasped his hands and satirically imitated the manner of a beggar. Henderson addressed the preliminary line, in a solemn tone, to the spectators of the interview between the *King* and *Regan,* saying "Do *you* but mark how this becomes the house," and as he knelt he took off his hat and dropped both that and the staff which he carried. Later the practice was adopted of addressing the whole speech directly and vehemently to *Regan.* The latter was Forrest's method, and at that point, with the ensuing explosion of impotent passion, he wrought the most overwhelming effect incident to his entire performance. In respect to details of mechanism in acting, Forrest,—who detested everything which he considered finical,—was unrefined, and often careless. In *King Lear* he walked "toed-in," and that expedient was a distinct blemish on his performance. In the Mad Scene he wore a crown of twisted straw which had been too artfully constructed to resemble an actual crown, but he did not, as some actors have done, carry a sword carefully whittled out of pieces of lath: his "sword" was a bit of sapling, his sceptre a handful of loose straw. Various silly old devices for theatrical effect still lingered on the stage in Forrest's time, and some of them,—such as the "trick sword," the blade of which can be rattled in the hilt, and thus made to accentuate the agitation and trembling of the wielder,—he did not, on occasion, disdain to use. His *King Lear*, however, was comparatively free from artifice, and on the whole was the simplest of his Shakespearean impersonations: by himself it was considered the best. "I *am* Lear" he once exclaimed. To the American public in general he became, in the course of his long professional life, more closely identified with that character than any other actor was who ever assumed it on our Stage. His *King Lear,* however, was not the most popular of his personations. The multitude preferred his

Metamora, a part which he, rightly, despised, but one with which he earned the most of his large fortune.

OTHER PLAYERS OF *KING LEAR.*

Among the players who performed *King Lear,* in the American Theatre, during the histrionic reign of Forrest and soon after it had ceased, were John M. Vandenhoff, 1837; W. C. Macready, 1844; Augustus A. Addams, 1848; Charles Walter Couldock, 1849; Edward L. Davenport, 1850; James Stark, 1852; J. W. Wallack, the Younger, 1852; James R. Anderson, 1854; John R. Scott, 1854; Edwin Booth, 1857; McKean Buchanan, 1857; Joseph Proctor, 1864; Charles Kean, 1865; George C. Boniface, 1865; Charles Dillon, 1867; Lawrence Barrett, 1876; John McCullough, 1877; George Edgar, 1879; and William E. Sheridan, 1884. Anderson and also Wallack presented the play in a suitably condensed form of the original, using only the text of Shakespeare. The excision in Wallack's Prompt Book, of which I have made a careful study, is somewhat too considerable, yet the arrangement is a good one. Wallack was an admirable actor, largely influenced by the style of Macready, some of whose peculiarities he copied, in this character and others,—more particularly *Macbeth.* His wife (Ann Duff Waring) coöperated with him in his production of "King Lear," giving a performance of the *Fool* which elicited thoughtful and earnest critical commendation. I saw many performances by Mrs. Wallack: she was highly intellectual, and was a consummate dramatic artist. Addams, a Boston actor, who died in 1851, after a career of about twenty years, was possessed of exceptional natural advantages and great talent, but his inebriety ruined him. There is no informing account of his *King Lear.* James Stark, whom I saw in the part in 1861, gave a respectable utilitarian performance. Joseph Proctor, distinguished as the *Jibbenainosay,* was not impressive as *King Lear*. Dillon's supreme merit in the part was simplicity. His tones were not sufficiently subdued in the closing scenes, but he did not rant at any time. In the portrayal of madness his sincerity was afflicting, and in the moment of the *King's* recognition of *Cordelia* his forlorn aspect of mingled doubt and tremulous, hesitant hope was affectingly piteous.

EDWIN BOOTH.

Four years of Edwin Booth's novitiate as an actor,—from July, 1852, till September, 1856,—were passed in California, the Sandwich Islands, and Australia, and in the course of that time he acted several of the leading Shakespearean characters, including *King Lear*. His performances, then, were modelled on those of his father. The elder Booth had acted in Tate's perversion of the tragedy, and it was in Tate's play that Edwin Booth first acted, and for several years, at irregular intervals, continued to act, presenting the conventional *King Lear* of the Theatre,—a half-crazed old man, preposterously restored to reason and sovereignty. About 1860 Booth discarded the part from his repertory, in order to forget it (as he told me long afterward) and thus to facilitate for himself a careful and thorough study of the original. That study he made, and when, November 16, 1875, at the Fifth Avenue Theatre, he effected, for the first time in New York, his presentment of "King Lear" according to Shakespeare's text (he had previously, in October, 1870, shown it at McVicker's Theatre, Chicago), his performance of the *King* was seen to be, not a loose, wandering, sporadic display of tumultuous emotions, but,—entirely in purpose, and almost entirely in result,—a comprehensive, sequent, fluent embodiment of the whole various character. His acting was uneven, and it always continued to be so; indeed, it was often so in every part he played. He lacked size and weight, in the opening scene of "King Lear," but he lacked nothing else. His spirit was intrinsically grand; his manner possessed, in perfection, the attribute of regal authority; and his humanity of feeling, as aroused and liberated under the stress of affliction, was sympathetic and exceedingly beautiful. He did not exhaust his strength in the invocation of Nature's curse upon the insolent *Goneril,* but, having wrought a thrilling effect with that tremendous speech, he transcended it in his utterance of the frenzied *King's* impotent threat, which presently follows. He was the heart-broken parent; he was the dethroned, dishonored, despised monarch; he was the great man, in ruin,—and therefore he was *King Lear.* The most affecting single passage in his personation (and in this he excelled all other actors of *King Lear* that I have seen) was that of the poor old man's awakening from the restorative sleep which brings him back, for a little while, to reason. I remember him,—indeed, who that saw him could ever forget?—sitting on a stool; his attenuated figure, his haggard face, his beseechful eyes, his bewildered glance at his clothing, his timid, hesitant, forlorn manner as he gazed on *Cordelia,* the doubting, questioning look which bespoke the slow recurrence of memory, the piteous, feeble movement of the hands, one upon the other, and the pathos of the heart-breaking voice, when he said:

"I am a very foolish, fond old man,
Fourscore and upward,—not an hour more nor less,—
And, to deal plainly,
I fear I am not in my perfect mind."

It was long customary on the English Stage, the business having been suggested by the learned commentator Steevens, for the actor of *King Lear* to take off his hat when he says, to *Edgar* and *Glo'ster,* "I will preach to thee," and then, after he has spoken one sentence, to look at his hat and suddenly break off, saying, "This is a good block." Booth repudiated that absurdity. The *King* should wear no hat. In the Storm Scene "unbonneted he runs," and in the scene on the plains near Dover his head is "crowned" with flowers and weeds, as distinctly specified by the text. This is the scene in which he begins that preachment which every reader earnestly wishes he had finished. Booth's business at this point was unique and skilful. The *"Gentleman* and *Attendants,"* sent by *Cordelia,* were brought on the scene a minute earlier than they are in the original, and they uncovered before the *King.* (The lines of *"A Gentleman"* had been given to *Curan.*) Booth caused the *King* to notice the hat that *Curan* was holding, and, with a look of vacuous curiosity, to take it from him and gaze at it, murmuring, "This is a good block." The scene was considerably cut, and was ended with the line "Kill, kill, kill, kill, kill, kill!"—I would here note that, although I edited Booth's "Prompt Books," of which there are sixteen, I did not always approve the cuts and transpositions of the text that he elected

From the Painting by Jarvis McEntee   Courtesy Volney Streamer, Esq.

EDWIN BOOTH AS *KING LEAR*

"Pray, do not mock me:
I am a very foolish, fond old man,
Fourscore and upward, not an hour more nor less."

Act IV., Sc. 7

to make, and which, of course, were made. In preparing "King Lear" for the stage I should make considerable restorations.

In his treatment of the madness of *King Lear* Booth discriminated between the acute agony of a mind which is vaguely conscious of its progressive decay and its vacant, babbling, pitiful frivolity when quite distraught. In this particular, however, he was less thorough and less affecting than John McCullough, who was the first to apply that treatment to the mental condition of the *King*. Booth was, unquestionably, the greater genius and the finer artist; but McCullough, for the part of *King Lear,* possessed the advantage of a more massive and powerful physique, and likewise more of that emotional quality which is best designated as elemental human sympathy. Booth was tender and affectionate, but he was highly intellectual and still more highly spiritual. When he was acting in London the poet Tennyson saw his performance of *King Lear,* and subsequently, at a social meeting, spoke to him about it, saying: "Most interesting, most touching and powerful,—but not a bit like *Lear.*" That incident Booth related to me, using precisely those words. His daughter, Edwina, Mrs. Ignatius Grossmann, in her "Recollections of My Father," prefixed to a collection of his letters, incorrectly states that "the poet praised, *above all else,* his performance of *Lear.*" Tennyson's ideal of the character is unknown; but it is pretty well understood that the great bard was not easily pleased with anything. Booth's *King Lear* deserved rank among the grandest achievements of the modern stage.

LAWRENCE BARRETT.

Lawrence Barrett (1838-1891) first acted *King Lear,* December 4, 1876, at Booth's Theatre, presenting the play in a version made by himself, strictly adherent to the original text. The stage setting was superb. Two of the scenes, a view of Stonehenge and a view of the Cliff at Dover, were indeed works of fine art. The cast was exceptionally strong, including E. L. Davenport as *Edgar,* William E. Sheridan as *Kent,* Frederick B. Warde as *Edmund,* E. K. Collier as *Cornwall,* Harry Langdon as *Albany,* Henry Weaver as *Glo'ster,* Stella Boniface as *Cordelia,* Gertrude Kellogg as *Goneril,* Dora Goldthwaite as *Regan,* and William Seymour as the *Fool.*

Barrett's personation of *King Lear* was deeply interpenetrated with the quality of paternal affection. It was "the kind old father who gave all" that he aimed to present, and in this respect he admirably fulfilled his purpose. The shattered mentality of the old man was, in the scenes of madness, touchingly portrayed, but the original grandeur of the sovereign was not indicated in the ruin of his sovereignty, and I remember thinking, as I watched the performance, that it might fitly be typified by a broken medallion rather than by a fallen statue. Barrett's elocution was beautiful. He brought out the meaning of every word that he uttered: the precisely right feeling was back of his delivery and enforced it. The speech beginning "I pr'ythee, daughter, do not make me mad" could not be better delivered than it was by him. The mingling of judicial austerity, forbearance, and ominous intimation of the sure justice of the avenging gods made this a superlative gem of dramatic speech. The words "Mend when thou canst, be better at thy leisure" were pathetically spoken, yet so as to cause a shudder of terror.

Barrett was, distinctively, among American actors, the most intellectual player of his time. He acted many parts, his restless ambition impelling him to wreak himself on the grandest and most difficult characters in the whole wide range of the legitimate drama, and frequently causing him to venture in parts new to the Stage. In his maturity he was adequate in every vein of dramatic art; in certain parts he was unrivalled. His *Cardinal Wolsey* was supremely fine. He was admirable in *King Richard the Third* and *Leontes,* and he stood alone in *Cassius.* In the expression of isolated intellectual supremacy, not entirely sequestered from human sympathy, yet pathetic in the loneliness inevitable to an austere mind, he had no superior. He was an extraordinary man, and as often as I think of him I remember the lines of Dryden:

> "A fiery soul which, working out its way,
> Fretted the pygmy body to decay,
> And o'er-informed the tenement of clay."

JOHN EDWARD McCULLOUGH.

Critical judgment was slow in recognizing the supreme excellence of John McCullough as a dramatic artist, and during his lifetime the custom considerably prevailed,—nor since his death has it been entirely discarded,—of disparaging him as merely "an imitator of Edwin Forrest," and dismissing him with the remark that "he was not a great actor." McCullough (1832-1885) was of low origin and of modest, unpretentious disposition, and he rose to eminence from a humble station; such men sometimes are obliged to wait long for a just recognition. It is quite true that in the early part of his professional career he was one of the many imitators of Forrest. Every actor, at first, copies a model, as well as he can: the alphabet must be learned,—it cannot be absorbed from the air. McCullough was uneducated, that is, unschooled, and he was constrained to learn wherever and as best he could. He respected, admired, and assiduously studied Forrest, in whose company and under whose guidance he acted, and he profited by study of that model, precisely as Forrest had done, in youth, by study of Edmund Kean and T. A. Cooper; but after he left Forrest's company, which he did, in San Francisco, in 1866-'67, and became a manager, and could act whatever parts he pleased to undertake, he speedily formed a style of his own, based, indeed, on that of Forrest, but, in its maturity, distinctively individual, and in its refinement, grace, delivery, spiritual exaltation, and naturalness of art decidedly superior to that of his exemplar; though McCullough did not equal Forrest in physical strength, leonine solidity, or reverberant vocal power. The statement that he was "not a great actor" is untrue; no competent judge of acting would make it who had seen him in his representative performances, which were *King Lear, Othello, Coriolanus, Virginius,* and *Damon.* His impersonation of *King Lear* was, in some respects, the best I have ever seen,—and I have seen many.

McCullough first acted *King Lear* in 1873, at the California Theatre, San Francisco, and his first performance of it in New York occurred, at Booth's

Theatre, April 23, 1877. He began by acting in the old stage version of the tragedy,—Tate's alteration, tinkered by Garrick and Kemble,—but it is significant of the independence of his mind that he perceived the inferiority of that version and reverted to the original, of which he made his own acting arrangement. At first, and for some time, his acting of the part was reminiscent of the more boisterous quality of the style of Forrest, and there was in the assumption a lack of complete identification with the character and of sustained uniformity in the expression of it. The actor had not yet succeeded in welding into a continuous chain the many links of his artistic fabric, and he appeared to be striving upward toward the part, rather than descending upon it; but that incertitude was, little by little, eradicated, and the impersonation finally became a perfectly unified embodiment of sovereign grandeur, shattered by misery and crumbling in decay. No actor can completely identify himself with *King Lear* unless he possesses a greatly affectionate heart, a fiery spirit, abundant and quick sensibility, and,—although the intellect must be shown in a state of progressive disintegration,—a regal mind. Within that forlorn, frenzied image of breaking manhood, reeling reason, and despoiled royalty the spirit must be noble and lovable. No puny, artificial, shallow person can ever successfully assume the investiture of that grand personality and that colossal sorrow. McCullough possessed exceptional qualifications to act *King Lear*,—imposing stature, expressive countenance, natural dignity, great compass and sympathy of voice, exceptional sensibility, and profound, passionate tenderness of feeling. His embodiment, at its best, combined these qualities, and it was formed, controlled, and guided by unerring intelligence. It was majestic and reverend in aspect; it was intrinsically imperial, possessing all requisite physical magnitude, imposing impression of personality, and authority of demeanor; it indicated a background of large experience and a prodigious reserve of power; it was moulded and shaded with judicious artistic skill; it was vitalized with the copious emotion of a deep and loving heart, and it sounded an unfathomable depth of grief.

An exceptional excellence of art in this remarkable achievement was the actor's comprehension and portrayal of madness. In this particular the performance was minutely, profoundly, afflictingly true,— without ever becoming offensive with literal realism. I know not whether McCullough studied insanity, as Garrick did, in a mad-house, but I have myself carefully observed it, there and elsewhere, and I know that he understood the subject. He embodied *King Lear* as, from the first of the play and indeed anterior to its opening, a man stricken in mind,—already the victim of incipient mental derangement; not entirely mad, but ready, *and certain,* to become so. There is an atmosphere of omen, a subtle apprehension of danger, all about the presence of the *King,* in the early scenes of the tragedy. He diffuses disquietude and vaguely presages disaster, and the observer looks on him with solicitude and pain. He is not yet wholly broken, but he will soon break, and the spectator of his irrational behavior and choleric vehemence is sorry for him and would avert the impending amentia, the destiny of woe, that is darkly foreshadowed in his condition and circumstances. McCullough's denotement of the earlier symptoms of mental failure, accompanied, as often it is, by the sufferer's own vague, fitful, piteous, indefinite yet terrifying sense of the disease that is in progress, was absolutely true and deeply pathetic. Over all the mood and conduct of the *King,* in his first scene with the *Fool,* when he has begun to doubt of his state and surmise himself neglected, he diffused a kind of autumnal sunset air, sweetly and sadly indicative of the troubled mind and the sorrowing heart. The invectives which follow were spoken as they should be, with impetuous violence, and yet as emanant from agony more even than from passion. The pathos of those tremendous passages is in their chaotic disproportion; in their lawlessness, their lack of government; in the evident helplessness of the poor old man who hurls them forth from a breaking heart and a distracted mind. He loves, and he loathes himself for loving: every fibre of his nature is in horrified revolt against such cruel lack of reverence, gratitude, and affection toward such a monarch and such a father as he knows himself to have been. The feeling that McCullough poured through those moments of terrible yet pitiable frenzy was overwhelming in its intense emotion, sonorous yet quavering volume of voice, and struggling, intermittent, agonizing energy of utterance.

It has long been customary on the stage to close Act I. of "King Lear" with the outraged father's frightful invocation of vengeance on *Goneril,* and to close Act II. with his wild threat of unspeakable "revenges" on both *Goneril* and *Regan,* and his heartbreaking paroxysm of agony, as he rushes off, vociferating "O Fool, I shall go mad!". McCullough adhered to the old custom. His delivery of the terrific speech, "Hear, Nature, hear! dear goddess, hear!", which is as much a pagan prayer as it is a curse, expressed to the full, and therein was overwhelming in commingled pathos and terror, the anguish of a breaking heart and the distraction of a maddened brain. In the scene of the *King's* subsequent meeting with *Goneril,* when his insane fury has subsided, giving place to confident expectation of refuge and royal treatment in the love and home of *Regan,* McCullough made afflictingly evident the forlorn condition of an old, infirm, mentally disordered man, already oblivious of the fearful imprecation that he had spoken, and,—as such sufferers usually are,—mindful only of himself: the disordered consciousness, imperceptive of much that is external, is acutely aware of its own painful disturbance and suffering, and is sensitive chiefly to those things that affect itself. As spoken by him the line, "We'll no more meet, no more see one another," was made to express all it means of the abject, forsaken, utterly desolate condition in which, unknowingly, the wretched old monarch stands. The frantic burst of impotent passion, generated and impelled by the sense of injury and insult, the revolt of scorned paternal affection, and the exasperating consciousness of self-contemning weakness, with which the *King* finally breaks away from all human ties and plunges into the night and storm was effected with prodigious power and with much felicity of vocalism, —the reckless fluency of desperate effort to speak being almost suffocated by the mixed and contending forces of emotional tumult. In his treatment of this passage McCullough did not try to equal the reverberant sonority with which Forrest delivered it, and he could not have equalled it if he had tried; but he used an artistic method more conformable to Nature

From a Photograph *Collection of Evert Jansen Wendell, Esq.*

JOHN McCULLOUGH AS *KING LEAR*
"A man may see how this world goes with no eyes!"

Act IV., Sc. 6

than that of the elder tragedian, and his action, while it had neither the ponderous precipitance of Forrest, nor the lurid, electrical, meteoric celerity that made Edwin Booth's *King Lear* superlatively thrilling at this point, was splendidly effective. McCullough had thoroughly learned that even in the utterance of the most tempestuous passion there should be "a temperance that may give it smoothness."

In the use of suggestiveness,—by pausing, by facial expression, by use of the eyes, and by inflection of voice,—McCullough's art was both expert and delicate. Thus, in *King Lear,* his maintenance of a sad preoccupation with memory and thought of the lost *Cordelia,* while he is talking with the *Fool,* was subtly signified: the remorseful words "I did her wrong" could not be more tenderly and meaningly spoken than they were by him: they are only four little words, but they bear the crushing weight of bitter compunction and a hopeless grief. There was great pathos in the portrayal of the *King's* "lucid interval,"—the dazed forlorn, piteous recognition of *Cordelia*. That passage in the play does so much for itself that no experienced actor could fail to make it effective: McCullough's treatment of it was perfect, in tenderness and simplicity.

In the mad scenes of *King Lear* McCullough was unique. I believe him to have been the first actor of this part to discriminate between the agony of a man while going mad and the vacant, heedless, volatile, fantastic condition,—afflicting to the beholder but no longer agonizing to the person diseased,—of a man who has totally lapsed into madness. Edwin Booth made the same discrimination, but not so strongly, and his adoption of this method was, I believe, consequent on the informing example of McCullough. Neither the elder Booth, nor Edmund Kean, nor Edwin Forrest indicated such a design. In the first Storm Scene, when the insane *King*

> "Strives in his little world of man to out-scorn
> The to-and-fro conflicting wind and rain,"

McCullough was the veritable image of distracted sublimity, and he spoke the apostrophes,—"Blow, winds," and "Tremble, thou wretch,"—in a wild strain of magnificent vocalism and a portentous and thrilling delirium of emotion, in perfect accord with the tumult in the outraged parent's mind and in the tempest that rages around him. In those and in kindred speeches which are distributed through the Mad Scenes there is denotement of the original quality of *King Lear's* nature, the wide reach of his imagination, and the kindness of his loving heart. It was the crowning felicity of McCullough's personation that he clearly and continuously indicated what the *King* had once been. His saying of the pitiful words, "Poor fool and knave, I have one part in my heart that's sorry yet for thee," was sweetly significant of innate goodness. In the talk with the Bedlamite, the disguised *Edgar,* the undertone of forlorn gentleness, discernible through outward denotements of settled misery,—the madness in the eyes, the disorder of the ravaged figure,—was inexpressibly touching. The whole conduct of the wonderful scene upon which the distracted *King* enters, "fantastically dressed with wild flowers," was perfect in its exposition of a great mind shattered, yet the sad spectacle afforded almost a sense of relief, by reason of contrast with preceding scenes of anguish, because the condition presented in it was that of established insanity, permeated indeed by the remembrance of filial ingratitude and cruelty, but no longer harrowing with the element of self-conscious disintegration.

> "Why, he was met even now
> As mad as the vex'd sea; singing aloud;
> Crown'd with rank fumiter and furrow weeds,
> With haddocks, hemlock, nettles, cuckoo flowers,
> Darnel, and all the idle weeds that grow
> In our sustaining corn."

With the doctrine announced by Lamb and approved by Hazlitt, that "the *Lear* of Shakespeare cannot be acted," it is not reasonably possible to agree. An undefined and indefinable *King Lear,* a *King Lear* endowed with attributes of soul, mind, and body transcending all possibilities of human nature, cannot be acted; but the *King Lear* of Shakespeare is distinctly drawn; it can be comprehended; and it has been acted, and acted exceedingly well, though not in the time of Lamb and Hazlitt.

ROBERT BRUCE MANTELL.

Since the period of John McCullough, whose last appearance on the Stage occurred September 29, 1884, and that of Edwin Booth, who acted for the last time April 4, 1891, only one important production of "King Lear" has been made in America,— that, namely, which was effected, November 27, 1905, at the Garden Theatre, New York, by Robert Bruce Mantell,—who then acted the *King* for the first time, —in partnership with, and under the business management of, William A. Brady. At the beginning Mantell's performance of *King Lear* was indefinite in ideal and vacillant in expression. It did not sufficiently denote the *King's* original individuality of greatness, and it did not discriminate as to continuously variable conditions, mental and physical, in the portrayal of the *King's* derangement: the madness was all of one piece, and it did not, in any way, manifest itself until the action had proceeded considerably far. That method of acting the part is sanctioned by precedent: it was used by such actors as Charles Kean, Barry Sullivan, E. L. Davenport, and Edwin Forrest: but it is not the best method, and Mantell, as shown by his later performances, has wisely departed from it, evincing a clear and right ideal of the massive personality and direful experience of *King Lear,* and portraying, truthfully and pathetically, the characteristics of "difference and decay," the fluctuations of condition consequent on progressive mania. This means that he has profited by study and thought, and that his embodiment of this great character, while it is not perfect in all its details, exhibits the quality of grandeur, the beauty of profound human feeling, and the terror and pathos of an altogether tragic experience. His impersonations of *Othello* and *King John* are those which most fully display his ample resources of emotional power, his breadth of imagination, and the robust quality of his executive style; but his embodiment of *King Lear,* which has continuously grown in poetic substance and artistic finish, ranks next to those fine works of art, and by itself would entitle him to the eminence which he justly holds as the leading tragedian of the American Stage. His exhibition of *King Lear's* regnant authority, senile egotism, wavering mind, and explosive temper,—indeed, the whole preliminary development of the character, culminating in the invocation of curses and the frenzied disruption of human ties,—is equally truthful in portraiture and splendid in passion. In the Storm Scene he presents a perfect example of "the paradox of acting" (as Diderot called it), the union of the weakness of extreme age with the power of a tremendously passionate expression, only possible to the vigor of manhood. In the afflicting scene in which the crazed *King,* decorated with weeds and flowers, encounters and talks with the blind, wretched *Glo'ster,*—"Ha! Goneril,—with a white beard!"—his use of pathos is overwhelming in its simplicity, and, alike in picture, personation, and utterance, he reaches a magnificent climax with the exclamation, superbly delivered, "Ay, every inch a King!" His management of the poor old father's recognition of his daughter, the use made of face and voice, to show the slow dawning of intelligence, the return of memory, the despairing grief over past unkindness, the abject consciousness of infirmity, the air of desolation,—all this is dramatic art of a high and exceedingly beautiful order. The version of the tragedy that Mantell uses is, practically, that which was made and used by Edwin Booth, a few speeches that Booth omitted being restored. When, however,

From a Photograph by White, N. Y. *Author's Collection*

ROBERT MANTELL AS *KING LEAR*

"*I remember thine eyes well enough. Dost thou squiny at me? No, do thy worst, blind Cupid; I'll not love!*"

Act IV., Sc. 6.

he made his latest appearance in New York as *King Lear,* at Daly's Theatre, 1911, he was censured in the newspaper press for not having followed Booth's example!

CONTINENTAL ACTORS OF *KING LEAR.*
ROSSI.—BARNAY.—SALVINI.—VON POSSART.—NOVELLI.

The actors from Continental Europe, speaking foreign languages, who have made professional tours of America within the last sixty years have customarily exerted their talents, sometimes brilliant and sometimes commonplace, in misrepresenting *Hamlet* and *Othello,* and in that employment they have been abundantly successful. Few of them, comparatively, have endeavored to act *King Lear.* Ernesto Rossi (1829-1896) made his first appearance on the American Stage in that character, at the Globe Theatre, Boston, October 3, 1881. His first appearance in New York was made on October 31, following, at Booth's Theatre, as *Othello:* on November 10 he performed as *King Lear.* The exhibition was, in every sense, melancholy. Rossi spoke Italian; the players associated with him spoke English: the result,—which is inevitable in all such experiments,—was gibble-gabble. *Edgar* was assumed by Milnes Levick, *Edmund* by Leslie Gossin, *Kent* by H. A. Weaver,

Goneril by Constance Hamblin, and *Cordelia* by Louise Muldener.

Rossi embodied *King Lear,* at the outset, as a querulous, testy old man, without either royalty, dignity, or personal distinction; later he provided a tiresome study of insanity. The invocation of Nature for curses on *Goneril* was volubly declaimed, causing no effect of either terror or pathos. As the action proceeded the *King* became more and more fractious, till at the last he broke down altogether. The collapse, however, was not that of a grand nature, a person innately royal, but that of a commonplace, domestic martinet, the middle-class Italian father-of-the-family. In no sense could the personation be deemed representative of Shakespeare's *King Lear.* But Rossi was a talented and experienced actor, and while, in playing this part, he did not even remotely suggest intrinsic majesty, either normal or in ruins, he correctly, pathetically, and effectively depicted feeble age, physical suffering, wounded feeling, and the pitiable irrationality of a dazed mind. In the scene of the *King's* temporary recovery and the recognition of *Cordelia,*—a scene which does much for itself, and in which no good actor could help winning sympathy,—his acting was excellent: the forlorn behavior, the enfeebled body, the wistful countenance, the imploring gaze, the quavering voice, the trembling hands, the manner of mingled mental wandering and hesitant intelligence,—these were affecting constituents of a piteous image of human misery. On January 17, 1882, Rossi began a brief engagement at the New York Academy of Music, repeating *King Lear,* and speaking a few lines of the text in English. The Italian version of Shakespeare's tragedy, in which he acted when in America, was a clumsy collocation of scenes, and well calculated to mislead an actor as well as to disappoint an English-speaking audience. Rossi, as he appeared on the American Stage, was best in comedy and romantic drama. He made an excellent impression as *Edmund Kean,* in the wild and whirling play concerning that eccentric dramatic genius written many years ago by Alexandre Dumas. He can hardly be said to have failed in "King Lear" for the reason that, reasonably speaking, he did not act in it.

Ludwig Barnay appeared as *King Lear,* February 10, 1883, at the Thalia Theatre, New York, acting in a German version of the tragedy, and giving a performance which, in proportion, symmetry, and the artistic treatment of details, was admirable. Barnay was one of the most thoroughly trained and competent of the Continental actors who have visited the American Stage. He knew exactly what he wished to do and exactly how to do it. His best performance in America was *Marc Antony,* in "Julius Cæsar." He was a stalwart person, of fine animal presence, and possessed of a powerful voice, hard in quality, but clear and resonant. He did not, and could not, personate *King Lear.* He did not, in the first half of the representation, indicate that the *King* is old,—except that he wore white hair,—and he did not, at any point in his performance, even remotely suggest that the aged monarch is of a superlatively affectionate nature, and intrinsically,—notwithstanding his faults, —a being so noble, so compounded of virtues, that, to those who truly know and therefore love him, his ruin seems the extinction of all goodness. Unless an actor of *King Lear* can make his auditors feel and know that the wreck upon which they are looking is that of a *great man* he cannot play the part as it stands in Shakespeare's tragedy. Barnay embodied as the *King* a man so ordinary that his commonness, though it could not justify the cruelty of his ingrateful daughters, explained their aversion. He was essentially unlovable, a cross-grained old tyrant, eminently capable of subduing opposition, and not in the least likely to suffer any heartbreak from filial ingratitude. In his portrayal of madness he made no effort to discriminate between the agony of the *King,* when going mad, and his levity, at once awful and piteous, when wholly insane. An excellent actor, in parts suited to his temperament and style, Barnay was wholly out of place in *King Lear.*

Tommaso Salvini, before he made his third professional visit to the United States,—which occurred in 1882-'83,—had adopted *King Lear* into his repertory, playing it,—of course in an Italian version of Shakespeare's tragedy,—at the Teatro Salvini, Naples, in 1882. His first performance of the part in New York was given, February 21, 1883, at the Academy of Music. He spoke Italian, and the actors associated with him spoke English. His acting afforded an impressive example of physical power and professional skill. His lofty stature, resonant voice, fluent delivery, and picturesque poses and gestures, combined with the vital force and occasional strong feeling which animated his impersonation, expressed a striking personality, but it was not that of *King Lear.* Salvini was a great actor, but not in Shakespeare.

Every actor operates within positive limitations, spiritual, mental, and physical. No actor has proved equally true and efficient in every kind of character. Salvini, as *Hamlet,* was unspiritual,—giving no effect to the haunted tone of that part, or its weird atmosphere,—while as *Macbeth* (in which part, as in *Othello,* he greatly admired himself) he was unimaginative, obscure, common, and inadequate. The only

Shakespearean character in which he excelled was *Othello,* and in that he excelled, not by impersonating the character as it stands in the author's page, but by embodying, with almost perfect art, a radically false, wrong, and degrading ideal of it. The attributes of his *Othello* were, almost exclusively, animal. The character was shorn of all magnanimity and all tenderness. The loftiest heights that the actor reached were those of grievous distraction and barbaric fury; but his personality was instinct with overwhelming power; his method was, in the highest degree, pictorial, and he diffused a vigorous magnetism which enthralled the senses and was well calculated to blind the judgment,—as, indeed, it generally did.

In his make-up for *King Lear* Salvini wore a profuse wig and beard of iron-gray color,—not white, —apparently to help the signification that the *King* is not decrepit but vigorous. His first entrance was made with the slow, heavy step of a large, portly, very old man, who yet is sturdy. He gave, at the beginning, no intimation of the breaking mind, no suggestion of mental disturbance, either present or impending: in fact, he introduced into his performance no tinge of madness till he reached the line about "a thousand with red burning spits," in the *King's* colloquy with the disguised *Edgar* and the *Fool,*—in the original, Act III., sc. 6. He decreed the partition of the kingdom in a nonchalant, subdued manner, wholly ineffective. The extravagant protestations of *Goneril* and *Regan* were received by him with a chuckle of satisfaction. The sensible words of *Cordelia* appeared to daze him with amazement. He spoke with harsh deliberation, in disclaiming her, became convulsed with hysterical fury, at *Kent's* attempt to expostulate, and then, curbing himself, and standing silent for almost a minute (which is a long time on the stage), delivered the edict of banishment of that nobleman in a perfectly self-controlled, judicial manner. The whole of his first scene was acted behind a table, and that foolish arrangement helped to mar it, by contributing to an effect of something commonplace. The ideal of *King Lear* as the ruin of a magnificent monarch and supreme man,—the ruler of all minds, the delight of all worthy hearts,— which is unmistakable in Shakespeare's pages, Salvini did not even suggest. The essential and dominant fact about *King Lear,*—which cannot be overemphasized,—namely, that the afflictions which befall him, while they awaken sympathy and inspire compassion, are not, of themselves, sufficient to constitute the tragedy, seemed never to have occurred to the Italian actor. The pity of it all is that these afflictions encompass, ravage, and ruin a being of such glorious mind and great and tender heart. The moment you make *King Lear* an *ordinary* man, you deprive the play of its central significance, and dissipate its colossal control over the imagination and the feelings. Salvini's *King Lear* was a selfish, choleric despot; formidable but not majestic; devoid of inherent grandeur; destitute of personal fascination; completely unsuggestive of ever having been a great man. The performance was not invested with either the terror that overwhelms or the pathos that melts. There were (as, indeed, with such an actor was inevitable) fine bits of action and moments of lovely speech. Exquisite points were made at "I gave you all" and "I'm cold myself." The more subtle and touching significance of the forlorn reference to *Cordelia,*—"No more of that—I have noted it well,"—was, however, altogether missed; and, strangely enough, the speeches "Beat at this gate" and "I will have such revenges," etc., went for nothing, because of the commonness with which they were spoken. In delivering the first speech in the Storm, "Blow, winds, and crack your cheeks," etc., Salvini walked slowly down a set "run-way," from the right of the stage, so that his figure was half-obscured by painted semblance of rocks, and he *grumbled* the speech, all the way, in a low, monotonous voice, producing no effect whatever, except of tedious ineptitude. Such a

King Lear as he presented may be good Italian; it is not good English, and it is not Shakespeare.

The grandest performance that Salvini ever gave in America,—or, as I conjecture, anywhere else,—was not in a character drawn from the works of Shakespeare, but in one depicted by his illustrious countryman Alfieri. He acted that poet's *King Saul,* and it was, as I believe, his success as *King Saul* that led to his assumption of *King Lear*. Alfieri's tragedy of "Saul" was written in 1782-'83, when the haughty, impetuous, passionate poet was thirty-four years old, and at the suggestion of the Countess of Albany, whom he loved. He had suffered a bereavement at the time, and he was in deep grief. The Countess tried to console him by reading the Bible, and when they came upon the narrative of Saul the idea of the tragedy was struck out between them. The work was written with vigorous impulse and the author has left, in his "Autobiography," the remark that none of his tragedies cost him so little labor. "Saul" is in five acts and it contains 1,567 lines,—of that Italian *versi sciolti* which inadequately corresponds to the blank verse of the English language. The scene is laid in the camp of *Saul's* army. Six persons are introduced, namely, *Saul, Jonathan, David, Michel, Abner,* and *Achimelech*. The time supposed to be occupied by the action,—or rather, by the suffering, —of the play is a single day, the last in the *King's* life. Act First is devoted to explanation, conveyed in warnings to *David,* by *Jonathan,* his friend, and *Michel,* his wife. Act Second presents the distracted monarch, who knows that God has forsaken him and that death is at hand. In a speech of terrible intensity he relates, to *Abner,* the story of the apparition of *Samuel* and the doom that the ghost has spoken. His children humor and soothe the broken old man, and finally succeed in softening his mind toward *David,*— whom he at once loves, dreads, and hates, as the appointed instrument of his destruction and the successor to his crown. Act Third shows *David* playing upon the harp before *Saul,* and chanting *Saul's* deeds in the service and defence of Israel,—so that he calms the agonized delirium of the haunted *King* and wins his blessing; but at last a boastful word makes discord in the music's charm, and *Saul* is suddenly roused into a ghastly fury. Acts Fourth and Fifth deal with the wild caprices and maddening agonies of the frenzied father; the ever-varying phenomena of his mental disease; the onslaught of the Philistines; the killing of his sons; the frequent recurrence before his mind's eye of the shade of the dead prophet; and finally his suicidal death. It is, in form, a classic tragedy, massive, grand, and majestically

KING LEAR

simple; and it blazes from end to end with the fire of a sublime imagination.

Lovers of Italian literature rank Alfieri's "Saul" with Shakespeare's "King Lear." The claim is, perhaps, natural, but it is not valid. In "King Lear," not to speak of its profound revelations of human nature, there is a vast scope of action, through which mental condition and experience are dramatically revealed; and also there is the deepest depth of pathos, because the highest height of afflicted goodness. In "Saul" there is simply,—on a limited canvas, without illustrative adjuncts, without any wealth of intellectual suggestion of resources, without the relief of even mournful humor, and with a narrative rather than a dramatic background,—the portraiture of a *condition;* and, because the man displayed is neither so noble nor so human, the pathos surcharging the work is neither so harrowing nor so tender. Yet the two works are akin in majesty of ideal, in the distressful topic of mental disease that shatters a king, and in the atmosphere of desolation that trails after each of them, like a funeral pall. It is not strange that Alfieri's "Saul" should be deemed the greatest tragedy in the Italian language. It attains to a superb height, for it keeps an equal pace with the severe simplicity of the Bible narrative on which it is founded. Salvini embodied the type of royalty, grandeur, passion, agony, and terror which is its central figure as no other actor within my remembrance could have done.

Possart played *King Lear* for the first time in New York, February 21, 1888, at the Bowery Theatre, and on a later occasion he repeated his performance, March 5, 1890, at the Amberg Theatre. His ideal was shown to be that of the afflicted father. In person, however, his monarch was stalwart, even athletic, while in mind he was potent and dominant. Such a *King Lear* as Possart embodied would not have abdicated his throne; or, having done so, would, on occasion, have readily resumed it. The actor's tones, strong and metallic, rang clearly, indicating force, firmness, and self-control. It was only when the repulsed and outcast father mentioned *Cordelia* or indirectly referred to her that his accents became tender: in the Recognition Scene the vocalism was sympathetic and touching. There was no royalty in the assumption, no denotement that *King Lear* had ever been anything but a consequential parent and arbitrary ruler: the performance moved strictly within the limits of domesticity. No suggestion was given of the dread of impending madness, nor of the contrasted states in the development of that malady. The wronged and insulted father's "abjurement of all roofs" was made consequent on the bolting of a door. After the terrific outbreak upon *Goneril* and *Regan* (in the original, Act II., sc. 4), closing with "O Fool, I shall go mad!" Possart's *King Lear,* having, most absurdly, been left alone upon the scene by all except the *Fool,* endeavored to enter *Glo'ster's* house, closed to him by his daughter's order, when suddenly the clicking of a bolt within startled him, and then, and not till then, he rushed away into the night and tempest. Prosy triviality of stage business (originated, in this instance, by memory of the *King's* figurative words, "And, in conclusion, to oppose the bolt against my coming in") could not be pushed much further. *King Lear's* incipient mania is not precipitated into raving madness by the closing of doors, but by the closing of hearts. In explosions of passion Possart was powerful, and he expressed the grief consequent on lacerated paternal affection and wounded vanity; also he expressed self-pity. His best acting was done in the scene of the *King's* colloquy with the disguised *Edgar,*—presented by a lithe and agile person who emerged from "this straw" attired in a snow-white sheet,—when showing the stimulative effect upon actual madness that is wrought by the spectacle of an artificial craze which the lunatic supposes to be real. Valuable as it is as an adjunct, much more is required for the representation of this character than the pathological consideration of madness. Possart was an exceptionally good actor,

—one of the best, in fact, that have visited America, from the Stage of Continental Europe,—but he showed that the part of *King Lear* was entirely beyond his reach.

Ermete Novelli, highly distinguished on the Italian Stage, presented himself as *King Lear,* March 19, 1907, at the Lyric Theatre, New York, and utterly failed. There was not, in his labored and generally ludicrous performance, any intimation of the disordered *King,* at first wasted by encroaching senility and, at last, precipitated into lunacy by the ingratitude and cruelty of his heartless daughters. The embodiment was characterized by denotement of ordinary attributes, such as a condition of self-pity, fractious resentment, querulous discontent, and incoherent wrath. The man whom Novelli called *King Lear* was so common and so commonplace that, in his decrepitude and misery, he was neither more important, more interesting, nor more pathetic, than an old, doddering pauper, picking oakum or polishing a pewter plate in the Poor House. His ideal of the monarch was seen to be a good man, of conventional, prosy order, a kind and indulgent father, and a worthy member of society, as is often said on gravestones. Attributes that might serve well enough for *Caleb Plummer* or *Daddy O'Dowd* do not serve for *King Lear,* and critical attention, accordingly, was soon diverted from the structural substance of Novelli's embodiment to observation of its technical, professional details, which were miserably inadequate. The actor missed almost every point of importance in the tragedy. His *King* was not even an old man, except that he had decorated himself with a prodigious quantity of gray hair, so that he looked like an aged he-goat. His utterance of the curse on *Goneril* was so puny as to be contemptible; he delivered it with his face half-averted from the audience, and he sputtered like a wet pin-wheel. When he reached the passage in that speech which is the Italian equivalent for

"Let it stamp wrinkles in her brow of youth,
With cadent tears fret channels in her cheeks," etc.,

he teetered across the stage and pinched *Goneril's* face! At the end of the scene with *Goneril* and *Regan* (in the original, Act II., sc. 4) he collapsed utterly, though, in Shakespeare, the *King* leaves the scene "in high rage," "calls to horse," and then traverses the heath, with the strength of madness,—speaking and acting with violent though transitory power, such as only augmentative delirium could impart to his aged, breaking body. In the scene with *Edgar,* who came forth from the hovel in an immaculate white nightgown, pinned up between his legs, Novelli's *King*

Lear indulged in a sort of game of "hop-scotch," and straddled a broom-stick, like a child, "playing horse." Such a performance is noticeable in the historical record only because given by a conspicuous actor and highly commended by enthusiasts of Continental Acting. Novelli was a proficient actor in parts indigenous to his language and suited to his temperament: he was generally better in comedy than in serious character: he was at his best as *Corrado*, in "Morte Civile"; *King Louis the Eleventh*, Goldoni's *Filiberto* and *Geronte* (as the latter, in "Il Bubero Beneficio," he was delightful), and as *Kean*. He was signally offensive in his pretentious efforts to act some of the great Shakespearean characters. The effort to claim for Novelli a professional equality with Salvini was not discreet: Salvini possessed personal magnetism, immense power, imposing presence, fine voice, and in artistic stature he towered above Novelli as Gibraltar towers above the Straits.

V.

THE TAMING OF THE SHREW.

It is, my lord, a kind of history,
An old, Italian tale of love and mirth;—
How pretty Katharine, that was a Shrew,
Dismay'd all suitors, till she met with one,—
Wilder than wind and fiercer than a flame,
With jovial rudeness and with stormy glee,—
Who shamed her into meekness: sir, a tale
Of woman's wayward temper, shrewish rage,
And turbulent rebellion, quite subdu'd
By man's determin'd will and sharper spleen.

ORIGIN, AND DATE OF COMPOSITION.

A PLAY entitled "The Taming of *a* Shrew" was published in London in 1594. It had been for some time extant and had been "sundry times" acted by the players who were in the service of the Earl of Pembroke. The authorship of it is unknown, but Charles Knight ascribes it to Robert Greene (1561-1592), that dissolute genius who is remembered as a detractor of Shakespeare and as the first English poet that ever wrote for bread. Alexander Pope and the German commentator Louis Tieck suppose that play to be a juvenile production of Shakespeare, but this is unwarranted conjecture. Harness is of the opinion that it was "probably written about the year 1590, either by George Peele or Robert Greene." Fleay believes that it was written by Marlowe and Shakespeare, as co-laborers, in 1589. It is, however, generally believed that Shakespeare had no hand in writing the *old* play. Furnival expresses the conviction that "an adapter, who used at least ten bits of Marlowe in it, first recast *the old play,* and then Shakespeare put into the re-cast the scenes in which *Katharine* and *Petruchio* and *Grumio* appear." The learned Gervinus declares that the earlier play is by "an unknown hand," and in regard to the First Folio "Shrew" he makes the statement that *"undoubtedly* the poet's own hand was more than once employed upon it." If the fact be as thus stated it is surprising that the final composition is not of greater merit. Harness considers that "the play, as a whole, is not in our author's best manner," but that "in the Induction and the scenes between *Katharine* and *Petruchio* the traces of his hand are strongly marked." It is generally agreed that Shakespeare wrote the Induction as it stands in the First Folio. Dr. Johnson, comparing the Shakespearean play with its predecessor, remarks that

THE TAMING OF THE SHREW

"the quarrel in the choice of dresses is precisely the same; many of the ideas are preserved without alteration; the faults found with the *cap*, the *gown*, the *compassed cape*, the *trunk sleeves*, and the balderdash about *taking up the gown*, have been copied, as well as the scene in which *Petruchio* makes *Katharine* call the sun the moon. The joke of addressing an elderly gentleman as a 'young, budding virgin, fair and fresh and sweet,' belongs also to the old drama; but in this instance it is remarkable that, while the leading idea is adopted, the mode of expressing it is quite different."

It is believed by several Shakespearean commentators (Payne Collier, Richard Grant White, Frederick James Furnival, and Edward Dowden being the most conspicuous of them) that Shakespeare either collaborated with another dramatist to make a new version of the old play of "The Taming of *a* Shrew," or else that he augmented and embellished a new version of it which had already been made by another hand. Collier feels assured that "Shakespeare had little to do with any of the scenes in which *Katharine* and *Petruchio* are not engaged." White says:

"The plot, the personages, and the scheme of the Induction are taken from the old play, which, however, is as dull as this is in most points spirited and interesting. In [this play] three hands at least are traceable; that of the author of the old play, that of Shakespeare himself, and that of a co-laborer. The first appears in the structure of the plot and in the incidents and the dialogue of most of the minor scenes; to the last must be assigned the greater part of the love business between *Bianca* and her two suitors; while to Shakespeare himself belong the strong, clear characterization, the delicious humor, and the rich verbal coloring of the recast Induction, and all the scenes in which *Katharine, Petruchio,* and *Grumio* are prominent figures, together with the general effect produced by scattering lines and words and phrases here and there, and removing others elsewhere, throughout the play."

Dowden's view is harmonious with White's. He says:

"In 'The Taming of *the* Shrew' we may distinguish three parts: (1) The humorous Induction, in which *Sly,* the drunken tinker, is the chief person; (2) A comedy of character, the *Shrew* and her tamer, *Petruchio,* being the hero and heroine; (3) A comedy of intrigue—the story of *Bianca* and her rival lovers. Now the old play of '*A* Shrew' contains, *in a rude form,* the scenes of the Induction, and the chief scenes in which *Petruchio* and *Katharine* (named in the original *Fernando* and *Kate*) appear; but nothing in this old play corresponds with the intrigues of *Bianca's* disguised lovers. It is, however, in the scenes concerned with these intrigues that *Shakespeare's* hand is least apparent. It may be said [many things *may be,* and *are,* said in Shakespearean commentary that might much better be left unsaid!] that Shakespeare's genius goes in and out with the person of *Katharina.* We would, therefore, *conjecturally* assign the intrigue-comedy to the [*conjectural*] adapter of the old play, reserving to Shakespeare a title to those scenes—in the main enlarged from the play of '*A* Shrew'—in which *Katharina, Petruchio,* and *Grumio* are speakers."

THE TAMING OF THE SHREW 485

This conjectural intermediation of an "adapter of the old play," to which Collier, White, Furnival, and Dowden,—all following Farmer,—have given their sanction, is mere moonshine, and is unworthy alike of the scholars who made it and those who have adopted it. The *Bianca* "intrigue comedy" did not seem to them sufficiently well written to satisfy their arbitrary standard of merit in Shakespeare; *"argal,"* Shakespeare did not write it, but *adopted it* from some other and unknown writer, who had already combined it with the *Sly-Fernando-Kate* material of *"A* Shrew." Such idle conjecture aptly illustrates the bad custom which Furness had in mind when he referred to "the uncritical method . . . whereby we attribute, as a rule, whatever is *good* to Shakespeare, and whatever is *less* good to some one else!"

There are, in "The Taming of the Shrew," as it is printed in the First Folio, 2,671 lines (Globe Edition numbering), including the Induction. Several assumptive computations have been made of the exact portions of the play which,—accepting the notion of an intermediary hand between that of the writer of *"A* Shrew" and that of Shakespeare,—should be ascribed to the latter. That made by Dowden is as follows:

"The Induction............................ 285
    Act II., sc. 1, lines 169-326............. 157
    Act III., sc. 2, lines 1-125
              and lines 151-241......... 215
    Act IV., sc. 1, Entire................. 214
    Act IV., sc. 3,   "   198
    Act IV., sc. 5,   "   79
    Act V., sc. 2, lines 1-180............. 180
                                            ——
    " Total .... 1328."

It will thus be seen that Dowden ascribes to Shakespeare only seven lines more than one-half of the play, as printed in the Folio.

The computation as made by Professor Tolman is as follows:

"Act II., sc. 1, lines 115-320............ 205
    Act III., sc. 2, lines 89-125
              and lines 186-241....... 91
    Act IV., sc. 1, Entire 214
    Act IV., sc. 3,   "   198
    Act IV., sc. 5,   "   79
    Act V., sc. 2,   "   181
                                            ——
    "Total........................... 968."

The Folio Induction is generally accepted as the work of Shakespeare: add its 285 lines to Tolman's computation of 968, and the grand total will amount to only 1,253, or eighty-two lines *less* than one-half

THE TAMING OF THE SHREW

of the play. Computations made by Fleay and Furnival nearly coincide with that by Tolman, except that both those commentators *add* Act III., sc. 2, lines 151-185,—which Rolfe thinks Tolman was right in rejecting. Thus doctors disagree!

Keightley describes "The Taming of the Shrew" as "a rifacimento of an anonymous play," and expresses the opinion that its style "proves it to belong to Shakespeare's early period." Various dates that have been assigned for the composition of Shakespeare's "The Taming of the Shrew" are

Drake, Knight, Delius, and Keightley..	1594
Malone, at first, 1606; finally..........	1596
Furnival	1596-'97
Dowden	1597
Chalmers	1598
Collier (with whom White is inclined to agree)	1601
Fleay	1601-'02

That which is *certain* concerning this question of authorship is that Shakespeare was acquainted with the old play of "The Taming of *a* Shrew" and based his play, as it stands in the Folio, on that drama. Knight's reasoning on the subject of the chronological place of the comedy (that Shakespeare, at the meridian of his career, after writing "Hamlet," "King Lear," "Othello," and "Macbeth," "would not have copied, somewhat servilely, an indifferent play in 1606 or a little earlier," and that he wrote "The Shrew" near the beginning of his career) is sound and conclusive. The date of the composition of "The Taming of the Shrew" should not be placed later than 1594. It was first published in the Folio, 1623, and there is only one quarto of it, published in 1631, eight years after the Folio, and printed from it. Collier maintains, theoretically, that *"The* Shrew" was *printed* in quarto many years before it was thus *published,*—perhaps as early as 1607, but he says it was suppressed, we know not why, till "some copies of it, remaining in the hands of Smithwicke, the stationer, were issued in 1631, with a new title page." It is, however, stated, on the authority of the Cambridge Editors, that an examination of Capell's copy of the 1631 quarto shows that "the paper on which it [the title page] is printed is *the same* as that used for the rest of the play," and that "the title page forms a part of the first quire, and has *not* been inserted": this disposes of Collier's notion as to the quarto of "The Taming of the Shrew."

The scheme of bewildering a drunkard, in the Induction, a plan common to both the "Shrew" plays, is ancient, being found, as an historical fact, in "The Arabian Nights," in the tale of "The Sleeper Awakened." Shakespeare did not know that work, but

THE TAMING OF THE SHREW

this tale of imposture,—said to have been practised upon Abu-l-Hassan, "the wag," by the Khaleefeh Er-Rasheed,—originating in remote Oriental literature, and repeated in various forms, may have been current long before his time. In that narrative Abu-l-Hassan is deluded into the idea that he is the Prince of the Faithful, and, as that potentate, he commands that much gold shall be sent to Hassan's mother and that punishment shall be inflicted upon certain persons by whom Hassan has been persecuted.

A variation of this theme occurs in Simon Goulart's "Admirable and Memorable Histories," translated into English by E. Grimestone, in 1607. In that work it is related that Philip, Duke of Burgundy, called the Good, found a drunken man asleep in the street, at Brussels, caused him to be conveyed to the palace, bathed, dressed, entertained by the performance of "a pleasant comedy," and at last once more stupefied with wine, arrayed in ragged garments, and deposited where he had been discovered, there to awake, and to believe himself the sport of a dream. Malone, by whom the narrative was quoted from Goulart, thinks that it had appeared in English prior to the advent of the old play of "The Taming of *a* Shrew," and may have been known to Shakespeare.

Another source of the dramatist's material is a play by Ariosto. In 1587 the collected works of

George Gascoigne were published, and among them there is a prose comedy called "The Supposes," a translation of Ariosto's "I Suppositi," in which occur the names of *Petrucio* and *Licio,* and from which Shakespeare borrowed the amusing incident of the *Pedant* personating *Vincentio.* Gascoigne, it will be remembered, is the poet to whom Scott was indebted, when he wrote his magnificent novel of "Kenilworth," —so superb in pageantry, so strong and various in character, so deep and rich in passion, and so fluent in style and narrative power,—for description of the revels with which the Earl of Leicester entertained Queen Elizabeth, in 1575.

In versification the acknowledged Shakespearean comedy is much superior to the older play. The Induction contains passages of felicitous fluency, phrases of delightful aptness, that crystalline lucidity of style which is characteristic of Shakespeare, and a rich vein of humor. The speeches uttered by the *Lord* have the unmistakable Shakespearean ring. The character of *Christopher Sly* is conceived and drawn in precisely the vein of Shakespeare's usual English peasants. Hazlitt likens *Sly* to *Sancho Panza.* The Warwickshire allusions are also significant—though Greene as well as Shakespeare was a native of Warwickshire; but some of the references are peculiar to the Folio comedy, and they inevitably suggest the

THE TAMING OF THE SHREW

same hand that wrote "The Merry Wives of Windsor." "Burton Heath" is, almost certainly, Barton-on-the-Heath, a village situated about two miles from Long Compton, not far from Stratford-upon-Avon. Knight, citing Dugdale, points out that in "Doomsday Book" the name of the village is written "Bertone." "Burton Heath" is only such a contraction as might naturally be made in colloquial reference to "Burton-*on-the*-Heath." Shakespeare's aunt, the wife of Edmund Lambert, and two of her sons, lived there. (Lee.) Shakespeare's own beautiful native shire,—as his works abundantly show,—was often in his mind when he wrote. It is from the region of Stratford that he habitually derives his climate, foliage, flowers, sylvan atmosphere, and romantic and always effective correspondence between nature's environment and the characters and deeds of mankind. Only Scott, Wilkie Collins, and Thomas Hardy, since his time, have conspicuously rivalled him in this latter felicity, and only George Eliot and Thomas Hardy have drawn such English peasants as his. "Ask Marion Hacket, the fat ale-wife of Wincot," is another of the Warwickshire allusions. There is a hamlet named Wincot about four miles from Stratford, on the road to Cheltenham, to which I have walked from Shakespeare's Birthplace. The allusion may be to Wilmcote,—which Malone says was called Wyncote,—

where lived Mary Arden, the mother of Shakespeare, in a cottage, still extant, old and weather-beaten now, in the parish of Aston-Cantlow, about four miles northwest of Stratford. And there is a Wilnecote, "near Tamworth, on the Staffordshire border of Warwickshire, at some distance from Stratford," said to have been "celebrated for its ale in the seventeenth century." (Lee.) The name "Hacket" has been found in the parochial registers of Quinton, the parish in which lies the hamlet of Wincot (Richard Savage), and "Sly" was a common name in and about Stratford, in Shakespeare's lifetime.

The scene of the Induction to "The Taming of the Shrew" is certainly Warwickshire, while that of the main action of the comedy is at Padua, and at the country-house of *Petruchio,*—who comes to Padua, from Verona. The period indicated is the sixteenth century, about the year 1535. The time supposed to be occupied by the action is four days. The name of Shakespeare's shrew is *Katharina Minola.* The Induction presents the only opportunity that Shakespeare's works afford for showing English costume of his own time,—unless "As You Like It" be placed in the Warwickshire Arden, and in the dramatist's own period. The Italian dresses required for the play are of styles such as were contemporaneous with the poet. An actor named Sincklo, who is mentioned

THE TAMING OF THE SHREW

in the quarto edition of "King Henry IV.," Part Second, and also in "King Henry VI.," Part Third, is supposed to have acted in "The Taming of the Shrew," as well as in those two histories, for the reason that a reference to him occurs in the old play. The line "I think 'twas Soto that your honor means" was originally given to Sincklo. It has been customary, since Garrick's day, in acting this play, to present *Curtis,* a serving-man in the original, as an old woman, and to allot two or three words to the servants who are named by *Grumio,* in his deprecatory appeal to his master, in the Arrival Scene.

OFFSPRING OF SHAKESPEARE'S "SHREW."

On the English Stage "The Taming of the Shrew" has been the parent of several popular plays. "Sawney the Scot," by John Lacy, soldier and actor (died, 1681), acted, April 9, 1667, at the Theatre Royal,—Killigrew's theatre, later called Drury Lane,—and published in 1698, is an alteration of "The Taming of the Shrew" and is not as good a play. Another derivative of this original is "The Cobbler of Preston," by Charles Johnson, a two-act farce, performed at Drury Lane and published in 1716. A play by Christopher Bullock, having the same title as that of Johnson, was acted at the same time, at Lincoln's

Inn Fields. Both seem to have been approved. John Fletcher's "Rule a Wife and Have a Wife" (1640) is perhaps the most notable type of the popular plays of this class. In that piece *Leon* pretends meekness and docility, in order to win *Margarita,* and presently becomes imperative for the control of her. Garrick personated *Leon,* in an alteration of the comedy attributed to his own hand. It is worthy of mention that Fletcher, whose views of women are somewhat stern and severe (he was the son of that Fletcher, Dean of Peterborough, who troubled the last moments of Queen Mary Stuart by his importunate religious exhortations to her on the scaffold at Fotheringay Castle), nevertheless wrote a sequel to "The Taming of the Shrew," in which *Petruchio* reappears,—*Katharine* having died,—with a second wife, by whom he is henpecked and subdued: this is entitled "The Woman's Prize, or the Tamer Tamed": it was printed in 1647. John Tobin's comedy of "The Honeymoon," 1805, based on ideas derived from Shakespeare, Fletcher, and Shirley, portrays a husband's conquest of his wife's affections by personal charm, manliness, and firmness of character; and this play is deservedly held in high esteem. *Petruchio's* method is to meet turbulence with still greater turbulence, remaining, however, self-possessed and determined throughout the stormiest paroxysms of violence, till at last his boisterous, rough, sinewy vigor and clamorous tumult overwhelm *Katharine* and disgust her with the exaggerated image of her own faults.

Aside from its rattling fun the subject of "The Taming of the Shrew" seems, in itself, to possess a particular interest for those numerous Britons whose chief article of faith is the subordination of woman to man. Long ago it became a settled principle of the common law of England that a man may beat his wife with a stick not thicker than his thumb. The ducking stool,—a chair affixed to the end of a beam, which rested on a pivot, and so arranged that the person bound into it could be repeatedly soused in a pond or river,—was used in England, to discipline a scolding woman, as late as 1809. John Taylor, the water-poet, counted sixty whipping-posts within one mile of London, prior to 1630, and it was not till 1791 that the whipping of female vagrants was forbidden by statute. The brank, a peculiar and cruel kind of gag, formerly in common use, has been employed to punish a certain sort of women within the memory of persons still alive. Thackeray's caustic ballad of "Damages Two Hundred Pounds" affords an instructive glimpse of the view that has been taken, by British law, of masculine severity toward women. It is not meant that the gentlemen of England are tyrannical and cruel in their treatment of the women; far from it; but that the predominance of John Bull, in any question between himself and Mrs. Bull, is a cardinal doctrine of the English law, and that plays illustrative of the application of discipline to rebellious women have found favor with the English audience.

EARLY REPRESENTATIONS.—BRITISH STAGE.—GARRICK'S ALTERATION.

"The Taming of the Shrew" was acted, by the associates of Shakespeare, at the Blackfriars Theatre, at the theatre in Newington Butts,—which the Shakespeare players occupied while the Globe Theatre was being built,—and, finally, at the Globe itself. No account has survived of those early representations. The version of "The Taming of the Shrew" which, in one form or another, has, for many years, been generally used on the stage, is the one made by David Garrick, produced March 18, 1754, at Drury Lane, and published in 1756, under the name of "Katharine and Petruchio." It was first presented as an after-piece to the tragedy of "Jane Shore," Henry Woodward acting *Petruchio* and Mrs. Pritchard acting *Katharine*. Genest says of it that "In altering 'Katharine and Petruchio' (*sic*) Garrick . . . has done little more than omit the weak points of 'The Taming

From an Old Print   Author's Collection

HENRY WOODWARD AS *PETRUCHIO*

*"I come to wive it wealthily in Padua;
If wealthily, then happily in Padua."*

Act I., Sc. 1

THE TAMING OF THE SHREW 497

of the Shrew,' and has thereby made the best afterpiece on the stage." That statement is measurably true: the chief objection that can reasonably be made to Garrick's alteration of the original (especially by those who believe, with Dowden, that "the genius of Shakespeare may be said to go in and out with the person of *Katharina*") is that in making his changes and condensations he did not do his work as well as it easily might have been done: he could have improved the construction so that the action would have been smoother.

Arthur Murphy, discussing this subject, remarks that "From the whole he [Garrick] had the judgment to select the most coherent scenes, and, *without intermixing anything of his own,* to *let Shakespeare be the entire author* of a very excellent comedy." One defect in Murphy's biographical and critical writings is misinformation, proceeding from the fact that he did not always take the trouble to acquaint himself with the subjects about which he wrote. His statement relative to this play is both untrue and ridiculous. Garrick, in re-arranging and condensing "The Shrew," made many material transpositions and inserted a considerable number of speeches, sometimes compounded of lines from the Folio text, sometimes composed by himself. He omitted the whole of the Induction, the entire secondary plot of the comedy,—involving the quadruple wooing of *Bianca,* and all the associated incidents,—together with the characters of *Gremio, Lucentio, Tranio, Vincentio,* the *Pedant,* and a *Widow;* and he introduced a *Music-Master,* to play *Hortensio's* "Broken Lute" Scene; gave to *Biondello* the descriptive speeches of *Gremio* about the wedding; introduced a servant, named *Pedro;* presented *Hortensio* and *Bianca* as wedded, and changed *Curtis* from an old man to an old woman. Thus his presentment, which is in three acts, goes directly "to Hecuba," concerns itself only with the main features of the turbulent wooing, the mad marriage, and the violent taming. It has, in the course of 160 years, been successfully presented hundreds of times, throughout the English-speaking world, and there can be no doubt of its effective qualities: it has justified itself and its adapter.

PLAYERS OF *KATHARINE* AND *PETRUCHIO.*—BRITISH STAGE.

The performances of *Katharine* and *Petruchio* that were given by Woodward and Mrs. Pritchard, in 1754, are nowhere particularly described. When, subsequently, 1756, Garrick's version was again brought out, Kitty Clive acting *Katharine* and Woodward still being the *Petruchio,* the play gained its first real success,—a popular favor by which it has

THE TAMING OF THE SHREW

ever since been attended. Woodward was extremely boisterous and at times downright brutal in his method of taming. Tate Wilkinson mentions that, on the occasion of his first performance with her, he "threw Mrs. Clive down," on making the exit in the Second Act, a proceeding which was resented with such practical indignation by the infuriated actress,—not over-amiable at the best of times,—that "her talons, tongue, and passion were very expressive to the eyes of all beholders." Davies, however, gives a different account, recording that "Woodward was, perhaps, more wild, extravagant, and fantastical than the author designed," and that "he carried his acting to an almost ridiculous excess: Mrs. Clive, though perfect mistress of *Katharine's* humor, seemed to be overborne by Woodward's manner, and to be really as much over-awed by his violence as *Katharine* is supposed to be in the play, for beyond throwing her down it is said he once stuck a fork into her finger. As it was well known that they did not greatly respect one another, it was believed that something more than chance contributed to these excesses." Murphy says that Mrs. Clive acted *Katharine* "in her true vein of comic humor" and "crowned the whole with success," —adding that *Grumio* was well played by Yates. *Katharine* can show a kind of spiteful "humor," but she is more serious than comic.

500   SHAKESPEARE ON THE STAGE

Numerous representations of Garrick's play have occurred on the English Stage since the time of Woodward and Mrs. Clive, and, occasionally, performances of Shakespeare's "The Shrew" and personations of *Katharine* and *Petruchio* have been given by Mrs. Gregory and Edward Shuter, 1757; Mrs. Greene and W. T. Lewis, 1774; Mrs. Crawford and William Crawford, 1781; Mrs. Siddons and John Philip Kemble, 1788; Miss Wallis and W. T. Lewis, 1796; Mrs. Charles Kemble (as Miss De Camp she first played *Katharine* in 1798) and J. P. Kemble, 1810; Mrs. C. Kemble and Charles Mayne Young, 1812; Eliza O'Neill and Young, 1817; Helena Faucit and Charles Kemble, and Ellen Tree and Charles Kemble, 1836; Mme. Vestris and Benjamin Webster, 1844; Mrs. Stirling and Benjamin Webster, 1848; Isabella Glyn and Barry Sullivan, 1855; Miss Atkinson and Henry Marston, 1856; Fanny Hughes and Henry Neville, 1864; Ellen Terry and Henry Irving, 1867; Miss Alleyne and Boothroyd Fairclough, 1870; Helen Barry and William Rignold, 1875; Bella Pateman and Henry Neville, 1880; Mrs. Bernard-Beere and Johnston Forbes-Robertson, 1885; Ellen Webster and W. H. Pennington, 1887; Ada Rehan and John Drew, 1888; Mrs. F. R. Benson and F. R. Benson, 1890; Ada Rehan and George Clarke, 1893 and 1897; Mrs. Beerbohm-Tree and Herbert

THE TAMING OF THE SHREW

Beerbohm-Tree, 1897; Lilly Brayton and Oscar Asche, 1904; and Nina de Silva and Martin Harvey, 1913.

Katharine and *Petruchio* are laborious parts for the players of them, but they are readily comprehensible, they tax the body far more than they do the mind, and though they can be properly performed only by experienced actors, all that they require is simple, direct, spirited treatment. Genest says that J. P. Kemble "played *Petruchio* very well," and that "Mrs. Siddons acted with spirit, but did not seem to be at home in the character of *Katharine*." It is not easy to believe that either of those grand actors was suited in parts not much more than farcical. John Bannister, speaking of J. P. Kemble's comedy, is said to have remarked "He is as cheerful as a funeral and as lively as an elephant"; and another of his contemporaries, referring to the same subject, likened him to a hearse stalled in a snow-storm. When Kemble "restored" the play, June 25, 1810, with Mrs. Charles Kemble as *Katharine*, his restoration was confined to the title, "The Taming of the Shrew"; he presented Garrick's version as an after-piece to "King John." Liston acted the *Tailor*. That wonderful fountain of tears, Miss O'Neill, must have been as much out of place as Mrs. Siddons certainly was in *Katharine*.

When Woodward and Mrs. Clive first acted in

Garrick's "Katharine and Petruchio" it followed "Florizel and Perdita," also adapted by Garrick, from "The Winter's Tale." Throughout its long career Garrick's version has, almost invariably, been used as an "after-piece," that is, as the farce with which, in old times, it was customary to close every theatrical entertainment. During the half-century immediately following its advent it was presented on various occasions, at either Drury Lane or Covent Garden, after "Macbeth," "The Rival Queens," "Douglas," "Jane Shore," "All for Love," and "The Merry Wives of Windsor." Such were the dramatic pleasures of Long Ago.

On May 14, 1828, at Drury Lane, Shakespeare's "The Taming of the Shrew" was presented as an opera, the arrangement of the text for musical treatment having been made by Frederick Reynolds. Four performances occurred. That, probably, was the first restoration to the Stage, though not in dramatic form, of the original play. The cast, accordingly, is notable:

Petruchio	J. W. Wallack.
Grumio	J. P. Harley.
Hortensio	John Braham.
Lucentio	Bland.
Tranio	J. Cooper.
Gremio	Browne.
Baptista	W. Bennett.
Vincentio	Gattie.

THE TAMING OF THE SHREW

Tailor	J. Russell.
Pedant	Paul Bedford.
Katharine	Fanny Ayton.
Bianca	Miss Grant.
Widow	Miss Nicol.
Curtis	Mrs. C. Jones.

The failure of this opera was followed, on May 20, by a revival of Garrick's farce. Wallack played *Petruchio,* to the *Katharine* of Miss Lawrence.

SHAKESPEARE *REDIVIVUS.*—WEBSTER AND PHELPS.

Benjamin Webster (1798-1882), whose career, notwithstanding his alleged slipshod managerial methods, was beneficial to the English Stage, effected a revival of "The Taming of the Shrew," presenting it, at the Haymarket Theatre, London, according to the text of Shakespeare, and also according to the putative stage custom of Shakespeare's time, in March, 1844. Tapestry hangings were used, to form a background, and written scrolls were displayed, designative of the respective scenes. Webster acted *Petruchio,* and the performance that he gave is recorded as brilliant and bold. He was an actor of rare ability, one of the finer comedians, successful in an exceedingly wide range of character, from *Triplet* to *Tartuffe,* and from *Dogberry* to *Robert Landry* and *Dr. Primrose.* On

December 7, 1847, at Covent Garden, Webster acted *Petruchio,* in scenes from "The Taming of the Shrew," for the benefit of the fund for the purchase of the Shakespeare Birthplace, at Stratford-upon-Avon.

The first genuine restoration of "The Taming of the Shrew," as an acting play, according to the usage of the modern stage, was effected by Samuel Phelps, at Sadler's Wells, November 15, 1856. F. G. Tomlins, a noted critic of that period, testifies that "the entire five acts were rigidly played," that "the dresses were particularly good," and that Henry Marston was a capital *Petruchio,*—"manly, hearty, humorous, but, withal, the gentleman." *Petruchio* portrayed as "a gentleman" is not portrayed as he is drawn by Shakespeare. Phelps impersonated *Sly,* and he must have been elaborately artistic. Morley commends his performance for "Dutch fidelity and characteristic humor." The man portrayed was a man "buried and lost in his animal nature, . . . brutish, . . . unleavened by fancy." According to that authority, Phelps banished from his face every spark of intelligence while representing *Sly;* partly "by keeping the eyes out of court as witnesses of it: the eyes were hidden, almost entirely, by the drooping lids, except when exposed in a stupid stare." *Sly* is not a difficult part, but good taste is specially requisite in the acting of it. *Sly* is a coarse, drunken lout, in a condition of

THE TAMING OF THE SHREW

bewilderment; there is a vein of vulgar humor in him, which can be elicited, to good dramatic effect, only by an actor, naturally refined, who possesses dexterity of art to show the comicality of the character and the situation without over-accenting the sottishness of the boor and so making him obnoxious instead of amusing. Phelps appears to have achieved that excellence, so that his critics marvelled at the facility with which he passed from *Hamlet* and *Brutus* to the drunken tinker of Burton Heath.

The revival by Phelps of Shakespeare's "The Taming of the Shrew" did not particularly prosper, and, indeed, the only presentment of that play, in its original form, that has notably prospered is the one made by Augustin Daly,—which was first effected in America. That production owed its great success mainly to the cogent and brilliant acting of Ada Rehan, as *Katharine*. Particular description of the many performances of *Katharine* and *Petruchio* by all the many performers of those parts who have been enumerated is not desirable, because it would be only a ringing of the changes on the several degrees of vigor and violence shown by the several *Petruchios,* and the several degrees of ill-temper and vixenly wrath shown by the several termagant *Katharines.*— The coöperation of Ellen Terry and Henry Irving as *Katharine* and *Petruchio* is memorable only because it marks the occasion when, December 26, 1867, at the Queen's Theatre, London, those two great performers acted together for the first time.

AMERICAN STAGE.—EARLY REPRESENTATIONS.

On the American Stage "The Taming of the Shrew," as Shakespeare wrote it, was never acted till Augustin Daly produced it, in New York, in 1887. Garrick's version, "Katharine and Petruchio," was invariably used until the time of Edwin Booth. The first presentment of it in America occurred, November 21, 1766, at the Southwark Theatre, Philadelphia. This was the cast:

Katharine	Margaret Cheer.
Petruchio	Lewis Hallam.
Grumio	Owen Morris.
Baptista	Tomlinson.
Hortensio	David Douglas.
Biondello	Wall.
Music-Master	Allyn.
Pedro	Stephen Woolls.
Bianca	Mrs. Wall.
Curtis	Mrs. Hallam.

The first representation of "Katharine and Petruchio" in New York was given, April 14, 1768, at the John Street Theatre, with the same cast as when first

THE TAMING OF THE SHREW 507

performed in Philadelphia, except that *Bianca* was performed by Maria Storer and *Curtis* by Mrs. Harman.

Margaret Cheer was a beauty and a fine actress. Her advent as the *Shrew,* in the Philadelphia production of "Katharine and Petruchio," was her first appearance on the American Stage. She first appeared in New York, December 7, 1767, at the John Street Theatre, as *Mrs. Sullen,* in "The Beaux' Stratagem." It seems probable that she passed a professional novitiate in England. She acted many parts, of the first order, on our Stage, in Shakespeare and in Old English Comedy, and, from the first, was deemed competent and admirable in them. Success of that kind implies experience. Mention is made of Mrs. Cheer's marriage, in 1768, to a Scotch lord named Rosehill and of her subsequent, though not immediate, retirement from the Stage. Dunlap says that she reappeared in 1794, as Mrs. Long, but had ceased to be attractive. The same authority states that Catharine Maria Harman was a granddaughter of Colley Cibber.

Among the players who conspicuously performed *Katharine* and *Petruchio* on our Stage were Mrs. Allen and Lewis Hallam, the Younger, 1785; Mrs. Mason and T. A. Cooper, 1814; Macready and Mrs. Darley, 1827; Fanny Kemble and Charles

Kemble (her father), 1832; William B. Wood and Mrs. Sharpe (Miss LeSugg), 1839; John M. Vandenhoff and his daughter, Charlotte Vandenhoff, 1839; Fanny Wallack and James R. Anderson, 1848; Mrs. J. W. Wallack and T. S. Hamblin, 1850; C. W. Couldock and Mrs. Hoey, 1850; Laura Addison and T. S. Hamblin, 1851; Mrs. Abbot and Robert Johnson, 1856; Susan Denin and James E. Murdoch, 1857; Mme. Ponisi and Barry Sullivan, 1859; Julia Dean and Barton Hill, 1860; Mrs. Scott-Siddons and James K. Mortimer, 1869; Clara Morris and Louis James, 1871; Kate Forsyth and John McCullough, 1881, and Jane Hading and Constant Coquelin, 1894. At one time or another, until Daly revived the Shakespearean original, almost every prominent performer who has appeared on our Stage made use of "Katharine and Petruchio."

EDWIN BOOTH AS *PETRUCHIO*.

Edwin Booth used a variant of Garrick's version of "Katharine and Petruchio," prepared by himself, reducing the farce to two acts, presenting it always as an after-piece,—often to the sombre, romantic play of "Ruy Blas," sometimes in association with "The Fool's Revenge." His *Petruchio* was a dashing spark, exceedingly virile, bluff, and boisterous. Booth was pictorial and engaging in appearance, in this character, manly in demeanor, fluent and various in delivery, and almost incessant in action. He made *Petruchio* a good fellow, but, properly, without the least pretence of exalted character. He had personal distinction and was blunt and reckless, but not coarse. He enjoyed acting *Petruchio,* and often did so, because the part provided him with opportunity for a frolic. The whip with which the shrew-tamer flagellates his terrified servants was plied by him with peculiar skill, vigor, and relish. I recall the personation as one that was almost continuously tumultuous and laughable. Booth was essentially a tragedian, and his temperament was radically melancholy; but he possessed both a strong sense and a fine faculty of humor, and in social intercourse with his few intimate friends those qualities were sometimes delightfully shown. In acting the comedy parts,—aside from *Richelieu,*—which were retained in his repertory, in the days of his high renown, he used far less art than it was ever his custom to use in acting those great serious or tragic characters with which his name is inseparably linked. No elaborate production of "Katharine and Petruchio" was ever made by him, though the play was always sufficiently well mounted and dressed. Among the performers associated with him as *Katharine* were Ada Clifton, Isabella Pateman, Rose Eytinge, and

Fanny Davenport, none of whom raised the part above mediocrity.

The German actress Marie Seebach, who made her first appearance in America, September 22, 1870, at the Fourteenth Street Theatre, New York, as *Gretchen,* in "Faust," presented, October 29, that year and at that theatre, a German version, in four acts, of "The Taming of the Shrew," and impersonated *Katharine.* Mme. Seebach was a great actress, but not in the *Shrew;* she was petulant where she should have been passionate, and ethereal where she should have been robust. A note, published with her version of the play, censuring the alteration made by Garrick, states that

> "It is not customary to take such liberties with the works of a great Bard on the German Stage, and the play as performed by Mme. Seebach and her company, with the exception of a few cuts and unimportant alterations, adheres to the original form."

That statement is untrue: the play as performed by Mme. Seebach and her associates (the adaptation was made by Philip Bonfort) was in four acts; it omitted the Induction and materially altered the sub-plot of *Bianca* and her lovers. The principal characters were cast as follows:

THE TAMING OF THE SHREW

Baptista	Mr. Mueller.
Katharine	Marie Seebach.
Vincentio	Mr. Paetsch.
Lucentio	Mr. Kraus.
Petruchio	Mr. Dombrowsky.
Gremio	Mr. Harry.
Tranio	Mr. Brinkman.
Tailor	Mr. Sage.

AUGUSTIN DALY'S REVIVAL.

The first presentment in America of "The Taming of the Shrew" in substantial accordance with the text of the play as it stands in the First Folio of Shakespeare was made, January 18, 1887, at Daly's Theatre, New York, under the management and stage direction of Augustin Daly. The production was one of unprecedented brilliancy, and it has not since been equalled. It gained an instantaneous success, its first "run" comprising 137 consecutive performances, and it profitably kept its place on the stage for many years. On the memorable occasion of Daly's revival the parts were cast as follows:

IN THE INDUCTION

(Never Before Acted in America, in Any Form.)

A Lord	George Clarke.
Christopher Sly	William Gilbert.

A Page (Representing a Lady) . . . . William Collier.
A Huntsman . . . . Thomas Patten.
Players . . . . { Frederick Bond.
                                John Wood.
Two Servants . . . . . Messrs. Ireton and Murphy.
The Hostess . . . . Miss May Sylvie.

IN THE PLAY PERFORMED

Baptista Minola . . . . Charles Fisher.
Vincentio . . . . John Moore.
A Pedant . . . . John Wood.
Lucentio . . . . Otis Skinner.
Petruchio . . . . John Drew.
Gremio . . . . Charles Leclercq.
Hortensio . . . . Joseph Holland.
Tranio . . . . Frederick Bond.
Biondello . . . . Edward P. Wilks.
Grumio . . . . James Lewis.
Nathaniel { Servants at Petruchio's } . Mr. Hamilton.
Philip . {   Country House   } . Mr. Ireton.
A Tailor . . . . George Parkes.
Katharine Minola . . . . Ada Rehan.
Bianca, her sister . . . . . . Virginia Dreher.
Curtis . . . . Mrs. G. H. Gilbert.
A Widow . . . . Miss Jean Gordon.

Shakespeare's play consists of a prelude, in two scenes, styled the Induction, and five acts, containing twelve scenes. There are eight speakers, mostly minor parts, in the Induction, and sixteen in the main body of the play, and the action is made to

From a Photograph by Sarony, N. Y.　　　Author's Collection
JOHN DREW AS PETRUCHIO
"I will be master of what is mine own."
ACT III., Sc. 2

From an Old Print　　　Author's Collection
JAMES E. MURDOCH AS PETRUCHIO
"Tush, tush! Fear boys with bugs!"
ACT I., Sc. 1

THE TAMING OF THE SHREW 513

proceed in eleven different places. Daly's version consists of five acts, no division being made between the end of the Induction and the beginning of the First Act, except such as is indicated by "a dark change," and it is limited to nine scenes, representing eight different places. The First Scene of the Induction is "Before an Ale House, on a Heath"; the Second is "A Bedchamber, in the *Lord's* House." The First Act is played in "A Public Place," a street, in Padua. The speeches that pass between *Sly* and his supposed wife, during the performance of the First Act, are retained. The Second and Third Acts are played in "A Room in *Baptista's* House." The Fourth Act is played in two scenes, the first "a front scene," "Before *Baptista's* House"; the second, "A Room in *Petruchio's* House in the Country." The Fifth Act, also, is played in two scenes,—the first, "Before *Lucentio's* House"; the second, "A Hall in *Lucentio's* House." The scenery was painted by James Roberts and Henry E. Hoyt and the costumes were made by Arnold & Constable after designs by E. Hamilton Bell.

In his work of coördination Daly aimed to avoid prolixity, expedite movement, and maintain the delicacy required by good taste. He therefore excluded all coarse language, all language employed in the original merely to supply the place of scenic picture, and all obscure or superfluous material,—such, for example, as *Sly's* Elizabethan slang, "Go by, Jeronimy!" (a kind of cant phrase from Kyd's play of "The Spanish Tragedy" which his contemporaries delighted to gird at), and much of the colloquy between *Lucentio* and *Tranio,* which begins the First Act. Shakespeare's play contains 2,671 lines; Daly's adaptation contains about 2,000, and of those few,—less than 200,—are either taken from Garrick or varied from the original text. A conspicuous and remarkably effective change made by Daly is that which transposes *Baptista's* Bargaining Scene with *Tranio* and *Gremio,* and leaves *Katharine* alone on the stage, to close Act II. with the telling speech,— written by Garrick, but sometimes imputed to Shakespeare:

"Is't so? Then watch me well, and see
The scornèd Katharine make her husband stoop
Unto her lure,
And hold her head as high, and be as proud,
As e'er a wife in Padua!
Or—double as my portion be my scorn!
Look to your seat, Petruchio, or I throw you:
Katharine shall tame this haggard; or, if she fails,
Shall tie her tongue up, and pare down her nails!"

In the original the act is ended with a jocose, tame speech by *Tranio,* signifying that in the interest of his

THE TAMING OF THE SHREW

master, *Lucentio,* with whom he has exchanged identity and habiliments, he will play a trick by "begetting a father" for himself, and thus deceive *Baptista,* and help *Lucentio* to win *Bianca.* The improvement made by giving the situation to *Katharine* is obvious: no person who ever heard Ada Rehan's delivery of that closing speech, and the repeated enthusiastic calls of her audience, could harbor a doubt of it. Other fortunate changes made by Daly are those which reserve the first entrance of *Katharine* to the beginning of the Second Act, and which restrict to one scene, played in *Petruchio's* country house, all the active expedients of his taming process,—which can easily be made tedious. The first entrance provided for *Katharine* affords an exacting yet grand opportunity to the actress, who must begin her performance at a high pitch of excitement, and thereafter, while avoiding rant, steadily rise to a climax of violent passion. The skilful and happy combination of the incidents of *Petruchio's* taming of his *Shrew* forestalls all possibility of tediousness in effect. In brief, Daly's version of Shakespeare's play is as faithful as it should be to the original, preserving the humorous Induction,—so characteristic of the dramatist,—presenting in bold relief all the essential points of the subsidiary plot, making brilliantly distinct the amusing conflict of two oppugnant wills, and fulfilling to the utmost the dramatic purpose of the composition, which was to show that

> "Where two raging fires meet together
> They do consume the thing that feeds their fury."

CHARACTERS OF *KATHARINE* AND *PETRUCHIO*.

The major characters in Shakespeare's plays, while not obscure,—his style being perfectly distinct and simple,—are complex, in the sense that they are compounded of many and various attributes, for which reason they are profoundly interesting subjects for close study and analysis. His minor characters, among which *Katharine* and *Petruchio* seem rightly placed, are, as a rule, instantly perspicuous. The *Shrew* and her *Tamer* are specially so. Both are young (*Petruchio's* age is thirty-two), sturdy, healthful, handsome, more animal than mental, and somewhat common. *Katharine,* intrinsically, is the better-natured, the finer, and the more interesting person. Commonness and hardness, in her, have resulted from lack of proper discipline; in *Petruchio* they are constitutional. Some enthusiasts of Shakespeare have, however, discovered in this character a virtue and a charm which commonsense is unable to discern. Thus, Hazlitt wrote of him:

"*Petruchio* is a madman in his senses; a very honest fellow, who hardly speaks a word of truth and succeeds in all his tricks and impostures. He acts his *assumed character* to the life, with the most fantastical extravagance, with complete presence of mind, with untired animal spirits, and without a particle of ill-humor from beginning to end."

Petruchio does, now and then, play a part, pretending to be more fractious, boisterous, belligerent, and violent than he really is, but mostly he is himself, and he does according to his nature. Clever actors can gloss the character, and make it advantageous to themselves, in representation,—as some of them have done: but *Petruchio,* as he stands in Shakespeare's play, is coarse, turbulent, contentious, domineering, tyrannical, and mercenary. His first act is to beat his servant, for not understanding an order. His first explanatory statement about himself, to his old friend *Hortensio,* is that he has inherited money, and that his object is to obtain more by marrying a woman who is wealthy:

"If you know
One *rich enough* to be Petruchio's wife
(As wealth is burthen of my wedding dance)
Be she as foul as was Florentius' love,
As old as Sybil, and as *curst and shrewd*
As Socrates' Xantippe, *or a worse,*
She moves me not, or not removes, at least,
Affection's edge in me. . . .
I come to wive it wealthily in Padua;
If wealthily, then happily in Padua."

On being told about *Katharine,* that she is rich, young, and handsome, but an intolerable shrew, he instantly declares that he "will not sleep" till he has seen her and bespoken her in marriage, and that he "will board her, though she chide as loud as thunder." His immediate resolve is to marry the *Shrew* for her money, and then to tame her by violence,—to "kill her in her own humor." No such resolve is formed by a gentleman, and no such conduct is possible to one. The character of *Petruchio* was drawn in a period of rude manners and for the coarser audience of the time. It typifies an old and obnoxious principle of English law whereby a wife's person, estate, goods, and earnings become the property of the husband. *Petruchio,* indeed, specifically proclaims that principle, vociferating, after the wedding, "I will be *master* of what is *mine own.* She is my goods, my house, my household stuff, my field, my barn, my horse, my ox, my ass, my *anything,"* etc. His position was strictly legal; for, as old Theophilus Parsons used to say, when lecturing at the Harvard Law School, in my student days, according to the English Common Law, "The husband and the wife are one, and *the husband is that one."* The spirit thus indicated was supreme in Shakespeare's time, and, notwithstanding the advance of civilization, it is still existent; and I believe that a considerable public sympathy with it underlies, to some extent,

THE TAMING OF THE SHREW

the enduring success of "The Taming of the Shrew."

The character of *Katharine,*—which also can be, and has been, glossed in representation and provided with various charms which are only faintly, if at all, indicated in Shakespeare's page,—is, nevertheless, more agreeable than that of *Petruchio.* She believes, as is not unnatural with elder sisters, that the elder sister should be married before the younger is, but it does not appear that she is either self-seeking or mercenary. She is, undoubtedly, a vixen. Her temper is red-hot; her conduct pugnacious and unruly. She binds and beats her sister; she threatens *Hortensio* with a noodle combed with a three-leggèd stool, and, later, when he is in his disguise as a *Music-Master* and endeavoring to teach her, she breaks his head with a lute; she strikes *Petruchio,* at their first meeting, and she openly flouts her father, in the presence of their wedding-guests. "A couple of quiet ones" in very truth—she and her "Mad-cap ruffian" of a husband! *Katharine's* meekness and her gentle speeches, after she has been married, and has been bullied into submission, are, perhaps, warrant for the belief that, all the while, she has been, inwardly, a sweet and lovely woman, but physically disordered,—though that seems an extreme theory, more fanciful than sensible. Her disposition is clearly shown to be imperious and her conduct almost ferocious. One valid ground of discontent she must be allowed, namely, her father's partiality for her younger sister: but that does not justify her in her perverse and quarrelsome proceedings. Such an unbridled young "devil" as the comedy surely implies might well deserve to be curbed in *Petruchio's* harsh way, and would not be amenable to any other discipline. This subject of feminine shrewishness, the disorder being in fact a malady, cannot be deemed agreeable, and it would be offensive on the stage, if seriously treated. Daly was judicious, therefore, when he caused the play to be acted as a farcical comedy, and cast *Katharine* to an actress as lovely in her nature as in her person, and well aware that the essence of farcical acting is absolute gravity, and sometimes the semblance of passionate ardor, in comically preposterous situations.

ADA REHAN'S *KATHARINE*.

According to Miss Rehan's ideal, the shrewishness of *Katharine* is largely superficial. She is externally a virago, but the loveliest qualities of womanhood are latent in her. She is at war with herself; a termagant in temper; haughty; self-willed; imperious; resentful of control; still more resentful of the thought of submission to love, yet, at heart, ardently desirous of it,

THE TAMING OF THE SHREW

and secretly impelled to seek for it. Her spirit is high and fiery, and while she longs for the triumph and the endearments of love, she rages against herself, contemning the weakness which permits her longing, but which really is her, as yet unrecognized, power. That ideal was implied by Miss Rehan's treatment of the character, and her art, in the implication and expression of it, was as nearly perfect as anything of human fabric can be. The vitality, sympathy, and delicious bloom of her *Katharine* could not be too freely extolled. By precisely what means she imparted a sense of *Katharine's* charm it would be difficult to say. Perhaps it would be exact to suggest that her latent loveliness was signified not by action but by condition,—by the personality of the actress, and by the feeling, relative to the character, with which she was wholly possessed and animated. The method and execution of her acting can be precisely described: Her appearance was magnificent. The raiment that she wore and the make-up of her face were exactly correspondent with the complex temperament of the ideal *Shrew* she had determined to represent. She wore ruddy golden hair, short and curly. Her first dress, dark red in color, consisted of a short skirt of velvet; an over-skirt of stiff, heavy, flowered silk, looped up at the left side, with a gold cord, so as to expose the velvet skirt; a short train; a long-bodied waist; inner sleeves, fitted close to the arms; and oversleeves, depending from the shoulders almost to the knees, with flame-colored lining. Around her neck she wore a single, close-fitting string of large, heavy, dark-ruddy beads. On her head was a small red cap, and from her ears depended massy gold ornaments. Her shoes were of satin, dark red in color, to match the dress. Her first entrance on the scene, as she swept in, driving *Bianca* along with her, affected her audience like the rush of a whirlwind. Her impetuosity was terrific, and yet she was majestic. Her every movement, lithe, graceful, and splendid, showed the abounding health and affluent energy of youthful womanhood. As she moved to and fro, in tempestuous rage, it became easy to appreciate the dread of her which had previously been expressed, by *Gremio* and *Hortensio*. After a moment, as *Bianca* ended her speech of supplication, she suddenly came to a menacing stand, towering over the frightened girl, and, in her first, deep-throated, tremulous, angry query, struck the key-note of *Katharine's* raging discontent:

"*Of all thy suitors*, here I charge thee, tell
Whom thou lov'st best: see thou dissemble not!"

In *Katharine's* subsequent scene with her father she was effectively rebellious and sullen. The sound of her voice, outside, exclaiming "Out of the house, you

From a Photograph by Sarony, N.Y.   *Author's Collection*

ADA REHAN AS *KATHARINE*
"They call me Katharine that do talk of me!"

Act II., Sc. 1

scraping fool!" plainly and comically signified the sorry plight of the unlucky *Music-Master,* and there was an expressive blending of rage and curiosity in the tone of her remonstrance, "Sir—father—surely—" spoken outside to *Baptista,* and by him curtly interrupted, with "Hence, Kate! ne'er tell *me!*" just before her entrance to meet *Petruchio.* In *Katharine's* first scene with that impudent wooer she evinced extraordinary vigor and variety of feeling and action, and, notwithstanding the intensity of her struggle with him and her fierce defiance of him, there was underlying her violence of demeanor and effervescence of wrath, a subtle denotement of resentful consciousness of being interested in and even attracted by him, and with this was mingled an agitation not unlike the tremor of fear. A gleam of gratified vanity showed itself in her face when *Petruchio* said:

> "For by this light whereby I see thy beauty—
> Thy beauty that doth make me love thee well!"

The threatening speech at the end of the act, already mentioned, was delivered with such magnificent savagery that sometimes I used to wonder whether *Petruchio,* if he had heard it, would have had the hardihood to make his appearance, according to promise, "on Sunday next." In the Third Act *Katharine* did not appear till the moment of the tumultuous return of the guests and bridegroom, after the marriage service, when, distracted between fear and fury, she was half dragged upon the scene by *Petruchio,* who compelled her to dance with him. Her imperative ejaculation to *Baptista,* "Father, *be quiet!*", instead of offending, merely amused. There was a singular blending of dread and supplication in her entreaty to *Petruchio,* spoken as though intended for his hearing only, "Now, if you love me, *stay!*" And there was a fiery "now or never" spirit in the "Nay, then, do what thou wilt, *I* will not hence to-day!" and in the mocking repetition, "No-o-o-o-o-o!" of *Petruchio's* interjected query. From that point onward, through the trial and tribulation of the Taming episode, the actress steadily held the sympathy of every spectator, largely by virtue of the potent charm of her natural womanly feeling. This was deftly used, as involuntary, to show *Katharine's* gradual change from turbulence to serenity, and from shrewishness to loveliness. Throughout the closing scenes, in illustrating the ideal which she had formed, Miss Rehan depicted the unfolding of a woman's nature under the stress of widely varied emotions,—showing pride, scorn, sarcasm, anger, bewilderment, terrified amazement, and, at the last, sweetly feminine tenderness. Her appearance was continuously lovely. *Katharine,* finally, was shown as indeed changed "as she had never been" from what she was at the opening of the play, yet, as indicative of the uniformity of the impersonation, she was seen to be unmistakably the same woman, only now her actual self.

The description which *Grumio* gives of the mishap of her fall with her horse, in the journey from Padua to *Petruchio's* house, was, for some inscrutable reason, ignored,—her dress remaining undamaged and in perfect condition: this was a blemish on almost perfect stage management. Another neglect of the prescription of the text occurred in the Last Act,—Miss Rehan wearing not a "cap," but a handsome wreath of dark green leaves, though *Petruchio* always spoke the lines,

> "Katharine, that *cap* of yours becomes you not;
> Off with that bauble, throw it under foot!"

In the acting of Ada Rehan there were many charming qualities;—obvious purpose, clearly seen and steadily pursued; complete identification with assumed character; unerring, responsive intelligence, which answers every look and word of others; ample breadth and fine denotement of gesture; prescient purpose; exact performance; invariable authority; that art which conceals art, producing an effect of perfect spontaneity; melodious, flexible elocution, which flows from deep feeling; and the refined physical luxuriance which at once pleased the imagination and satisfied the eye: but the most delightful of all its qualities was its healthful vitality,—an impartment of freshness and purity, as of roses in their morning bloom. No taint infected it; no element of morbidity underlaid it; no hint of coarseness ever defaced it; and the observer was conscious of a large, fine, breezy, vigorous nature, a lovely temperament, diffusive of happiness and stimulative of noble thoughts and genial feelings. The figure of her *Katharine,*—splendid with beauty, stormy with arrogant passion, diversified with continuous fluctuation of mood, subtle with revelations of the woman's true heart, and beautiful with symmetry of treatment and melody of speech,—stood out with royal prominence, and it has rightly passed into theatrical history as one of the few really great and perfect dramatic creations of its time. It was all that could have been in Shakespeare's mind when he wrote, and it *far transcended* what is depicted in his text of "The Shrew." That performance, fine as it was, did not mark the highest range of Ada Rehan's achievement. Her *Rosalind, Lady Teazle, Portia,* and *Beatrice* were all works of art of at least equal beauty, of greater variety, and illustrative of higher ideals of womanhood: but her *Katharine* was an epitome of her powers, and, being condensed, concise, and continually active, it was widely popular. Moreover, its great *brilliancy* gave it an emphasis that public observation could not mistake.

DISCURSIVE COMMENT.

Daly's version of "The Taming of the Shrew," with Miss Rehan as *Katharine*, was presented far and wide, not only in the United States and Canada, but in England, France, and Germany, and everywhere it was opulently successful. When Miss Rehan first acted *Katharine*, the favorite comedian John Drew was associated with her, as *Petruchio*, and he was the first actor, in America, to play the part in what is, substantially, the original comedy,—if comedy it can be called which partakes so considerably of the nature of farce. After Drew left Daly's company, 1892, and became a star, George Clarke played *Petruchio*, to Miss Rehan's *Katharine*, and later, after Daly's death, 1899, the part was acted, in association with her, first by Charles Richman, and then by Otis Skinner. Drew invested the swaggering wooer with a charm of manly grace, and contrived to make the Taming process sufficiently boisterous, without any infusion of the brutality which could easily be justified, from Shakespeare's text, by the actor who should choose to employ it, but which would cause a disagreeable effect. Clarke was the best *Petruchio* seen on our Stage since the time of Edwin Booth,—making him a rough, resolute, rollicking, devil-may-care young man, shrewd and sensible in mind, abrupt in manner and speech, and tempering his fiery behavior with a certain quizzical, even kindly humor. His first entrance was superbly made. He seemed an incarnation of vigorous health, a person in the full enjoyment of life, careless of everything, and free and happy. His performance was all of one piece and it never flagged: it possessed the brightness and fluency of the acting which is governed by a clear design and vitalized by right feeling well controlled. Richman and Skinner, who were acquainted with Clarke's personation, followed the general course which he had indicated. Richman "looked" the part exceedingly well, and his fine person, animated countenance, and boy-like amiability of temperament made him agreeable in it, though he did not impersonate the character. Skinner's *Petruchio* was a pictorial, dashing blade, who revelled in the tumult of the Taming Scenes.

The brilliant representation of "The Taming of the Shrew" that was given in Paris, in the summer of 1888, at the Gaiety Theatre, by Augustin Daly's company of comedians, headed by Miss Rehan, aroused extraordinary public interest, and it was attended by at least one important consequence. The

THE TAMING OF THE SHREW

eminent French comedian Constant Coquelin (1841-1909), having seen Daly's production, became desirous of acting *Petruchio,* and, under his auspices, with himself in that character, an adapted French version of Shakespeare's play presently made its appearance on the Paris Stage. That version, made by Paul Delair, is entitled "La Mégère Apprivoisée." It is based on Daly's arrangement of the original, in as far as the scenes implicating *Katharine* and *Petruchio* are concerned, but it largely curtails the incidents of the wooing of *Bianca,* and it excludes the Induction. It is comprised in four acts. On January 24, 1892, Coquelin appeared in that play, at Abbey's Theatre (now, 1914, the Knickerbocker), New York, acting *Petruchio,* in association with the accomplished actress Jane Hading, as *Katharine,* and gave a spirited, artistically finished performance, again showing himself to be a capital low comedian and a master of the technical resources of his vocation. Jane Hading gave a weak imitation of Miss Rehan, devoid of charm, and,—which was singular, considering how clever she had elsewhere shown herself to be,—devoid of art: probably the part did not interest her. One piece of Coquelin's stage business indicated the notion he had formed of *Petruchio's* character. In the course of the Taming *Katharine,* overcome with weariness, fell asleep, and thereupon *Petruchio,* with much parade of affectionate solicitude, covered her person with his cloak, to keep her from the cold,—coincidently, as is the absurd custom of the French Stage, signifying to the audience, by elaborate pantomime, the chivalric beauty of his uxorious conduct. Yet this loving husband (in Shakespeare's play) has declared his disposition and purpose by remarking:

> "If she chance to nod, I'll rail and brawl,
> And with the clamor keep her still awake."

And that he is true to his word is ruefully certified by *Katharine* herself, who plaintively declares:

> "I, who never knew how to entreat, . . .
> Am starv'd for meat, *giddy for lack of sleep*,
> *With oaths kept waking*, and with brawling fed."

The production of "The Taming of the Shrew" that was effected by Elsie Leslie, first at the Colonial Theatre, Peekskill, May 11, 1903, and (afternoon) May 12, at the Manhattan Theatre, New York, is remembered as the first, and, indeed, the only one, thus far, ever made, combining Garrick's version of Shakespeare's play with the Induction as it stands in the original. Miss Leslie acted *Katharine,* and Jefferson Winter acted *Petruchio.* At the time of that venture Daly's superb revival was fresh in public recollection, and the presentment made by

THE TAMING OF THE SHREW

those young players was, by some judges,—forgetful that "comparisons are odorous,"—viewed as presumptuous, and censured as exemplifying the enormity of taking "liberties" with Shakespeare. That censure seemed odd, in view of the world-wide acceptance which has been accorded to Garrick's alteration of "The Shrew," and likewise to the Farmer-White-Dowden doctrine that Shakespeare was really not the author of the play, but only a contributor to it, of the Induction and the *Katharine* and *Petruchio* scenes. If that be authentic (which I do not believe) it would follow that Miss Leslie and her associates spoke the purest "Shakespearean text" of "The Taming of the Shrew" that has ever been spoken, because they acted only the Induction and the scenes in which *Katharine* and *Petruchio* appear. The freaks of criticism, however, are more amusing than important. Miss Leslie and her players were, I believe, the first to appear conspicuously in *Katharine* and *Petruchio*, in New York, subsequent to the time when Daly's sumptuous production had made "The Shrew" almost the exclusive property of that manager and Miss Rehan. With Daly's production they could not hope, and did not attempt, to compete. The scenery with which they invested the play was "sharked up" in haste, and the setting was insignificant. Some of the stage furniture, though, was part of that which had been used by Daly,—hired from an auction company. The dresses were appropriate, in every instance, some of them being rich and handsome. Elaborate and agreeable incidental music was specially composed for the production, by that excellent musician Frederick W. Ecke. The acting, throughout, was exceptionally good.

Miss Leslie had formed a clear and correct ideal of *Katharine,* and she expressed it in bold yet graceful demeanor, simple, natural action, and a fluent delivery. Her *Shrew* was a spoiled young beauty, high-spirited, self-willed, impulsive, of a fiery temper, discontented with her circumstances and with herself, impatient of restraint, yet not unwomanly,—not lacking in latent amiability. She maintained a vigorous spirit throughout the scenes of conflict, made every point neatly and precisely, and evinced a peculiar gentleness of temperament at the close. In her delivery of such speeches as "I pray you, husband, be not so disquiet," and "The more my wrong, the more his spite appears," there was a certain plaintive, wistful note, almost pathetically indicative of *Katharine's* rueful sense of unavoidable, and not wholly unwelcome, impending subjugation. The sweetly submissive closing speeches were spoken with finely simulated feeling. The pervasive characteristic of the performance was fantastic girlishness of condition, now bitter, now sweet. The

From a Photograph by White, N. Y.   Author's Collection
JULIA MARLOWE AS *KATHARINE*
"Where did you study all this goodly speech?"
ACT II, Sc. 1

From a Photograph by Otto Sarony Co., N. Y.   Author's Collection
ELSIE LESLIE AS *KATHARINE*
"I'll see thee hang'd on Sunday first!"
ACT II, Sc. 1

impersonation of *Petruchio* by Jefferson Winter was marked by sustained vigor, rough humor, continuous action, and fluent, expressive vocalism. If the performance had been given by an actor of established repute,—such, for example, as Walter Montgomery or Lawrence Barrett, in old times,—it would have been universally and cordially approved. By the public the merit of the performance was immediately recognized, and it did not entirely lack critical commendation; but relationship of the actor to a veteran dramatic critic was remarked, and the opportunity then occurent to evince hostility toward the father by disparagement of the son was not altogether neglected. Among Miss Leslie's associates excellent performances were given by the veteran, Edwin Varrey (one of the best of actors and of men) as *Baptista*, Robert Payton Gibbs as *Grumio*, Richard Webster as *Sly*, Thomas Hadaway as *Biondello*, Spottswoode Aiken as the *Tailor*, and Annie Alliston as *Curtis*.

A revival of "The Taming of the Shrew" was accomplished by E. H. Sothern and Julia Marlowe, September 18, 1905, at Cleveland, Ohio, and on October 16, following, they presented their production at the Knickerbocker Theatre, New York. The scenery was good and the dresses were handsome. The Induction was omitted, and the play was condensed to four acts, which had been so unskilfully cut and arranged as, practically, to make the story incoherent, and also to render the performance almost unintelligible, except to persons familiar with the original. The acting, at its best, was extravagant and turbulent, and, in general, it was commonplace. There is, undoubtedly, warrant in the text for performing "The Shrew" in a farcical spirit, but there is no warrant for degrading it into an exhibition of clamor and empty buffoonery. Miss Marlowe, as *Katharine,* was, at times, beautiful to see, but, because of her frequent use of shrill vocalism, seldom agreeable to hear. Her delivery of the text was, of course, intelligent, and, likewise,—which was not true as to that of her associates in the representation,—it could be understood. No intimation was given by her, at any point, of latent, woman-like sweetness in *Katharine's* nature, and her performance was rendered the more unsympathetic by pervasive self-consciousness and by her obvious disposition to amuse herself rather than to interpret the character and amuse her audience. Sothern, as *Petruchio,* was indistinct in articulation, harsh, sharp, brittle, and explosive in vocalism and, seemingly, intent on an expeditious exemplification of fume and bluster. The associate players, aiming at rapidity, only succeeded in augmenting a distressing effect of confusion and chatter. Mr. Sothern and Miss Marlowe have gained their worthy professional reputation and prosperity by many thoughtful, careful, often admirable productions and performances: it is a pity that actors so important and influential should ever forget that whatever is worth doing at all is worth doing well. They have practically dropped "The Taming of the Shrew" from their repertory.

The eminent Italian actor Ermete Novelli,—who made his first appearance in New York, March 18, 1907, at the Lyric Theatre, as *Papa Lebonnard,*—presented an Italian version of "The Taming of the Shrew," April 13, that year, and performed as *Petruchio*. Signora O. Giannini played *Katharine*. Novelli, in several comedy characters which he impersonated on our Stage, proved himself an excellent comedian. His *Petruchio* was spirited and jovial, and to that extent, if no other, was commendable. He introduced some of the same inappropriate stage business which had been done by Coquelin,—the cloaking of *Katharine,* in her sleep, etc. But Shakespeare in Italian fares even worse, if that be possible, than he does in French. Novelli's achievement as *Petruchio* was merely casual. He closed his first New York season with that performance, April 13; acted in three short plays, April 15, at the Waldorf Hotel, and on April 17 sailed for Italy.

The most recent production of "The Taming of the Shrew" which requires notice in this chronicle is that made by Margaret Anglin, who appeared in it as *Katharine*. The first performance occurred, October 10, 1908, at Melbourne, Australia; on September 22, 1913, Miss Anglin first acted the part in America, at the Columbia Theatre, San Francisco; and, on March 19, 1914, she presented it, at the Hudson Theatre, for the first time in New York. Miss Anglin's revival of "The Shrew" is chiefly notable as being *the first* presentation of it in America strictly according to the original. The text was somewhat cut, but no words were used other than those in the Folio. At first Miss Anglin presented the Induction; later, before bringing her version to New York, she excluded it. The play, as presented here, was comprised in four acts, divided into ten scenes, showing eight places. The scenery was commonplace and uninteresting, but it served its purpose. The dresses were appropriate, and in some instances rich and handsome. The frequent changes of scene and the prolix display of the Taming incidents caused an effect of extreme tediousness. The cast included Eric Blind as *Petruchio,* Miss Ruth Holt Boucicault as *Bianca,* Pedro de Cordoba as *Lucentio,* Sidney Greenstreet as *Biondello,* and Max Montesole as *Grumio.* The performance, as a whole, was execrable,—slow, heavy, colorless, and inane.

Miss Anglin's assumption of *Katharine* was the

worst embodiment of hers that I have seen. The *Shrew*, however curst and froward, is "young and beautiful": Miss Anglin presented her as ponderous, mature, and frumpish, without distinction, charm, vivacity, or even a suggestion of latent sweetness of womanhood. Her utterance was shrill and painful. During the First Act she emitted, at frequent intervals, a parrot-like screech, as indicative of her rage at *Petruchio's* behavior. Throughout the play she was pettish, fretful, and unpleasant; never either forceful, sympathetic, or interesting. If that is the *Shrew* that Shakespeare drew, then the sooner she is permitted to "die in oblivion" and the public, as far as she is concerned, to "return unexperienced to the grave," the better it will be. In the scene at *Petruchio's* country house Miss Anglin's *Katharine* wore a nondescript dress, put on, presumably, because of injury to her raiment when "her horse fell, and she under her horse." Much of her stage business was trivial,—such, for example, as climbing on a chair and turning back the hands of a clock, before she would assent to *Petruchio's* assertion that at two o'clock 'tis seven. On the journey back to *Baptista's* House this *Katharine* became overcome by fatigue and fell asleep, whereupon *Petruchio* threw away his whip, and,—though there had not been the slightest intimation of even good-will between them,—developed a touching solicitude for his shrewish wife, raised her in his arms, wrapped his cloak around her, and supported her from the scene, she, meanwhile, clinging to him, with an air of affectionate dependence. Miss Anglin, finally, delivered the speech "Fie, fie, unknit that threatening, unkind brow," etc., as if it were mere mockery,—implying that it is hypocritical, a jest, secretly understood between *Petruchio* and his wife.

Mr. Blind is large and muscular in person and loud and strident in voice; crude in method, though apparently experienced, as an actor; and perfectly self-satisfied. "How was Mellish?" whispered Henry Irving,—stretched upon a sick bed,—when Mellish had, as an understudy, taken his place, as *Napoleon.* "Mellish," answered Harry Loveday, "Mellish—why —Mellish—why—he *was firm as a rock!*" "Ah, yes," said Irving; "'firm as a rock,'—and just about as interesting, I fancy!" Mellish is one of the best actors on our Stage to-day, but there are many who are fairly described as about as interesting as a rock, and Mr. Blind is one of them. He spoke the lines of *Petruchio,* made the motions, did the usual business, and "got through." There are scores of such commonplace actors on our Stage any one of whom would give a performance just as good and just as unimportant. Mr. Montesole as *Grumio* and Mr. Greenstreet as *Biondello* deserve special record, for the

THE TAMING OF THE SHREW

reason that they were so completely and wickedly bad. Many of the low-comedy parts in Shakespeare are mere bits,—quaint, whimsical, eccentric, interesting for a few moments, and useful as cogs in his dramatic machinery. It has, unhappily, come to be thought essential that every actor who appears in any one of these minor parts should make a pother about it, assert himself, and in every possible way intrude upon public attention. That was the method (in as far as there was any method) exhibited in these two performances. *Biondello* is a comic bit, and he has one exceptionally difficult speech to deliver. Mr. Greenstreet presented him as a gross caricature of humanity, a clumsy, greasy, loathsome lout, and his treatment of that speech,—"Petruchio is coming, in an old hat and a new jerkin," etc.,—with its wheezy, inarticulate, meaningless utterance and clown-like grimace, would have disgraced the callowest amateur that ever afflicted his friends in back-parlor entertainments at a country house. Mr. Montesole, as *Grumio,* was even worse,—a scarecrow, with hair and complexion never seen on any human being, except in this sort of "Shakespearean revival," with two heavy semicircles of brown paint drawn around his chin and lower face, and blotches of blue paint as big as half-dollars around his eyes; idiotically grotesque, inhuman in method and speech, and altogether a prodigy of abominable ineptitude and indurated self-conceit. That woful exhibition was sapiently pronounced to be "Shakespearean": perhaps, in the worst possible sense, it was. Shakespeare seems to have seen some such fellows, and he has left a description of them: fellows that, "neither having the accent of Christians, nor the gait of Christian, pagan, nor man," address themselves to the "barren spectators," "capable of nothing but inexplicable dumb shows and noise"!

VI.

JULIUS CÆSAR.

*"There is no warrant for this fatal deed,
And howsoever just your cause may be
It cannot prosper, for you do usurp
Divine prerogative, ordaining death.
Besides, the act, though done in face of day,
Is base with treachery, and I foresee
A heavy doom and lamentable end."*
—OLD PLAY.

COMPOSITION, AND SOURCE OF THE PLOT.

THE magnificent tragedy of "Julius Cæsar," which, whether it be regarded as a study of man's nature, a transcript of actual life, a work of dramatic art, or an example of superb style, is one of the great creations of the human mind, has held its place in Literature and on the Stage for more than three hundred years, and, seemingly, is destined to survive as long as civilization endures. It is agreed, substantially, by the careful and diligent commentators who have investigated the question of its chronological place among the plays of Shakespeare that it was written about 1600 or 1601, and also that it was produced, for the first time, in the latter year, at the Globe Theatre. The testimony of Shakespeare's contemporary, Leonard Digges, provides authentic evidence that when it was thus produced it was received by the public with abundant favor, and was successful from the beginning. That testimony is contained in two pieces of verse by Digges, one prefixed to the First Folio of Shakespeare, the other included, as a prefatory encomium, in a collection of Shakespeare's poems, published in London, in 1640. These lines occur in the latter:

> "So have I seen, when *Cæsar* would appear,
> And on the stage at half-sword parley were
> *Brutus* and *Cassius*, O how the audience
> Were ravish'd! With what wonder went they hence!"

"Leonard Digges," says Halliwell-Phillips, "was an Oxford scholar, whose earliest printed work appeared in the year 1617, and who died, at that University, in 1635." His tribute to the poet, from which these four lines are extracted, is superscribed "Upon Master William Shakespeare, the deceased author, and his poems," and Halliwell-Phillips expresses the opinion that "it bears every appearance of having been intended for one of the Commendatory Verses prefixed to the First Folio, perhaps that for which his shorter piece in that volume may have been substituted." The essential fact is that the testimony of Digges is that of an eye-witness: he saw performances of the play, and observed and recorded that the favorite scene with the audience was that of the quarrel between *Brutus* and *Cassius*,—a scene which has been the popular favorite ever since. Davies, writing in 1783, remarks that "the scene between *Brutus* and *Cassius* was the admiration of the age in which the author lived, and has maintained its important character to this hour." The lapse of more than a century and a quarter since then has not lessened it in the general esteem.

The dramatist derived the historical material on which his tragedy is based from Plutarch's "Lives," a translation of which, 1597, by Sir Thomas North (1535-after 1601), made from the French translation by Jacques Amyot (1513-1593), Bishop of Auxerre, was widely circulated and well known in Shakespeare's time; and so closely did he follow North's text that he copied its errors, and also, in several instances, paraphrased its words. The exceeding great felicity of invention, however, with which he varied the historical incidents, so as to make them contributory to dramatic effect, is brilliantly exhibitive of his genius, —as the student perceives, when comparing related passages in the tragedy and the biography. Dyce remarks that "it is not impossible that there was a much earlier drama about Julius Cæsar, from which he [Shakespeare] may have derived something." That earlier dramas about Julius Cæsar existed is certain. Collier cites authentic record of a play bearing that title, which was acted "by the gentlemen of the Inner Temple," February 1, 1561, before Queen Elizabeth and her Court, at Whitehall, and he considers that this was "the earliest instance of a subject from the Roman History being brought upon the stage." Stephen Gosson (1554-1623), a clergyman, who wrote much in denunciation of the Drama, about the middle of the reign of Queen Elizabeth, mentions, in his "School of Abuse," 1579, a play, then existent, called "The History of Cæsar and Pompey." A Latin play, by Richard Eedes (died, 1604), of Worcester, called "Epilogus Cæsaris Interfecti," was acted at Oxford University, in 1582. Allusion to early plays about Julius Cæsar occurs in Henslowe's "Diary," 1594. No proof, however, has been adduced that Shakespeare was acquainted with any drama on the subject, before he wrote his tragedy. Rolfe suggests that very likely he knew of the Eedes play, because of the reference made in "Hamlet," Act III., sc. 2, to the enacting of *Julius Cæsar* by *Polonius,*—which histrionic exploit, as the garrulous old statesman has told the *Prince,* occurred "i' the university."

JULIUS CÆSAR

No quarto of "Julius Cæsar" was published. The play first appeared in the First Folio. As there printed it is divided into acts, but not into scenes. The stage directions are ample and explicit. The text is uncommonly free from errors. Some students of Roman History,—of whom I am one,—believing that Julius Cæsar was the greatest man of his time, have ventured to think that the dramatist, in his incomplete and almost contemptuous depiction of *Cæsar's* character, was historically incorrect: it is to be remembered that in order to magnify *Brutus* it may have been deemed necessary to depreciate *Cæsar:* and also that Shakespeare did not lack historical authority for his position. *"Jure cæsus existimetur"* (Suetonius).

OLD PLAYS ABOUT JULIUS CÆSAR.

William Alexander, Earl of Stirling (1581-1640), wrote a play on the story of Julius Cæsar, in either 1604 or 1607. Malone gives the latter date, and believes that the play was printed before that of Shakespeare was acted. Alexander's tragedy is in five acts, each of them beginning with a long speech (one opening address, containing 240 lines, is delivered by *Juno*) and ending with a Chorus. *Cæsar* is unceasingly loquacious, until slain,—after Act IV. *Cicero* also talks freely, closing the proceedings with an exhortation to peace. Dulness is the chief characteristic of Alexander's style. This author's "Julius Cæsar" was published, with his other plays,—"Darius," "Crœsus," and "The Alexandræan Tragedy,"—in a small folio, in 1637: it never was acted, and probably Shakespeare never heard of it.

John Sheffield, Duke of Buckingham (1648-1721), having observed that there are two plots in Shakespeare's tragedy, derived from it, by the process of adaptation, two plays, the first called "Julius Cæsar," the second called "Marcus Brutus": they were published in 1722. They are clumsy in construction and laborious in style. *Brutus,* in one scene, is depicted as a lover! *Junia,* sister to *Brutus,* and wife of *Cassius,* is one of the characters. The address of *Brutus* to the populace, after the assassination of *Cæsar,* is turned from Shakespeare's carefully phrased prose into bad blank verse. *Brutus* comes upon the scene before *Cassius* dies. The *Ghost of Cæsar* appears twice,—the last time just before *Brutus* kills himself. Each act, in both plays, is ended with a Chorus: two of the Choruses were written by Pope. Much of Shakespeare's text is used, but it is considerably altered, and it is freely interspersed with that of the adapter.

Voltaire wrote a tragedy called "The Death of Cæsar," in which he borrowed from Shakespeare some-

JULIUS CÆSAR

thing of *Antony's* speech to the people, over the corpse of the murdered *Dictator*. In that play the Conspirators make their plans by daylight, at the Capitol, and *Cæsar* is killed outside,—that is, off the scene. Voltaire aimed at classic form, the unities, etc., and regarded Shakespeare's methods as barbaric. Voltaire's play contains no females. Aaron Hill (1685-1750) based on Voltaire's "The Death of Cæsar" a tragedy called "The Roman Revenge," 1753, which was acted at Bath,—where it failed. Quin, and also Garrick, refused to act in it. Both Voltaire and Hill adopted the absurd notion that Brutus was the son of Cæsar, by Servilia, sister of Cato: yet Cæsar was less than fifteen years old when Brutus was born. Hill makes *Portia* and *Calphurnia* (the Roman spelling of the one name is Porcia, of the other Calpurnia) intimate friends, from childhood. Hill's play was admired by Bolingbroke, to whom it was dedicated, and by Pope.

Mention is made, in the "Biographia Dramatica," of "The Tragedy of Julius Cæsar, with the Death of Brutus and Cassius, written originally by Shakespeare; altered by Sir William Davenant and John Dryden. Acted at Drury Lane, 12mo., 1719"; and the statement is added that it was performed at Covent Garden, with Thomas Walker (1700-1744) as *Brutus*. The scene ending Act IV., in which the

Ghost of Cæsar appears, is closed by *Brutus* with this piece of fustian:

> "Sure they have raised some devil in their aid,
> And think to frighten Brutus with a shade;
> But ere the night closes this fatal day
> I'll send more ghosts this visit to repay."

No credible authority is known for ascribing the authorship of this mutilation of Shakespeare's "Julius Cæsar" to either Davenant or Dryden. No allusion occurs in the voluminous writings of Dryden to any association of his with that play, nor is any such association mentioned in the biography of that poet by Sir Walter Scott. Dryden admired and in some ways imitated Davenant, who was twenty-six years his senior, had been Poet Laureate, and was a literary leader of his time; and because it was known that Dryden had worked with Davenant on an alteration of Shakespeare's comedy of "The Tempest" it seems to have been gratuitously assumed that those dramatists colabored on an alteration of "Julius Cæsar." Genest remarks that "it is morally certain that Davenant never assisted in altering 'Julius Cæsar,' that being one of the plays assigned to Killigrew, and which consequently Davenant could not act at his own theatre."

JULIUS CÆSAR

EARLY REPRESENTATIONS.—BRITISH STAGE.

Nothing is known of the first performance of Shakespeare's "Julius Cæsar," except that it was successful. The cast of the parts has not been preserved. A reasonable conjecture is that *Brutus* was acted by Burbage, and *Cassius* by Taylor. No information is obtainable as to the manner in which the play was arranged for representation, or as to the costumes that were worn by the actors. The stage custom then prevalent was to dress theatrical characters in the raiment of the contemporary period. The history of the play from its advent in the Theatre until after 1660 is, practically, a blank. In the course of the first twenty years of the seventeenth century, while Burbage was living, it, presumably, was acted many times. There is mention in the record kept by Sir Henry Herbert, Master of the Revels, that a play named "Julius Cæsar" was presented before King Charles the First and his Queen and courtiers, at Hampton Court, January 31, 1637. That play, probably, was Shakespeare's: King Charles the First read, admired, and cherished the writings of the great poet: it was acted by the King's Company of Players, headed by Lowin and Taylor. Not till after the momentous episode of the Cromwell Protectorate and the re-establishment of the

Theatre, under the patronage of King Charles the Second, does the explorer of theatrical annals again strike the trail of Shakespeare's "Julius Cæsar." Downes mentions that it was one of the "principal old stock plays" which were acted by Thomas Killigrew's company, at various places in the capital, 1660-'61-'62-'63, and intimates that after Killigrew had opened, April 8 (or, according to another account, May 7), 1663, the new theatre in Drury Lane, this tragedy was one of the plays presented there. The date of its representation is not stated. Genest is of opinion that it must have been revived about 1671. The chief features of the cast were these:

Julius Cæsar	——— Bell.
Cassius	Michael Mohun.
Brutus	Charles Hart.
Antony	Edward Kynaston.
Calphurnia	Ann Marshall.
Portia	Mrs. Corbet.

CHARLES HART AND HIS ASSOCIATES.

Charles Hart (died, 1683), the grand-nephew of Shakespeare, was an actor of the first order,—an impersonator. When on the stage he invariably maintained absolute identification with the character he had assumed, and he claimed to be at all

JULIUS CÆSAR

times, when acting, utterly unconscious of the audience. His person was stately, his face handsome, his voice melodious, his action graceful. Downes, who saw him, testifies that *Brutus* was one of his best parts. Thomas Rymer, the antiquary, who also saw him, is cordial in praise of his acting. "To the most wretched character," says that writer, "he gives a lustre which . . . dazzles the sight." Mohun, who had seen military service and obtained the rank of Major, was distinguished, as an actor, for correctness, skill, dignity, and grace. Rymer styles him the Roscius of his day. He was slight in figure, but of a noble spirit, which could awe and impress. Hart and Mohun, as *Brutus* and *Cassius,* could always attract a numerous audience. "That we have no memoirs or relations but what can be gathered from Downes, and some traditional scraps and slight notices of poets and critics of these two great actors, is to be lamented" (Davies). Kynaston also was an accomplished actor. He had early been accustomed to act women, and had acquired a naturally imposing gravity of mien and stateliness of step and movement. His features were regular, his person was fine, his glance imperious and piercing, his delivery clear, incisive, sometimes impetuous. Colley Cibber says that, when acting *King Henry the Fourth,* Kynaston conveyed, in his penetrating whisper, to *Hotspur,*—

"Send us your prisoners, or you'll hear of it," etc., —a more terrible menace than the loudest intemperance of voice could have expressed. Macready, more than a century later, acting the same part,—in which he gained great celebrity,—adopted the same method. Kynaston's capability of giving a perfect performance of *Julius Cæsar,* a part which incarnates the spirit of supreme authority, appears justly inferential from Cibber's relation.

THOMAS BETTERTON.

Betterton, who succeeded Hart, was accounted unrivalled in *Brutus.* He played the part for the first time in 1684, at the Theatre Royal (Drury Lane), and thereafter he acted it many times, retaining it in his repertory to the end of his career, which befell in 1710. Cibber affords an illuminative glimpse of his performance:

"When the Betterton *Brutus* was provoked, in his dispute with *Cassius*, his spirit flew only to his eye; his steady look alone supplied that terror which he disdained an intemperance in his voice should rise to. Thus with a settled dignity of contempt, like an unheeding rock, he repelled upon himself the foam of *Cassius.* . . . Not but in some parts of the scene, when he reproaches *Cassius*, his temper is not under this suppression, but opens into that warmth which becomes a man of virtue; yet this is that hasty spark of anger which *Brutus* himself endeavors to excuse."

Betterton's associates, on the occasion of his first performance of *Brutus,* were, almost without exception, distinguished actors: the cast is highly remarkable:

Cassius	Smith.
Antony	Kynaston.
Cæsar	Goodman.
Casca	Griffin.
Octavius	Perrin.
Ligarius	Bowman.
Metellus Cimber	Mountfort.
Decius Brutus	Williams.
Messala	Wiltshire.
Titinius	Gillow.
Trebonius	Saunders.
Artemidorus	Percival.
Cinna	Jevon.
Portia	Mrs. Cook.
Calphurnia	Lady Slingsby.
Plebeians,—Cave Underhill, Antony Leigh, and —— Bright.	

William Smith (died, 1696) seems to have been greatly esteemed in his profession and in polite society. Barton Booth, who wrote his Epitaph, in Latin,—though he never saw him,—records therein what was known to be true, that "he was Betterton's contemporary and friend, and very near him in merit." Cardell Goodman, talented as an actor, was the contemptible rascal,—highwayman, forger, spy, traitor, paid paramour of the disreputable Duchess of Cleveland, and generally called "Scum Goodman,"—who was afterward implicated in the Sir John Fenwick plot to assassinate King William the Third. Readers who recall the excellent play of "Lady Clancarty," by Tom Taylor, will remember that it makes skilful use of the story of the Fenwick plot, and that *Goodman* is one of the characters in it. Macaulay, in his wonderfully pictorial and eloquent "History of England," Chapter XXIII., suggested that story as furnishing "a good subject to a novelist or dramatist." Griffin was much admired, socially and professionally: he was soldier as well as actor, and held the rank of Captain. Wiltshire also served in King William's army, became a captain, and was killed in battle, in Flanders. Jacob Bowman (1651-1739) acted the "sick man," *Caius Ligarius,* "to the life." That actor kept this part in his repertory for more than fifty years. It is very slight, but, properly acted, it can be made peculiarly effective. Davies, who saw Bowman act it when he was past eighty, says that "he assumed great vigor and a truly Roman spirit." William Mountfort (1659-1692) was the ill-fated young man, treacherously stabbed to death by the ruffian Captain Richard

JULIUS CÆSAR

Hill,—with the connivance of the blackguard Lord Mohun,—because reputed to be the favored lover of beautiful Anne Bracegirdle. "In tragedy he was the most affecting lover within my memory," wrote Cibber, in 1739. His person was tall and symmetrical, his face handsome, his complexion fair, his voice melodious and winning. The Stage suffered a great loss, in his untimely death. Joseph Williams played several parts of conspicuous importance, and, like Percival, was a useful and respectable actor. "Griffin, Mountfort, Williams, Gillow, Jevon, Underhill, and Leigh, all very eminent actors, thought it no diminution of their consequence to play the inferior parts." Thomas Jevon (1652-1688) played such parts as *Osric,* in "Hamlet"; the *Gentleman Usher,* in Tate's "King Lear," and the *Poet,* in Shadwell's adaptation of Shakespeare's "Timon of Athens." Lady Mary Slingsby, widow, is mentioned as the performer of a few unimportant parts, most of them in obscure plays. She died in 1693. Betterton, it will be seen, had the coöperation of a good dramatic company. Description of the particular performances has not been found.

LATER PLAYERS OF *BRUTUS.*

The predominant character in the tragedy is *Brutus;* upon the exposition of that character the dramatist exercised his utmost skill. *Cassius* is more executive; *Antony* is more brilliant; *Brutus* incarnates moral grandeur and exemplifies intellectual supremacy. No actor can fully and truly impersonate *Brutus* whose nature does not combine intellectual power, in the widest sense of that phrase, with, at least, a perfect and sympathetic comprehension of intrinsic moral excellence. *Brutus,* from first to last, is shown more in thought than in action, and he impresses more by what he is than by what he does. Not many actors have completely triumphed in this part, though many have assumed it. Among its representatives on the English Stage, in the course of the eighteenth century, were Barton Booth, 1709; Theophilus Keen, 1718; James Quin, 1718; Thomas Walker, 1725 (?); Dennis Delane, 1732; Thomas Sheridan, 1755; Robert Bensley, 1773; and John Palmer, 1780. The accounts which have survived of their performances are widely scattered and, when assembled, are, generally, superficial, indefinite, and inconclusive. Barton Booth was transcendently majestic in bearing, and he seems to have been supremely excellent in characters that are instinct with intellectual domination, inherent royalty, and the stately calm of conscious virtue. He spoke the perilous taunt to *Cassius,* "No, for your soul, you durst not," in a thrilling tone, just above a whisper, meanwhile looking him steadfastly in the face.

JULIUS CÆSAR

The custom was, and Booth followed it, to substitute the word "soul" for the word "life," in that line (an execrable change!) and for the angry generals to draw their swords half-way, and make the hilts of them clash and repel each other, at that juncture in the quarrel: that stage business, probably, was traditional; a usage established at the Globe Theatre, in Shakespeare's time; the "half-sword parley," mentioned by Digges. Keen appears to have imitated Booth; he is chiefly commended for majesty of demeanor, in this part. Quin's personation was expert and impressive,—that of a competent, experienced actor. He was exceptionally felicitous in speaking the line "No man bears sorrow better—Portia is dead." His pause before saying the last three words was exceedingly effective, and his look and tone, when he said them, were extremely affecting. Delane was a handsome young actor, of respectable abilities, and nothing more. Sheridan, the father of the great orator and dramatist, was more a declaimer than an impersonator: his son maintained that his best performance was that of *King John*. Walker was a pleasing actor of gay libertines; also a good *Hotspur* and a good *Edmund;* effective as the enraged tyrant, and ruinously addicted to the bottle. His person was manly, his voice strong and pleasing, his face expressive, and he could exceedingly well assume the condition of despotic and vehement anger. The part of *Brutus* seems to have been beyond his capability, but in that of *Antony,* which he acted in 1722, he was excellent. He must have possessed frolicsome humor, for he gave a capital performance of *Macheath,* in "The Beggar's Opera," in which his singing was delightful, particularly because of the incidental action with which he enforced it. As to Bensley and Palmer, it is inconceivable, considering what is recorded of their characteristics, professional and personal, that either of them could have been anything but mechanic as *Brutus.*

EARLY PLAYERS OF *CASSIUS.*

On the English Stage, in the eighteenth century, prominent performers of *Cassius,* who contributed to both the making and the transmission of stage customs in the performance of that part, were John Verbruggen, 1706; Thomas Elrington, 1715; Richard Ryan, 1718; Antony Boheme, 1722; William Milward, 1734; William Smith, 1766; Thomas Hull, 1773, and John Henry, 1780. Verbruggen is warmly praised for "nature without extravagance and freedom without licentiousness. When he acted *Cassius,* to Betterton's *Brutus,* you might behold the grand contest, whether Nature or Art excelled" (Aston). The

JULIUS CÆSAR

justifiable inference would seem to be that his talents lacked thorough cultivation. His *Cassius,* probably, was rugged and forcible, lacking the dexterity of subtle insinuation which is an essential attribute of the part. The most correct and effective of the personations of *Cassius* given by the other actors mentioned appear to have been those of Ryan and Smith. The meagre accounts which survive, as to all of them, leave the reader upon a sea of conjecture.

WILKS.—GARRICK.—BARRY.—MOSSOP.—MILWARD.

Robert Wilks, among the earlier actors of *Antony,* seems to have towered above all rivalry. Dignity and grace were, at all times, prominent among his characteristic attributes. One proceeding of his, as *Antony,* shows how well he understood the part and how admirably he played it. When he entered the Senate Chamber, after the assassination of *Cæsar,* he took no notice of the Conspirators assembled there, or of anything except the dead body of his murdered friend, to which he walked very swiftly, and beside which he knelt, in passionate grief. For some time his agitation overwhelmed him, so that he was unable to speak. Then, in heart-breaking tones, he began the apostrophe, "O mighty Cæsar! dost thou lie so low?" Wilks acted *Antony* for the first time, January 14,

1707, at the Haymarket Theatre, London. He was then associated with Betterton as *Brutus,* Verbruggen as *Cassius,* and Booth as *Cæsar.* On January 24, 1715, he again presented *Antony,* this time with Booth as *Brutus,* Thomas Elrington as *Cassius,* and John Mills as *Cæsar.* On December 9, 1724, at Drury Lane, he was the *Antony* in Cibber's tragedy, "Cæsar in Egypt." He long retained Shakespeare's *Antony* in his repertory, and the business which he invented has become traditional.

Garrick never acted in "Julius Cæsar." He was attracted by the part of *Cassius,* and at one time expressed the intention to assume it, acting in association with Quin, as *Brutus;* but his purpose was abandoned. Being of comparatively low stature,—according to an epigram written by himself he "scarce reached to five feet, four,"—and slender in figure, Garrick disliked to wear Roman dress,—which seems to have been more or less expected in the garniture of plays on Roman subjects. This dislike, though, need not have embarrassed him, relative to playing *Cassius,* since it was his custom to disregard propriety of costume, whenever his fancy prompted him to do so. He wore English court dress as *Hamlet* and English military dress as *Macbeth.* The audience that accepted him as *Horatius, Regulus,* and *Antony,* in "Antony and Cleopatra," and even applauded his

Virginius (in Samuel Crisp's dull tragedy of "Virginia"), would have accepted him as *Cassius,* whatever might have been his attire; and, probably, he would have been superb in the part, for besides that he was a consummate actor, he was of precisely the nervous, impetuous temperament required for "that spare Cassius," and so vital in action that one of his critics was moved to say "he could never stand still": an exaggeration, of course, yet it helps to explain him. Garrick's personation of *Antony,* in "Antony and Cleopatra," was given, January 3, 1759, at Drury Lane. The stage version of the play then presented was one made by the Shakespeare scholar and editor Edward Capell (1731-1781) and Garrick. The tragedy was handsomely mounted and richly dressed. Mrs. Yates played *Cleopatra.*

Spranger Barry never acted either *Brutus* or *Cassius,* but he excelled as *Antony.* His first performance of the part was given, March 28, 1746, at Drury Lane, in company with Delane as *Brutus* and Isaac Sparks as *Cassius.* He had previously, in Ireland, played Dryden's *Antony* (Dublin, 1745) and had repeated that performance in London. He is said to have possessed a vocal capability in making a burst of grief,—an artifice of voice akin to Edmund Kean's famous sob, so potent in later years,—which was unique and irresistibly affecting: it must have served him well in his delivery of *Antony's* pathetic apostrophe to the dead *Cæsar*. All available testimonies relative to this actor concur in the affirmation that his particular excellence was shown in moments of passionate emotion. In the utterance of the touching appeal with which *Antony* closes his artful harangue to the Roman populace his sympathetic, magical voice wrought a prodigious effect.

Henry Mossop, it is believed, acted *Brutus,* when in Ireland, where his much vexed career began, and where for some time, intermittently, it continued. He certainly acted *Cassius* there, in his first season on the stage, Dublin, 1749, his chief associates in the representation being Thomas Sheridan as *Brutus* and West Digges as *Antony:* later he acted the part in London, showing extraordinary ability and winning renown. His mental concentration, superb vocal power, splenetic temperament, and amazing capability of bursts of passion peculiarly fitted him for this character, and he was esteemed one of the best players of it that had ever appeared. The Quarrel Scene, between *Brutus* and *Cassius,* requiring exasperation, with difficulty curbed, and a tumult of hysterical emotion, provided precisely the kind of situation in which, according to contemporaneous testimony, his acting was supremely effective.

William Milward seems to have emulated Wilks as

JULIUS CÆSAR

Antony. His person was commanding, his demeanor dignified. Several competent contemporary authorities commend his voice, for strength and sweetness: Aaron Hill wrote that it comprehended and expressed "the utmost compass of harmony." Davies says that in delivering *Antony's* address to the people, when showing to them the butchered body of *Cæsar,* "he began in a low, but distinct and audible voice, and by gradual progress rose to such a height as not only to inflame the populace on the stage, but to touch the audience with a kind of enthusiastic rapture." Milward first acted *Antony* in 1734. Later, 1737, he acted *Cassius.*

JOHN PHILIP KEMBLE AND CHARLES MAYNE YOUNG.

Kemble, on the British Stage, gained renown for an excellence in the impersonation of Roman characters, in the poetic drama, unequalled in his day, and, apparently, never surpassed. Shakespeare's *Coriolanus* and *Brutus* and Addison's *Cato* were the Roman parts in which he was supreme. He acted *Brutus* for the first time, February 29, 1812, at Covent Garden. Boaden, who almost worshipped him, might, naturally, be expected to extol the performance, but as between his *Cato* and his *Brutus* that critic gave the preference to his *Cato.* Many authorities concur in opinion that his *Coriolanus* was the best of his Romans: it was in *Coriolanus* that he took leave of the Stage, in 1817. The version of "Julius Cæsar" that he presented was one that he had himself made, and the reader of his biography is apprised that it shows "some very judicious alterations and arrangements." It was not published, and I have not been able to verify that assurance. Kemble's performance of *Brutus,* says Boaden, "exhibited all that purity of patriotism and philosophy which [historically] has been, not without some hesitation, attributed to that illustrious name." John Doran (1807-1878), who wrote so much about the Stage, confirmed himself in the belief, though he never saw Kemble, that "his *Brutus* was perfect in conception and execution."

It is recorded, relative to Kemble's revival (1812) of "Julius Cæsar,"—a production which, in scenery and costumes, was sumptuous, for its period,—that on the night of the first performance the brilliant acting of Young as *Cassius* made a profound impression, eclipsing that of Kemble as *Brutus* and Charles Kemble as *Antony:* but it is added that before the end of the first week of the run the acting of Kemble as *Brutus* had practically obliterated that of all his associates. Young, however, according to the best contemporary testimony, was perfectly *Cassius* as depicted by Shakespeare. His symmetrical figure and thoughtful, pallid countenance; his impetuous temper, seething under restraint; his expressive action, of which a nervous pace is mentioned as a notably fine peculiarity, and his intense feeling, now passionate and now pathetic, combined with finished execution and with charm of voice to make this embodiment a noble and memorable work of art. I have, in studious examination of the theatrical records, found no reason to believe that it was ever equalled, except by the entirely great personation of *Cassius* given, sixty years later, on the American Stage, by Lawrence Barrett. Young's performance of *Brutus,* shown subsequently, first at Bath and later in London, while artistically competent, appears to have been much less distinctive. Kemble acted (1787) *Antony,* in Dryden's impassioned and pathetic tragedy "All for Love, or, the World Well Lost" (1678), but it does not appear that he ever acted either *Antony* or *Cassius* in "Julius Cæsar."

The casts of "Julius Cæsar," on the English Stage, in the early years of the nineteenth century, are often striking, in their exhibition of distinguished names, but the rehearsal of them would be tedious. Few English-speaking actors have risen to distinction in tragedy without having acted *Brutus,* or *Cassius,* or *Antony.* *Antony,* with actors, has generally been the favorite,—which is not surprising, because the part allows exhibition of a fine person and admits of much variety of dramatic action and of a brilliant and affecting elocutionary display. Charles Kemble was highly renowned as *Antony*. Beauty of elocution, exquisite grace of manner, subtle, discriminative intelligence in depiction of character, and a beguiling air of spontaneity with which he executed his representative embodiments were the dominant characteristics of his acting. His performance of *Antony* was deemed perfect. Particular commendation was accorded to the skill, variety, and wonderfully winning charm of his delivery of *Antony's* address to the Roman populace;—his genuine grief and assumed humility; his specious disclaimer of all purpose to disparage *Brutus,* or any one else; his artful suggestion of *Cæsar's* many virtues; his finely feigned reluctance to read the dead man's Will; and, finally, his passionate delivery of the appeal,—"If you have tears, prepare to shed them now,"—that swept the multitude into a tumult of frenzy by its glowing and overpowering eloquence. There is no reason to doubt that he gave a grand performance of *Antony*.

WILLIAM CHARLES MACREADY.

Macready, writing about *Brutus,* expressed the opinion that "it never can be a part that can inspire a person with an eager desire to go to the theatre to

EDWARD L. DAVENPORT AS *BRUTUS:* WILLIAM C.
MACREADY AS *CASSIUS*

*"There is my dagger
And here my naked breast!"*

Act IV., Sc. 3

see it represented." He also designated that noble Roman as possessing "a gentle, loving, self-subdued mind," and specified, as attributes of his character, "tenderness, reluctance to deeds of violence, instinctive abhorrence of tyranny, open simplicity of heart, and natural grandeur of soul"; and he intimated that among the requisites to the acting of the part are "dignified familiarity" in delivery of the text and "enthusiastic inspiration of lofty purpose," in the spirit of the performance. Those words show his right comprehension of the character. His acting of *Brutus,* however, while it was extolled as impressive and admirable, seems not to have aroused such enthusiasm as attended his acting of *Cassius.* This would not necessarily prove that his *Brutus* was not the better impersonation. *Brutus* is the more difficult part to make effective. *Cassius* is the mainspring of the action: *Cassius* acts; *Brutus* is acted upon. As to the exact manner in which Macready played either of those parts there is no ample and definite testimony. Lewes says that in *Cassius* he was "great"; another critic declares that his *Cassius* was "almost universally admired." The quality of his "greatness" in the part and the grounds of the "universal" admiration are not specified. It is readily credible that he could, and did, exhibit, with exemplary fidelity, the irascible temperament of *Cassius,* one reason being that his own was of much the same kind,—inherited from his father (William Macready, 1753-1829), whose disposition was excessively fractious, and whose behavior and language were sometimes almost brutal. On the other hand, it is not to be doubted that he was one of the most intellectual, virtuous, conscientious, and high-principled of men, and exceptional for sensibility,—in those respects profoundly sympathetic with the character of *Brutus,* and eminently fitted for the just representation of it. He played *Cassius,* for the first time, June 8, 1819, at Covent Garden, doing so,—as he records,—to oblige Young, who, taking a benefit, appeared as *Brutus.* In 1822 he again acted *Cassius,* and as to this occurrence he writes: "I entered *con amore* into the study of the character, identifying myself with the eager ambition, the keen perception, and the restless envy of the determined conspirator, which, from that time, I made one of my most real impersonations." He seldom appeared as *Antony,* but in his fragment of "Autobiography" he speaks of having played that part, in 1813, at Glasgow: he was then only twenty-one. He acted *Antony,* in "Antony and Cleopatra," in association with Louise Anne Phillips, at Drury Lane, November 21, 1833; the play had a short run. His performance of *Brutus* was shown in New York, October 12, 1848, at the Astor Place Opera House, on which occasion *Antony* was acted by George Vandenhoff, *Cassius* by John Ryder, and *Portia* by Catherine Wemyss. He played *Cassius* in 1827, at the old Park Theatre, with William Augustus Conway as *Brutus*. He seems to have liked both those parts, yet he seldom appeared in either of them. In the course of his management of Covent Garden, 1837-'39, and of Drury Lane, 1841-'43, the tragedy was represented, in all, only six times.

JUNIUS BRUTUS BOOTH.

The elder Booth acted *Cassius* for the first time, December 7, 1820, at Drury Lane, with James W. Wallack, the Elder, as *Brutus;* John Cooper as *Antony*, Alexander Pope as *Cæsar,* and Mrs. West as *Portia*. Booth's acting of *Cassius* was not extraordinary. In the delivery of the speech in which *Cassius* disparages *Cæsar* as weak and sickly his elocution was expert and expressive, and when, with the other conspirators, he left the Senate Chamber, after the assassination, he strode swiftly and indifferently across the head of the murdered *Dictator,* as if unaware of the presence of the corpse, or contemptuous of it,—a striking piece of stage business, but of questionable suitability either to the situation or the character. He was the inventor of that business, and it has been adopted by some of his successors in *Cassius*. His son Edwin used it, when acting in the scene in Cibber's version of "King Richard III.,"—taken from "King Henry VI.," Part Third, Act V., sc. 6,—in which *Glo'ster* murders *King Henry*. Booth did not often play *Cassius* and he never played Shakespeare's *Brutus*. Gould states that he acted *Cassius*, "about the year 1837," in Boston, with Edwin Forrest as *Brutus*, but I have found no explicit record that Shakespeare's *Brutus* was ever assumed by Forrest. At the Park Theatre, New York, November 13, 1834, Booth performed *Cassius*, with the elder Wallack as *Brutus*, William Wheatley as *Antony*, that fine old comedian William Chippindale as *Casca*, and stately Mrs. Sloman as *Portia*. In 1851, at the old Chestnut Street Theatre, Philadelphia, he presented *Cassius* for the last time, acting with James E. Murdoch as *Antony* and Jean Davenport as *Portia*. There is no account of him as *Antony*, but Edwin Booth told me that his father did act that part, and the investigator of theatrical records finds it judicious to remember that the old-time actors, in making their way to distinction, were accustomed to act any and every sort of part that chance brought to them. The *Brutus* in which the elder Booth gained exceptional renown was the hero of Payne's tragedy, "Brutus, or, the Fall of Tarquin," first acted, December 3, 1818,

JULIUS CÆSAR

at Drury Lane, with Edmund Kean in the chief character.

SAMUEL PHELPS.

Phelps gained distinction in both *Brutus* and *Cassius*. His first performance of *Cassius* was given, February 20, 1838, at Covent Garden, in the revival of "Julius Cæsar" then effected by Macready. In making up for the part he wore a bald wig and a dark beard. Edward William Elton was the *Antony;* Bartley the *Casca*. Macready acted *Brutus*. Phelps was again the *Cassius,* when Macready revived "Julius Cæsar," May 1, 1843, at Drury Lane. His interpretation of the intense, brooding, unquiet spirit of the old Roman schemer seems to have been strikingly effective. He did not play *Brutus* till after he had assumed management of Sadler's Wells, when he produced "Julius Cæsar," May 5, 1846. *Cassius* then was played by Creswick; *Antony* by Henry Marston. At various times Phelps associated with himself, as either *Antony* or *Cassius,* James R. Anderson, James Prescott Warde, E. W. Elton, and Barry Sullivan. His admiring friend and cordial eulogist John Coleman mentions having seen a representation of "Julius Cæsar" in which the leading participants were J. M. Vandenhoff as *Brutus,* Phelps as *Cassius,* Sheridan Knowles as *Antony,* George Bennett as *Cæsar,* and

Mrs. West as *Portia*. Vandenhoff, he declares, was "stately and turgid"; Knowles spoke with "a brogue as thick as butter." Phelps as *Brutus* was admired for the stateliness of his demeanor and for his smooth, persuasive elocution. In the Quarrel Scene he maintained an impressive dignity, only once permitting a flash of passion, and later he was specially felicitous in the denotement of compassionate consideration for the sleeping boy, *Lucius,* and in his subtle intimation of a sense of awe and dread, in the Ghost Scene. The portrait of him in this character shows a stalwart person, in the customary dress of a Roman patrician. The head is dressed with a wig of thick, curly, dark hair. The face is clean-shaven and heavily lined, dignified and severe in expression, and indicative of a mind heavily burdened with care. It was in the character of *Brutus* that he closed (1862) his memorable career, lasting eighteen years, of management of Sadler's Wells Theatre, where, intermingling them with other dramas, he successfully produced thirty-one of the plays of Shakespeare. *Brutus* was acted by him as late as 1865, at Drury Lane, and the part was retained in his repertory till the end. The last part he played (March 1, 1878) was *Cardinal Wolsey*. On November 6, following, he died.

JULIUS CÆSAR

BEERBOHM-TREE'S PRODUCTION.

After the time of Phelps "Julius Cæsar" was, practically, banished from the London Stage for more than thirty years. It was played at Drury Lane, in German, by Ludwig Barnay, as *Antony,* and the Saxe-Meiningen Court Theatre Company, June 30, 1881, and an inconspicuous presentation of it was made by Edmund Tearle, April 16, 1892, at the Olympic Theatre. A scenically opulent revival of it was effected at Her Majesty's Theatre, January 22, 1898, by Herbert Beerbohm-Tree, who appeared as *Antony.* *Brutus* was assumed by Lewis Waller, *Cassius* by Franklin M'Leay, *Cæsar* by Charles Fulton, *Casca* by Louis Calvert, *Portia* by Evelyn Millard, and *Calphurnia* by Lily Hanbury. Mrs. Tree appeared as *Lucius.* That production gained popular success; the play, thus handsomely mounted, had a long run, and it has since been several times revived. The scenery and dresses, designed by Sir Lawrence Alma-Tadema, were devised with knowledge and taste, and were rich and warm in color. Much emphasis was laid on adroit use of the incidental mobs. The play was arranged in three acts, the first of which, in representation, lasted two hours, the continuity being at intervals momentarily broken by a drop curtain. The purpose pursued and accomplished was that of exaggerating the prominence and importance of *Antony*. The method employed to exploit *Antony* was the obvious one,—inartistic and improper,—of obscuring and depressing the more essentially important characters of *Brutus* and *Cassius,* and thus marring the whole dramatic fabric. As a natural consequence the climax of the action was reached in the scene of *Antony's* speech over the corpse of *Cæsar,* and that scene was accompanied by so much elaboration of tumult and display as to make it disproportionately conspicuous and to cause the remainder of the play to seem tame and superfluous. Tree, temperamentally, is well suited to exhibit the specious, wily, sensual character of Shakespeare's *Antony,* a resourceful and "shrewd contriver"; but, having known him as an actor for more than thirty years, and having seen him in many different characters, I do not recall any prominent player less suited to assume the part: he has neither person nor face for *Antony;* he is eccentric, almost to grotesqueness, ungraceful, and unmagnetic; his voice is unsympathetic, and his elocutionary method is execrable. I have not, however, seen him as *Antony,* and some observers who have seen him in that part declare that his performance is excellent.

JULIUS CÆSAR

AMERICAN STAGE.—EARLY REPRESENTATIONS.

The first performance of "Julius Cæsar" ever given in America occurred, April 20, 1774, at a theatre which had been opened in the previous December, in Charleston, South Carolina. The players were members of David Douglass's American Company. The cast of parts is not known. Douglass, it is probable, since he was the leading actor as well as manager, played *Brutus,* while *Cassius* would, naturally, have been cast to John Henry, and *Antony* to Lewis Hallam, the Younger. Henry, in his youth, in Ireland, had been taught by old Thomas Sheridan: he was an excellent all-round actor. Hallam, an actor of brilliant ability, then aged thirty-three, was in his prime of vigor. The company comprised, among others, Wools, Hughes, Davis, Roberts, Morris, Dermot, Mrs. Douglass, Mrs. Morris, and Miss Storer. No account of the representation has survived. Repetitions of "Julius Cæsar" were not frequent in the early American Theatre. Mention occurs of the announcement of it to be performed, April 20, 1788, at the John Street Theatre, New York,—where, possibly, the performance occurred,—and of a production of it, January 29, 1791, at the Southwark Theatre, Philadelphia. It was acted at the John Street Theatre, March 14, 1794, with an excellent cast, which Ireland declares to be "the first found in New York," and of which these were the principal features:

Brutus	Hallam.
Cassius	Henry.
Antony	Hodgkinson.
Cæsar	Richards.
Octavius	Martin.
Portia	Mrs. Melmoth.
Calphurnia	Mrs. Hallam.

John Hodgkinson (1767-1805) was deemed a superb *Antony*. His height was five feet ten inches. His person, though inclined to stoutness, was symmetrical, except that his legs were clumsy. His neck was long, straight, and massive, the muscles being strongly developed and prominent. His chest, shoulders, and arms were specially well formed, suggesting both strength and grace. His face was surprisingly expressive: Dunlap says he could express everything "but the delicate or the sublime." His complexion was pallid, his hair dark brown. His eyes were gray, with dark lashes and very dark brows. His voice was melodious and of wide compass. He appeared to the greatest advantage in long, flowing drapery, and, accordingly, his appearance in the Roman toga was majestic. As *Antony* he was a picture.

JULIUS CÆSAR

Thomas Abthorpe Cooper (1776-1849), whose range in acting was remarkably wide, his repertory comprising 264 parts, impersonated on the American Stage, at various times and places, and with invariably equal success, *Brutus, Cassius,* and *Antony.* The career in America of that great actor began, December 9, 1796, at the Chestnut Street Theatre, Philadelphia, and continued till October, 1838, when, at Albany, he made his last appearance. Joseph T. Buckingham (1779-1861), the honored old Boston journalist, whose "Personal Memoirs" and "Recollections" are of much value to the historian, wrote of Cooper, whose acting he carefully studied: "His *Antony* was a model of popular eloquence and his *Brutus* displayed the calm, unimpassioned yet persuasive eloquence of the philosopher. . . . All his accents speak the voice of nature." Robert Treat Paine (1773-1811), esteemed a leading critical authority in his day, declared, 1808, that "in the natural gifts and requisites of an actor Cooper has never had a competitor on the American Stage." His early ventures in "Julius Cæsar" are not recorded; they, probably, were made on the English provincial Stage, prior to his appearance in London, 1795, at Covent Garden, where he acted both *Hamlet* and *Macbeth.* In America his first performance of *Antony* was given in 1818. In 1824, at the old Park Theatre, New York, he acted

Brutus, with William Augustus Conway as *Antony.* At the same theatre, in 1828, he acted *Brutus,* with Forrest as *Antony.* In 1831 he acted *Antony,* with Hamblin as *Brutus,* and in the same year, in Philadelphia, repeated the performance, with the elder Booth as *Cassius.* In 1834 he acted at the Bowery Theatre, New York, as *Cassius,* with Forrest as *Antony,* and at the same theatre, in 1835, he appeared as *Antony,* with Hamblin as *Brutus* and Booth as *Cassius.* Ireland, who saw his performances, says that he possessed "a fine, mellow voice, of wonderful capacity of modulation, unusual dignity of manner and grace of action, and a most forcible and eloquent style of declamation, which, in such speeches as *Marc Antony's* on the death of *Cæsar,* was, in his day, unapproached."

Edwin Forrest did not play either *Cassius* or (unless Gould's dubious mention be correct) *Brutus,* and he only occasionally played *Antony,* and not at all in the last quarter-of-a-century of his career. I did not see him in that part. It is one to which he was exceedingly well fitted, by person, aspect, voice, temperament, and physical power, and I have no doubt he was supremely fine in it.

JULIUS CÆSAR

LATER PLAYERS OF *BRUTUS, CASSIUS*, AND *ANTONY*.

It would be a prolix and wearisome descant that should expatiate on all the players who have presented on the American Stage the three great characters of *Brutus, Cassius,* and *Antony,* in the tragedy of "Julius Cæsar." Mention of some of them, however, is essential to the completion of the record. Since the great days of Cooper, *Brutus* has been acted, in America, by the elder Wallack (who first played the part, in London, in 1820), 1829; William Goodall, 1852; Wyzeman Marshall, 1854; Edward Loomis Davenport, 1857; Edwin Booth, 1864; William Creswick, 1872; F. C. Bangs, 1872; Louis James, 1885; William E. Sheridan, 1886; Frederick Warde, 1886; Thomas Keene, 1889; Robert D. Maclean, 1889; Mathier Pfiel, 1891; Richard Mansfield, 1902; Robert Bruce Mantell, 1906, and Tyrone Power, 1912.

Cassius has been acted by John R. Duff, 1826; George H. Barrett, 1826; Henry Wallack, 1829; Edward Eddy, 1852; James W. Wallack, the Younger, 1857; Junius Brutus Booth, Jr., 1864; Lawrence Barrett, 1870; Edwin Booth, 1872; William Creswick, 1872; Milnes Levick, 1878; John Lane, 1886; Joseph Haworth, 1902; and Frank Keenan, 1912.

Antony has been assumed by Henry Wallack, 1826; T. S. Hamblin, 1829; James R. Scott, 1843; William

Wheatley, 1843; Charles Pope, 1854; Henry Loraine, 1857; George C. Boniface, 1860; John Wilkes Booth, 1864; Walter Montgomery, 1870; F. C. Bangs, 1871; Edwin Booth, 1872; Frederick Warde, 1878; Charles B. Hanford, 1882; Ludwig Barnay, 1883; Franz Tichy, 1891; Henry A. Langdon, 1892; Arthur Forrest, 1902; and William Faversham, 1912.

EDWIN BOOTH'S PRODUCTION.

Edwin Booth produced "Julius Cæsar," December 25, 1871, at his theatre, in New York, and the play thereafter held its place successfully till March 16, 1872. Eighty-five consecutive representations were given. The cast of parts is worthy of preservation:

Brutus	Edwin Booth.
Cassius	Lawrence Barrett.
Antony	F. C. Bangs.
Casca	James Stark.
Cæsar	D. W. Waller.
Octavius	John W. Norton.
Trebonius	John Wilson.
Decius	Nelson Decker.
Cimber	Frederick Bernard.
Cinna	Frederick Monroe.
Popilius	J. Rooney.
Soothsayer	Augustus W. Fenno.
Titinius	J. P. Deuel.

From a Steel Engraving — Author's Collection

LAWRENCE BARRETT AS CAIUS CASSIUS

"The last of all the Romans, fare thee well!
It is impossible that ever Rome
Should breed thy fellow."

ACT V., Sc. 4

After the Bust by J. C. Hartley — Courtesy of David Belasco, Esq.

EDWIN BOOTH AS BRUTUS

"This was the noblest Roman of them all. . . .
His life was gentle, and the elements
So mix'd in him that Nature might stand up
And say to all the world, 'This was a man!'"

ACT V., Sc. 5

JULIUS CÆSAR

Ligarius	David C. Anderson.
Flavius	Henry Hogan.
Varro	Charles North.
Pindarus	G. H. Harris.
Lepidus	John Taylor.
Servius (Servant to Antony)	T. F. Brennan.
Strato	F. Intropidi.
Clitus	A. Curtis.
Lucius	Frank Little.
First Citizen	Robert Pateman.
Second Citizen	Charles Rosene.
Portia	Bella Pateman.
Calphurnia	Theresa Selden.

The setting and dressing of the play were magnificent. The attainment of right and splendid dramatic effect, rather than scrupulous observance of historical exactitude, had been steadily kept in view, and the result was a gorgeous spectacle,—one of the most impressive ever shown on our Stage, yet one in which Embellishment was kept ever secondary to Acting. The tragedy was divided into six acts, exhibiting seven scenes. The whole of Act I. was performed in a Public Place in Rome. The sets that followed were, the Orchard of *Brutus,* in which the Conspirators assemble at dead of night; a Room in *Cæsar's* Palace; the Senate Chamber in the Capitol; the Forum; the tent of *Brutus,* at Sardis; and the Plains of Philippi. Every scene was massive and spacious. The painting showed bold design and delicacy of color. The Rome so grandly depicted was not that of Julius Cæsar (B.C. 100-44) but that of Augustus (B.C. 63-A.D. 14), who became Emperor B.C. 31. "Augustus found Rome of brick and left it of marble" (Poynter), and, because the Rome of Augustus suggests a stately and beautiful setting for this superb tragedy, Booth chose it as a basis for scenic embellishment. The general custom of the modern stage, indeed, has been to ignore considerations of historical correctness as to the showing of the Rome of Julius Cæsar. No part of the scenery used in Booth's production gave, or pretended to give, an idea of the Rome that Julius Cæsar knew.

Booth's stage was uncommonly large. The distance from the footlights to the back wall was fifty-five feet. The width of the proscenium opening was seventy-six feet. Beneath the stage there was a cavity thirty-two feet deep, into which an entire scene set could be sunk. (The depth of the subterraneous pit at the present Metropolitan Opera House, 1914, is twenty-seven feet, while that at the Academy of Music is only fourteen.) At Booth's Theatre scenic effects of the most extraordinary kind were feasible, and some effects were produced there which have never been surpassed. The grandest of the scenes displayed in Booth's production of "Julius Cæsar" were

JULIUS CÆSAR

those representing the Senate Chamber and the Forum. The former, in which the assassination was depicted, was an exceedingly beautiful reproduction, slightly altered for theatrical use, of Gérôme's marvellous painting of that terrible spectacle. There, as elsewhere, Picture was subordinated to Acting. The approach to the dreadful climax was made with superlative skill, creative in the audience of fervent interest and almost breathless suspense, and culminative in a perfectly electrical tumult of emotion. Every part of the tragedy received equally thoughtful, competent, and effective treatment. The most poetical of the scenes were those of the Orchard of *Brutus* and the apparition of the *Ghost of Cæsar,* in both of which the atmosphere was sombre and weird, a sense being imposed by them of mysteriously impending peril. I remember, particularly, as one of the most perfectly poetical illusions of reality ever created on the stage the picture of that shadowy garden and the sinister forms of the conspirators when all action was suddenly arrested by the admonition, "Peace! count the clock," and far away the bell struck three.

The persons represented in "Julius Cæsar," thirty-five in number, as designated in the standard Library Editions of Shakespeare, are set down in the following order, and with the appended nomenclature and description:

Julius Cæsar.
Octavius Cæsar, ⎫ Triumvirs,
Marcus Antonius, ⎬ after the
M. Æmil. Lepidus, ⎭ Death of Cæsar.
Cicero, ⎫
Publius, ⎬ Senators.
Popilius Lena, ⎭
Marcus Brutus, ⎫
Cassius,
Casca,
Trebonius, ⎬ Conspirators Against Julius Cæsar.
Ligarius,
Decius Brutus,
Metellus Cimber,
Cinna, ⎭
Flavius, ⎫ Tribunes.
Marullus, ⎭
Artemidorus, A Sophist of Cnidos.
A Soothsayer.
Cinna, a Poet.
Another Poet.
Lucilius, ⎫
Titinius,
Messala, ⎬ Friends to Brutus and Cassius.
Young Cato,
Volumnius, ⎭
Varro, ⎫
Clitus,
Claudius, ⎬ Servants to Brutus.
Strato,
Lucius,
Dardanius, ⎭
Pindarus, Servant to Cassius.
Calphurnia, Wife to Cæsar.
Portia, Wife to Brutus.

Edwin Booth's stage version of the play omits *Cicero, Publius, Marullus, Artemidorus,* the poet *Cinna* and *Another Poet, Lucilius, Messala, Young Cato, Volumnius, Claudius,* and *Dardanius.* The name of *Servius* is a stage-manager's coinage, given to the servant of *Antony,* who brings *Antony's* message to the Conspirators, after the murder of *Cæsar.*

Some interesting changes in the cast were made in the course of the run of "Julius Cæsar" at Booth's Theatre. On February 19, 1872, Junius Brutus Booth, Jr., Edwin's elder brother, succeeded Lawrence Barrett, as *Cassius.* On March 4 Edwin Booth acted

JULIUS CÆSAR

Cassius and William Creswick appeared as *Brutus*. On March 11 Creswick played *Cassius,* Bangs assumed *Brutus,* and Edwin Booth presented *Antony.* Thus Edwin Booth was seen in all three of the great characters of the tragedy.

EDWIN BOOTH AS *BRUTUS* AND *ANTONY.*

Booth acted all sorts of parts when he was in California, at about the beginning of his career, and he may have acted *Brutus* there, but I have found no record of his appearance in the tragedy of "Julius Cæsar" of earlier date than November 25, 1864, when, at the Winter Garden Theatre, for the benefit of a fund for the erection of a statue of Shakespeare in the Central Park in New York, he coöperated, as *Brutus,* in a representation of that play, his elder brother, Junius Brutus Booth, Jr., appearing as *Cassius,* and his younger brother, John Wilkes Booth, appearing as *Antony.* The occasion was interesting and the performance, though not brilliant, was earnest and commendable. Edwin Booth did not again act in the tragedy till Christmas night, 1871, when he produced it at Booth's Theatre. From that time onward he retained *Brutus* in his regular repertory, and he acted that noble Roman many times, with splendid ability and great success.

The agonizing conflict proceeding in the mind of *Brutus*,—a high-principled, conscientious, just, and noble person,—impelled to an act which he believes imperative for the public good, yet as to the rectitude of which he is unsure, runs, like a pervasive, recurrent motive, throughout the play. It is indicated in the first colloquy between *Brutus* and *Cassius;* it is fully portrayed in the prelude to the midnight meeting of the Conspirators, in the Orchard,—or, as it is usually called, the Garden,—of *Brutus,* when finally the death of *Cæsar* is determined: it shows itself in the hesitancy of *Brutus* at the supreme moment, and in his comparatively tame and ineffective speech to the populace, in the Forum; it is perceptible in the vigil of *Brutus,* in "the deep of night," at Sardis, when that "monstrous apparition," the *Ghost of Cæsar,* comes upon him and indicates his imminent doom; and finally, it is subtly implied in his farewell words to *Cassius,* so touchingly significant of his premonition of failure and death, as the inevitable consequence of a fatal action, well intended but intrinsically wrong. From first to last there is a cloud of doubt upon the mind of *Brutus.* He is first wishful to take a right course, and then doubtful whether he has taken it. "They say blood will have blood": a tyrant is slain, but the heart of his slayer is cleft by his own sword, in expiation of that mistaken act. In this way Booth comprehended the character, and in the exhibition of it, as thus conceived, he was perfect. At the beginning the trouble of his mind was shown in his care-worn face, and the cause of it was told in his simple utterance of the words "I fear the people choose Cæsar for their king!" His manner and tone in saying, "I would not, Cassius; yet I love him well," were beautiful. His delivery of the difficult soliloquy,—"It *must* be by his *death*,"—expressed afflicting mental perturbation, and his embodiment, then and thenceforward, was suffused by a lofty, pathetic solemnity. The dominant beauties of the personation were poetry of condition, massive self-poise, and gentle spirit. In the Quarrel Scene the predominating look of authority in his eyes inspired awe. He was one of the few actors ever seen in our time who, fully meeting the exigency of stage requirement, could, in the presence of an imagined spirit, make the spectator see and feel the supernatural quality of the visitation.

In his portrayal of *Antony* Booth exhibited, with exceeding skill, the graceful, refined, urbane patrician and courtier who, under the stress of personal bereavement and at a perilous crisis in public affairs, suddenly shows himself a man of deep and strong feeling and formidable character, a wily politician, and an able, dangerous demagogue. His person, features, and demeanor were exactly suited to the part. His figure was slender and symmetrical; his eager, animated countenance instantly attractive by reason of its great mobility of expression, his movement graceful, his voice deeply sympathetic. In the First Scene he made the manner of *Antony* toward *Cæsar* that of perfect suavity commingled not with servile homage, but profound respect. The tone in which he said, referring to *Cassius,* "Fear him not, Cæsar; he's not dangerous," was exceedingly gentle, and it was expressive of a self-centred mind. The massive personality beneath the placid, genial manner might have been inferred from it. Shakespeare's intent that *Antony* should be understood in this way,—as a man whose resolute will and ample capability of action are latent under a calm, even a blithe, exterior,—can be gathered from observation of the sharp contrast between what his compatriots say he is and what his conduct presently shows him to be. *Cæsar* says of him that he "loves plays" and "revels long o' nights." *Brutus* remarks that "he is given to sports, to wildness and much company." *Cassius* designates him "a brawler and a reveller." In the end he is the victor. *Brutus* and *Cassius,* at the beginning, however, are not ignorant of his inherent strength: to the one he is "a wise and valiant Roman"; to the other "a shrewd contriver." In the sequel he stands revealed,—politic, crafty, stern, fierce in nature, unscrupulous and treacherous as a statesman, intrepid as a soldier, a person vastly unlike the supple runner of the race, at the Feast of the Lupercal. In the representation of the tragedy the passage (Act IV., sc. 1) in which *Antony* flippantly consents that his innocent nephew shall be slain, and treacherously arranges that his associate, *Lepidus,* shall be deceived and disgraced, is omitted, so that the ignominious aspect of the character does not appear. Booth's personation emphasized all that is fine in the dramatist's conception, and left the rest in shadow. He made the manifestation of *Antony's* grief over the dead *Cæsar* that of sincere feeling, the genuine emotion of a heart-broken friend. His demeanor toward the Conspirators, after the assassination, was splendidly effective in its ingenuous assumption of candor: while *Antony's* passion of sorrow was genuine, his rage of resentment was completely dissembled. Not till he had been left alone with the corpse of *Cæsar* was the pent-up emotion of fury permitted a free way; but then, in his utterance of the prophecy of "blood and destruction," "domestic fury and fierce, civil strife," the great tragic actor liberated all his power and rose to the summit of passionate eloquence. His delivery of *Antony's* address to the multitude, when showing the wounded body of *Cæsar,* provided an exquisite illustration of the union of perfect elocution with a truly wonderful example of skill in verbal artistry. The speech, so well known and so much admired, is a model of adroit, specious, inflammatory declamation, and Booth's expert treatment of it was worthy of its felicity. His manner at first was deferential to the people. He spoke in a low tone, and as if struggling to curb emotion. He watched, without seeming to watch, the effect of every sentence. He did not assume success. The advance was gradual, the feeling cumulative. The acted grief seemed real. The performance was a triumph.

CHARACTER OF *CASSIUS*.

The method of critical study which derives from Shakespeare's portrayal of character the richest and therefore the best significance deducible from it is rational, and certainly his text warrants the ascription to *Cassius* of a commanding intellect and a virtuous aim. He is a conspirator, and the means to which he resorts for the accomplishment of his design are, intrinsically, criminal; but he is a conspirator in the service of the most sacred of all causes, Human Liberty, and the means that he chooses are chosen only because there is no alternative. That is the theory of the dramatist, in the tragedy of

"Julius Cæsar." *Cassius* is an intellectual ascetic and a moral enthusiast. He has been first saddened and then embittered by looking "quite through the deeds of men." His lot has been cast in an iron age. He sees a tyrant, holding unlimited sway over his country, and he feels that,—in the circumstances which exist,—the tyrant must be slain in order that the liberty of the country may be saved. His large, unselfish, inspiring motive is not a merely personal one. To himself his purpose is humanitarian and righteous, the noblest purpose that a patriot can pursue. *Cassius,* as drawn in this play, is the emblem, incarnate, of bitter, burning deadly animosity toward imperial despotism as a principle in the government of mankind. The conclusion to which he arrives, and on which he acts, is the same that is reached by the more judicial, magnanimous, compassionate *Brutus,* a man entirely unimpassioned and of the loftiest integrity,—the friend whom he loves and venerates, and by whom,—as it is important to remember,—he is dearly loved. "It must be by his death," says *Brutus,* long meditating on the despotic attitude of *Cæsar.* In this conviction these erring patriots concur; upon it they proceed: and in the end both of them atone for their error by a violent death. *Cassius* possesses one practical advantage over *Brutus:* that he sees things as they are, and not as they should be.

The life of *Antony* is spared, against his judgment,—for the Conspirators an obvious mistake; against his judgment *Antony* is allowed to make his fatal address to the Populace; against his judgment the battle is fought on the plains of Philippi: " 'Tis better that the enemy seek us" is wise counsel, given by him, but overruled by *Brutus,* to whom, out of respect and affection, he defers. *Brutus* incarnates grandeur of mind, rectitude of principle, virtue of intention, purity and beauty of life. As to Shakespeare's meaning, in the portrayal of that character, there can be no doubt. For the right comprehension of *Cassius* it is essential to consider the estimate of him that is spoken by *Brutus,* over his dead body, and almost in the hour of his own death:

"Thou last of all the Romans, fare thee well!
It is impossible that ever Rome
Should breed thy fellow! Friends, I owe more tears
To this dead man than you shall see me pay.
I shall find time, Cassius, I shall find time."

EDWIN BOOTH AS *CASSIUS.*

Edwin Booth's embodiment of *Cassius* was remarkable for beauty and nobility of aspect and demeanor, and for the magnetic quality of the feeling by which it was animated and which it continuously diffused. There was, about this actor, a charm of personality,—

the magic of genius. When he was on the scene he absorbed attention, and when he left it the thought of the spectator followed him. The spirit of his *Cassius,* without ceasing to be poetically refined, was wild, impetuous, violent, vindictive,—as if inspired more by loathing of the tyrant than by hatred of tyranny. A part of his make-up was a close-fitting wig of curly, gray hair. His figure was slender, and in the Roman dress seemed tall. His face, cleanshaven, was thin, pallid, and expressive of deep and wasting thought. His elocution, at all times correct and mellifluous, was, in this part, singularly trenchant. As a whole the achievement impressed by brilliancy of expression more than by moral grandeur of ideal,—without which the character is lessened in esteem.

LAWRENCE BARRETT AS *CASSIUS*.

Lawrence Barrett's personation of *Cassius* possessed every constituent of the character as it is drawn by Shakespeare, and it was a consummate work of art. The figure was gaunt; the face pale and haggard; the dark eyes, stern and gloomy in expression, seemed ablaze with inward light; the hair, which had been dark, was thin and almost entirely white; the voice was clear, copious, penetrating, instinct with fervent emotion; the demeanor was that of enforced self-control at a high pitch of excitement; the action was at times vigilantly deliberate, at other times nervous and rapid; the passion was ever intense, but the intellect predominant, and while the man was ascetic and morally fanatical, there was in him a vein of lovely human tenderness. The appeal to *Brutus,* in the First Scene, considered merely as a piece of elocution, was, in Barrett's delivery, marvellous for variety of expression and fire of eloquence, but far transcendent of the splendid manner was the tremendous sincerity of feeling and meaning that illumined the words. In fervent bursts of passion Barrett was customarily superb, but I never knew him to surpass this feat, except on those occasions, not invariably occurrent,—because the play was often shortened in representation,—when the night Storm Scene was acted, in which *Cassius* and *Casca* meet, and their talk is about the terrific portents that threaten Rome: the opportunity there provided is great, and he greatly rose to it. At the midnight meeting of the Conspirators his vitality of fatal purpose animated the scene and the whole sinister throng, and it caused a thrilling sense of dread and terror. His advisement of the killing of *Antony*—"Let Antony and Cæsar fall together"—was spoken with such deadly earnestness as caused a shudder.

His demeanor in the Senate Scene,—at first a watchful calm, the silence of concentrated purpose, then the awful energy of the dagger thrust, and then the wild, half-joyous, half-frenzied outburst of triumph,—made and sustained a complete illusion. He was not an instant out of the character: he scarcely touched the extended hand of *Antony;* his convulsive start, when *Brutus* assented that *Antony* should speak in the funeral of *Cæsar,* and the quick, sharp tone in which he said, "You know not what you do!" and at the moment of exit his fierce turn backward toward *Antony,* as if then and there to kill him, were exactly consistent. No dramatic scene could have been made more actual in effect than the terrible scene of the assassination was made, when Lawrence Barrett and Edwin Booth acted in it. Both could perfectly maintain the appearance of deadly earnestness. In the Quarrel Scene they were about equally matched, Barrett having the advantage, as to effect, that accrues from violent passion, becoming at last spasmodically grieved and then pathetic. On both sides the art was beautifully refined. In the exchange of farewells, which the dramatist has made so touching that the spirit of it cannot be missed, while both were affecting, Barrett manifested the more acute sensibility. In Booth's manner and voice there was great solemnity; in those of Barrett great sorrow; he spoke as if possessed by dark presentiment—like a man who intuitively knows that his life is drawing to an end. From first to last his performance of *Cassius* carried the entire sympathy of his auditors, steadily maintaining anxious solicitude for his safety and success. It was, unequivocally, an achievement of genius. One cause of the sympathy that *Cassius* wins is the sentiment of pity, mingled with poignant regret, which he inspires that such a man should go wrong, should make the terrible mistake, from which his great mind ought to have saved him, of adopting bad means for the attainment of a good end,—means that, in themselves, cannot rightly be construed for anything but what they are, savage, treacherous, and wicked. It rests with the actor, however, to elicit this feeling. Barrett did so, and I remember that on the first night when Booth and Barrett played together in "Julius Cæsar" his *Cassius* bore away the highest honors of the occasion. Barrett, indeed, had before acted *Cassius,* December 27, 1870, at Niblo's Garden, E. L. Davenport being the *Brutus,* Walter Montgomery the *Antony,* and Mark Smith the *Casca;* Booth had only once, and that many years before, acted *Brutus,* and his embodiment of that part, which later became so magnificent, was not then, nor for some time afterward, matured.

JULIUS CÆSAR

J. B. BOOTH, JR.—CRESWICK.—BANGS.—MONTGOMERY.

Junius Brutus Booth, Jr. (1821-1883), appeared at Booth's Theatre, for the first time, February 19, 1872, presenting himself as *Cassius*. This actor had, at that time, been on the stage for thirty-eight years, and he possessed the advantages of long and varied experience. He was not, however, a man of genius in his profession, nor did he evince any extraordinary talent. He admired the style of Edwin Forrest, and the fact was evident in his acting that he had been influenced by it. In person he was of medium height, short and heavy. His head was unusually large, his face aquiline, and his eyes and complexion were dark. In youth he may have shown something of the Booth spirit; he did not show it in his representation of *Cassius*. He could neither "look" the part nor act it. He did the stage business which had customarily been done, including his father's action of striding with contemptuous indifference across the head of the corpse of *Cæsar*, but all that he did was mechanical. His voice was weak and hard, and he was frequently at fault in the text. In the scene of the assassination his vocalism and his action were tame, and in the Quarrel Scene the personality that he denoted was radically common. This actor was one of the many who, while useful, lack the imagination and executive capability requisite for signal achievement in the higher walks of the Drama. He acted well in the illustration of domestic themes, but he was out of place in poetic tragedy.

Creswick appeared as *Brutus,* May 8, 1872, giving a performance that was definite in ideal, precise in method, gentle in spirit, and impressive in effect. This actor was naturally dignified. His aspect was benign, his manner finely courteous. He was a scholar, and his professional training had been thorough. He lacked the quality of magnetism, but he was a master of the technical mechanism of acting. He exhibited *Brutus* as a noble gentleman, chivalrous toward *Portia,* exquisitely refined, constitutionally grave and sad, not only because perceptive of an odious social wrong which he is imperatively constrained to redress, but because of a natural propensity to brood upon the melancholy vicissitudes of human experience. He was the stoical philosopher as well as the patriot and the soldier.

Creswick's performance of *Cassius* signified comprehension of the character, but it was heavy and more laboriously vehement than naturally passionate. The splenetic temper was indicated. The form was correct, the spirit incommunicative of emotion. Creswick was a man who, had he lived in *Cæsar's* time, would have sympathized with the mind and feelings

of *Brutus,* but not with those of either *Cassius* or
Antony. He played many parts exceedingly well.
He was a fine actor and a person of exemplary virtue, known to a wide circle of friends, and honored
by all to whom he was known.

Francis C. Bangs possessed a robust person, a loud
voice, an aggressive disposition, and an intuitively
discriminative sense of character, combined with
enough of the faculty of impersonation to enable him
to give a respectable performance. As *Antony* his
action was vigorously demonstrative and his delivery
was vociferous. His method, in treatment of the
funeral oration, lacked subtlety, flexibility, and
variety, but it was forcible and effective, especially
in the simulation of *Antony's* grief when showing
the wounded body of *Cæsar.* At that point he manifested knowledge of the tradition associated with the
part which has descended from Wilks, Barry, and
Charles Kemble, in England, and Hodgkinson and
Cooper in America. His dress for *Antony,* in the
Forum Scene, was black, from head to foot,—consisting of black tights and shoes and black tunic and
toga. The black toga was correct, the other garments were not. The dress of a Roman Senator
comprised a belted tunic, of white linen, having long,
close-fitting sleeves, fringed at the wrists, and a broad
purple stripe across the breast; an ample toga, of

white woollen cloth, and leather shoes, either scarlet or purple in color. A black toga was worn, for mourning, or the toga was discarded. The *Antony* presented by Bangs was efficient,—the achievement of a mechanical actor whose experience was more ample than his ability: Bangs considered it to be sublime. The best of his performances on the New York Stage was that of the *Duke of Alba,* in Sardou's "Patrie," given at the Grand Opera House, in 1871.

Walter Montgomery—whose performance with Barrett and Davenport has been mentioned,—possessed many personal advantages: a fine figure; a handsome face, though the eyes were small; a naturally graceful demeanor; and a voice which, though neither powerful nor ample, was sympathetic and pleasing: it often failed him toward the latter part of any exacting performance. He was of a gentle, genial temperament and had a fine and well cultivated mind. Next to Edwin Booth he was the best, because the most pictorial and convincing, of the various players of *Antony* whom I have seen. He exhibited, at first, the bland courtier and complacent voluptuary, and then the resolute and dangerous man of action. He did not obtrude himself at the beginning, nor, indeed, at any time; but he kept his exact place in the picture and the action. He was, at the outset, content to please the eye. When the supreme moments for *Antony* were reached he was equal to them in force, if not always in voice. He delivered the apostrophe to the dead *Cæsar* with fervent emotion, and he vociferated the prophecy of calamitous war with all the requisite imaginative perception of impending horrors and sufferings. In his treatment of the speech over the corpse he was specious, various, and impassioned. He was a fine actor, and in his death our Stage suffered a grievous loss.

THE BOOTH AND BARRETT ALLIANCE.

Booth and Barrett formed a professional alliance, in the summer of 1886, when the former actor was visiting the latter, at his seaside home, in Cohasset, Massachusetts. The alliance was suggested by Barrett. The first Booth and Barrett season began, September 12, 1886, at Buffalo, New York, but Booth and Barrett did not act together, under this compact, till the season of 1887-'88: Barrett was the manager, and he travelled with a company of his own. "Julius Cæsar" was presented by Booth, at Buffalo, to begin the season. John A. Lane, Benjamin G. Rogers, Owen Fawcett, Edward J. Buckley, Charles B. Hanford, Minna Gale, Gertrude Kellogg, and Elizabeth Robins were members of the company. When, later, the two stars joined their forces, Booth played

SHAKESPEARE ON THE STAGE

Brutus and Barrett played *Cassius,* as they had done when at Booth's Theatre, in 1871-'72. This alliance continued, and it was a source of much pleasure and advantage to the public, till the death of Barrett,—a bereavement causing deep and lasting grief to many friends,—on March 20, 1891. Booth died, universally lamented, June 7, 1893. In the season of 1889-'90 the beautiful Mme. Modjeska was associated with Booth and Barrett.—This is one of the casts of "Julius Cæsar" as given by those actors:

Brutus	Edwin Booth.
Cassius	Lawrence Barrett.
Antony	Charles B. Hanford.
Julius Cæsar	John A. Lane.
Decius	Charles Collins.
Casca	Benjamin G. Rogers.
Octavius Cæsar	Lawrence Hanley.
Cimber	William Stafford.
Popilius Lenas	M. C. Stone.
Titinius	James Morris.
Trebonius	Frederick Vroom.
Cinna	Beaumont Smith.
Soothsayer	W. H. DeWitt.
Pindarus	Charles Koehler.
Servius	Walter Thomas.
Flavius	Melvin Field.
Lucius	Agnes Acres.
First Citizen	Owen Fawcett.
Second Citizen	Oliver Dowd.
Portia	Minna K. Gale.
Calphurnia	Gertrude Kellogg.

JULIUS CÆSAR

JARRETT AND PALMER'S PRODUCTION.—
EDWARD LOOMIS DAVENPORT.

Henry C. Jarrett and Henry David Palmer, who, for many years, were partners in theatrical management and highly influential in the field of the acted drama, revived "Julius Cæsar," December 27, 1875, at Booth's Theatre, using the scenery which had been devised for the production made by Booth in 1871, supplemented with a tableau pictorial of the pyre erected for incineration of the body of *Brutus*. This scene,—originally used in a revival of "Coriolanus" effected by William Wheatley, November 2, 1863, at Niblo's Garden, with Edwin Forrest as the arrogant patrician,—was shown before an auditorium shrouded in darkness, and the spectacle was gloomily magnificent. The play was acted 103 times in New York and many times in other cities. The cast included E. L. Davenport as *Brutus* and Barrett as *Cassius*, those performances being its chief features. Bangs was *Antony*, Milnes Levick *Cæsar*, Henry A. Weaver *Casca*, Mary Wells *Portia*, and Rosa Rand *Calphurnia*.

Davenport was a consummate artist and a marvel of versatility. Since his day no actor has been seen who could impersonate equally well *Macbeth* at one extreme, and *William*, in "Black-Ey'd Susan" at the other. His embodiment of *Brutus* was grandeur incarnate. He was suited to the part by physique and by temperament. His figure was massive, without being ponderous; his head was noble, his face expressive of thought, kindly feeling, and the sad patience which comes of long experience of the vicissitudes of fortune. He was unusually handsome, in the grand style. His features were regular, his eyes blue, and very eager and sweet in expression. His voice was copious, flexible, and, at moments of excitement, characterized by a ringing quality which was singularly affecting. His movements were marked by the involuntary ease that is an attribute of strength. His gestures were broad and fine. He completely identified himself with the character and never lapsed from it. The solidity and perfect mental poise which are the main constituents of *Brutus* were signified at the beginning simply by his presence. There was a certain melancholy abstraction in his demeanor, when listening to *Cassius,* which at once enlisted sympathy. He seemed even then the authentic image of heroic virtue foredoomed to ruin. He made the manner of *Brutus* toward *Cæsar* touchingly expressive of mental struggle between fervor of friendship and sense of imperative duty, and into the manner of *Brutus* toward *Cassius* he infused a beautiful spirit of comradeship, gentle and loving, without insipidity or any trace of ebullience. In the

Senate Scene he was magnificent in his stately bearing, dominant over all the elements of fear and horror, and his voice, exclaiming "People and Senators, be not affrighted," rang like a clarion. In the Ghost Scene, at "How ill this taper burns," his sense of the awe and dread that come upon *Brutus* was so completely assumed that it conveyed itself to his audience. No actor within my long observation has played that difficult scene more fitly or so as to cause a more thrilling effect. The embodiment, as a whole, formal, stately, sometimes, perhaps, declamatory,—for the actor was not always "in the vein,"— was true to the author's conception, impressing the mind and touching the heart: at its best it was without a flaw. The spectator of it saw the genuine Roman patrician,—born, not made,—the ideal gentleman of Shakespeare.

Much has been said in the contemporary press, and much can be heard in the talk of the day, about the alleged "artificial," "stagey," "unreal" methods of actors of "the old school." I had the good fortune of making acquaintance with the old school of actors more than sixty years ago, and I can testify that the actors of the present day, with very few exceptions, and those only such as have followed in their footsteps and preserved something of their style, are not comparable with them, in any particular.

The disparagement of them, by persons who never saw them, and who know nothing about them, is sickening nonsense. Burton, Warren, Owens, Jefferson, Wallack, Gilbert, Blake, Murdoch, Vandenhoff, Booth, Hackett, Adams,—no one of them could be matched now. No such actor as Davenport is extant. He was like the burning-glass, which concentrates every light to which it is exposed. He could act, and excel in, tragedy, comedy, melodrama, burlesque, —anything and everything. He "knew all qualities with a learnéd spirit" of the profession which he loved and adorned. He was a master of the dramatic art: "When comes there such another?" I, certainly, shall never again look upon such a noble performance of *Brutus* as was given by him, nor upon such an actor. He has gone, with so many others, the brightest spirits of a gentler age than this, the comrades of my better days,—

"And fallen into the dusty crypt
Of darkened forms and faces."

Davenport acted, as a member of the company supporting Macready, in the last engagement that was filled by that famous actor,—extending from October 28, 1850, to February 3, 1851, at the Haymarket Theatre, London. Macready's mentions of him, in his "Diary" (published in full, for the first time, in 1912), are singularly ungracious and, like some other remarks in that extraordinary medley of egotism, piety, and wrath, painfully discreditable to the writer,—a good man, cursed with a jealous disposition and a bad temper:

1850.
"November 16. Mr. Davenport very feeble and inefficient in *Othello*.
" 19. My power and spirits were affected by the wretched bad acting of Mr. Davenport's *Iago*.
1851.
"January 14. ["Werner"] Much distressed by Mr. Davenport's incorrectness in text. [Davenport played *Ulric*.]
" 27. The audience were cold, and, as Mr. Howe observed, 'slow.' But this could scarcely be otherwise, with such an atrocious stick in *Iago* as Mr. Davenport: it was really and utterly devoid of all meaning."

A sufficient comment on these ebullitions of ill nature is furnished by Bayle Bernard, who was a spectator of the acting, and a reviewer of it, throughout Macready's farewell season, and who makes this comprehensive and informing statement:

"Davenport was engaged by Mr. [Benjamin] Webster to play with Mr. Macready during the Farewell performances of that last of great tragedians; and if the fact is undeniable that at the time when public sympathy was converged on its departing favorite and every last performance proved that he was departing in his prime,—no lack of thought or fire, of force, physical or mental, being apparent in his efforts,—if, we say, it is undeniable that Mr. Davenport was able to maintain his ground beside him, and even on occasions to divide the impressions of the night, we presume we have said enough in attestation of his merits."

JOHN EDWARD McCULLOUGH.

McCullough's impersonation of *Brutus* was seen for the first time in New York, May 24, 1878, at Booth's Theatre, where he acted in association with Milnes Levick, as *Cassius,* and Frederick Warde, as *Antony.* In spirit it was noble, in demeanor majestic. The large, symmetrical figure, stately head, dignified countenance, and naturally deliberate movement of this actor combined with the equable quality of his mind and the sweetness of his temperament to make him an exceptionally fit representative of *Brutus.* He loved the part, and his performance of it was natural and beautiful. Magnanimity and gentleness are prominent characteristics of *Brutus,* and to be magnanimous and gentle McCullough had only to be himself. He was a born comrade, and while he did not in the least lessen or impair the dignity of *Brutus* in his manner toward *Cassius,* he made that manner delicately fraternal. Throughout the early part of the performance there was a well-sustained undertone of perplexity and sadness, and in the latter part of it there was suggestion of a continuous presentiment of impending calamity. A special felicity of the performance was the facial expression. When *Brutus* first entered his face was pale and thoughtful, but not yet wholly void of its natural serenity; after the assassination, when some time had passed, and he appeared in his tent, at Sardis, his face was worn and haggard, exhibiting the ravages of care and sorrow. Artistic beauties of this kind, significant of careful study and fine intuition, were perceptible in the Senate Scene,—the slight shudder, instantly repressed, with which *Brutus* shrank from touching the hand of *Cæsar,* and the effort and his horror of it when he struck the fatal blow. In the colloquy, after the quarrel, the bleak grief of his voice when he said "Portia is dead," the tender, protective act of covering with his mantle the sleeping boy, *Lucius,* and, later, the tremor of apprehension, just before the entrance of the *Ghost of Cæsar,*—as if he were vaguely conscious of something awful at hand,—were exquisite touches of art. Only once did he liberate his ample physical resources of vocalism and action, and then,—it was after the assassination, when sonority of speech and celerity of movement are imperative,—the effect was thrilling.

AT THE CINCINNATI DRAMATIC FESTIVAL.

An elaborate and opulent production of "Julius Cæsar" was effected at Cincinnati, as one of the incidents of a Dramatic Festival which occurred in that city, lasting from April 30 to May 5, 1883, several renowned actors participating in the representation, and making it important and memorable. The performance was given in a theatre of great size, called the Music Hall. The auditorium, as arranged for the occasion, contained seats for 3,785 persons, and standing-room for 1,000 more. The stage was prodigious, the proscenium opening being sixty-six feet wide and sixty-nine feet high. Imposing scenes were set for "Julius Cæsar," and besides the necessary actors 226 auxiliary persons assisted, presenting the processions, the mobs, and the military combatants. The "properties" were numerous. Everything essential was provided to enhance magnificence of display. A statue of Pompey, one of the embellishments of the Senate Chamber, cost $1,000. The scene showing "the Orchard," in which the Conspirators assemble at midnight, was one of great extent and weird beauty. It was closed by a hedge of cedar shrubbery, displaying the name *Brutus,* deftly carved in the foliage, and there was about it an air of stately affluence, mystery, and melancholy splendor, singularly in keeping with the austere and dread theme it was designed to invest and exploit. The makers of it, Messrs. Waugh and Piggott, were justly credited with having provided a masterpiece of scenic art. Another prodigious scene was a tableau, showing the Battlefield of Philippi, after the fight had ended,—a wide plain, strewn with chariot wheels, broken weapons and standards, dead men and horses; a medley of ruins; in its realism excessive; in its suggestiveness terrible to contemplate. As a spectacle the exhibition thus made was impressive and commendable, but the play was overloaded with embellishments, and, necessarily, in such a huge place, the acting was obscured and practically lost. *Brutus* was played on that occasion by John McCullough, *Cassius* by Lawrence Barrett, *Antony* by James Edward Murdoch, and *Cæsar* by Henry A. Langdon.

Murdoch was then seventy-one years old, and he could not resemble *Antony,* but he made a gallant and not wholly fruitless effort to revive the splendid fire of his youth and to animate the scene. Later, when the play was repeated, *Antony* was undertaken by Edmund Collier, an actor of respectable ability, who made the part statuesque and stentorian.

THE SAXE-MEININGEN PRODUCTION IN AMERICA.

The dramatic company,—or a considerable part of it,—from the Court Theater of the Duke of Saxe-Meiningen, making a professional visit to America, appeared, November 17, 1891, at the Thalia Theatre, New York, in the well-known and esteemed German version of Shakespeare's "Julius Cæsar" made by Augustus Wilhelm von Schlegel (1767-1845). That company had gained at home a high reputation for acting and for fidelity to detail in the setting and embellishment of the drama, and its much heralded advent in America was cordially welcomed, not only by the German but also the American audience, and the local press, with its customary obsequiousness toward foreign actors, bestowed its approbation with copious liberality.

The choice of "Julius Cæsar" as a medium for the introduction of the Meiningen Company to America proved eminently judicious. The field in which specially it excelled was that of Realism: it was strong in the display of Mobs, and for mob scenes that play provides copious opportunity. There is one for *Casca,* one for *Cæsar,* one for *Brutus,* and one for *Antony,* and toward the close there are soldiers in conflict. All the way from the festival of the Lupercal, at Rome, to the Battlefield at

JULIUS CÆSAR

Philippi, the movement implicates numerous auxiliaries, and, accordingly, there is occasion for much variety of person, stature, countenance, raiment, weapons, colors, voices, groupings, gestures,—everything that is involved in theatrical tableau and action. The stage director of the Meiningen actors improved that occasion with intelligence, taste, skill, and patient labor, —all resultant in a series of living pictures, in which, while the force of contrast was strikingly exemplified, there was complete harmony of details, the total effect being that of reality. In respect to the felicity of exhibition which results from competent stage management, the Meiningen Company justified its high repute. In other respects it proved a disappointment. The acting did not, in any particular, transcend the level of respectable mediocrity. No member of the company evinced either exceptional talent or special charm. The most effective performance was that given by Hismar Knorr, who played *Cæsar,* and who correctly simulated intrinsic egotism, austere temperament, and despotic authority. *Portia* was well played by Anna Haverland, who seemed to possess much latent emotional force. Mathier Pfeil, appearing as *Brutus,* attracted attention chiefly by excessive play of feature (which, in a native actor, would have been considered "mugging") and much responsive heaving of the chest, while listening. *Cassius,* the embodiment of concentrated intellect, was made trivial by Gustav Kober, a voluble person, in a continuous condition of fluster. *Casca,* a phlegmatic man, bluff in demeanor and blunt in speech, was made agile and explosive by Gustav Rickeit. The representative of *Antony,* Franz Tichy, elicited abundant applause by a performance completely devoid of the spirit and effect of sincerity, but pictorial and vigorous. The lack of subtle and discriminative characterization in the acting of the leading parts in the tragedy was truly surprising. *Brutus,* for example,—suiting the action to the word,—immediately before the assassination, literally kissed the hand of *Cæsar,* and *Cassius* grasped the hand of *Antony* (whom he distrusts and would slay, if not overruled) as casually as though it had been a pump-handle, in the crucial scene immediately after it. Such blunders are close denotements of imperfect study and defective art. The Meiningen actors presented a useful example of disciplined professional coöperation, but they taught nothing which was not already known, and their acting, at its best, was not in any way superior to that which had ordinarily been seen, and was then current, on the American Stage.

A realistic method of treatment, which would be inappropriate if used for the expression of a poetic ideal, is suitable to the exhibition of prosaic masses of persons, yet such treatment can easily be carried so far as to defeat itself by its profusion. A little of the Mob is sufficient. If there were nothing in the play of "Julius Cæsar" except its portrayal of the fickle, clamorous rabble of Rome it would be insufferably tedious. The Stage imparts nothing valuable when it imparts only a sense of superficial, commonplace fact. The ultimate consequence of realism in the Theatre is the impoverishment of Art. The stage manager accomplishes his best work, and all that is rationally desired of him, when he provides just enough of seeming fact to beguile and stimulate the imagination of the spectator, and impose upon the senses an illusion of truth. The lamented Planché, that eminent authority on Heraldry and Costume, was only ridiculous if, as is alleged, he stopped a dress-rehearsal of an historical play because one of the "supers" employed in it was wearing a pair of spurs of the thirteenth instead of the fourteenth century. The effect of Daly's lovely epitome of dramatic meaning in the Garden Scene of "Twelfth Night" was not in the least marred because, by chance, the moon was caused to rise in what had been indicated as the west: probably not ten persons who saw the performance ever noticed the fact. Fine scenery, correct attire, and appropriate historical properties are desirable and commendable; judicious fidelity to fact is a virtue; but it is not the body, it is the soul that conquers; not the word that gives life, but the spirit. Over all the achievements of the painter, the costumer, the carpenter, the machinist, and the stage manager, the Genius of Acting bends like a blue sky, with the sun at meridian and the earth beneath it suffused with its lustre. All that obscures the picture by over-enrichment of the frame, all that exalts embellishment at the sacrifice of meaning, is useless and hurtful.

VARIOUS LATER PRODUCTIONS.

Many presentations of "Julius Cæsar" have been made on the New York Stage, and subsequently in other American cities, within the last twenty-five years, but mostly they have been of the ordinary and conventional kind, and unsuggestive of particular remark. Embodiments of *Brutus, Cassius,* and *Antony,* set before the public by Frederick Barkham Warde, Charles Barron, Joseph Haworth, Louis James, John E. Kellerd, and Robert D. Maclean, among others, have shown ability and worthy ambition and have gained public applause. It would, however, be supererogatory to examine each of them, and of no benefit to the reader. As I review them, and many others like to them, in remembrance, I do not

From a Photograph by Lutz   *Author's Collection*

RICHARD MANSFIELD AS *BRUTUS*
"I know my hour is come."

Act V., Sc. 5

JULIUS CÆSAR

recall any instance of marked felicity in ideal or in method of art. Warde has, in a long, laborious, and honorable career, shown uncommon versatility of talent. His *Antony* was fiery, fluent, and expeditious. James, who began as a light comedian, surprised the public by his sudden revelation of capability in tragedy, and, but for his deplorable propensity to trifle with serious subjects and make light of everything, he might have gained high renown. Haworth, who had been taught by McCullough, possessed rare ability, pursued his art with ceaseless, glowing fervor, accomplished much, but died in the morning of his fame. Barron, an actor finely gifted by Nature and matured by ample professional experience, often played the noble Roman, and could worthily exemplify the thoroughness of style peculiar to the old school in which he was trained: he began acting as long ago as 1850. Much might be said of all those players, and of others who have striven and toiled in the difficult pathway of artistic emulation; but there must be a limit, somewhere, even to the most liberal commemoration and critical commentary, and numerous inconspicuous performances which have been given, in the tragedy of "Julius Cæsar," are therefore only indicated here, as among the ordinarily creditable endeavors of talented and worthy actors. European Continental performers, visiting America, have seldom presented themselves in this play. A pictorial, intelligent, finely finished, splendidly effective personation of *Antony* was given by the distinguished German actor Ludwig Barnay.

RICHARD MANSFIELD.

Mansfield produced "Julius Cæsar," October 14, 1902, at the Grand Opera House, Chicago, acting *Brutus* for the first time, and on December 1, following, presented the play in New York, at the Herald Square Theatre. The cast, at first, included Barry Johnstone as *Cassius,* Arthur Forrest as *Antony,* Arthur Greenaway as *Cæsar,* W. H. Denny as *Casca,* Dorothy Hammond as *Portia,* and Maude Hoffman as *Calphurnia:* later the representative of *Cassius* was superseded by Joseph Haworth,—a judicious choice for that exacting part. The play was elaborately and well mounted and richly dressed. Some of the scenes and costumes were selected from those designed by Alma-Tadema for Henry Irving's production of "Coriolanus," at the London Lyceum, April 15, 1901, and they were appropriate and beautiful. It is an interesting fact in the history of "Julius Cæsar" on the stage that Mansfield presented it throughout the entire theatrical season of 1902-'03, and that, although his impersonation of *Brutus* was, by various censors, severely and even bitterly condemned, his production of that play was the most profitable one that he ever made. Salient characteristics of his performance were dignity, authority, intense feeling, the self-absorption of a man whose sense of duty is fanatical, and the pathetic outward calm which covers, without wholly concealing, grief, remorse, and vague apprehension. His depiction of conflict in the mind,—the painful struggle between restraining doubt and impelling duty,—was impressively faithful. In the turmoil subsequent to the assassination his distracted aspect was pitiful, the more so that he signally expressed the tremendous effort of *Brutus* to quell the commotion and vindicate the awful sacrifice. His treatment of the Ghost Scene was novel: a weird, ominous voice was heard, but the spectre remained invisible except to himself. There were other impersonations by Mansfield which more fully revealed and more explicitly determined the quality of his genius and the felicity of his art; but his embodiment of *Brutus* signally exemplified the warmth and scope of his imagination and his exceptional capability to grasp a poetic ideal and make it actual. In the Death Scene of *Brutus* he was exceedingly pathetic, an image of moral grandeur, ruined and desolate.

ROBERT BRUCE MANTELL.

Mantell acted *Brutus* for the first time, November 26, 1906, at the Academy of Music, New York: Cecil Owen acted *Cassius,* Francis McGinn *Antony,* Alfred Hastings *Cæsar,* and Marie Booth Russell *Portia.* Mantell's impersonation of *Brutus,* noble in aspect, refined in style, intense in feeling, and continuously sustained, was signally expressive of the melancholy isolation and haunted loneliness of a highly intellectual man who, perplexed by conflicting motives and blinded by moral enthusiasm, sheds the blood of a fellow creature, and thereafter lives on, grief-stricken and anxious, however resolute, in the vague, troubled consciousness of an impending retributive doom. In the Orchard Scene his denotement of mental conflict was painfully true and his management of the difficult soliloquy,—for an actor the most exacting single passage in the play,—remarkably expert. In the midnight meeting with the Conspirators his dignity, simplicity, and solemnity of demeanor imparted to the scene an awful sense of sinister purpose and of danger. His wild passion, with difficulty controlled, immediately after the assassination, was splendidly effective, and his delivery of the address of *Brutus* to the Roman populace,—a speech so much more notable for sober reason than for persuasive eloquence,—was made electric with a tremendous passion of earnestness: in this latter respect his method differed from that of other actors who have played the part within my remembrance, the almost invariable custom having been to match the barren calm of the words with an equally barren calm of manner. The effect was an instant surge of real emotion in his audience before the curtain, as well as the prescribed emotion of the multitude behind it. In that part of the Tent Scene which follows the quarrel between *Brutus* and *Cassius,* and which is the more difficult part of it, because of its draft upon tender sensibility and upon haunted imagination, he rose to his full stature as a tragedian. It was when slowly becoming aware of the chill and dread presaging supernatural apparition that he wrought his finest effect,—that of seeming to feel, and making the spectator feel, an emotion of awe and terror. At all points his performance, after he had given it a few times, was adequate, but at this point it was superb. Among the tragedians of the period,—who are few,—Mantell is the best. He has strength, poise, authority, a commanding figure, an expressive voice, which though worn is still sympathetic and of wide compass, sensibility, exact knowledge of art, and ready command of its resources. His level speaking is melodious and finely expressive, and he can sustain himself at a high pitch of simulated excitement, never losing self-control. He is unequal and, particularly in playing *Brutus,* I have known him, for the sake of effect on "the groundlings," to substitute vehemence for true feeling, and to close the Tent Scene with an almost hysterical outcry to his officers, "Go and commend me to my brother Cassius," etc., and then almost collapse, embracing *Lucius* and vociferating "My boy! my boy!!" But such flaws and starts are unusual with him. His performance deservedly ranks among the highest achievements in tragedy that have been seen on the contemporary Stage.

WILLIAM FAVERSHAM'S PRODUCTION.

A specially important revival of "Julius Cæsar," memorable by reason of much of the acting that vitalized and graced it, was effected by William Faversham, who produced the play October 7, 1912, at Toronto, Canada, and presented it, November 4, following, at the Lyric Theatre, New York,—subsequently making a tour with it, throughout the country. Faversham appeared as *Antony;* Tyrone Power, and, later, Burton Churchill and then Robert D. Maclean, appeared as *Brutus;* Frank Keenan, and, later, Edwin Arden as *Cassius;* Fuller Mellish as *Cæsar,* Julie Opp as *Portia,* and Jane Wheatley as

Calphurnia. My views of the performance, as given in New York, have been recorded in my "Lives of the Players: I.—Tyrone Power," and I cannot do more justice to the subject than by here reprinting salient portions of them:

The version of the tragedy presented by Faversham follows the text of Edwin Booth's "Prompt Book," but is disfigured by some injudicious restorations, excisions, and innovations, made by himself. A usual managerial error is here again exemplified,—that in reviving a Shakespearean play novelty of treatment is imperative. That notion is as foolish as a search would be for new sunlight to illumine the marbles of Michael Angelo. The essential requirement in presenting a Shakespearean play is Dramatic Art,— the capability of assuming, exhibiting, and making actual the massive and complete ideals of character in which that marvellous writer has delineated the whole of human nature. Great *Acting* is the originality that should be sought,—not the paltry novelty of a restoration of needless lines or the introduction of crotchets of stage business. . . . Experience has proved the wisdom of closing the Assassination Scene with *Antony's* passionate, prophetic speech, when left alone with the corpse of *Cæsar.* Faversham not only restored the unnecessary colloquy between the *Servant* and *Antony,* but introduced the widowed

Calphurnia, distracted in speechless grief, in order to make a picture. The effect was that of anti-climax. The Quarrel Scene between *Brutus* and *Cassius* was seriously marred by the expedient of showing both the men in armor. The meeting of *Brutus* and *Cassius* at Sardis,—in the play as written, —occurs in front of the Tent, into which they enter, and then their colloquy ensues. In representation in the modern Theatre a far finer effect is caused by showing *Brutus* in his Tent, attired as a military officer naturally would be when resting, and causing *Cassius,* who comes at the head of his horsemen, to enter, precipitately, in full martial accoutrement, impatiently and injudiciously ejaculating his impetuous anger. The calm majesty of *Brutus,* subduing but not concealing a noble resentment, and the fiery wrath of *Cassius* are contrasted in that scene, and the force of the contrast would be heightened by dissimilarity of their garb. Bigoted deference to tradition is foolish, but customs which have been tried and proved should not be lightly discarded. Innovation merely for the sake of seeming to be novel is unwise.

In the Apparition Scene as treated by Faversham the part of *Brutus* is foolishly subordinated to the part of the *Ghost* and to the mechanical trick of the appearance of that phantom. The time is midnight. *Brutus* is trying to compose his mind by reading, before,—in his own phrase,—he shall "niggard the necessity of nature with a little rest." The intention of the scene is to impart that chill of dread which, in superstitious belief, widely prevalent in the time when Shakespeare wrote and not yet entirely extinct, always accompanies ghostly visitation. *Brutus,* an imaginative man, of sensitive temperament, becomes vaguely and fearfully conscious of a strange influence, a preternatural presence, and, in stage representation, as he looks up from his book he should see the *Ghost of Cæsar* before it is seen by the spectators in the theatre, and his face should be visible to them, in order that they can see and feel the effect produced on him by the apparition. In Faversham's arrangement of the scene *Cæsar's Ghost,* unspiritual and commonplace, appears at the rear of the stage, behind *Brutus,* who, accordingly, must turn his back toward the audience, in order to see it. No atmosphere of awe and terror, such as the poet designed, could possibly be created under those conditions, and Power, as *Brutus,* did not, because he could not, cause the thrilling effect which otherwise he might have produced. . . .

Faversham, as *Antony,* merited admiration. His athletic person is exactly suited to the part. His manly bearing and buoyant, cheery aspect, in the Lupercal

Scene, were exactly consonant with those of *Antony*. His passion, in the lament over the dead *Cæsar,* was completely simulated and truly pathetic. His simplicity and candor, in the plausible compact with the Conspirators, were thoroughly well assumed, and the lapse that *Antony* makes into grief and lamentation was expertly managed, so as to cause the effect of natural conduct. His utterance of the wild and terrible prophecy of "blood and destruction" was fluent, vociferous, and fraught with fiery energy, and he spoke the blank verse with unexpected felicity of modulation. That passage is, for *Antony,* the most exacting in the play, since it is a climax which must surpass the preceding climax of the assassination of *Cæsar* and must augment an excitement already hysterical.

Faversham's delivery of *Antony's* funeral speech was skilfully diversified by expressive changes of tone and of facial expression, together with an expert use of inflection, gesture, and pause. The exposition of actual sorrow permeated by artifice was, indeed, specially ingenious, and the use of the expedient of transparency (by which an actor shows the capability of seeming to be one thing to his associates on the scene and simultaneously the same and yet a different thing to the spectators in the theatre) was adroit and highly effective. The personation somewhat

JULIUS CÆSAR

lacked inherent patrician quality, and at moments the actor evinced an inappropriate peculiarity of deportment which might almost be called supercilious. All the same, his performance of *Antony* proved a delightful surprise,—an extraordinary effort, a worthy and auspicious achievement, and it has met with general commendation.

Frank Keenan is an actor of marked ability, proved many times and in many characters, but not in Shakespearean tragedy and not in any form of poetic drama,—to which, indeed, he has, as *Cassius,* shown himself to be unsuited, alike in mental quality, person, voice, and style. . . . The person presented as *Cassius* was crack-brained, malignant, turbulent, addicted to bombastic utterance and fantastic gesticulation, a "plug-ugly," and a spouter. Concentration of mind, for which *Cassius* is remarkable, was indicated, and therein lay the chief merit of this performance; but the actor was abrupt and harsh where he should have been fervidly passionate; spasmodic where he should have been intense; slow where he should have been torrentially swift; artificial where he should have been pathetic; and his rough delivery of Shakespeare's verse marred its melody. *Cassius* is fanatical in his love of freedom and hate of tyranny, and fiery in temper, but those facts afford no warrant for gyration and bluster in the stage representative of him. . . .

Perhaps some notion of being what is called "natural" in treatment of a poetic part may have prompted Keenan's singular exhibition of mistaken judgment and erratic procedure. He exhibited great energy, earnestness, and force, but nearly everything he did was wrong and overdone, and there was no definite, fixed purpose apparent in his wild gesture and feverish prodigality of exertion and vociferation. His exuberant and empirical conduct not only marred his own part in the tragedy, but to some extent embarrassed his associates. . . .

The stage-management of the two essential scenes, for *Brutus,* in Faversham's revival was extraordinarily bad: had it been deliberately intended to "kill" the performance of *Brutus* it could not have been more ingeniously harmful and wrong. Faversham is known,—and he is known to be a generous, sympathetic actor, incapable of envy and the meanness that envy inspires. The fact remains, however, that the Garden Scene, in his production, as shown in New York, was so restricted by badly devised scenery, and so obscured by bad lighting, as to lay a disheartening and needless blight on the actors in it, and especially on Power. The Tent Scene, which ought to occupy the whole stage, and which assuredly should be so illuminated that, in the Quarrel, every variation of expression, every look, should be visible, was set as,

From a Photograph by Sarony, N. Y.   Author's Collection

WILLIAM FAVERSHAM AS ANTONY

"*Stay, ho! and let us hear Mark Antony!*"

Act III., Sc. 2

From a Photograph by White, N. Y.   Author's Collection

TYRONE POWER AS BRUTUS

"*I do fear the people
Choose Cæsar for their king.*"

Act I., Sc. 1

practically, a front-scene,—there being only about eight feet between the back drop and the footlights; and moreover it was crowded and cluttered and so dimly lit that, except for persons in the foremost seats, much of the facial expression of Power and Keenan was absolutely invisible. . . .

The choice of Power for *Brutus* proved eminently wise and fortunate. His impersonation of the noblest Roman was a triumphant success. It does not possess the melancholy beauty and the perfect elocution that made Edwin Booth's *Brutus* a marvel of acting, but it is true to the poet's conception, it is saturated with the actor's strong and original personality, it is characterized by inherent and potent charm, and, while duly observant of good tradition, it is not, in any particular, an imitation. Power was seen to possess qualifications, both mental and physical, admirably fitting him for the part of the illustrious conspirator,—commanding stature, stately demeanor, deliberate movement, an expressive countenance, an intense and acutely sensitive temperament, a deep, resonant, melodious voice, the involuntary repose which accompanies strength, and the mental self-possession which can maintain complete control over passionate feeling.

In *Brutus,* with whom deliberation is temperamental, a certain uniformity of bearing is not only appropriate but essential. Except at the climax of the Assassination, at that of the Ghost Scene, and momentarily in the Quarrel, his massive reticence is steadily preserved. Monotony of style, therefore, is not a detriment to Power's assumption of this character. His natural dignity and observant, anxious calm, in the opening conversation with *Cassius* and *Casca,* indicated, at the outset, his perception of the quality of the part. His revealment of the tortured mind of *Brutus,* wherein patriotism contends with friendship, in the Garden Scene, was truthful and deeply touching,—although the meditative soliloquy ("It must be by his death," etc.) had been ruthlessly cut and practically spoiled. He rose splendidly from watchful self-restraint to wild, passionate excitement at the culmination of the Senate Scene. His stern predominance and flickering anger, in the Quarrel Scene, were finely illuminative of the character, and in the parting scene between *Brutus* and *Cassius* he touched the heart by spontaneous expression of that deep tenderness, that humanity, and that unaffected, lovely, winning simplicity which no man can show who does not possess those qualities. His excellence in the pathetic passages was unequivocal.

INDEX

NOTE

*This Index, though not as comprehensive and minute as I wish it were, and as it would be if space permitted, contains more than 7,000 references, and it should meet all usual requirements of an index. It is, for convenience, arranged in four divisions,—*ACTORS AND THEATRICAL MANAGERS; CHARACTERS, *in Plays and Novels;* TITLES, *and* MISCELLANEOUS SUBJECTS.

W. W.

INDEX

ACTORS AND THEATRICAL MANAGERS

A

Abbott, William (1789-1843): as *Orsino*, in "T. N.," 27; as *Romeo*, 127-128.
Abbott, Mrs.: 47.
Abington, Mrs. Frances (Miss Fanny Barton: 1739-1815): as *Olivia*, 20; on Mrs. Siddons, 238.
Actresses: first on B. S., 112.
Adams, Edwin (1834-1877): as *Mercutio*, 163; 606.
Adams, Maude (Kiskadden: 1872-19—): as *Juliet*, 189, *et seq.*
Addison, Edward Philip (1808-1874): acts *Sir Toby Belch*, 40.
Addison, Laura (Miss Wilmshurst: 1822-1852): acts *Juliet*, 130.
Alexander, Sir George, kt. (1858-19—): acts *Orsino*, 34.
ALLEN, VIOLA (Mrs. Peter Duryea: 1867-19—): produces "T. N.," 76; her production of that play considered, 76-83; her performance of *Viola*, 80-82; mentioned as *Imogen*, 81; stricken while acting *Viola*, 82.
ANDERSON, MARY ANTOINETTE (Mrs. Antonio de Navarro: 1859-19—): presentment of "R. & J." by, 123; 136; 150; 165; revival of "R. & J." by, described and considered, 172, *et seq.*; her *Juliet* censured by C. Scott, 176; her *Juliet* described and analyzed, 176-179; presents "A. Y. L. I." at Stratford, 293, *et seq.*; as *Rosalind*, described and considered, 295-301.
ANGLIN, MARGARET (Mrs. Howard Hull: 1876-19—): produces "T. N.," 93; her production of, and version of, "T. N.," considered, 95-106; her dress, as *Viola*, 97; her personal appearance as, and performance of, *Viola*, 98; arrangements of Shakespeare's plays by, 101; produces "A. Y. L. I.," 313; her production of that play, and her performance of *Rosalind*, described and considered, 313-315; produces "T. T. of T. S.," 335; as *Katharine*, 536-538.
Armin, Robert: 46; actor of *Fools* or *Clowns*—acted *Feste*, in "T. N."(?), 13.
Atchmet, Mrs. (Miss Egan): 144; as *Juliet*, 145.

B

Bangs, Francis C—— (1834-1908): as *Antony*, in "J. C.," and his dress as, 599-600.
Bannister, John (1760-1836): as *Sebastian*, in "T. N.," 21; as *Malvolio — Mercutio — Gratiano,* — as *Walter*, in "Children in the Wood," 25.
Barnay, Ludwig (1842-19—): acts *King Lear,* and his performance of, 467-469; acts *Antony* in "J. C.," 468; the same, in London, 573; as *Antony*, 618.
Barrett, George Hooker (1794-1860): 45; acts *Sir Andrew Aguecheek*, 49.
BARRETT, LAWRENCE P. (1838-1891): acts *Sebastian*, in "T. N.," 50; 60; 160; 183; acts *King Lear,*
Barrière, Henry (th. man.): 47.

450; his *King Lear* considered, 450-451; representative performances of, and his quality as an actor, 451-452; his *Cassius,* 565; 584; as *Cassius,* 593-596; alliance of, with Booth, 601; 603; 611.

Barrow, Julia Bennett (Mrs. Jacob Barrow): acts *Viola,* 49; quality of, and first appearance of, in America, 59; as *Viola,* 60.

BARRY, SPRANGER (1719-1777): acts *Romeo,* 114; leaves D. L.—his *Romeo,* 115-117; 118; enamored of Miss Nossiter, and his *Romeo* to her *Juliet* described—marries Mrs. Dancer, 142; 143; 160; his *King Lear* described and considered, 360-365; as *Romeo*—as *Othello,* 361; his quality as an actor, 364; his sense of Garrick's superiority, 365; 392; as *Antony,* in "J. C.," 561-562.

Barry, Mrs. Spranger (Anne Street, Mrs. Dancer, Mrs. Barry, Mrs. Crawford: 1733-1801): as *Viola,* 20; marriage with Barry, 142; acts *Juliet,* 143; as *Rosalind,* 234-235.

Barrymore, William (Bluett: died, 1846): acts *Orsino,* in "T. N.," 27.

Bateman-Hunter, Leah (1892-19—): acts *Olivia,* in "T. N.," 91; her performance of that part, 93.

Bayfield, St. Clair: as the *Sea Captain,* in "T. N.," 88.

Beerbohm-Tree, Sir Herbert, kt. (1853-19—): bad stage business introduced by, in "T. N.," 106; produces "J. C."—acts *Antony,* and his performance of, 573-574; qualities of, as an actor, 573.

Bellamy, George Anne (1733-1788): acts *Juliet,* 115; her performance of that part, 116-170.

Bellew (Higgin), Harold Kyrle (1845-1911): acts *Romeo,* 158; his performance of, 184-185; *Voysin* his best personation, 185.

Bensley, Robert (died, 1817): as *Malvolio,* 20; the same, 21; the same, 22-23; as *Brutus,* 558.

Beringer, Isme: as *Romeo,* 200.

Bernard, John (1756-1828): on Bensley, 23; on Edwin, 24; 157.

BETTERTON, THOMAS (1635-1710): 15; as *Sir Toby Belch,* in "T. N.," 15-16; ment. as *Mercutio* in "R. & J.," 17; 18; 111; dress of, as *Mercutio,* 119; 120; as *King Lear,* 351-353; no *proof* that he acted Shakespeare's *King Lear,* 353; 418; as *Brutus,* 552-553; 555; 558; 560.

Betterton, Mrs. Thomas (Mary Saunderson: 1637-1712): 15; 112.

Blagden, ———: 15.

Blair, John (18—-19—): acts *Malvolio,* 55; the same, 76; his performance of *Malvolio,* 77-78.

Blake, William Rufus (1805-1863): acts *Malvolio,* 48; excellence of his acting—characters of, mentioned—his performance of *Malvolio,* 50; 55; 606.

Blanchard, William: acts *Feste,* in "T. N.," 26; acts *Sir Andrew Aguecheek,* 27; 45.

Bland, ——— (brother of Mrs. Jordan): as *Sebastian,* in "T. N.," 22.

Blind, Eric: as *Petruchio,* 538-539.

Boheme, Anthony (died, 1731): personal appearance of, and his performance of *King Lear,* 356-357.

Booth, Agnes (Marion Agnes Land, the second Mrs. Junius Brutus Booth, Jr., Mrs. John B. Schoeffel: 1847-1910): as *Juliet,* 166.

BOOTH, BARTON (1681-1733): as *King Lear,* 354-356; epitaph by, 553; as Brutus, 556-557.

BOOTH, EDWIN THOMAS (1833-1893): " R. & J." presented by, 123; 152; 161; as *Romeo,* described, 162; his opinion of his *Romeo,* 165; 166; 170; restores Shakespeare's "K. L.," 446; his *King Lear,* 445-450; Tennyson on his *King Lear,* 449; treatment of insanity by, in "K. L.," 460; last appearance of, 462; 464; as *Pe-*

INDEX

truchio, in "K. & P.," 506; 508-509; art of, 509; 570; his production of "J. C." described, &c., 580-584; his stage version of "J. C.," 584-585; acts *Brutus, Cassius,* and *Antony,* 585; as *Brutus,* 585-587; as *Antony,* 587-590; as *Cassius,* 592-593; alliance of, with Barrett, 601; 603; 606.

Booth, John Wilks (1839-1865): acts *Antony,* in "J. C.," 585.

BOOTH, JUNIUS BRUTUS (1796-1852): as *King Lear,* 393-395; 403; as *King Lear,* 435-436; 460; as *Cassius,* 569-570; acted *Antony,* in "J. C.," and as Payne's *Brutus,* 570.

Booth, Junius Brutus, Jr. (1821-1883): 166; succeeds Barrett as *Cassius,* 584; 585; his *Cassius,* and his rank, 597-598.

Booth, Mrs. (Hester Santlow): acts *Rosalind,* 232.

Booth, Sally (1793-18—): acts *Viola,* 27.

Bosworth, Hobart (18—-19—): notable performance of *Charles, the Wrestler,* in "A. Y. L. I.," by, 278-280.

Bourchier, Arthur (1863-19—): quarrels with Daly, and place taken by C. Clarke, 72.

Boucicault, Ruth Holt (18—-19—): as *Olivia,* in "T. N.," 102; 103.

Bowman, Jacob (died, 1737): as *Caius Ligarius,* in "J. C.," 554.

Bracegirdle, Anne (1663-1748): 555.

Brady, William A—— (1865-19—): 462.

Brereton, William (1741-1787): acts *Romeo,* 144; the same, 146.

Brougham, John (1810-1880): acts *Sir Toby Belch,* and quality of his performance of, 54.

Buckstone, John Baldwin (1802-1879): 45.

Bulkley, Mrs. (Mrs. Barresford: died, 1792): as *Viola,* 21.

Burbage, Richard (1568?-1619): first actor of *Romeo,* 111; dress of, as *Romeo,* 119; acts *King Lear,* 351; first player of *Brutus*(?), 549.

Burton, William Evans (1804-1860): his production of "T. N.," 48, *et seq.;* as *Sir Toby Belch,* and compared with J. E. Owens, 49; 50; 59; 78; 606.

Busley, Jessie (Mrs. Ernest Joy: 1869-19—): acts *Maria,* in "T. N.," 91.

C

Calhaem, Stanislaus: acts *Feste,* in "T. N.," 34.

Calvert, Charles (1828-1879): Miss Faucit acts for benefit of, 246.

Calvert, Louis (1859-19—): acts *Sir Toby Belch,* 91; 92; 93.

Campbell, Mrs. Patrick (Beatrice Stella Tanner; Mrs. Cornwallis West: 1865-19—): acts *Juliet,* 136; her performance of, 137-138.

Carlyle, Francis (18—-19—): acts *Orsino,* 72.

Carlyle, Sybil: 72.

Cavendish, Ada (Mrs. Frank Marshall: 1847-1895): as *Juliet,* 167-168.

Chapman, Thomas (died, 1747): as *Touchstone,* 327.

Cibber, Colley (1671-1757): description of Underhill by, 17; 129; acts *Jaques,* in alteration of "A. Y. L. I.," 232; 551; 552; 555; 560.

Cibber, Jane: plays *Juliet,* 113.

Cibber, Theophilus (1703-1758): alters "R. & J."—plays *Romeo*—appearance of, 113; on Garrick and Barry as *King Lear,* 363.

Cibber, Mrs. Theophilus (Susanna Maria Arne, 1714-1766): acts *Juliet,* 114; leaves D. L., 115; her *Juliet,* 116-117; 118.

Clarke, Creston (1865-1910): takes Bourchier's place—acts *Orsino,* in "T. N.," 72; 193.

Clarke, George (1844-1906): acts *Malvolio,* 55; his performance of that part, 57; acts *Malvolio,* 64; his performance of, 69; 72; as *Jaques,* 276; as *Petruchio,* 527.

CLIVE, MRS. KITTY (Catherine Raftor: 1711-1785): as *Olivia*, in "T. N.," 18; the same, 20; her dressing of "chambermaids," 121; acts *Celia*, in first recorded restoration of "A. Y. L. I.," 233; 235; Davies on—Dr. Johnson on, 236; acted *Rosalind—Celia—Portia*—ambition of, 283; as *Katharine*, in "K. & P.," 498-499.

COGHLAN, CHARLES F. (1842-1899): as *Mercutio*, 138; as *Orlando*, 263-264; his *Jaques*, 321; described and considered, 318-319.

Colas, Stella (Mme. Stella de Corvin): as *Juliet;* 150-151; acts at Shakespeare tercentenary celebration, 151.

Coleman, John (1832-1904): on C. Cushman's *Romeo*, 210; on Miss Faucit as *Rosalind*, 249.

Collier, James W.: acts *Romeo*, and other parts, 160.

Collins, Cecil, as *Feste*, in "T. N.," 87.

Colman, George, the Elder (1732-1794): his alteration of Tate's "K. L.," 373.

Compton (Mackenzie), Edward: acts *Malvolio*, 55; his performance of that part, 57.

Conway, William Augustus: as *Romeo*, 127.

Conway, Mrs. Frederick Bartlett (Sarah E. Crocker: 1834-1875): as *Romeo*, 204.

COOKE, GEORGE FREDERICK (1756-1812): as *King Lear*, 391-392; his best parts—early popularity of, 391; saw Garrick and Barry as *King Lear*, 392; 403.

Coombs, Jane (Mrs. F. A. Brown): acts *Olivia*, in "T. N.," 49.

COOPER, THOMAS ABTHORPE (1776-1849): as *Brutus*, *Cassius*, and *Antony*, 577-578.

Coquelin, Benoit-Constant (1841-1909): as *Petruchio*, 529-530; 535.

Couldock, Charles Walter (1815-1898): 211.

Craig, John (18—-19—): acts *Orsino*, in "T. N.," 72; his performance of that part, 76-77; manages Castle Square Theatre, Boston, 77.

Cranch, Mrs.: as *Olivia*, in "T. N.," 21.

Crane, William Henry (1845-19—): as *Sir Toby Belch*, 53-54.

Crawford, Mrs. *See* Barry, Mrs. Spranger.

Crawley, John: as *Sir Andrew Aguecheek*, 87-88.

Creswick, William (1814-1888): as *Brutus*, 580; the same, 598; as *Cassius*, 598-599.

Crosman, Henrietta (Mrs. Maurice Campbell: 1865-19—): acts *Celia*, in "A. Y. L. I.," 275; as *Rosalind*, 311-313.

Currier, Frank: acts *Sir Andrew Aguecheek*, 76; his performance of, 79.

CUSHMAN, CHARLOTTE SAUNDERS (1816-1876): acts *Viola*, 45; restores "R. & J.," 129; 155; acts *Romeo*, 200; her *Romeo* described and considered, 205-211; "The London Times" on her *Romeo*, 207; J. S. Knowles on her *Romeo;* G. Vandenhoff on, 209; J. Coleman on, 210; her male characters, 211.

Cushman, Susan (Mrs. James Sheridan Musprat: died, 1859): acts *Olivia*, in "T. N.," 46; studies with her sister—first appearance of—marries Dr. Musprat, 206.

D

DALY, AUGUSTIN (1838-1899), (theatrical manager and dramatist): 53; his Shakespearean revivals, 62; revivals of "T. N.," 63, *et seq.;* best presentment of "T. N.," 64; methods of, 65, *et seq.;* his defence of omission of Dungeon Scene, in "T. N.," 68-69; 74; 75; 76; 77; manages Booth's Theatre, 165; 241; Shakespearean plays produced by—his company in 1869-'70, 260; his revivals of

INDEX   637

"A. Y. L. I." described and considered, 260-283; his stage version of "A. Y. L. I.," 267; death of, mentioned, 277; 505; 506; his revival of "T. T. of T. S.," and his stage version of, described and considered, 511-516; 531; 616.

Dancer, Mrs.: *see* Barry, Mrs. Spranger.

Davenant, Sir William (1605-1668): his company at the Duke's Theatre, 15; 17; 547; 548.

Davenport (Hoyt) Adolphus ("Dolly" Davenport: 1831-1873): 59.

Davenport, Mrs. Adolphus: *see* Weston, Lizzie.

Davenport, "Mrs.": as *Viola*, 15.

DAVENPORT, EDWARD LOOMIS (1815-1877): as *Mercutio*, 198; his performance of *Jaques*, 318; acts *Brutus*, and the performance described and analyzed, 603-606; versatility of, 603-604; acts with Macready—disparagement of, and refuted, 606-608.

Davenport, Fanny Lily Gypsy (1850-1898): as *Viola—Nancy*, in "Oliver Twist"—*Lady Teazle*, 60; as *Maria*, in "T. N.," 64; as *Rosalind*, 263.

Davidge, William Pleater (1814-1888): acts *Sir Toby Belch*—his artistic range—his performance of *Sir Toby*, 52; acts *Malvolio*, 55; his performance of, 56; acts *Sir Toby*, 64; as *Touchstone*, 329.

Davies, Thomas (also theatrical historian and biographer: 1712-1785): as *Feste*, in "T. N.," 21; 117; on Mrs. Clive, 236; on the Quarrel Scene, in "J. C.," 543; 551; 554; 563.

Davies, Mrs. Thomas (died, 1786): 15.

Dean, Julia (Mrs. Arthur Hayne, Mrs. James Cooper: 1830-1866): 171.

de Cordoba, Pedro (1881-19—): as *Orsino*, in "T. N.," 102.

Delane, Dennis (died, 1750): as *Brutus*, 556.

Denin, Susan (1835- —): as *Romeo*, 204.

Devlin, Mary (the first Mrs. Edwin Thomas Booth: 1840-1863): acts *Juliet* to *Romeo* of C. Cushman, 211.

Dixey, Henry E. (1859-19—): acts *Malvolio*, 52; his performance of, 56-57; acts *Malvolio*, 72.

Dodd, James William (173 -1796): as *Sir Andrew Aguecheek*, 20; the same, 21; described as *Sir Andrew*, 24-25; 45.

Downes, John (prompter, and first historian of the English Stage): "T. N." mentioned by, 15; 233; 351; 353; 550; 551.

Dowton, William (1766-1851): as *Feste*, in "T. N.," 25; first time as *Malvolio*—as *Falstaff*—as *Sir Peter Teazle*—his acting, 26.

Drew, John, Jr. (1853-19—): 45; acts *Orlando*, 275; as *Petruchio*, 527.

Dunlap, William (1766-1839) (th. man, and first historian of the Am. S.: 1832): on Mrs. Jordan's *Viola*, 21; on Palmer and Dodd, in "T. N.," 24; 253; 254; 255; on Hodgkinson, 576.

Dunstall, John: as *Sir Toby Belch*, 20.

Durang, Mrs.: acts *Maria*, in "T. N.," 48.

Dyott, John (1812-1876): acts *Sir Andrew Aguecheek*—and qualities of his acting, 54-55.

E

Edgar (Biddle), George (18—-18—): trains Margaret Mather, 181.

Edwin, John (1749-1790): as *Sir Andrew Aguecheek*, 21; the same, 24.

Elliott, Maxine (Mrs. George A. McDermott, the third Mrs. Nathaniel Cheever Goodwin: 1871-19—): 72.

Elliston, Robert William (1794-

1831): as *Romeo*, 127; acts *Romeo*, 146.
Emery, John (1778-1822): acts *Sir Toby Belch*, 2; the same, 27.
Emery, Winifred (Mrs. Cyril Maude: 1862-19—): acts *Olivia*, 34.
Entwhistle, Mrs.: acts *Olivia*, in "T. N.," 218.
Esten, Mrs. (Miss Bennett): acts *Juliet*, 145.

F

Farren, Elizabeth (Countess of Derby: 1759-1829): acts *Olivia*, 24.
Farren, William (1791-1861): acts *Malvolio*, and quality as an actor, 27; 28; acts *Malvolio*, 39.
FAUCIT, HELENA (Lady Theodore Martin, 1820-1898): as *Juliet*, 129; opinion of "R. & J.," 148; as *Juliet*, 149-150; as *Rosalind*, 245-249; her range, and quality of, as an actress, 246, *et seq*.
Faversham, William (1868-19—): as *Romeo*, 188; produces "J. C.," 622; his production of "J. C." described and considered, 623-625; his *Antony*, 625-627.
Fawcett, John (1769-1837): acts *Feste*, in "T. N.," 27.
Fechter, Charles Albert (1824-1879): 285.
Field, B. A.: as *Sir Toby Belch*, 87.
Finn, Henry J. (1790-1840): acts *Sir Andrew Aguecheek*, 47.
Fisher, Charles (1816-1891): acts *Malvolio*, 49, 50; first appearance in America—acts *Malvolio*—his artistic range, 51; 55; 57; acts *Malvolio*, 64; acts *Romeo*—and *Mercutio*, 159; as *Jaques*, 264-265.
Fisher, David (1806-1887): acts *Sir Toby Belch*, 34.
FORBES-ROBERTSON, SIR JOHNSTON, kt. (1853-19—): 123; as *Romeo*, 136-137; plays *Romeo* in first recorded "open-air" performance of a Shakespearean play, 337; as *Orlando*, 331.
Forbes-Robertson, Norman (Norman Forbes: 1859-19—): acts *Sir Andrew Aguecheek*, 34; the same, 62.
FORREST, EDWIN (1806-1872): 160; 170; acts *King Lear*, 437; his version of "K. L.," 437-439; his performance of *King Lear*, 439-444; 460; as *Antony*, in "J. C.," 578; 597; acts *Coriolanus*, 603.
Frohman, Charles (1860-19—): designation of "Ben" Greet's method by, 87; 185; production of "R. & J." by, described and considered, 187, *et seq*.

G

Gale, Minna K. (Mrs. Archibald C. Haynes: 1869-19—): acts *Juliet*, 183.
GARRICK, DAVID (1718-1779): 18; alters, and produces, "R. & J.," 114; acts *Romeo*—his performance of, 115-117; anecdote of, and C. Macklin, 117; anecdote of, and Mrs. Bellamy, 118; his dress for *Hamlet*—for *Macbeth*, 119; 120; 126; 129; acts *Romeo*, 143; 160; 173; as *Mercutio*, 196, 199, 282; his *King Lear* described and considered, 358-360; quality as actor, and as man, 364; farewell of, 365; 392; 414; his dress as *King Lear*, 417; 434; 442; his study of *King Lear*, 455; alters "T. T. of T. S.," 496, *et seq.*; 514; 531; planned to act *Cassius*, and never appeared in "J. C.," 560; his stage dresses, and acts *Antony*, in "A. & C.," 560-561.
Gibbs, Anne: as *Olivia*, 15; 17; acts *Maria*, in "T. N.," 27; the same, 28.
Gilbert, John Gibbs (1810-1889): 600.
Glover, Mrs. (1782-1850): 27.
Gottschalk, Ferdinand (1865?-19—): acts *Sir Andrew Aguecheek*, 91; his performance of, 93-95.
Green, Mrs.: acts *Olivia*, 28.
Greenstreet, Sidney (1880-19—): as *Sir Toby Belch*, 102; 103; as *Bi-*

INDEX 639

ondello, in "T. T. of T. S.," 538-540.
Greet, "Ben" (18—-19—): revives "T. N.," and acts *Malvolio*, 83; introduced "Everyman," to Am. S., 84; his "Elizabethan method" considered, 84-87; his production of "T. N." considered, 87-88; his performance of *Malvolio*, 88-89.
Gresham, Herbert (18—-19—): 45; as *Touchstone*, 277.
Griffiths, George H. (1822-——): acts *Malvolio*, 55; his performance of, 56; 62.

H

Hackett, James Henry (1800-1871): 205; 606.
Hackett, James Keteltas (1869-19—): as *Mercutio*, 189.
Hading, Jane (Jeannette Hadingue: 1859-19—): as *Katharine*, in "T. T. of T. S.," 529.
Hallam, Isabella (Mrs. William Mattocks: 1746-1826): as *Olivia*, 20; 21; as *Juliet*, 144.
Hallam, Lewis, Sr. (17—-after 1794): 253; 433.
Hallam, Lewis, Jr. (1736-1808): acts *Romeo*—acts *Mercutio*, 156; 433; 575.
Hallam, Mrs. Lewis (Miss Tuke, Mrs. David Douglass: died 1773): acts *Olivia*, 47; acts *Juliet*, 156.
Handyside, Clarence (18—-19—): acts *Sir Toby Belch*, 76; his performance of, 78-79.
Hanford, Charles Barnum (1859-19—): acts *Mercutio*, 187.
Harley, John Pritt (1786-1858): acts *Feste*, in "T. N.," 40; 46; 415; costume of, as *Kent*, in "K. L.," 418.
Harper, Miss: as *Olivia*, 21.
Hart, Charles (died, 1683): quality of—and as *Brutus*, 550-551.
Hartley, Mrs. Elizabeth (died, 1824): as *Olivia*, 20.
Harris, Henry (——-——): mentioned, 15; as *Sir Andrew Aguecheek*, 15-16; mentioned as *Romeo*—and as *Cardinal Wolsey*, 16; 45; as *Mercutio*, 112; dress of, as *Romeo*, 119.
Harwood, John E. (1771-1809): acts *Sir Toby Belch*, 47.
Haworth, Joseph (1855-1903): acts *Malvolio*, 55; the same, 89; acts *Romeo*, 190; 616; as *Cassius*, 617; same, 618.
Heath, Caroline (Mrs. Wilson Barrett: 1835-1887): 130.
Heminge, John (1556-1630): acted *Sir Toby Belch*(?)—original of *Falstaff*, 13.
Henderson, John (1747-1785): Kemble's opinion of, in *Shylock*—plays *Malvolio* first time, 21; Genest's opinion of, 21; as *King Lear*, 386-387.
Henry, John (died, 1795): 156; 253; 254; 575.
Henry, Mrs. John: acts *Viola*, 47; acts *Juliet*, 156.
Herbert, Sidney (18—-19—): as *Touchstone*, and notable range of, 277.
Hill, Charles John Barton (1830-1911): acts *Malvolio*, 55; his performance of, 56; 313.
Hill, James M.: produces "R. & J.," 179.
HODGKINSON, JOHN (1767-1805): acts *Romeo*, 156; acts *Jaques*, 254; as *Jaques*, 321; as *Antony*, in "J. C.," and personal appearance of, 576.
Hoey, Mrs. John (Josephine Shaw: 1824-1896): as *Viola*, and quality of her acting, 55.
Holden, "Mrs." (at D. L.: 1663): 15.
Holman, Joseph George (1764-1817): acts *Romeo*.
Howard, Edward, acts *Feste*, in "T. N.," 76; his performance of, 79.

I

IRVING, SIR HENRY, kt. (original name, John Henry Brodribb: 1838-1905) (also theatrical manager): as *Malvolio*, 32-35; produces "T. N.," 33; 104; presentment of "R.

& J." by, 123; his production of "R. & J." considered, 130-133; as *Romeo*, 132; 174; his commendation of Miss Faucit's conception of *Rosalind*, 248; 402; acts *King Lear* — performance of — alleged "change of conception," 427-432; anecdote of, and Mellish, 538; 618.

J

Jackson, A. W. ("Black Jackson," th. man.): 59.
Jackson, John (historian Scotch Stage): 144; 145.
Janauschek, Mme. (Francesca Romana Magdalena Janauschek, Mrs. Frederick Pilot: 1834-1904): as *Jaques*, 340.
Jarrett and Palmer, theatrical managers (Henry C. Jarrett: 1827-1903—Henry David Palmer: died 1879): manage Booth's Theatre, 165; their production of "J. C." described and considered, 603-608.
Jefferson, Joseph (*Rip Van Winkle*: 1829-1905): 20.
Jefferson, Thomas (founder of the Jefferson Family of Actors: 1728-1807): 20.
Jennings, "Mrs.": 15.
Jennings, Mrs. (Clara Simpson, Mrs. Daniel C. Kingsland): as *Rosalind*, 261.
Jewett, Henry (18—-19—): acts *Malvolio*, 55; performance of, 83.
Johnson, John (1759-1819): acts *Sir Andrew Aguecheek*, 47; acts *Adam*, in "A. Y. L. I.," 255.
Johnson, Mrs. D.: acts *Viola*, 26.
Johnson, Mrs. John (Miss Ford: 1770-1830): acts *Viola*, 47; quality of her acting, and as *Viola*, 58; acts *Juliet*, 156; first player of *Rosalind* in N. Y., 254; 255.
Jones, Mrs. W. G. (Miss Wagstaff, Mrs. J. M. Cooke: 1828-1907): as the *Nurse*, in "R. & J.," 188; as *Romeo*, 202.
JORDAN, DORA, "Mrs." (Dorothea Bland: 1762-1816): 19; first acts *Viola*, 21; as *Sir Harry Wildair*— her artistic method—Boaden and Reynolds on her acting—*Viola* to her brother's *Sebastian*, 22; 23; 24; 25; 39; as *Viola*, compared with Ellen Tree, 40; 44; acts *Juliet*, 146; 234; as *Rosalind*, 238-240; superior to Mrs. Siddons as *Rosalind*—and Boaden on, 240.

K

KEAN, CHARLES JOHN (1811-1868): married to Ellen Tree, 41; as *Romeo*, 127; as *Mercutio*, 196; produces "K. L.," and acts *King Lear*, 425-427.
KEAN, EDMUND (1787-1833): as *Romeo*, 125-127; effect of his acting on Byron, 126; 149; 208; as *King Lear*, 393-395; quality of, and rank as actor, 396, *et seq.*; quality of, as actor, 402; 403; 435; 460; 561.
Keeley, Robert (1794-1869): acts *Sir Andrew Aguecheek*, 40.
Keenan, Frank (18—-19—): acts *Cassius*, 622; his performance of, 627-628.
Keene's: Laura Keene's Varieties Theatre, 49.
KEMBLE, CHARLES (1775-1854): as *Romeo*—as *Mercutio*, 125; *Romeo* to his daughter's *Juliet*, 157; 197; as *Antony*, in "J. C.," 564; same, 566.
Kemble, Mrs. Charles (Anne Theresa Decamp: 1774-1838): acts *Olivia*, 27.
KEMBLE, FANNY (Frances Anne Kemble, Mrs. Pierce Butler: 1810-1893): as *Juliet*, 127; on W. Abbott's *Romeo*, 128; as *Juliet*, 147-148; *Juliet* to her father's *Romeo*, 157; as *Juliet* to Ellen Tree's *Romeo*, 199; *Juliet* to Miss Cushman's *Romeo*, 211.
KEMBLE, JOHN PHILIP (1757-1823): his opinion of Henderson's *Shylock*, 21; 22; 23; dresses of, 121; as *Romeo*, 125; revives "A. Y. L. I.," 242; his acting version of "A.

INDEX 641

Y. L. I."—and his license as an adapter of Shakespeare, 243; as *Orlando*, 329-330; his alteration of "K. L.," 373; as *King Lear*, 388-391; Scott on, 389; his supreme excellence, 390; 396; as *Petruchio*, in "K. & P.," 501; Roman parts of—and acts *Brutus*, 563; his *Coriolanus*—and development and effect of his *Brutus*, 564-565.

Kemble, Mrs. Stephen (Eliza Satchell): acts *Juliet*, 146.

Kenna, Mrs.: first player of *Rosalind* in N. Y., 253; 254.

Kennedy, Charles Rann (1871-19—): as *Orsino*, 88.

Kilner, Thomas: acts *Sir Toby Belch*, 47.

King, Thomas (1730-1805): as *Malvolio*, 20; as *Touchstone*, 328.

Knight, Edward: as *Sir Andrew Aguecheek*, 26.

Knowles, James Sheridan (1783-1862): on C. Cushman's *Romeo*, 208; 209; 210.

Kynaston, Edward (1640-1706): quality of—and as *King Henry the Fourth*—as *Julius Cæsar*, 551-552.

L

Ladnowski, Boleslaw: acts *Romeo*, 171.

Lang, Matheson (1879-19—): acts *Orsino*, 91; his performance of, 93.

Langtry, Mrs. Lillie (Emily Charlotte Le Breton, Mrs. Edward Langtry, Mrs. Hugo de Bathe, Lady de Bathe: 1852-19—): as *Rosalind*, 289-290.

Leclercq, Carlotta (Mrs. John Nelson: 1838-1893): as *Rosalind*, 285-286.

Leclercq, Charles (died, 1895): as *Antonio*, in "T. N.," 72.

Leclercq, Rose (Mrs. Mellish: 1845-1899): acts *Olivia*, 34.

Leslie, Elsie (Elsie Leslie Lyde, Mrs. [William] Jefferson Winter: 1880-19—): produces "T. T. of T. S.," acts *Katharine*, etc., 530-533.

Lester, Mr. *See* Wallack, Lester.

Levick, Milnes (died, 1896): as *Edmund*, in "K. L.," 465; 603.

Lewis, Catherine (Mrs. Donald Robertson: 18—-19—): as *Maria*, in "T. N.," and quality of, 71-72.

Lewis, Mrs. Henry (Miss Harvey: died, 1854): as *Romeo*—and acts other male parts, 201.

Lewis, James (1838-1896): acts *Sir Toby Belch* in "T. N.," 52; the same, 69; his quality as an actor, and his performance of *Sir Toby* considered, 70-72; as *Touchstone*, 276.

Liston, John (1777-1846): as *Malvolio*, 27.

Long, "Mrs.": 15.

Lovell, Thomas: as *Malvolio*, 15-16.

Lowin, John (1575-1658): 549.

M

McCullough, John Edward (1832-1885): acts *Romeo*, 167; critical judgment regarding, etc., 452; quality, etc., and first acts *King Lear*, 453; his *King Lear*, 454-461; death of, 462; as *Brutus*, 608-609; 610; 617.

Macklin, Charles (M'Laughlin: 1690-1797): as *Malvolio*, 18; as *Malvolio*—*Shylock*—*Sir Pertinax Macsycophant*, mentioned, 19; anecdote of, and Garrick, 117; 125; 143; 358; on Garrick's *King Lear*, 359.

Macklin, Maria (1733-1781): as *Juliet*, 143-144.

Maclean, Robert D. (Shepherd): produces "R. & J.," 186; as *Romeo*, 187; acts *Brutus*, 617.

Macready, William Charles (1793-1873): as *Romeo*, 128-129; acts *Jaques*, 244; 245; 248; 249; 250; 262; his restorations of "K. L.," 374; 387; 395; as *King Lear*, 397-402; refuses to act *King Lear*, 397; how led to restore "K. L.," 398; opinion of, regarding the *Fool* in "K. L.," 399; the acting of

402-404; 422; 423; 424; 552; his views on *Brutus,* 566; as *Brutus,* 567; as *Cassius,* 567-569; 571; farewell engagement of, 606; disparagement of Davenport by, and refuted, 607-608.

Malone, John (1854-——): as *Jaques,* and anecdote of, 313.

MANSFIELD, RICHARD (1854-1907): as *Brutus,* 618-619.

MANTELL, ROBERT BRUCE (1853-19—): as *Romeo,* 170; acts *King Lear,* 462; his performance of that part described and considered, 462-465; version of "K. L.," used by, 464; as *Brutus,* 620-622.

MARLOWE, JULIA (Sarah Frances Frost—Fanny Brough—Mrs. Robert Taber—Mrs. Edward Hugh Sothern: 1867-19—): first time as *Viola,* 89; her *Viola,* 89-90; presentment of "R. & J." by, and E. H. Sothern, 123; her *Juliet* described and considered, 190-192; appears in "R. & J." with Sothern, 192, *et seq.;* as *Rosalind,* 303-305; produces "T. T. of T. S.," with Sothern, 533; as *Katharine,* 534.

Marshall, "Polly": acts *Maria,* in "T. N.," 49.

Martin, John G. (1770-1807): acts *Malvolio,* 47.

MATHER, MARGARET (Margaret Finlayson, Mrs. Emil Haberkorn, Mrs. Gustav Pabst: 1859-1898): performance of *Juliet* by, described and considered, 179, *et seq.*

Mathews, Charles James (the Younger: 1804-1878): 45; 50; 59.

Matthison, Edith Wynne (Mrs. Charles Rann Kennedy: 18—-19—): acts *Viola,* 83; introduced to America in "Everyman," 84; her performance of *Viola,* 88.

Mattocks, William: 144.

McVicker, Mary F. (Miss Runnion, the second Mrs. Edwin Thomas Booth: 1849-1881), as *Juliet,* 164.

Meadows, Drinkwater (1795-1869): acts *Malvolio,* 40.

Medbourne, Matthew: 15.

Mellen, Miss: as *Maria,* 25.

MELLISH (HAROLD) FULLER (1865-19—): acts *Sebastian,* in "T. N.," 35; acts *Malvolio,* 55; as *Malvolio,* 102; 103; his performance of, considered, 104, *et seq.;* his *Jaques* described and considered, 316-317; anecdote of, and Irving, 538; acts *Julius Cæsar,* 622.

Merry, Mrs. (Anne Brunton, Mrs. T. Wignell, Mrs. W. Warren 1769-1808): acts *Juliet,* 157.

Milton, Maud (1859-19—): acts *Olivia,* 62.

MODJESKA, MME. HELENA (Helen Opid, Mrs. Gustave S. Modrzejewska, Mrs. Charles [Karol] Bozenta Chlapowska: 1840-1909): acts *Viola,* first time—and mentioned as *Isabella,* in "M. for M.," 61; personal appearance of, as *Viola,* and her performance of that part, 61-62; as *Juliet,* 136; 150; as *Juliet* closes Booth's Theatre, 165; her *Juliet* described and analyzed, 171-172; 177; as *Rosalind,* 291-293; plays *Juliet,* in first recorded "open-air" performance of Shakespearean play, 337; associated with Booth and Barrett, 602.

Mohun, Major Michael: 551.

Montesole, Max: as *Grumio,* in "T. T. of T. S.," 538-540.

MONTGOMERY, WALTER (Richard Tomlinson: 1827-1871): acts *Romeo,* 151; as *Orlando,* 330-331; as *Antony,* in "J. C.," 600-601.

Mosley, John: 15.

Mossop, HENRY (1729-1773): as *King Lear,* 365-366; death, and burial of, 366; acts *Brutus*—and as *Cassius,* 562.

Mountfort, William (1659-1692): murdered, &c., 554.

Mowatt, Mrs. (Anna Cora Ogden, Mrs. James Mowatt, Mrs. William F. Ritchie: 1819-1870): acts *Juliet,* 200.

INDEX 643

Munden, Joseph (1758-1832): as *Malvolio,* 26.

Murdoch, James Edward (1813-1893): acts *Romeo,* 159; acts *Antony,* in "J. C.," 570; 606; 611.

N

NEILSON, LILIAN ADELAIDE (Elizabeth Ann Bland, Mrs. Philip Lee: 1846?-1880): acts *Viola,* 39; mentioned as *Juliet,* 41; her "consummate impersonation" of that part, analyzed and described, 41-45; her dress as *Viola*—mentioned as *Juliet,* 43; 57; Ada Rehan acts with, in "T. N.," 73; 150; an English girl, 151; her *Juliet* described and analyzed, 151-155; 165; 177; as *Rosalind,* 284-285.

Nelson, John (1830-1879): acts *Romeo,* 151.

Noakes, James (right name Noke; died about 1692): 15.

Nossiter, Miss: enamoured of Barry, and her *Juliet* to his *Romeo,* 142.

Novelli, Ermete (1851-19—): as *King Lear*—and his rank and ability as an actor, 478-480; produces "T. T. of T. S.," and as *Petruchio,* 535.

O

O'Brien, William: as *Sir Andrew Aguecheek,* 20.

O'Neill, Eliza (Lady Wrixon Becher: 1792-1872): as *Juliet,* 127; 129; as *Juliet,* 147.

Owens, John Edmond (1823-1886): likened to Burton, 49; 78.

Owen, William Florence (1844-1906): acts *Sir Toby Belch,* 52; his performance as, 53; 62; acts *Sir Toby* with Daly's company, 72.

P

Palmer, John (1742-1798): as *Sir Toby Belch*—as *Sebastian,* in "T. N.," 20; as *Sir Toby,* 21; the same, 24-25; as *Brutus,* in "J. C.," 558.

Parker, Amelia: acts *Olivia,* 50.

Parsons, William (1736-1795): as *Feste,* 21; 46.

Payne, John Howard (1792-1852): 28.

Pepys, Samuel (1632-1703): his "Diary," mentions of "T. N." in, 14; Harris characterized by, 16.

PHELPS, SAMUEL (1804-1878): presents "T. N.," 28; his *Malvolio,* 28-30; stage business of, as *Malvolio,* 106; restores "R. & J.," 129; as *Mercutio,* 130; the same, 197; on Mrs. Nisbett, and Miss Faucit, as *Rosalind,* 249-250; produces "K. L.," and acts *King Lear,* 421-425; 426; restores "T. T. of T. S.," and acts *Sly,* 504-505; as *Sly,* 504-505; as *Brutus,* and as *Cassius,* 571-572; death of, mentioned, 572; 573.

Piercey, Samuel: acts *Romeo,* 168.

Placide, Henry (1800-1870): acts *Feste,* in "T. N.," 48, 50.

Plympton, Eben (1853-19—): as *Romeo,* 179.

Ponisi, Mme. (Elizabeth Hanson: 1818-1899): as *Romeo,* 204.

Pope, Mrs. (William) Coleman (died, 1880): as *Romeo,* 204.

Possart, Ernst, Ritter von (1841-19—): as *King Lear,* 476-478.

Potter, Mrs. (Cora Urquhart, Mrs. James Brown Potter: 1859-19—): as *Juliet,* 185.

Powell, Charles Stuart: opened theatre in Boston, 47.

Powell, George (1658-1714): as *King Lear,* 353-354.

Powell, Snelling (1758-1821): 47; as *Romeo,* 158.

Powell, Mrs. Snelling (Miss Harrison: 1774-1843): 47.

Powell, William (1735-1769): as *King Lear,* 386.

Power (Frederick) Tyrone (1869-19—): acts *Brutus,* 623; his performance of, 628-630.

Price, Joseph: 15.

Prince, Adelaide (Mrs. ———

——, Mrs. Creston Clarke: 1866-19——): acts *Olivia*, 72.
Pritchard, Hannah (Miss Vaughan: 1711-1768): as *Viola*, 18; acts *Lady Capulet*, in "R. & J.," 143; acts *Rosalind* in first recorded restoration of "A. Y. L. I.," 233; the original *Katharine*, in "K. & P.," 498.
Pritchard, Miss: as *Juliet*, 143.

Q

Quick, John (1747-1831): as *Sir Andrew Aguecheek*, 20.
Quin, James (1694-1766): 23; 115; qualities of, and as *King Lear*, 357; 556; as *Brutus*, 557.

R

Raymond, Emiline (Mrs. G. F. Marchant: died, 1858): acts *Viola*, 49.
Raymond (O'Brien), John T. (1836-1887): 78.
Redmund, William (18——-19——): as *Mercutio*, 186.
Rees, Alys: as *Olivia*, 87.
REHAN, ADA (Ada Crehan: 1860-19——): 19; her impersonations of *Katharine* and *Rosalind* characterized, 63; mentioned as *Rosalind*—as *Katharine*—first acts *Viola*, 73; her performance of *Viola*, 73-75; her performance of *Rosalind*, 265; the same, described and considered, 271-275; chief associates of, in "A. Y. L. I.," 275-280; superiority of her *Rosalind*, 302; highest achievements of, 426; delivery of speech, as *Katharine*, 515; her *Katharine*, 520-527; qualities in the acting of, 525; 531.
Richards, ——: 15.
Riche, ——: his "Apolonius and Silla," 8.
Rich, John (1692-1761): embellishment of "R. & J." by, 115.
Richman, Charles (J.): as *Orlando*, 278; as *Petruchio*, 528.
Riddle, George: as *Antonio*, in "T. N.," 88.

Rigby, ——: acts *Romeo*, 156.
Rignold, George (1838-1912): 60; acts *Romeo*, 167.
Robinson, Henry Crabb (1775-1867): description of "T. N." in German by, 35; 238.
Robinson, Frederick Charles Phelps (1830-1912): 130.
Robinson, Mrs. (Mary Darby, "Perdita": 1758-1800): 21; 121; acts *Juliet*, 144; as *Rosalind*—and significant friends of, 236.
Robson, Stuart (1836-1903): as *Sir Andrew Aguecheek*, 53-54.
Ross, David (1728-1790): acts *Romeo*, 124.
Rossi, Ernesto (1829-1896): as *Romeo*, 168-169; acts *King Lear* in America, and professional associates of, in "K. L."—his *King Lear* considered, 465-467.
Rowe, George Fawcett (1834-1889): 78.
Russell, Annie (Mrs. Eugene Presbey, Mrs. Oswald Yorke: 1864-19——); acts *Viola*, 91; her performance of, 92.
Ryder, John (1815-1885): acts *Antonio*, in "T. N.," 40; acts *Cassius*, 569.

S

SALVINI, TOMMASO (1829-19——): 170; acts *King Lear*, 469; rank and quality of, 469-470; his *King Lear* described and considered, 470-473; his "grandest performance," as *King Saul*, described and considered, 473-476; 480.
Sandford, Samuel: 15.
Saunderson, Mary: *see* Betterton, Mrs. Thomas.
Schancke, John: 13.
Schlegel, William Augustus von (1767-1845): translated "T. N.," 35; translation of "J. C." by, 612.
Scott-Siddons, Mrs. (Mary Frances Scott-Siddons [Mr. Scott-Siddons' name was Canter, but he changed it to Scott-Siddons]: 1844-1896): acts *Viola*—her performance of—

INDEX

and personal appearance, 64; as *Rosalind,* 260-262.

Seebach, Marie (Mrs. Niemann: 1837-18—): acts *Juliet,* 165; produces "T. T. of T. S.," in German, and acts *Katharine,* 510.

SHAKESPEARE, WILLIAM (1564-1616): one of actors in first performance of "T. N.," 3; 4; regarding question of his knowledge of foreign languages, 6; belief that he was acquainted with "Gl' Ingannati," 7; age of, when he wrote "T. N.," 8; 11; his disregard of laws of form, 12; 13; testimony as to early popularity of his plays, 14; 22; 24; 40; 41; his *Clowns* or *Fools,* 46; 62; 69; plays of, on the modern stage, Dr. Johnson on, 68; methods of acting his plays in his own time, 83; 85; 86; 95; First Folio of, 101; "modern" spirit in treatment of his plays, 106; actor at Curtain Theatre, 108; First Folio of, 110; 111; 113; customs of stage dressing in time of, 118; 119; 123; 125; 126; 129; 130; 133; 140; 142; 143; tercentenary celebration of birth of, 151; 168; 174; 189; 200; 206; 212; 213; scene of boyhood "exploration and adventure," 216; 217; poetry "incidental and natural" with—temperament of, discernible, 219; 222; characters in "A. Y. L. I." invented by, 223; motives and methods of, in his work, 224, *et seq.;* mood of, in "A. Y. L. I." 226; feeling of, toward *Rosalind,* 227; tradition of, acting *Adam,* 228-230; popularity of, and editions, of his writings, 231; two plays of, mangled by Dryden, 232; 236; 245; 247; 265; 268; 270; plays of, in which musical embellishment is required, 280, *et seq.;* 284; 290; 293; 294; 308; taste in time of, and purity of, as a writer, 309-311; prompted to write "King Lear," 344; 345; 346; 347; 348; 352; 353; "Tatefication" of, 366; 367; 368; 369; 390; 416; 417; 418; 420; 434; 436; Forrest on, 437; 444; 466; 469; 473; 479; 481; his authorship of "T. T. of T. S.," etc., discussed, 482-493; residence of, and of relatives of, 490-492; 494; 496; 497; 502; 503; 504; 511; 512; 514; 515; scope and quality of his characters, 516, *et seq.;* 517; 526; 530; 531; 535; 539; 540; 590; 592; 605; 612.

Shaw, Mrs. (Eliza Ann Marian Trewar, Mrs. Thomas Sowerby Hamblin: died, 1873): rank of, and first appearance in America, performs *Viola,* 58-59; as *Romeo,* 201-202; as *Rosalind,* 255-256.

Sheppy, Thomas: 15.

Sheridan, Thomas (1721-1788): 556; as *Brutus,* 557.

SIDDONS, MRS. WILLIAM (Sarah Kemble, 1755-1831): as *Juliet,* 145; 155; as *Rosalind,* 237-238; inferior to Mrs. Jordan as *Rosalind,* 240; Boaden on—Mrs. Clive on, 302; as *Katharine,* in "K. & P.," 501.

Singleton, John: acts *Mercutio,* 156.

Skinner, Otis (1858-19—): acts *Romeo,* 182; as *Petruchio,* 528.

Smith, Mark, Sr. (1829-1884): acts *Feste,* in "T. N.," 49; as *Friar Lawrence,* in "R. & J.," 163; as *Casca,* in "J. C.," 596.

Smith, William (died, 1696): 15; as *Edgar,* in "K. L.," 553.

Smith, Mrs. W. H. (Miss Riddle: died, 1861): acts *Maria,* in "T. N.," 50.

SOTHERN, EDWARD HUGH (1859-19—): acts *Malvolio,* 55; same, 89; his performance of, 90-91; presentment of "R. & J." by, and Julia Marlowe, 123; appears in "R. & J." with Miss Marlowe, 192; as *Romeo,* 193; as *Jaques,* 304-305; produces "T. T. of T. S.," with Miss Marlowe, 553; his *Petruchio,* 534.

Spiller, William: acts *Feste,* in "T. N.," 47.

Stirling, Mrs. Edward (Fanny Hehl, stage name, at first Fanny Clif-

646 INDEX

ton, 1816-1895): as the *Nurse*, in "R. & J.," 131.
St. John, Margaret: 72.
Suett, Richard (1755-1805): as *Feste*, in "T. N.," 21; as *Sir Andrew Aguecheek*, 25.

T

Taber, Robert (1865-1904): 193.
Taylor, Joseph (1583?-1653): acted *Malvolio*(?)—succeeded Burbage as *Hamlet*, 13; first performer of *Cassius*, 549.
Taylor, Mary: acts *Maria*, in "T. N.," 48.
Terriss, William (Lewin: 1848-1897): acts *Orsino*, 34; acts *Romeo*, 124.
Terry, Ellen Alice (Mrs. George Frederick Watts, Mrs. Charles Kelly [Charles Wardell], Mrs. James Usselmann [James Carew]: 1848-19—): as *Viola*, 34; place taken by her sister, 35; as *Juliet*, 177; on *Cordelia*, 420; acts *Katharine*, in "K. & P.," 500; 505.
Terry, Fred (1863-19—): acts *Sebastian*, in "T. N.," 34.
Terry, Kate (Mrs. Arthur Lewis: 1844-19—): as *Viola*—and "doubled" with *Sebastian*, 35.
Thompson, Lysander (1817-1854): first American appearance of, 51.
Thorne, Mrs. Sarah (1827-1889): 152.
Thurgate, Lillian: as *Maria*, in "T. N.," 102; 103.
Tilbury, Zeffie (Mrs. Arthur Lewis, Mrs. L. D. Woodthorpe: 1862-19—): 76; as *Maria*, 79.
TREE, ELLEN (Mrs. Charles John Kean: 1806-1880): acts *Viola*, first time, 39; as *Viola*, 39-41; married, 41; as *Romeo*, 198-199; as *Rosalind*, 244-245; first appearance in America, 255.
Tree, Maria (Mrs. Bradshaw: 1802-1862): as *Viola*, 27-28; quality of her singing, and first singer of "Home, Sweet Home," 28.
Tyler, Odette (Kirkland, Mrs. R. D. Maclean [Shepherd]: 1869-19—): as *Juliet*, 186.

U

Underhill, Cave (1623?-1715): mentioned, and as *Feste*, in "T. N.," 15; his personation of *Feste*, and described as the *First Grave-Digger*, in "H."—his *Trinculo*, in "The T.," and *Sir Sampson Legend*, in "Love for Love," 17; 46.

V

Vandenhoff, George (——-——): on Miss Faucit's acting, 150; as *Mercutio*, 196; on Miss Cushman's *Romeo*, 209; as *Brutus*, in "J. C.," 606.
Veneta, Mlle.: as *Romeo*, 166.
Verbruggen, John (died, 1707): as *Cassius*, 558-559.
Vining, George J. (1824-1875): acts *Mercutio*, 151.

W

Wainwright, Marie (Mrs. Louis James, Mrs. Franklyn Roberts: 1853-19—): produces "Twelfth Night," 56; experience of, 60; as *Viola*, 60-61.
Walcot, Charles Melton, Sr. (1816-1868): 45; acts *Sir Toby Belch*, 54; quality of his performances—characterized as *Touchstone* and as *Sir Andrew Aguecheek*, 55.
Walker, Thomas (1700-1744): as *Brutus*, 547; the same, and quality of, and performances by, 557-558.
Wallack, Fanny (1822-1856): acts *Juliet*, 157; as *Juliet*, 203.
Wallack, Henry John (1792-1870): acts *Malvolio*, 47; artistic quality of, 48.
Wallack, James William, the Elder, (1795-1864: also theatrical manager): 48; revives "T. N.," 54; 159; 205; acts *Brutus*, 570.

INDEX

Wallack, James William, the Younger (1818-1873): acts *Mercutio*, to Miss Cushman's *Romeo*, 110.
Wallack, Lester (John Johnston Wallack: 1820-1888): 45; 48; as *Orsino*, in "T. N.," 50; the same, 54; 130; 185; 203; 261.
Warren, William, the Elder (1767-1832): acts *Sir Toby Belch*, 47.
Warren, William, the Younger (1818-1888): as *Touchstone*, 329.
Webster, Benjamin (1798-1882): acts *Malvolio*, 39; 46; restores "T. T. of T. S.," and acts *Petruchio*, 503.
Wendell, Jacob, Jr. (1869-1910): acts *Feste*, in "T. N.," 91; as *Feste*, 93.
Wenman (Newman), Thomas Edmund: 1844-1892): acts *Sir Toby Belch*, 34; the same, 52; and his performance of, 53.
Weston, "Lizzie" (Elizabeth Jackson, Mrs. Adolphus Hoyt [Davenport], the second Mrs. Charles James Mathews, Jr.) (18—-18—): acts *Viola*, 48; her quality, and her performance of *Viola*, 59.
Wheatley, William (1816-1876): acts *Romeo*, 159.
Widdecombe, Wallace: 103.
Wigan, Horace (1818-1885): 45.
Wilkinson, Tate (1734-1803): on Barry and Mrs. Cibber, 117; on stage costumes, 120; on Barry and Miss Nossiter, 142.
WILKS, ROBERT (1666-1732): acts *Orlando*, 232; as *King Lear*, 234; as *Antony*, in "J. C.," 561-562.
Wilson, Mrs.: as *Maria*, in "T. N.," 20.
Winter, (William) Jefferson (1878-19—): as *Petruchio*, 530, 533.
Woffington, Margaret (1718-1760): as *Viola*, 19; 115; meagre wardrobe of, 121; as *Rosalind*—and death of, 234.
Wood, William B. (1779-1861): acts *Malvolio*, 47.
Wood, Mrs. John (Matilda Charlotte Vining: 1833-19—): 72.
Woodward, Henry (1717-1777): as *Sir Andrew Aguecheek*, 18; the same, 20; 45; acts *Mercutio*, 114; his dress for *Mercutio*, 120; as *Mercutio*, 194; as *Petruchio*, in "K. & P.," 498-499.
Worthing, Frank (Francis George Pentland: 1866-1910): acts *Orsino*, 72; as *Orlando*, 278.
Wroughton, Richard (true name Rotton: died, 1822): as *Romeo*, 124; acts *Romeo*, 146.
Wyatt, Francis: acts *Sir Andrew Aguecheek*, 34.

Y

Yates, Richard (1706-1796): 19; acts *Malvolio*, 20; 46.
Yorke, Oswald: acts *Malvolio*, 91; his performance of, 92.
Young, Charles Mayne (1777-1856): on Mrs. Siddons as *Rosalind*, 237; as *King Lear*, 387; 389; as *Cassius*, 564-565.

CHARACTERS, IN PLAYS AND NOVELS

A

Adam, in "A. Y. L. I.": 227; tradition of Shakespeare's acting, 228-230; Johnson acts, 255; Fisher as, 276; Varrey as, 277.

Adrastus, in "Ion"; 54.
Alfred Evelyn, in "Money": Macready as, 129.
Antigone, in "Antigone": 149.
Antonio in "T. N.," Ryder acts, 40; G. Riddle acts, 88; 96.

648 INDEX

ANTONY (*Marcus Antonius*), in "J. C.": Barry as, 468; 547; quality of, 556; Wilks as, 559; Mills as, 560; Barry as, 561-562; Milward as, 562-563; C. Kemble as, 564; same, 566; Macready acts, 568; Cooper acts, 569; J. B. Booth acts, 570; Beerbohm-Tree as, 573-574; Hodgkinson as, 576; Cooper as, 577-578; Forrest as, 578; players of, Am. S., named, 1826-1912, 579-580; E. Booth as, 587-590; 592; 595; Bangs as, and his dress for, 599; Montgomery as, 600-601; Ward as, 608; Murdoch as, 611; 612; Tichy as, 614; various players of, 616; Warde as, 617; Barnay as, 618; McGinn acts, 620; Faversham as, 625-627.
Antony, in "A. & C.": 561.

B

Beatrice, in "M. A. A. N.": Mrs. Shaw as, ment., 58; Mrs. Barrow as, ment., 59; 245.
Beau Farintosh, in "School": Fisher as, ment., 51.
Belvidera, in "Venice Preserved": 142.
Bianca, in "Fazio": 205.
Bishopriggs, in "Man and Wife" (play): 52.
Bob Tyke, in "The School of Reform": L. Thompson as, ment., 51.
BRUTUS (*Marcus Brutus*), in "J. C."; Betterton as, ment., 16; 543; 545; 546; Walker as, 547; Hart as, 550; Betterton as, 552; predominant character in "J. C.," 555, *et seq.;* eighteenth century representatives of, named, 556; Quin—Keen—Delane as, 557; 558; 560; Delane acts, 561; Mossop acts, 562; J. P. Kemble as, 563-565; Macready as, 567; Phelps as, 571-572; Walker as, 573; Cooper as, 577-578; players of, Am. S., 1829-1912, named, 579, 580; 581; 583; 584; E. Booth as, 585-587; quality of, 586; 588; 595; 596; Creswick as, 598; Davenport as, 603-606; McCullough as, 608-609; 611; 612; Pfeil as, 513; various players of, 616; Mansfield as, 618-619; Mantell as, 619-622; Power as, 628-630.

C

Caius Ligarius, in "J. C.": Bowman as, 554.
Caius Marius, in "Caius Marius": 113.
Caliban, in "T. T.": 52.
Cardinal Wolsey, in "K. H. VIII.": 31.
CASSIUS (*Caius Cassius*), in "J. C.": 543; 545; 546; 550; Mohun as, 551; quality of, 556; eighteenth century players of, named, 558; Garrick planned to act, 560; Sparks acts, 561; Mossop as, 562; Young as, 564-565; Barrett as, 565; Macready as, 567-569; J. B. Booth as, 569-571; Phelps as, 571-572; M'Leay as, 573; Cooper as, 577-578; players of, Am. S., named, 1826-1912, 579; 586; 588; character of, 590-592; E. Booth as, 592-593; Barrett as, 593-596; Creswick as, 598-599; 603; Levick acts, 608; Barrett acts, 611; Kober as, 614; Haworth as, 617; same, 618; Keenan acts, 622; Keenan's performance of, 627-628.
Celia, in "A. Y. L. I.": 227; Mrs. Baddeley acts—"Cuckoo Song" sung by Mrs. Clive as, 235; 236; 244; Mrs. Cleveland acts, 254; Mrs. Broadhurst acts, 255; Mrs. Abbott acts, 256; character of, 269; Henrietta Crosman acts, 275; often acted by Mrs. Clive—Mrs. Mattocks acts, 283; 295; 296; 297; 299; 305; 323.
Charles, the Wrestler, in "A. Y. L. I.": notable performance of, by Bosworth, 278-280; "Jem" Mace as, 284.
Cicely Homespun, in "The Heir-at-Law": Mrs. Barrow ment. as, 60.

INDEX 649

Constance, in "The Love Chase": Mrs. Shaw as, 58.
Cordelia, in "K. L.": character of —and players of, 419-421.

D — E

Desdemona, in "O.": 145.
Duke Theseus, in "A. M. N. D.": Fisher as, ment., 51:

Edgar, in "K. L.": players of, 415.

F

Fabian, in "T. N.": 32.
Fabrito, in "Gl' Ingannati": 7, 8.
Falstaff: Sir Toby Belch compared to, 70-71.
Feste, in "T. N.": the character original with Shakespeare, 8; 11; 13; Underhill's performance of, 17; Yates acts, 19; Davies acts— Suett acts — Parsons as, 21; Blanchard acts, 26; Fawcett acts, 27; 29; 32; S. Johnson acts, 34; Calhaem acts, 34; Harley acts, 40; character of, and various actors of, named and considered, 45-46; Spiller acts, 47; Placide acts, 48; Mark Smith acts, 50; 62; J. Cooper acts, 62; 68; E. Howard acts, 76; his performance of, 79; Collins acts, 87; 90; Jacob Wendell, Jr., acts, 91; his performance of, 93; M. Montesole as, 102.
First Grave-Digger, in "H.": 19.
Flamineo, in "Gl' Ingannati": 7; 8.
Fool, the, in "K. L.": 46; restored by Macready, 398, *et seq.*
Friar Lawrence, in "R. & J.": Macready acts, 129; 135; 157.

G — H — I

Gratiano, in "T. M. of V.": Bannister as, 25.
Geoffrey Dale, in "The Last Man": Blake acts, 50.
Goneril, in "K. L.": character of, 419.

Haller, Mrs., in "The Stranger": 126.
Hamlet, in "H.": 5; Betterton as, ment., 16; 119; Hazlitt's comparison of, and *Romeo,* examined, 133-136; 465; 469.
Hermione, in "T. W. T.": 149.
Hippolyta, in "She Would and She Would Not": Mrs. Barrow as, ment., 59.

Imogen, in "C.": Miss Neilson as, ment., 43; Viola Allen as, 81; 149; compared with *Rosalind,* 270.
Imoinda, in "The Grecian Daughter": 144.
Isabella, in "Gl' Ingannati": 78.

J

JAQUES, in "A. Y. L. I.": 220; the character invented by Shakespeare, 223; 227; C. Cibber acts, in alteration of "A. Y. L. I.," 232; Quin acts, on occasion of first recorded restoration of "A. Y. L. I." since time of Shakespeare, 233; Love acts, 235; Kemble as, speaks *First Lord's* lines, etc., 243; Macready acts, 244; Hodgkinson acts, 254; the same, 255; Hamblin acts, 256; Wallack acts, 258; Fisher as, 264-265; 266; 267; character of, commented on, 266; Clarke as, 276; Davenport acts, 284; Waller as, 287; Tearle as, 288; Malone as, 313; Mellish acts, 315; Mellish's performance of, described and considered, 316-317; character of, analyzed, 317; Davenport excels all players as, 318; Coghlan as, 318-319; many players of, named, 319-320; Quin— Henderson — Cooke — Jefferson — Young—Phelps—Anderson —Vandenhoff—Hodgkinson—Cooper as, 320-321; Mme. Janauschek as, 340.
Jesse Rural, in "Old Heads and Young Hearts": 50.
JULIET, in "R. & J.": Miss Neilson as, ment., 43; first actor of, 111; 113; Mrs. Cibber as—Mrs. Bellamy as, 115-117; dressing of,

650 INDEX

119; male players of, 120; Mrs. Robinson's dress for, 121; Fanny Kemble's dress for, 122; Ellen Terry as, 131-132; character of, analyzed and considered, 138-141; various players of, B. S., 1750-1800, named and considered, 141-148; defined by Campbell, 146; players of, B. S., nineteenth century, named, 146-147; Miss O'Neill as, 147; Fanny Kemble as, 147-148; Helena Faucit as, 148-150; Stella Colas as, 150-151; Miss Neilson as, 151-155; early performers of, Am. S., 156-157; Mary McVicker as, 164; first performer of, 167; Mme. Modjeska as, 171-172; Mary Anderson as, 176-178; Miss Mather's performance of, 179, *et seq.;* Julia Marlowe acts, 123; Odette Tyler as, 186; Cecilia Loftus acts, 188; Maude Adams as, 189, *et seq.;* Julia Marlowe as, 190-192; 306.

Julius Cæsar, in "J. C.": 545; 552; 553; 560; 563; 566; 569; 573; 578; 581; 583; 586; 587; 589; 591; 595; 599; 601; 602; 603; 604; 609; 611; 612; 613; 618; 619; 620; 622; 624; 625; 626.

Justice Shallow, in "K. H. IV.": *Sir Andrew Aguecheek* likened to, 71.

K

KATHARINE (*Minola*), in "T. T. of T. S." and "K. & P.": Miss Rehan as, ment., 73; players of B. S., 1754-1913, named, etc., 498-501; Mrs. Siddons as, 501; character of, 516-520; players of, Am. S., 507-508; players of, with E. Booth, 509; Marie Seebach as, 510; character of, 516-520; Miss Rehan as, 520-527; Jane Hading as, 529; Elsie Leslie as, 530-533; Julia Marlowe as, 534; O. Gianini as, 535; Margaret Anglin as, 536-538.

Kent, in "K. L.": players of, 414-415.

King John, in "K. J.": 463.

KING LEAR, in "K. L.": 46; first player of, 351; Betterton as, 351-353; (N. B.—All players of, appeared in character, according to Tate, till Macready, 1833); Powell as, 353-354; Barton Booth as, 354-356; Boheme as—Quin as, 356-357; Garrick as, 358-360; Spranger Barry as, 360-365; rivalry of Garrick and Barry as, and their performances of, compared, 361-365; T. Cibber on Garrick and Barry as, 363; Mossop as, 365-366; Wilks as, 384; Mills—Digges—Delane as, 385; W. Powell as, 386; Henderson as, 386-387; Pope and Young as, 387; Brooke as, 388; J. P. Kemble as, 388-391; Cooke as, 391-393; J. B. Booth, and E. Kean as, 393-395; Macready as, 397-402; Macready's view of the character, 400; the personality and character of, 404, *et seq.;* insanity of, 405-406; condition of, and original quality of character, considered, 407-412; 415; Phelps as, 421-425; C. Kean as, 425-427; Irving as, 427-432; Irving's views of, 429; first player of, in America, 432; various players of, early Am. S., 434; J. B. Booth as, 435-436; Forrest acts, 437; Forrest's performance of, 439-444; custom in acting, 442; various players of, Am. S., named, 444; E. Booth as, 445-450; Tennyson on Booth's performance of, 449; Barrett as, 450-451; McCullough as, 454-461; treatment of, by J. B. Booth—E. Kean—Forrest—McCullough, 460; not possible to agree with Lamb and Hazlitt on, 461-462; actors of, Am. S., 1884-1905, 462; first played by Mantell, and his performance described and considered, 462-465; method in, of C. Kean—Sullivan—Davenport—Forrest, 463; Continental actors in, 465, *et seq.;* Rossi, 465-467; Barnay as, 467-469; Salvini as, 469-473; Possart as, 476-478; Novelli as, 478-480.

INDEX   651

L

Lady Macbeth, in "M.": 145; 149.
Lady Teazle, in "T. S. for S.": 59; 60.
Lavinia, in "Caius Marius": 113.
Lelia, in "Gl' Ingannati": 7; 8.

M

Macbeth, in "M.": Betterton as, ment., 16; 119; 469.
Major Vavasour, in "Henry Dunbar": Fisher as, 51.
MALVOLIO, in "T. N.": the character original with Shakespeare, 8; that name given to "T. N." instead of its right title—first performer of the part, 13; Lovel acts, 15; Macklin acts, 18; Yates acts, 19; Bensley acts, 20; Henderson as, 21; Bensley as, 21; same, 23-24; Bannister acts, 25; Munden as, 26; Dowton acts, 26; Liston as, 27; Phelps as, 27-30; character of, and experience of, analyzed, 31-32; 35; Webster acts—Farren acts, 39; Wood acts, 47; Blake acts, 48; Fisher acts, 49; his performance of, 51; Walcot acts, 54; 55; later performers of, on American Stage, named and considered, 55-57; Griffiths acts, 62; Clarke acts, 64; 68; 73; Blake acts, 76; his performance of, 77; Jewett as, 83; Sothern acts, 89; his performance of, 90-91; Yorke acts, 91; his performance of, 92; 101; Mellish acts, 102; his performance of, 103, *et seq.*
Maria, in "T. N.," 8; 11; Mrs. Wilson acts, 20; Miss Mellen acts, 25; Mrs. Gibbs acts, 27; 28; Mrs. Durang acts, 48; Mary Taylor acts, 48; "Polly" Marshall acts, 49; Mrs. Smith acts, 50; Clara Fisher acts, 62; 68; Catherine Lewis as, 72; Zeffie Tilbury acts, 76; her performance of, 79; Lillian Thurgate as, 102; 103; 104.
Mariana, in "The Wife": 58.
Marius, the Younger, in "Caius Marius": 113.

MERCUTIO, in "R. & J.": Betterton as, ment., 16; Fisher as, ment., 51; 110; Harris as, 112; Woodward acts, 114; Macklin acts, 114; Woodward's performance of—and Macklin's, 115-116; dressing of, 119; Woodward's dress for, 120; C. Kemble as, 125; Terriss as, 131; Coghlan as, 138; early players of, Am. S., 156-157; Redmund as, 186; Hackett as, 189; Dr. Johnson on—Woodward as, 194; players of, named—Palmer—Lewis—Bannister as, 195; Garrick—Dodd—Jones—C. Kean—Vandenhoff as, 196; Phelps—C. Kemble—Everill as—and various American players of, 197; Davenport as, 198.
Micawber, in (play) "David Copperfield": 78.
Mr. Hardcastle, in "She Stoops to Conquer": 50.
Mr. Peggotty, in "David Copperfield": 51.
Mr. Squeers, in (novel) "Nicholas Nickleby": 100.
Mr. Toodle, in "The Toodles" ("A Widow Hunt"): 78.

N

Nancy, in (play) "Oliver Twist": Fanny Davenport as, ment., 60.
Nicholas Rue, in "Secrets Worth Knowing": 51.
Nurse, the, in "R. & J.": Mrs. Stirling as: 131-132; 155.

O

Olivia, the Countess, in "T. N.": 8; 9; Mrs. Gibbs acts, 15; Mrs. Clive acts, 18; Mrs. Hartley acts—Mrs. Clive acts, 20; Elizabeth Farren as, 24; Mrs. Glover acts—Mrs. Charles Kemble acts, 27; 29; 30; Rose Leclercq acts—Winifred Emery acts, 34; 35; 37; 38; 39; Mrs. Hallam as, 47; Mrs. Entwhistle acts, 48; Jane Coombs acts, 49; Amelia Parker acts, 50;

652 INDEX

Maud Milton acts, 62; 64; 66; 67; Maxine Elliott—Sybil Carlisle—Margaret St. John—Adelaide Prince act, 72; 80; Alys Reese as, 87; 91; Leah Bateman-Hunter acts, 91; her performance, 93; 94; 95; 96; Ruth Holt Boucicault acts, 102; her performance, 103; 104; 105.
Ophelia, in "H.": 134; 135.
ORLANDO, in "A. Y. L. I.": 220; quality of, indicated, 227; Wilks acts, in alteration of "A. Y. L. I.," 232; Milward acts, on occasion of first *recorded* restoration of "A. Y. L. I." since time of Shakespeare, 233; Palmer acts, 235; Cleveland acts, 254; Martin acts, 255; Coghlan as, 263-264; 265; 272; 273; 274; Drew acts, 275; quality of the part, and how generally regarded—Worthing as —Richman as, 278; Thorne acts, 284; 286; 288; Pitt as, 289; 295; 296; 299; 300; Forbes-Robertson acts, 302; James as, 303; Plympton as, 304; 305; 306; 307; 310; 311; 312; Kemble as, 329-330; character of, 330; Montgomery as, 330; Forbes-Robertson as, 331; many players of, named, 331-332.
Orsino, the Duke, in "T. N.": 8; 9; 11; Abbott acts—Barrymore acts, 27; Alexander acts—Terriss acts, 34; 35; 37; 38; 39; 44; Lester Wallack acts, 54-55; 62; 66; 67; Craig acts—Carlyle acts—Worthing acts—Clarke acts, 72; 74; Craig acts, 76; his performance of, 76-77; Kennedy as, 88; 91; M. Lang acts, 91; his performance of, 93; 96; costume of, in Margaret Anglin's production, 97; 99; bad stage business for, 100; de Cordoba as, 102.
Othello, in "O."; Betterton as, ment., 16; 463; 465; 469; 470.

P

Paris, in "R. & J.": 110; 131.
PETRUCHIO, in "T. T. of T. S."

and "K. & P.": players of, B. S., 1754-1913, named, &c., 498-501; J. P. Kemble as, 501; Webster as, 503; Marston as, 504; players of, Am. S., named, 507-508; E. Booth as, 508-509; character of, 516-520; Drew as—Clarke as, 527; Richman as—Skinner as, 528; Coquelin as, 529-530; Winter as, 533; Novelli as, 535; Blind as, 536.
Polonius, in "H.": 17.
Portia, in "T. M. of V.": compared with *Rosalind,* 270.

Q

Queen Katharine, in "K. H. VIII.": 31.

R

Regan, in "K. L.": character of, 419.
ROMEO, in "R. & J.": first actor of, 111; 113; 114; Harris as, ment., 16; dressing of, 119; various players of, 1760-1882, and Wroughton as, 124; Garrick as—Barry as — rivalry of Garrick and Barry as, 115-118; J. P. Kemble as—C. Kemble as—E. Kean as, 125-126; various notable performers of — Elliston — Conway — C. Kean—Abbott—Macready—Anderson—Creswick—Robinson, 127-130; 131; 132; character of, and compared with *Hamlet,* 133-136; Irving as, 132; Forbes-Robertson as, 136-137; *Romeo,* 139; 140; Garrick acts, 143; 144; 154; 155; early performances of, Am. S., 156-157; same, and down to 1904, named and considered, 158-160; Booth as, 162; Rossi as, 168-169; Signor Canona as, 169; Mantell as, 170; Plympton as, 179; Bandmann as, 183; Bellew as, 184; Faversham as, 188; Sothern as, 193; female players of, described and considered, 198, *et seq.;* same, Am. S., 200, *et seq.;* C. Cushman as, 205-211.
ROSALIND, in "A. Y. L. I.": com-

INDEX 653

pared with *Viola,* 37; Mrs. Shaw as, ment., 58; Ada Rehan as, ment., 73; 81; 101; Miss Macklin acts, 144; Mrs. Esten acts, 145; 149; 220; impossibility of disguising, 221; played by males, 223; Shakespeare's feeling toward, 227; clearly depicted, 228; Mrs. Booth acts, in alteration of "A. Y. L. I.," 232; Mrs. Pritchard acts, on occasion of first *recorded* restoration to stage since time of Shakespeare, 233; various players of, named, 1741 to 1799, 233-244; Mrs. Woffington as, 234; Mrs. Dancer as, 234-235; "Cuckoo Song" sung by players of—and question of Mrs. Clive's ever playing, considered, 236; Mrs. Siddons as, 237-238; Mrs. Jordan as, 238-240; Mrs. Jordan superior to Mrs. Siddons as, 240; various players of, named, 1804-1896; 240-241; Mary Anderson first acts—Ada Rehan acts at Stratford, 241; Miss Duncan as—Miss Smith as, 242; Mrs. Mattocks acts—Mrs. Johnson acts, 243; Ellen Tree as, 244-245; Helena Faucit as, 245-250; Mrs. Nisbett acts, 250; the same as, 251; Fanny Kemble's ideal of— and various players of, 252-253; Alice Marriott—Amy Sedgwick— Mrs. Rousby — Mrs. Kendal— Eleanour Calhoun act, 253; Mrs. Kenna first to play, in New York, 253; Mrs. Johnson acts, 254; Mrs. Shaw acts, 255; Miss Cushman as, 256-257; Mrs. Mowatt as, 258-259; Laura Keene as, 258-259; Mrs. Barrow acts, 259; Mrs. Scott-Siddons as, 260-262; Mrs. Jennings as, 261; Fanny Davenport acts, 262; the same as, 263; the character of, analyzed and described, 268-271; compared with *Viola*— with *Portia*—with *Imogen,* 270; Ada Rehan as, described and considered, 271-275; Rose Evans as, 284; Adelaide Neilson as, 284-285; Carlotta Leclercq as, 285-286; Ada Cavendish as, 287; Rose Coghlan as, 288; Mrs. Langtry as, 289-290; Mme. Modjeska as, 291-293; Mary Anderson acts, at Stratford, 293; *et seq.;* condition of, when first seen, 294; Miss Anderson as, described and considered, 295-301; Miss Anderson's singing as, 298; Miss Rehan's superiority in, 302; various players of, named—Miss Wainwright as, 303; Julia Marlowe as, 303-305; Julia Arthur as, 305-307; view of character as affected by misreading "father's child," 307-311; Henrietta Crosman as, 311-313; Margaret Anglin as, 314-315; dressing of, discussed, 334-336; 526.

S

Sea Captain, a, in "T. N.": St. Clair Bayfield as, 88; 98.
Sebastian, in "T. N.": 8; 11; Bannister as, 21; —— Bland as, 22; Fred Terry as, 34; Fuller Mellish as—the part "doubled" with *Viola,* 35; Lawrence Barrett as, 50; 66; 80; 96.
Shylock, in "T. M. of V.": 19.
SIR ANDREW AGUECHEEK, in "T. N.": the character original with Shakespeare, 8; 11; 17; Henry Woodward as, 18; Dodd as—Edwin as, 21; Edwin as, 24; Dodd as, 24-25; Suett as, 25; Knight acts, 26; Blanchard acts, 27; 32; Wyatt acts, 34; Norman Forbes (-Robertson) acts, 34; the same, 62; Keeley acts, 40; character of, and actors of the part, 45-46; Johnson acts, —— Finn acts, 47; George H. Barrett acts, 49; Stuart Robson as, 53-54; 70; attitude of *Sir Toby* to, 71; Herbert Gresham, 72; Frank Currier acts, 76; his performance of, 79; John Crawley as, 87-88; Ferdinand Gottschalk acts, 91; his performance of, 93-95; Wallace Widdecombe as, 102; 103.
Sir Anthony Absolute, in "The Rivals": 52.

Sir Giles Overreach, in "A New Way to Pay Old Debts": 126.

Sir Harry Wildair, in "The Constant Couple": Mrs. Jordan as, 22.

Sir Peter Teazle, in "T. S. for S.": Farren as, ment., 27; 52.

SIR TOBY BELCH, in "T. N.": the character original with Shakespeare, 8; 11; first performer of, 13; Betterton as, 15-16; Dunstall as, 20; Palmer as, 20-21; the same, 24-25; Emery acts, 26-27; 32; D. Fisher acts—Wenman acts, 34; Addison acts, 40; Kilner acts—Harwood acts—Warren, Sr., acts, 47; notable performances of, on American Stage, 52-53; Brougham acts, 54; Crane as, 53-54; Dyott acts, 54; Davidge acts, 64; 68; attributes of the character—compared with *Falstaff* — correct method of acting, and James Lewis' performance of, 70-72; Handyside acts, 76; his performance of, 78-79; B. A. Field as, 87; Louis Calvert acts, 91; his performance of, 92-93; Sidney Greenstreet as, 102; 103.

Sly (*Christophero Sly*), in "T. T. of T. S.": Hazlitt on, 490; Phelps as, 504.

Squire Broadlands, in "The Country Squire" ("The Fine Old English Gentleman"): 248.

T

TOUCHSTONE, in "A. Y. L. I.": 46; Walcot as, ment., 55; the character of, invented by Shakespeare, 223; 227; omitted from alteration of "A. Y. L. I.," 232; Chapman acts, on occasion of first *recorded* restoration of "A. Y. L. I." since time of Shakespeare, 233; Hallam acts, 254; Burton acts, 256; Walcot acts, 258; Davidge acts, 260; 267; 273; Lewis as, 276; Gresham as—Herbert as, 277; Pateman as, 287; 288; Elton as, 289; 297; identity with *Clown* of the First Act, discussed, 322-325; first player of —many performers of, 1740-1907, named, 325-326; character of, 326-327; Chapman as, 327; King—Hare—Wolcot as, 328; Warren and Davidge as, 329; costume of, 336.

Triplet, in "Masks and Faces": Fisher as, ment., 51.

Tybalt, in "R. & J.": 131; 137.

V — W — Y

Viola, in "T. N.": 8; 15; Mrs. Pritchard acts, 18; Mrs. Woffington acts, 19; Mrs. Yates acts, 20; Mrs. Bulkley acts—Mrs. Robinson acts, 21; 22; 24; Mrs. Johnson acts, 26; Sally Booth acts, 27; Maria Tree as, 27-28; Kate Terry as, 35; character of, and experience of, analyzed, 35-39; compared with *Rosalind,* 37; Adelaide Neilson acts, 39; Ellen Tree as, 39-41; "consummate impersonation of," and character of, 41-45; Mrs. Johnson as, 47; Mrs. Hoey as—"Lizzie" Weston as, 48; Emiline Raymond (Mrs. Marchant)—Mrs. Barrow act, 49; various performers of, on the American Stage, named and described, 57-62; Mrs. Scott-Siddons acts—and her performance of, 64; M. Wainwright as, 60-61; Modjeska as, 61-62; Adelaide Neilson acts, 64; 67; Ada Rehan acts, 73; her performance of, and dress for, 74-75; Viola Allen acts, 76; and her performance of, 80-82; Miss Allen stricken with illness while acting, 82; Edith Wynne Matthison as, 88; Annie Russell as, 91-92; Margaret Anglin's dress as, 97; her performance of, and business, 98-100; 101; compared with *Rosalind,* 270; 285.

Violante, in "The Wonder": 59.

Widow Delmaine, in "The Serious Family": 60.

Young Mirabel, in "The Inconstant": 159.

INDEX

TITLES

A — B — C

"All for Love, or the World Well Lost" (Dryden): 565.
"Antony and Cleopatra" (S.): 560; 561; 568.
"As You Like It" (S.—*cir.* 1598): 12; 62; 81; 101; 178; chapter on the comedy, 215-341; scene of action of, 217, *et seq.*; based on novel of Lodge—French names in—and "correct" dressing of, 217; composition, and spirit of the play, 218, *et seq.*; composition, 221; state of the text and sources of the plot, 222, *et seq.*; author's mood and inspiration in writing, 223, *et seq.*; affluence of mentality in, 225; incidents and characters of, considered, 226-228; first production of, 228; early performances of, 230; long absence from the stage, 231; at the Globe—and alteration of, 232; revival of—and cast of principal parts in, 233; at Drury Lane, 237; various revivals, 1804 to 1896, 240; acting version of, J. Kemble's, 243; early representations on American Stage, 253, *et seq.*; on the Am. S. since 1860—and Augustin Daly's revivals of, 259, *et seq.*; Daly's revivals of, described and considered, 260—262—265 *et seq.*; Daly's stage version of, 267; music of, 280, *et seq.*; various later productions, 1871 to 1885, 284, *et seq.*; Mary Anderson's revival, described and considered, 293, *et seq.*; Miss Anderson's stage version of, 301; later revivals, 1885 to 1914, 302, *et seq.*; a bad reading in, 307; Margaret Anglin's revival of, described and considered, 313 *et seq.*; theory of an earlier play, as basis of, considered, 322; "correct" costume for, 332; curiosities in presentation of—"open-air performances" —"all women cast," 337, *et seq.*; fundamental difficulty in acting of, 340; quality of, 341.

"Black-Ey'd Susan" (Jerrold): 603.

"Cæsar in Egypt" (Cibber): 560.
"Caius Marius" (Otway): "conveyance" of "R. & J." in: 113.
"Camille" ("La Dame aux Camélias": Dumas): 51.
Comedy of Errors," "The (S.—*cir.* 1591): ment., 5; alteration of, by Kemble, 243.
"Coriolanus" (S.—*cir.* 1608): altered, 366; 603; 618.
Country Squire," "The ("The Fine Old English Gentleman," ———): 48.
"Cymbeline" (S.—*cir.* 1633): 43.

D — E — F — G

"David Copperfield" (play): 51.
Death of Cæsar," "The (Voltaire): 546; 547.
Deceits," "The ("Gl' Inganni"): ment., 5.
"Diary," Manningham's: discovery of—and claimed by Collier, 2; 5.
"Diary," Pepys': mentions of "T. N." in, 14.
"Diary," Sir Henry Herbert's: payment for presenting "T. N." recorded in, 13.
Dunciad," "The: 232.

"Epilogus Cæsaris Interfecti" (Eedes): 544.
"Everyman" ("Morality" play, time of K. Edward IV., 1441-1483): 84.

"Fazio" (Milman: 1818): 205.

656 INDEX

"Gl' Inganni" ("The Deceits"): mentioned by Manningham, 5; 6; Prologue to, quoted—and Latin translation of, 7; 8.

Grecian Daughter," "The (Arthur Murphy: 1772): 144.

H—I—J

"Hamlet" (S.—*cir.* 1602): name in, similar to "Gonzaga," 5; 17; 188; 219; 544; 555.

Heir-at-Law," "The (Colman, Jr.): 60.

"Henry Dunbar" (Tom Taylor): 51.

History of Cæsar and Pompey," "The: 544.

"Ion" (Talfourd): 54.

"JULIUS CÆSAR" (*cir.* 1600-1601): 188; 219; chapter on, 541-630; composition, and source, 541, *et seq.;* testimony, i.e., first production of, 542; early dramas on subject of, 544; the same, 545-548; no quarto of (before Folio), 545; alleged alteration of, by Davenant and Dryden, 547; first performance of, and acted before King Charles the First, 549; early performances of, 550-552; notable cast of, 553; eminent actors play small parts in, 555; J. P. Kemble acts in—version of, and effect of, 563-565; seldom presented by Macready, 569; at C. G., 571; Beerbohm-Tree's production of, described and considered, 573-574; first performance of, in America —and early American representations of, 575-578; Booth's production—the cast, 580; described and considered, 580-584; Booth's stage version of, 584; for benefit of Shakespeare Statue Fund—the three Booths act in, 585; a cast of, presented by Booth and Barrett, 602; at the Cincinnati Dramatic Festival, 610-611; the Saxe-Meiningen production of, in America, described and considered, 612-616; Schlegel's translation of, 612; various productions of, 616-618; Mansfield's production of, 618-619; Mantell's production of, 619-622; Faversham's production of, 622-630.

"Julius Cæsar" (Sheffield): 546.

K

"KATHARINE AND PETRUCHIO" (Garrick's alteration of "T. T. of T. S.," *q. v.:* 1753: described and discussed, 496-498; repetitions of B. S., 1757-1913, 500; first acted in America—in N. Y., 506; 507.

"King Henry VIII" (S.—*cir.* 1612-'13): 188; 189.

"KING LEAR" (S.—*cir.* 1606): Tate's version of, alluded to, 54; 220; chapter on, 342-480; old stories of, 342; Shakespeare prompted to write, 344; first published, 345; sources of, 347, *et seq.;* question of the play preceding, or following, "the ballad" on same subject, 347-349; first performance of, 350; Burbage acts in, 351; Betterton in, and alteration of, by Tate, 351-352; Tate's version of, 357; Garrick produces, 358; alterations of, by Tate, and others, examined and considered, 366, *et seq.;* Dr. Johnson on Tate's alteration of, 367; Davies on, 368; cast of, in 1681, 369; Tate's dedication of his alteration of, 370; Addison on Tate's alteration of, 371; Garrick's changes in Tate's version, 372; Colman's version—Kemble's version, 373; Macready's restoration of, 374; Genest on the alterations of, 374, *et seq.;* omission of the *Fool* from, 382; impossibility of "happy catastrophe" to, 382-383; specimens of the style of Tate in, 384; element of action in, and aspect of the story, 412, *et seq.;* Booth's "Prompt Book" of, 414; "historical period" of, and dress-

INDEX

ing of, 416-419; produced by Phelps, 421; C. Kean produces, 425; produced by Irving, 427; Irving's views regarding, 429; first performance of, in America, and in early days of the American Stage, 432, *et seq.;* not popular, 434; last act of, never given by Kean and Booth, 436; Forrest's version of, 437-439; Forrest's "Prompt Book" of, 439; scope of, 441; restored according to S., 444; restored by E. Booth, 446; produced by McCullough, 453; produced by Mantell and Brady, 462; 487; Tate's, 555.

"King Richard II." (S.—*cir.* 1593-1594): altered, 366.

L

"Lady Clancarty" (Taylor): 554.
"Laelia" (Latin translation of "Gl' Ingannati"): acted at Queen's College, Cambridge, 7.
Last Man," "The: 50.
Love Chase," "The (Sheridan Knowles): 58; 256.
"Love for Love": 17.
"Love in a Forest" (alteration of "A. Y. L. I."): produced, 232.
"Love's Labor's Lost" (S.—*cir.* 1590): 62; 235.

M — O

"Macbeth" (S.—*cir.* 1606): bad production of, by "Ben" Greet, 87.
"Malvolio": 52.
"Man and Wife" (play, Collins-Daly): 52.
"Marcus Brutus" (Sheffield): 546.
"Masks and Faces" (Reade): 51.
"Menechmi": 5.
Merchant of Venice," "The (S.—*cir.* 1596): 62.
Merry Wives of Windsor," "The (S.—*cir.* 1592): 62.
Midsummer Night's Dream," "A (S.—*cir.* 1594): 51; 62.
"Much Ado About Nothing" (S.—*cir.* 1599): 62.

"Oh, It's Impossible" (Kemble's alteration of "T. C. of E."): 243.
"Old Heads and Young Hearts" (Boucicault): 50.
"Oliver Twist" (play, on the novel): 60.
"Othello" (S.—*cir.* 1604): 487.

R

"Romeo and Juliet" (S.—*cir.* 1591-'95): 51; chapter on, 107-214; Shakespeare's first tragedy—date of composition, 107, *et seq.;* published, 108; based on poem, 110; first performers in, 111; presented by Davenant—and first alteration of, 112; in abeyance—alteration of, by Otway—"revived and altered" by T. Cibber, 113; expedient taken from Bandello—Garrick alters, and produces, 114; presented at D. L. and C. G., 115; rivalry of Garrick and Barry, &c., in, 115-118; setting and costume—historical, and proper, 118-123; method of dressing in best modern revivals of, 123; various revivals of, 123-127; restored by Miss Cushman, 129; produced by Irving—acted before Q. Victoria, 130; Miss Faucit on, 148; on B. S., 1850-1884; 150; Booth's T. opened with, 152; first performance, and early, on Am. S., 156-157; E. Booth's production of, described, &c., 161-165; freak performance of—six *Juliets* to one *Romeo,* 167; acted with music, 169; Hill produces, with Miss Mather as *Juliet,* described, &c., 179, *et seq.;* various productions of, Am. S., 1885-1914, 183, *et seq.;* C. Frohman's production of, described, etc., 187, *et seq.;* "consummate tragedy of love"—the spirit and influence of the play, 212-214; 219.
"Rosalynde, or Euphues' Golden Legacye" (Lodge's novel of): 217; 222; 223; 269.
"Roscius Anglicanus" (Downes): 233; 353.

S

"Saul" (Alfieri): described, and Salvini in, 473-476; compared with "K. L.," 475.
"School" (Robertson): 51.
"School of Abuse": 544.
School of Reform," "The (Thomas Morton): 51.
"Secrets Worth Knowing" (Thomas Morton): 51.
Serious Family," "The (Morris Barret): 60.
"Shancke's Ordinary" (Shancke): produced, 13.
"She Stoops to Conquer" (Goldsmith): 50.
"Some of Shakespeare's Female Characters" (book of studies): 148; 246.
"Still Waters Run Deep" (Tom Taylor): 187.
Story of My Life," "The (Terry): 34.

T — V — W

"Tale of Gamelyn" (Coke): 222.
TAMING OF THE SHREW," "THE (cir. 1594); see also "Katharine and Petruchio": 62; 101; chapter on, 481-485; origin, date of composition, &c., 481-493; assumptive computations regarding authorship of, 485-487; that which is certain regarding — Knight on chronological place of, approved, 487-488; superiority of versification in, 490; scene of, 492; offspring of, 493, et seq.; subject illustrated by, and popularity of, 495-496; first acted, and alterations of, 496-498; presented as opera, 502; restored by Webster, 503; same, by Phelps, 504-506; on Am. S., 506, et seq.; produced in German, by Marie Seebach, 510; restored by Daly, and his revivals of, described and considered, 511-516; Daly's version of, 513-516; minor defects in Daly's production of, 525; players in Daly's version of, 527, et seq.; acted in Paris by Daly's company, 528; produced, in French, in N. Y., 529; produced by Elsie Leslie, 530, et seq.; produced by Sothern and Marlowe, 533, et seq.; Italian version of, produced, in N. Y., by Novelli, 535; Margaret Anglin's production of, described and considered, 535-540.
Tempest," "The (S.—cir. 1610): 62; 65.
Theatrical Inquisitor," "The: on Macready's Romeo, 129.
Thief," "The (Chambers, from Bernstein): 185.
Times," "The London: on C. Cushman's Romeo, 207.
"Titus Andronicus" (S.—cir. 1588): 107.
Tragical History of Romeus and Juliet," "The (Brooke poem): S.'s "R. & J." based on, 110.
"TWELFTH NIGHT, or What You Will" (S.—cir. 1599): chapter on, 1, et seq.; significance of title of, 1; chronologic place of—publication —and first recorded performance of, 2; source of plot, 5, et seq.; belief that was founded on "Gl' Ingannati," 7; Hunter's comparison of the two plots, 7-8; spirit of, and construction of, 9, et seq.; characters in, distinctively English—scene of, specified, 11; costume for—supposed first performance of—difficulty in assigning time and place, 12; mention of in audit-office record, 13; mentioned by Pepys—revived by Davenant—testimony as to early popularity of, 14; mentioned in "Roscius Anglicanus," 15; revived at Drury Lane, 18; performed as an opera, 27; presented by Samuel Phelps, 28; produced by Irving, 33-34; translated by Schlegel, and German performance of, described, 35; 43; first performance in America—in New York, 47; perversion of, produced by Robson and Crane, 53-54; Wallack's

INDEX 659

revival of, 54; Marie Wainwright produces, 56; length of—and of Daly's version of, 69; presented in London by Daly, 72; the persons in, how to be considered, 80-82; produced at the New Theatre, N. Y., 91; production there considered, 91-95; produced by Margaret Anglin, 95; Miss Anglin's associates in, 102; asinine stage business in, 103.

Two Gentlemen of Verona," "The (S.—cir. 1592): 62; 64.

"Venice Preserved" (Otway): 142.

"Was Ihr Wollt" ("T. N."): 35.
Wife," "The (Knowles): 58.

MISCELLANEOUS

A

Academy of Music, N. Y.: 171; 304; 468; 469.
Addison, Joseph (1672-1719): on Powell, 354; 563.
Alexander, William, Earl of Stirling (1581-1640): play by, 545.
Alfieri, Victor (Italian poet: 1749-1803): 473.
Alma-Tadema, Sir Lawrence (1836-19—): 573; 618.
Amberg, T., N. Y.: 476.
Anne, Queen of England, 119; 232.
"Apology," George Anne Bellamy's: 116.
Arden, Forest of, in England: described, 215; scene of action of "A. Y. L. I.," 217.
Arne, Dr. Thomas Augustus (musician: 1710-1778): music by, for "A. Y. L. I.," 266; same, 281.
Astor Place O. H., N. Y.: 210; 256.

B

Bacon, Francis, Viscount St. Alban, Baron Verulam (1561-1626): 12.
Bandello, Matthew (clergyman and novelist: 1480-1562): 5; 6; 8; 111; 114.
Bernard, William Bayle (d. a. & c.: 1808-1875): on Phelps' *Malvolio*, 30; on Mrs. Mowatt's *Rosalind*, 257; on Davenport and Macready, 607-608.
Bishop, Sir Henry Rowley (musician: 1780-1855): 28; music for "A. Y. L. I." by, 281.

Blackfriars T., London: 13; 225; 496.
Boaden, James (dramatist and d. c.: 1763-1839): on Mrs. Jordan's *Sir Harry Wildair*, 22; on Bensley, 23; on Kemble as a lover, 125; on Mrs. Siddons as *Rosalind*, 302; on Kemble as *King Lear*, 388; 564.
BOOTH'S THEATRE, N. Y.: "T. N." at, 57; first Am. appearance of Miss Neilson made at, 152; opened, 161; E. Booth retires from—various managers of—and closed, 165; 166; 167; 168; 284; 285; 286; "K. L." at, 450; 465; "J. C." at, 580, *et seq.*
Boston Museum, Boston, Mass.: 160; 260.
Bowery T., old: 59; 204; 255; "K. L." at, 1826, 437; 476.
Broadway Theatre, old: 59; 157; 183; 255.
Brooke (Broke), Arthur (died, 1563): 110; 111.
Byron, George Gordon, Lord (the poet: 1788-1824): opinion of Kean, 126-127; 141.

C

Cæsar, Julius (B.C. 100-44): 544; opinion regarding, 545; absurd notion about, and Marcus Brutus, 547; 582.
Campbell, Thomas (the poet: 1777-1844): definition of *Juliet* by, 146; on Mrs. Siddons as *Rosalind*, 237; on Kemble's *King Lear*, 389.
Canongate T., Edinburgh: 146.

660 INDEX

Capell, Edward (S. editor: 1713-1781): on source of "T. N.," 6.
Castle Square T., Boston: 77.
Century T. (the New Theatre): 91.
Chambers Street T. (Burton's), N. Y.: 49; 51.
Chappell, William (S. Music, 1809-1888): on chron. of "T. N.," 3; 4.
Charles, the First, King of England, &c.: changed title of "T. N.," 30; 31; 119; 231; 549.
Charles, the Second, King of England, &c.: 228; 550.
Chatham Garden T., N. Y.: 47.
Chaucer, Geoffrey (1328-1400): 222.
Chestnut Street T., Phila.: "T. N." at, 47.
Cole, John William (d. bio.): on Miss Tree's *Viola*, 40.
Coleridge, Samuel Taylor (the poet: 1772-1834): 42.
Collier, John Payne (S. editor, &c.: 1789-1883): claimed discovery of Manningham's "Diary," and first published same, 2; on source of "T. N.," 8; 111; 483.
Collins, William Wilkie (the novelist: 1824-1889): 287.
Congreve, William (dramatist: 1670-1729): 17.
Corsair," "The (Byron): lines in, applied to Kean, 126.
Costume, stage: old-time, and for "R. & J.," 118-123; for "A. Y. L. I.," discussed, 332-336; for "K. L.," 416-419.
Court T., London: "R. & J." produced at, 130.
COVENT GARDEN, Theatre Royal, London: 20; 21; 25; 26; 27; "R. & J." at, 115; 118; costumes at, 1750, 120; "R. & J." at, 127; same, 129; 141; 145; 149; 198; 234; 239; 242; 245; 247; 283; 374; 387; 394; 395; "K. L." at, 397; 398; 547; 571.
Crow Street T., Dublin: 143; 144.
"Cuckoo Song," so called: introduced into "A. Y. L. I."—and who sung by, 235-236; when and how so introduced, 282-283.
Curtain T., London: 108.

D

DALY'S THEATRE, N. Y.: "T. N." at, 56; 72; "K. L.," 165; "R. & J." at, 184; "A. Y. L. I." at, 265; "T. T. of T. S." at, 511, *et seq.*
Davenant, Sir William (1605-1668): presents "R. & J."—also alteration of, 112.
de Belleforêt, François (1530-1583): 6; 8.
De Quincey, Thomas (1785-1859): on Miss Faucit, 249.
Digges, Leonard (died, 1635): 14; testimony of, *re* "J. C.," 542; 543; 557.
Doran, Dr. John (th. historian: 1807-1878): on C. Kemble's *Mercutio*, 125; on J. P. Kemble's *Brutus*, 564.
Dowden, Edward (S. commentator: 1843-19—): 483-484.
Drama: affected movements in society, 230.
DRURY LANE, Theatre Royal, London: "T. N." revived at, 18; 19; 20; 21; 22; 24; 26; 27; "R. & J." produced at, 114; 118; 125; 143; Mrs. Siddons acts *Rosalind* at, 237; 238; 242; 282; 283; 372; 373; 385; 387; 394; 395; "K. L." at, 397; 415; 493; 547; 550; 552; 561; 568; 569; 572.
Dryden, John (dramatist, &c.: 1631-1701): 112; tradition, *re* "R. & J." recorded by, 194; 383; 547; 548; 561; 565.
Dumas, Alexandre: 467.
Dyce, Rev. Alexander (S. ed.: 1798-1869): 3; on Chappell, 4; on Shakespeare's knowledge of Italian, 6.

E — F — G

Eedes, Rev. Richard (died, 1604): 544.
Elizabeth, Queen of England, &c.: gift by, ment., 3; Italian actors play before, 6; 83; 84; 119; 120.
Essex, Earl of: 119.

INDEX 661

Fifth Avenue T., N. Y.: 41; "T. N." at, 53; same, 63; 64; 171; "R. & J." at, 172; Miss Anderson's first N. Y. appearance made at, 173; Daly's, 260; 262; "K. L." at, 446; 503.

Fourteenth Street Theatre, N. Y.: 510.

Furness, Dr. Horace Howard, Sr. (S. ed., &c.: 1833-1912): dedication of this volume to, viii.; on song in "T. N.," 4; on source of plot of "T. N.," 5, *et seq.;* 223; 309.

Furnival, Frederick James (S. ed., &c.: 1825-1910): 485.

Garden T., N. Y.: "K. L." at, 462.

Genest, Rev. John (th. historian: 1764-1839): on the alterations of "K. L.," 374, *et seq.;* on the omission of the *Fool* from "K. L.," &c., 382.

George, the Second, King of England: 119.

George, the Third, King of England: 30; 119.

George, the Fourth, King of England: 31.

Globe Theatre, London: "T. N." at(?), 12; 225; 496; 542; 558.

Globe T., Boston: "K. L." at, 465.

Godwin, Edward W. (antiquary & artist): on dressing of "K. L.," 417.

Gonzaga, Curtio: 5; 8.

Gosson, Rev. Stephen (1554-1623): 544.

Grand O. H., N. Y.: 167; 183.

Greene, Robert (dramatist: 1561-1592): authorship of *"A* Shrew" ascribed to, 481.

H — I — J

Halliwell-Phillipps, James Orchard (S. biographer, &c.: 1820-1889): on first performance of "T. N.," 3; 346; 348; 542.

Hapgood, Norman (journalist, 1868-19—): chatter precipitated by, 307.

Harlem O. H.: N. Y.: 82.

Haymarket Theatre, London: 20; 39; "R. & J." at, 113; 146; 200; run of "R. & J." at, 206; 207; 244; 260; 503; 606.

Hazlitt, William (essayist: 1778-1830): his designation of *Romeo* examined, 133-136; on Mrs. Jordan's attributes, 240; impossible to agree with, *re* "K. L.," 461-462.

Henry, the Third, King of England: 216.

Herbert, Sir Henry, Master of the Revels (1595-1673): his "Diary," quoted, 13.

Herbert, William, Earl of Pembroke: 230.

Her Majesty's T., London: "J. C." at, 573.

Higgin, Rev. John Montesquieu Bellew: 185.

Hill, Aaron (1685-1750): play by, 547.

Hook, Theodore: 127.

Howard, James: alteration of "R. & J." by, 112.

Hudson T., N. Y.: "T. N." at, 95; "A. Y. L. I." at, 313.

Hunt, James Henry Leigh (d. c., p., &c.: 1784-1859): 25; on Bannister, 26.

Hunter, Rev. Joseph (S. ed., &c.: 1783-1861): discovery of Manningham's "Diary" by, 2; "Gl' Ingannati" discovered by, 5; statement of resemblance between "T. N." and "Gl' Ingannati" by, quoted, 7-8.

Illinois T., Chicago: first joint performance of E. H. Sothern and J. Marlowe given at, 192.

Imperial T., Warsaw: 171.

Ireland, Joseph Norton (hist. Am. T.: 1817-1898): on Ellen Tree's acting, 244; 255.

James, the First, King of England: 13; 83; 120; 230.

Jewsbury, Geraldine Endsor (novelist: 1812-1880): on Miss Faucit's *Rosalind,* 248.

INDEX

Johnson, Charles (1679-1748): his alteration of "A. Y. L. I." produced, 232.
Johnson, Dr. Samuel (S. Ed., E., c., &c.: 1709-1784): 19; on Shakespeare on the Stage, 68; on *Mercutio*, 194; on Mrs. Clive, 236; on Tate's alteration of "K. L.," 367; on "T. T. of T. S." and its predecessor, 482-483.
John Street T., N. Y.: "R. & J." at, 156; first performance of "A. Y. L. I." in N. Y. given at, 253; 507; 575.

K — L

Keese, William Linn (th. biographer: 1835-1869): on Burton's *Sir Toby*, 49.
Knickerbocker T., N. Y.: "T. N." at, 76; 82; 83; "T. N." produced at, by Sothern and Marlowe, 89; "T. T. of T. S." at, 529; same, 533.
Knight, Charles (S. ed., &c.): opinion of, re "R. & J.," and author on, 109; 366; 481.
Knight, Joseph (d. c.: 1829-1907): on Stella Colas, 151.

Lamb, Charles (1775-1834): 20; 44; not possible to agree with, re "K. L.," 461-462.
Leicester, Robert Dudley, Earl of (1532-1588): 119.
Lennox, Mrs. Charlotte (S. comm.: 1720-1804): 6.
Lewes, George Henry (dramatist and critic: 1817-1878): on Stella Colas, 151.
Lincoln's Inn Fields T. (the Duke's T.): opened with "T. N.," 14; 17; 112; 120.
Linley, William (musician: 1771-1835): music by, for "A. Y. L. I.," 281.
Lloyd, W. W. (S. commentator): surmise by, re "A. Y. L. I.," 223.
Lodge, Thomas (1555-1625): 217; 222; 269.
Lyceum T., London: "T. N." at, 33; "R. & J." at, 130; same, 136;
Mary Anderson's production of "R. & J." at, 173; "K. L." at, 427; 478.
Lyceum T., N. Y.: 185.

M — N — O

Macaulay's T., Louisville, Ky.: 554.
Malone, Edmond (S. ed., &c.: 1741-1812): 109; 545.
Manningham, John (law student, &c.: temp. Q. E.): his "Diary" discovered, and published, 2; 4; his opinion, 5.
Marlowe, Christopher (dramatist: 1564-1593): 140; 221.
Marylebone T., London: 200.
Meres, Francis (1565-1647): his "Palladis Tamia," 4; 221.
Metropolitan T. (Burton's), N. Y.: 49; 204.
Middle Temple, London: "T. N." at, 2; 3; 84.
Moore, Thomas (the poet: 1779-1852): 10; 141.
Morley, Prof. Henry (1822-1894): on Phelps' *Malvolio*, 29.
Morley, Thomas (musician: 1557-1603): 3; compilation of musical works by, 4.
Murphy, Arthur (dramatist, biographer, &c.: 1727-1805): 114; 144; 359; on Garrick's "K. & P.," 497.

National T., N. Y.: 205; 210.
Newington Butts T., London: 496.
New Theatre (Burton's—Tripler Hall — the Metropolitan — Laura Keene's Varieties T.): 49.
New Theatre, the, N. Y.: "T. N." at, 91; same, 103.
New York T. (Daly's), N. Y.: 260.
Niblo's Garden T., N. Y.: 211; 257; 284.
North, Sir Thomas (1535-after 1601): 543.

Oldys, William (antiquarian: 1687-1761): tradition re S. preserved by, 222-229.
Olympic T., London: 35; 168.

INDEX

Otway, Thomas (1651-1685): "conveys" "R. & J.," 113; 142.

P — (Q)

Park T., N. Y. (old): "T. N." at, 47; 58; 157; 201; 206; opened with "A. Y. L. I.," 254; incidents of opening of, 255; 256; 257; 415; 434.
Planché, James Robinson (1796-1880): 217; 615.
Plautus, Titus Maccius (died 184 B.C.): 5; 8.
Plutarch (46?-120?): 113.
Pollock, Walter Herries (poet, critic, editor, &c.: 1850-19—): on Irving's *King Lear*, 430; 431.
Pope, Alexander (the poet: 1688-1744): 481; 546.
Princess' T., London: opened by C. Kean, 39; 40; 285; "K. L." at, 425.

R — S

Reynolds, Sir Joshua (1723-1792): on Mrs. Jordan's acting, 22.
Richmond Hill T., N. Y.: 201.
Robinson, Henry Crabb (1775-1867): on Liston's *Malvolio*, 27.
Rolfe, William James (S. ed.: 1827-1910): 544.
Rose T., London: "K. L." at, 345.
Royalty, the New, T., London: 152.
Ryan, Richard: on singing of Maria Tree, 28.
Rymer, Thomas (antiquary: 1641-1713): on Hart—on Mohun, 551.

Sadler's Wells T., Islington, London: "T. N." at, 28; 129; "K. L." at, 421; 504; 571; 572.
Scenic illustration: right methods of, 84, *et seq.*
Scott, Clement (d. c., &c.: 1841-1904): 200; on Miss Anderson's *Juliet*, and controverted. 175.
Scott, Sir Walter (1771-1832): 147; 237; 490; on dressing of "K. L.," 548.
Secchi, Nicolo: 5; 8.

Sex: abnegation of improper artistic expedient in acting *Viola* and *Rosalind*, 81-82.
Shakespeare, Gilbert (brother of W. S.): tradition of his seeing his brother play *Adam*, 228-229.
Sheffield, John, Duke of Buckingham (1648-1721): plays by, based on S.'s "J. C.," 546.
Stadt T., N. Y.: "R. & J." at, 166.
Star T. (old, at 13th St.): "T. N." at, by Irving, 33; same, by Miss Marlowe, 89; "R. & J." at, 179; 303.
Stebbins, Emma (sculptor and biographer, died 1882): 205.
Steevens, George (S. ed., &c.: 1736-1800): once owns King Charles the First's Shakespeare F. F., 30.

T — V

Tate, Nahum (the poet-laureate and playwright: 1652-1715): 54; his alteration of "K. L." first presented, &c., 352; his alterations of plays by S., 366; his alteration of "K. L." examined and considered, 366, *et seq.;* dedication of his alteration of "K. L.," 370; specimens of his style, 384; 434; 555.
Taylor, Douglas (th. antiquary, &c.: 1830-1913): 209.
Taylor, John (died, 1832): on Mrs. Dancer's *Rosalind*, 235.
Taylor, Tom (dramatist: 1817-1880): 554.
Thalia T., N. Y.: 467.
Theatre Royal, Birmingham, Eng.: 170.
Theatre, the, in Federal St., Boston: 47.
Tieck, Louis (S. com.: 1773-1853): 482.
Tripler Hall, N. Y.: 49.

Venetian Republic: 12.
Victoria, Queen of England, &c.: "R. & J." acted before, 130.
Vining, Fanny (Mrs. Edward Loomis Davenport: 1829-1891): as *Romeo*, 200.

INDEX

Voltaire (Jean François Marie Arouet: 1694-1778): play by, on Julius Cæsar, 546; 547.

W

Wallack's Lyceum, N. Y.: "T. N." revived at, 54; "A. Y. L. I." at, 258.

Wallack's T., N. Y.: 48; 55; "A. Y. L. I." at, 287, *et. seq.;* same, 305, *et seq.*

Walnut St. T., Phila.: Miss Cushman acts *Romeo* at, 209.

Webb, Charles (playwright): 53.

Webb, Henry (playwright): 53.

White, Richard Grant (S. ed.): 222; 483.

Widmer, Henry (musician: 1845-1895): 65.

William, the Third, King of England, 554.

Wingfield, Hon. Lewis: 174.

Winter Garden T., N. Y.: 59; burnt, 161; 211; 259; 585.